AMERICA'S
TEST KITCHEN

America's Test Kitchen

Cocktails
ILLUSTRATED

400+ Recipes for the Home Bartender, from Spirit Forward to Zero Proof

Library of Congress Cataloging-in-Publication Data has been applied for.

ISBN 978-1-948703-41-3

America's Test Kitchen
21 Drydock Avenue, Boston, MA 02210

Printed in Canada

10 9 8 7 6 5 4 3 2 1

Distributed by Penguin Random House Publisher Services

Tel: 800-733-3000

Pictured on front cover: Classic Negroni (page 333)
Pictured on back cover: Whiskey Sour (page 208)

Photography by Steve Klise
Editorial and Cocktail Advisor: Nick Korn

Editorial Director, Books: Adam Kowit
Executive Food Editor: Dan Zuccarello
Deputy Food Editor: Stephanie Pixley
Executive Managing Editor: Debra Hudak
Project Editors: Valerie Cimino and Sacha Madadian
Senior Editors: Camila Chaparro and Joe Gitter
Senior Photo Test Cook: José Maldonado
Test Cooks: Olivia Counter, Laila Ibrahim, Hannah Smokelin, and Stephanie Winter
Kitchen Interns: Janna Claassan and Lilly Morrison
Additional Recipe Development: Nick Korn
Assistant Editor: Julia Arwine
Creative Director, Editorial: Lindsey Timko Chandler
Associate Art Director and Designer: Kylie Alexander
Photography Director: Julie Bozzo Cote
Senior Photography Producer: Meredith Mulcahy
Senior Staff Photographers: Steve Klise and Daniel J. van Ackere
Staff Photographer: Kritsada Panichgul
Food Styling: Joy Howard, Catrine Kelty, Chantal Lambeth, Ashley Moore, Elle Simone Scott, Kendra Smith, and Christine Tobin
Project Manager, Books: Kelly Gauthier
Senior Print Production Specialist: Lauren Robbins
Production and Imaging Coordinator: Amanda Yong
Production and Imaging Specialist: Tricia Neumyer
Production and Imaging Assistant: Chloe Petraske
Copy Editor: Karen Wise
Proofreader: Ann-Marie Imbornoni
Indexer: Elizabeth Parson

Chief Executive Officer: Dan Suratt
Chief Content Officer: Dan Souza
Senior Content Adviser: Jack Bishop
Executive Editorial Directors: Julia Collin Davison and Bridget Lancaster
Senior Director, Book Sales: Emily Logan

Contents

Welcome to America's Test Kitchen

This book has been tested, written, and edited by the folks at America's Test Kitchen, where curious home cooks become confident cooks. Located in Boston's Seaport District in the historic Innovation and Design Building, it features 15,000 square feet of kitchen space including multiple photography and video studios. It is the home of *Cook's Illustrated* magazine and *Cook's Country* magazine and is the workday destination for more than 60 test cooks, editors, and cookware specialists. Our mission is to empower and inspire confidence, community, and creativity in the kitchen.

We start the process of testing a recipe with a complete lack of preconceptions, which means that we accept no claim, no technique, and no recipe at face value. We simply assemble as many variations as possible, test a half dozen of the most promising, and taste the results blind. We then construct our own recipe and continue to test it, varying ingredients, techniques, and cooking times until we reach a consensus. As we like to say in the test kitchen, "We make the mistakes so you don't have to." The result, we hope, is the best version of a particular recipe, but we realize that only you can be the final judge of our success (or failure). We use the same rigorous approach when we test equipment and taste ingredients.

All of this would not be possible without a belief that good cooking, much like good music, is based on a foundation of objective technique. Some people like spicy foods and others don't, but there is a right way to sauté, there is a best way to cook a pot roast, and there are measurable scientific principles involved in producing perfectly beaten, stable egg whites. Our ultimate goal is to investigate the fundamental principles of cooking to give you the techniques, tools, and ingredients you need to become a better cook. It is as simple as that.

To get inspiration and expert instruction, download the America's Test Kitchen app or check out our social media channels for kitchen snapshots, exclusive content, video tips, and much more. You can watch us work (in our actual test kitchen) by tuning in to *America's Test Kitchen* or *Cook's Country* on public television or on our websites. Listen to *Proof* (AmericasTestKitchen.com/podcasts) to hear engaging, complex stories about people and food. Want to hone your cooking skills or finally learn how to bake—with an America's Test Kitchen test cook? Enroll in one of our online cooking classes.

However you choose to visit us, we welcome you into our kitchen, where you can stand by our side as we test our way to the best recipes in America.

facebook.com/AmericasTestKitchen
instagram.com/TestKitchen
youtube.com/AmericasTestKitchen
tiktok.com/@TestKitchen
x.com/TestKitchen
pinterest.com/TestKitchen

AmericasTestKitchen.com
OnlineCookingSchool.com

JOIN OUR COMMUNITY OF RECIPE TESTERS

Our recipe testers provide valuable feedback on recipes under development by ensuring that they are foolproof in home kitchens. Help the America's Test Kitchen book team investigate the how and why behind successful recipes from your home kitchen.

The Front Bar

Becoming a Great Home Bartender

A cocktail is about so much more than the liquid in the glass. The proportions of the ingredients, how long you stir or shake, how you strain, the quality of the ice, the choice of glass, the style of garnish: Many elements are integral to the experience of a transcendent, give-me-more cocktail. And a cocktail is indeed an experience—in the crafting as well as in the enjoying.

When you order a cocktail at a bar or restaurant, a professional bartender crafts the experience for you. If you've ever wondered how to replicate that cocktail experience at home with ease, you've picked up the right book. For the recipes and techniques alike, we tested, and retested, and then tested again, always with the home bartender in mind. The result is that *Cocktails Illustrated* teaches you everything you need to know to make the very best drinks so that you can impress your friends—and yourself. Here's how.

Build a storehouse of good ingredients. You needn't splurge, but don't skimp either. As with cooking, better-quality ingredients lead to superlatively delicious results. We offer advice on what bottles to start with and how to build your collection over time. Our side-by-side tastings of spirits, liqueurs, fizzy waters, syrups, and more informed our knowledge to share about which ones are acceptable substitutes for others.

Work with the right tools. Your choice of shaker, or mixing glass, or bar spoon may be in part a stylistic one, but it's a very practical matter too, and we help you figure out what tools you need and how to select them based on both your preferences and what we used successfully in our recipe development.

Practice, practice, practice techniques. We teach you what they are and when to use them, from different ways to stir and shake correctly to muddling herbs and fruits for the best flavor extraction to making various sizes and shapes of perfectly clear cocktail ice. During testing, we shook dozens of cocktails with egg whites and substitutes to figure out how to achieve the best foam. We stirred even more martinis than that to determine the ideal serving temperature and how to achieve it. And we experimented with advanced techniques like aging, clarifying, infusing, and fat washing until we were satisfied that they were perfectly adapted for the home bartender.

Understand cocktail formulas and ratios. Knowing that the formula for a "classic" martini is 5 parts gin to 1 part vermouth lets you customize the ingredient ratios to make a wet martini, or a dry martini, or a reverse martini. Knowing that a basic sour cocktail is 2 parts spirit to 0.75 part citrus juice to 0.75 part sweetener allows you to mix and match ingredients and still end up with a delicious drink. Understanding concepts like these allows you to make adjustments and substitutions to create a custom cocktail that fits your palate.

Appreciate the science. Cocktail making involves science as well as art, and learning the science helps you better practice the art. If you overshake a daiquiri (or other drink), it won't keep getting colder—it will actually start to warm up. If you're making homemade seltzer, controlling the temperature of the water will let you achieve more fizz, or less, as you prefer. Understanding the qualities that alcohol brings to a cocktail also helps you craft praiseworthy zero-proof cocktails (and you'll find 50 of those in these pages).

As with everything to do with food and drink, subjectivity and opinions abound in the cocktail world. We made informed decisions about including particular drinks in the chapters you'll find here, but feel free to debate some of our choices—preferably while enjoying the cocktail in question.

So raise your glass—with the full confidence that the cocktail you've crafted meets the moment perfectly.

10 Ways to a Cocktail

Once you learn the fundamental principles surrounding cocktail formulas, flavor pairings, and crafting techniques, then you will be able to customize cocktails to suit your own palate like a pro. This book teaches you about those elements so that you can make the classics with ease and then use your knowledge to build off the formulas to create personalized versions of classics as well as brand-new cocktails. Let's use the Daiquiri (page 205) as an example to illustrate the many ways you will learn how to customize a cocktail.

Most chapters start with a

Fundamental Formula

For the Sours chapter (where you'll find the daiquiri), it's spirit + citrus juice + sweetener, shaken with ice and served up.

1 Scale up: Throughout the book, you will find "fridge door cocktails," larger batches that you can make ahead and keep chilled. Fridge Door Daiquiris (page 207) serve 6 people. Make two batches while you're at it to serve 12.

2 Switch up serving style: The cocktail police won't come after you if you serve a traditionally up drink like the daiquiri on the rocks. See page 24 to learn about shaking times and page 23 to learn about stirring times.

3 Add flavors using technique: Shake in fresh basil leaves to make a Basil Daiquiri (page 206) or muddle in chopped strawberries to make a Strawberry Daiquiri (page 206).

4 Swap citrus: Instead of using lime juice, swap in lemon, grapefruit, yuzu, or tangerine juice. See page 12 to learn about juicing citrus and page 202 for more about swapping citrus.

5 Sub sweetener: Instead of using plain simple syrup, make a flavored Citrus Syrup (page 458), Berry Syrup (page 458), or Herb Syrup (page 459) from the Backbar chapter, or swap in agave or honey.

6 Revisit spirits: Our daiquiri suggests white rum, but you can swap in aged rum. See page 236 to learn more about rum styles.

7 Split spirit base: Using two types of the same spirit can add depth and nuance. Instead of 2 ounces of white rum, use 1 ounce of white rum and 1 ounce of aged rum. Or use 1½ ounces of white or aged rum and ½ ounce of rhum agricole. See the Tropical chapter to learn more about splitting a rum base.

8 Infuse spirits: Infuse the rum with pineapple or makrut lime leaves, or fat-wash the rum with coconut oil. See the Infused and Fat Washed chapter to learn how to infuse and fat-wash spirits.

9 Incorporate egg white: Shake in 1 ounce of egg white for a silkier texture and fuller body. See pages 203 and 372 to learn about using egg whites in cocktails.

10 Gild with garnishes: Instead of a simple citrus slice, turn to the Backbar chapter for inspiration and instructions for adding a dehydrated citrus slice (see page 455) or rimming the glass with Vanilla Rim Sugar (page 454) or Citrus Rim Salt (page 453).

Ingredients

Whether you're stirring or shaking cocktails or sipping spirits on their own, quality matters, so purchase the best you can afford. We don't suggest you buy a $100 bottle of single-malt Scotch to make the Seelie Sipper (page 233)—save that for enjoying by itself. Conversely, the lowest-end bottle of whiskey is not likely to make an elevated cocktail. The same goes for liqueurs, which can be expensive. Making some of your own liqueurs and mixers gives you excellent quality control as well as cost savings; see The Backbar chapter for some versatile recipes. We tested and developed all of the cocktails in this book using midpriced bottles.

Spirits

Given the vast world of choices, we recommend reading labels, doing independent research, and not hesitating to talk with both merchants and bartenders about what kind of flavors you like and what level of quality you can get for what you're willing or able to spend. Let the merchant or bartender know what you're planning to use the spirits for, so they can offer advice to help you make the best choices. You can taste spirits at bars (and some higher-end liquor stores) before committing to buying a bottle.

GIN

Gin starts as a neutral base spirit (often distilled from various grains), which is imbued with many different botanicals, notably juniper. We developed our recipes using London dry gin, the standard-bearer of modern gin, which has an extremely versatile juniper-citrus flavor profile. That's what we recommend for a basic home bar, but there are thousands of gins made all over the world, often incorporating ingredients from far-flung locales. We also use Old Tom, which is sweeter and less herbal than London dry; this is the style against which London dry was differentiated. The assertive flavors of gin stand up to other assertive flavors in a cocktail, including muddled celery in the Celery GImlet (page 208) and Bénédictine and pineapple in the Seaport Sling (page 238). They also stand up well with minimal additional ingredients—think of the classic Gin and Tonic (page 95) or Gin Martini (page 155).

Aquavit Like gin, aquavit (or akvavit) is a neutral spirit flavored with botanicals. Meaning "water of life," aquavit has its roots and tradition grounded in Scandinavia. It may be made from various grains or potatoes and is often flavored with caraway, dill, or coriander. The types of botanicals used and the geographic region it's associated with differentiate aquavit from gin.

VODKA

The most neutral-tasting spirit, vodka in some form was made in Russia way back in the 14th century. It was traditionally distilled from potatoes, although in modern times it's at least as likely to be distilled from various grains. It can also be made from fruits, including apples or grapes. Vodka is sometimes taken for granted in the modern bar because of its neutral flavor, but we love it in our Herb Martini (page 161). It can also balance and temper other, stronger flavors, as it does with the tea liqueur and muddled kiwi in our Kiwi Blossom (page 78). And it's an excellent candidate for infusing and fat-washing—try the Olive Oil Martini (page 307) and see for yourself.

WHISKEY

Whiskey is made all over the world, with the top-producing countries being India, Scotland, the United States, Ireland, Japan, and Canada. (The United States and Ireland use the term "whiskey," while most other countries use "whisky.") All whiskey is made from grain, but different rules apply depending on the country of origin, and many factors affect flavor profile. In developing cocktails, we sometimes chose whiskeys that best suited certain flavors in the drink. For other recipes, including the Whiskey Highball (page 67) and the Whiskey Smash (page 139), you can easily make swaps among your favorite whiskeys. To make the recipes in this book, start with rye and bourbon; purchase additional types according to your preference.

American Whiskey Bourbon is the quintessential American whiskey. It must be made from at least 51 percent corn and be aged in new charred-oak containers. It must be made in the United States (but not necessarily in Kentucky). The corn contributes a certain sweetness and round, full body to the whiskey. We prefer it in our Old-Fashioned (page 123).

Rye, which has many of the same legal production and aging requirements as bourbon, must be made from at least 51 percent rye. This results in a drier, spicier flavor than corn-heavy bourbon. We think it's ideal in cocktails that have a sweeter element, such as the Manhattan (page 181), which uses sweet vermouth.

Tennessee whiskey has the same legal requirements as bourbon for raw materials and aging but must be produced in Tennessee. Charcoal filtering prior to aging tends to result in a lighter-bodied, smoother-textured whiskey.

Scotch Scotch has strict production and aging requirements. It must be made in Scotland and aged in oak containers (often used bourbon barrels). Many Scotches are made from malted barley, though other grains can be used. There is a whole lexicon of terms used in relation to Scotch, each of which comes with specific requirements. The majority of Scotch is blended, and that's what we recommend for cocktail making. Some Scotch may bring a smoky or peaty note to cocktails.

Irish Whiskey The word "whiskey" is derived from the Gaelic phrase "uisce beatha," meaning "water of life." Generally made from malted barley or other grains, Irish whiskey tends to have less smoky or peaty flavors than Scotch and often makes a great sub for bourbon in cocktails. We think it's a must in Irish Coffee (page 405).

Canadian Whisky Canadian whisky can be made from corn, wheat, or rye. Most well-known Canadian whiskies are blended and can be a good sub for Tennessee whiskey or even rum in cocktails.

Japanese Whisky Japanese whisky has a style that is strongly influenced by Scotch, but it generally has a silkier, smoother texture. Also like Scotch, single malts command higher prices than blends.

RUM

Rum can be a complicated spirit to understand because it is made all over the world, and just as with whiskey, rules for making it vary by locale. Rum's history—and present—is firmly rooted in imperialism, slavery, and international trade, so perhaps more than any other spirit, rum is often a blend of products from different parts of the world. Raw materials, distillate, and aged rums can come from multiple locations and then be blended and bottled under a label that doesn't tell you anything about where and how it was made.

The one thing all rums have in common is that they start with sugarcane. Rum is most typically made from molasses, but its siblings rhum agricole, cachaça, and clairin are made from fresh sugarcane juice and are highly regulated in their production and location. Arrack may be made from sugarcane or molasses, which is often combined with other ingredients.

Classifications based on color can be misleading. While most rum is aged to some degree, a darker rum does not mean it's older. Many white rums, notably from Cuba and Puerto Rico, are in fact aged and then filtered to remove the color imparted by the barrel. On the other end of the spectrum, so called black rums are young—often clear—rum with coloring and/or flavoring added.

A good way to understand rum styles is to learn about what they are made from, their production methods, their aging times, and their flavors. For our cocktails, we rely primarily on two categories: white rum (an unaged or lightly aged—1 to 4 years—rum that may have been filtered) and aged rum (aged 5 years or more). White rum is great for daiquiris and mojitos, while tropical drinks in particular can benefit from the more complex flavors of aged rum. For more information on rum styles, see page 236.

MEZCAL AND TEQUILA

Mezcal and its subcategory, tequila, are made from the agave plant. Many different types of agave may be used for mezcal, while only one species (blue Weber agave) may be used for tequila. The agave used for mezcal is often roasted, which is what can give some mezcal its signature smoky quality, while the agave used for tequila is often steamed. Tequila can be bottled young (blanco or joven) or be aged for up to 1 year (reposado) or 1 to 3 years or longer (añejo or extra añejo).

We find that blanco and reposado tequilas are sometimes interchangeable in cocktails. Broadly speaking, blanco will give your Fresh Margarita (page 214) a brighter, cleaner flavor, whereas reposado will bring more nuanced, toasted notes to your drink. When we have a preference, as we do for reposado in our Tequila Old-Fashioned (page 129), we note it in the recipe.

Smoky mezcals work especially well with bold complementary flavors. We like them with coffee in Bone in Her Teeth (page 344), our take on a mezcal espresso martini, or the MonMez Coffee (page 407), an Irish coffee variation.

BRANDY AND PISCO

Brandy is essentially distilled wine, of which Cognac, made in the Cognac region of France, is considered the apex. But "distilled wine" doesn't have to mean grape wine; it can mean any fruit. Calvados and applejack are types of brandy made from apples. The cocktails in this book use Cognac-style brandy unless otherwise specified. We suggest seeking out a brandy that is moderately aged, such as VSOP, which is aged for at least 4 years.

Pisco is a type of brandy made in Peru and Chile from specific grape varieties. Unlike many other brandies, it's never aged in wood, meaning its flavors and aromas are closer to its fruit source. Try it in the classic Peruvian cocktail El Capitán (page 163).

SOJU AND BAIJIU

Soju is a distilled spirit with deep roots in its home country of Korea. It's extremely popular globally. Typically made from fermented rice, barley, wheat, or sweet potatoes, soju has a clean, smooth flavor and is relatively low in alcohol compared to other spirits. In Korea it is often enjoyed straight in shot glasses (multiple times over the course of an evening), but it's used in cocktails, too. Try it in our Just Peachy (page 78) or Kimchi Bloody Marys (page 322).

Baijiu is a traditional spirit from China that is usually distilled from fermented sorghum but can also be made from rice, barley, or wheat. It has a high ABV, or alcohol by volume (higher than vodka), and an earthy flavor, with subtle sweetness and sourness. Baijiu is categorized by aroma: strong aroma, sauce aroma, light aroma, and rice aroma, with many subcategories. Year over year, baijiu is the world's most produced and most consumed spirit. Get on the baijiu bandwagon with our Monkey of the Mind (page 248).

LIQUOR DISTILLATION

Machines called stills distill spirits by heating fermented liquid, consisting of alcohol and water, until it boils, then capturing the vapor. The process transforms a low-alcohol base into a high-proof spirit. There are two main types: pot stills and column stills.

A pot still has a large chamber with a long, tapering arm that ends in a condensing coil. The chamber is filled with base and then heated. Volatile components, including ethanol, boil first, and the vapor travels through the arm to the coil, where it condenses. The character of the spirit that emerges is influenced by the distiller's oversight of the still's temperature and exactly which portion of the distillate to collect from the condenser. Pot stills are often used for spirits like tequila, malt whiskey, and rum. They distill a single batch at a time. Finished spirits may achieve a final strength of perhaps 70 percent alcohol.

In a column still, the vapor fills a vertical column lined with sequential perforated plates that form a series of chambers. As the vapor contacts each plate, it condenses into liquid and trickles down to be instantly redistilled. The difference in temperature from the bottom to the top of the column means that at each plate, the ratio of alcohol to water that condenses is different—higher proof at higher plates. Depending on where along the column's height the vapor is extracted, the distiller can achieve a consistent strength, all the way up to 95 percent alcohol in some column stills. Additionally, impurities are further removed every time the liquid is condensed and evaporated. Many distillers run their wash and vapor through multiple columns to achieve the desired results. A column still can operate continuously, producing a steady flow of spirit. Column stills are often used for vodka, gin, and American whiskey.

Fruits of the Forest Liqueur

Liqueurs

A liqueur is simply alcohol that has extracted flavors from added ingredients (or had flavorings added in other ways) and then been sweetened. Anything can be turned into a liqueur, from bitter herbs to savory vegetables to sweet fruits. Dozens of liqueurs act as major or supplemental players in cocktails. The more liqueurs you have, the more expansive your home-bartending options will be. On the flip side, there's nothing worse than puchasing a bottle for one drink, and then having it hang around like an albatross on your bar cart for years. We try to be intentional about which ingredients we call for in our recipes, and offer alternatives (and recipes to make your own) when possible. Here's a brief overview of some major categories.

ORANGE LIQUEUR

Orange liqueur is an essential and fundamental building block for countless cocktails, including the Fresh Margarita (page 214), Sidecar (page 225), and Corpse Reviver No. 2 (page 226). But if you've found yourself stumped by which orange liqueur to buy, you're not alone. They go by different names (many of which aren't legally protected) and can have different spirit bases, alcoholic strengths, and sweetness levels. Curaçao was historically a brandy- or rum-based orange liqueur made from bitter oranges grown on the Caribbean island of the same name. Nowadays, neutral spirits are also used, colors can be added, and curaçao can come from anywhere. Triple sec was originally an orange liqueur of French origin, made from a neutral-flavored clear spirit. Cointreau is one of the most famous and readily available brands of triple sec. Grand Marnier, another well-known brand of orange liqueur, is often called a curaçao-style orange liqueur due to its Cognac base.

Which orange liqueur you use can make a difference in your cocktail's flavor profile. If you're going to buy just one bottle, we suggest Cointreau or a similar high-quality triple sec. This style generally makes for a brighter, cleaner orange flavor in cocktails, particularly those using "lighter" spirits (like gin, tequila, or vodka). Just be aware that there is a wide range of alcohol content, sweetness, and flavor profiles across brands of triple sec. If you are able to buy a second type of orange liqueur, also try a brandy-based version, like Grand Marnier, which complements drinks that have deeper flavors or use darker spirits, like the Sidecar. You can even make your own Orange Liqueur (page 465).

OTHER FRUIT LIQUEURS

There are several different styles of cherry liqueur. The most important and versatile for cocktail making (and the one we use the most in this book) is maraschino liqueur, which is distilled from Marasca cherries; it is clear in color and lightly sweet. Liqueurs labeled "cherry liqueur" may be distilled from cherries or may be made of neutral spirits flavored with cherries. They are often deep red in color and may be noticeably sweeter than maraschino liqueur. Then there is cherry brandy, which may be either a grape brandy infused with cherries and sweetened (like a liqueur) or an unsweetened spirit distilled from cherries (as is kirsch).

Berry liqueurs, like Chambord (made from black raspberries) and crème de cassis (made from black currants), are great in punches or mixed with sparkling wine. Make your own Fruits of the Forest Liqueur (page 466) to use in the Frutti di Bosco Punch (page 54) or the Royal Berry (page 46).

Chiles are botanically fruits, and chile liqueur brings warmth and nuanced spiciness to cocktails such as the Tumbleweed (page 222). Purchase a dark chile liqueur or try our homemade Ancho Chile Liqueur (page 468), which can be customized by using tequila, vodka, or bourbon as the base spirit (and by using different chiles).

Amaretto, while not technically a fruit liqueur, is fruit-derived, being typically made from the bitter kernels found inside stone fruit pits (though some brands contain almonds). It has an almondy flavor profile, and it's worth buying for the Amaretto Sour (page 211) alone.

HERBAL LIQUEURS

Bénédictine, Strega, and Chartreuse are examples of sweeter-style herbal liqueurs. Italian aperitivi and amari (an extremely broad category) are often more lightly sweet or bittersweet (or even quite bitter). These herbal liqueurs are frequently consumed on their own, either before or after a meal, but they also regularly make their way into cocktails. The spritz family (pages 48–52) is among our favorite uses for herbal liqueurs. See page 328 for more information about aperitivi and amari.

Anise liqueur plays a small but important role in cocktails, including the Sazerac (page 128). The most famous version is absinthe, which is delicious but expensive. In our testing, we found that Herbsaint (originally made as an absinthe substitute), a dry pastis (such as Ricard), or an anisette labeled dry is an excellent alternative. Arak is a Middle Eastern anise-flavored spirit that is distilled from grapes or dates; try it in From Beirut with Love (page 142).

COFFEE, TEA, AND CHOCOLATE LIQUEURS

These aren't just-for-dessert drinks. Make a sophisticated, not-too-sweet Espresso Martini (page 343) to serve anytime with our Coffee Liqueur (page 467) or a store-bought version. Tea Liqueur (page 468) can be made from any type of tea and is used in the Bourbon Mint Tea Mule (page 109) and the Hole in One (page 76). And crème de cacao is a must for the Brandy Alexander (page 392) and our Keoke Coffee (page 407).

Fortified and Aromatized Wines

Fortified wines are wines that have had a distilled spirit (such as grape or grain alcohol) added to them to increase their alcohol by volume; this increases their longevity and may stop fermentation. Some fortified wines are also aromatized with botanicals. For longer shelf life, refrigerate your fortified and aromatized wines after opening.

SHERRY

This fortified wine is made in Spain from specific Spanish grapes. Production methods can vary according to the style being produced. There are several styles, but we call for three in this book: Fino is the driest, most saline style; amontillado is richer and nuttier; and oloroso is richer and more complex still.

PORT

Made in several styles (and subcategories of those styles), port is a rich fortified wine from Portugal that can be dry or sweet. We use ruby and tawny ports in our cocktails. The former is generally more fruit forward, while the latter can feature more nutty, spiced flavors.

MADEIRA

This category of fortified wine from a small island off the coast of Portugal has a long history of being enjoyed—alone and in cocktails—in America. There are many types, from extra-dry to sweet. A medium-sweet variety is a versatile bottle to keep on hand.

VERMOUTH

Vermouth is an aromatized wine made from a base of wine that is infused with botanical flavoring ingredients before fortification. Sugar and coloring are other possible add-ins. Vermouth is made in many different countries and in a multitude of nuanced varieties and styles. What traditionally distinguished vermouth from other aromatized wines (like Lillet) is the inclusion of an herb called wormwood (from which the word "vermouth" is derived). Although there are many varieties, the two primary ones are dry and sweet.

Dry Vermouth

Dry vermouth is made from white wine, botanical flavorings, and a small amount of sugar. It tends to have a more herbal flavor profile. For more information, see page 152. Our DIY version is on page 469.

Sweet vermouth is also made from a white wine base, but with more sugar, different botanicals, and a red-brown color from caramel, spices, and/or red wine. It tends to have more floral and spiced flavors in addition to herbs. For more information, see page 178. To make your own, see page 470.

Vermouth bianco, which can be clear or pale yellow in color, is semisweet, falling between dry and sweet vermouths in terms of sweetness level.

Rosé vermouth may be made from white wine or a blend of white and red wines. Its sweetness level is similar to that of vermouth bianco and it offers floral aromas.

OTHER AROMATIZED WINES

The category of aromatized wines goes far beyond vermouth to encompass other styles that are enjoyed solo and in cocktails. Often called aperitivo wines, examples that we use in this book include Cocchi Americano, an Italian version made from Moscato d'Asti wine; and Lillet, a French version made from Semillon and Sauvignon Blanc grapes.

Wine, Beer, and Sake

Wine, beer, and sake are invaluable for making lower-ABV cocktails. For more information on using wine in cocktails, see pages 34 and 350. For more information on using beer in cocktails, see page 350.

There are several different categories of sake, and the terms are often combined on labels, which can be confusing if you are new to this fermented beverage. Junmai means "rice and water only." Essentially this tells you that no other alcohol has been added. (Another type, honjozo, has brewer's alcohol added to round out the flavors.) Genshu sake is undiluted, often meaning that the sake has a higher ABV than other styles. We find genshu sake to have a bold flavor, which is helpful when you want the sake to stand up to other flavors in a cocktail, as in our Kappa Cocktail (page 361). Nigori sake is unfiltered or coarsely filtered, giving it a creamy mouthfeel. Different thicknesses are available, but you can use any of them in our Dew Drop (page 283). Ginjo refers to polish; polishing the rice leads to a sake with fruity and floral aromas and flavors. Ginjo is not the highest polish level available, but it's high enough to notice a difference in your cocktail.

Spirit-Free Bottles

Production—and quality—of nonalcoholic spirits has stepped up in recent years to meet increasing consumer demand, with more choices on store shelves and many cocktail bars devoting sections of their menus to nonalcoholic cocktails.

A surprising fact: According to the Food and Drug Administration, a beverage can contain up to 0.5 percent alcohol by volume (ABV) and still be considered nonalcoholic in the United States. Also noteworthy: Fruit juice and bread can contain similar levels of alcohol due to the presence of fermentation.

We enjoy using nonalcoholic aperitivi and amari, plus nonalcoholic wine and beer, in cocktails. Zero-proof aperitivi and amari can taste like what you'd expect from the alcohol-containing versions. See page 329 for more information on them, and to try out some zero-proof recipes using them, see our Bitter and Bubbly (page 116) and Bitter with the Sweet (page 221). For more information on using nonalcoholic wine and beer in cocktails, see pages 350–351.

When it comes to zero-proof spirits, we found in our tastings that while they can be delicious, they generally don't taste like the spirit they are supposed to be replacing. Zero-proof spirits tend to have unique flavors that are brand specific, and you need to craft a specific cocktail around a particular branded product.

Instead, we focused our energy on making nonalcoholic cocktails using ingredients and techniques that mimic some of the experiential qualities of alcohol, such as tea, unsweetened juices, vegetable glycerin, and proper shaking technique. See pages 14–15 for our best practices for making showstopping zero-proof cocktails.

Juices

CITRUS

Our single most important piece of advice regarding citrus is to always juice fresh fruit—never use juice from a bottle or carton.

It's easy enough to squeeze citrus for one or two cocktails, but what if you're making big-batch cocktails? Do they suffer in quality if you squeeze ahead of time? The short answer is no. Lemon and lime juices can be squeezed a few hours ahead with no problem; in fact, some tasters felt they even improved in flavor. We do recommend squeezing oranges right before you plan to use them, since they contain a compound that turns bitter when exposed to air.

Citrus yields:

- 1 lime = about 1 ounce juice
- 1 lemon = about 1½ ounces juice
- 1 orange = about 4 ounces juice
- 1 grapefruit = about 8 ounces juice

For the easiest, highest-yield juicing, make sure the citrus is at room temperature, roll the fruit on the counter before cutting it to tear the juice sacs, and use a press-style juicer (see page 18). We strain our freshly squeezed juices to remove any pith before using them.

OTHER JUICES

For juices beyond citrus, always look for 100 percent unsweetened juice rather than juice blends. We do sometimes use nectar if a certain juice is harder to find commercially, such as guava or pear. Nectars tend to be a bit thicker than juices and don't have to be 100 percent fruit; they can also have added sugar and water.

And sometimes we make our own juice, as for the Cucumber-Dill Spritzer (page 85) and the Bubbly Beet (page 87). Use an electric juicer or these instructions and the chart opposite for making 4 ounces of fresh juice without a juicer.

How to Make Fresh Juice Without a Juicer

1 Add produce and water, if specified, to food processor. Process until mixture is finely pureed, 30 seconds to 2 minutes, scraping down sides of bowl as needed.

2 Strain mixture through fine-mesh strainer into bowl, pressing on solids to extract as much liquid as possible. Rinse and dry strainer.

3 Strain mixture again through strainer (do not press on solids).

INGREDIENTS

Fruit/Vegetable	Prepped	Amount	Added Water
Apple (green or red)	Peeled, cored, cut into 1-inch pieces	10 ounces	½ ounce
Beet	Scrubbed, trimmed, cut into 1-inch pieces	14 ounces	4 ounces
Carrot	Scrubbed, trimmed, cut into 1-inch pieces	12 ounces	3 ounces
Celery	Cut into 1-inch pieces	8 ounces	½ ounce
English cucumber	Halved lengthwise, cut into 1-inch pieces	8 ounces	0
Melon (cantaloupe, honeydew, or watermelon)	Peeled, seeded, cut into 1-inch pieces	8 ounces	0
Pineapple	Peeled, cored, cut into 1-inch pieces	12 ounces	½ ounce

Waters, Fizzy and Still

Water and its diluting effects are critical to nuanced, balanced cocktails. Typically water is incorporated by shaking or stirring the ingredients with ice. Additionally, some cocktails include seltzer, and some cocktails are served on the rocks.

In testing, we found that it was worth the effort to pay attention to the quality of water used, whether you're adding it to a big-batch cocktail or using it to make ice. Tap water contains particulates that can affect flavor and clarity. We recommend using filtered water to make ice for stirring and shaking cocktails and also when you are adding water to a cocktail, as for Fridge Door Daiquiris (page 207). If you want to achieve the clearest possible Practically Clear Ice (page 28), we suggest distilled water.

Seltzer is simply carbonated water, with no added ingredients. It's indispensable in cocktail making, particularly for highball-style cocktails that are built right in the glass, including the Tom Collins (page 71) and the Paloma (page 74).

Club soda is slightly different in that it has added minerals, which do affect its flavor. But it can be used instead of seltzer. Likewise, sparkling mineral water may be used for cocktails, but it is often less carbonated than seltzer, and since it commands a higher price as well, it's really not worth it. See pages 88–89 for more info on fizzy waters.

Tonic water is essential for many cocktails, including the Gin and Tonic (page 95) and Lillet Tonique (page 100). Commercial brands vary quite a bit in their levels of sweetness, bitterness, and quality. See page 92 for our favorites, as well as a recipe for our bright, citrusy homemade Tonic Syrup that lets you make your own tonic water.

Tonic Syrup

Sweetening Syrups

Sweetness is an important element in many cocktail formulas. Since sugar granules don't dissolve readily in a cold fluid, syrups are often used to add balance, flavor, texture, and body. There are many varieties to meet different needs.

Simple syrup refers to a 1:1 mixture of sugar and water. You can purchase this, but it's easy and far cheaper to make your own (see page 458). Incorporate herbs, spices, or citrus fruits to make flavored syrups; see pages 458–459 for recipes.

Grenadine is a tart-sweet pomegranate-flavored syrup that's versatile enough to use in cocktails ranging from the ATK 25 (page 43) to the Rum Runner (page 249). Our version (page 460) is made from all-natural ingredients.

Orgeat, traditionally made from almonds and sometimes flavored with orange blossom water, is often used in tropical cocktails. See our DIY version on page 459.

Shrub syrups are sweetened fruit-and-vinegar syrups. Our fruit shrubs (see pages 460–461) are great for keeping on hand to mix with a spirit and seltzer (or just seltzer).

A Distilled Guide to Making Great Zero-Proof Cocktails

Crafting a zero-proof drink so that it transcends being a mere juice-seltzer blend and instead becomes an elevated cocktail involves evoking the flavor, texture, and body that alcohol brings to a cocktail. You don't have to mimic a one-to-one replacement for a particular cocktail—and you often shouldn't try. But there are important contributions that alcohol makes, and a great zero-proof cocktail emulates them.

First is **flavor**: Any spirit or liqueur has a level of complex flavor. And because alcohol is an efficient solvent, it can also strengthen the other flavors in a drink. Second is **aroma**: Alcohol promotes the release of aromatic compounds that enhance the sensory experience of enjoying a cocktail. Third is **body and texture**: Alcohol interacts with other ingredients to increase viscosity, and it often has an astringent textural mouthfeel. Fourth is **balance**: Alcohol balances the sweetness and acidity of other ingredients.

Check out the Traverse City recipe on page 198 for just one example of how we applied these principles. We developed all of our nonalcoholic recipes as meticulously as we did our spirited cocktails, with the hope that they become part of your regular cocktail rotation.

- **Alcohol-free replacements** for aperitivi, amari, wine, and beer are high quality and can faithfully mimic their alcohol-containing counterparts in drinks including Bitter and Bubbly (page 116) and Bitter with the Sweet (page 221).
- **Unsweetened juices** such as cherry, pomegranate, or cranberry or fresh vegetable juices add flavor and balance without being too sweet, letting you craft cocktails such as Spiced Cranberry-Orange Punch (page 57) and Cucumber-Dill Spritzer (page 85).
- **Strongly brewed tea** adds body and astringency. We use a hibiscus tea concentrate in the Hibiscus-Lime Buck (page 113) and Lapsang souchong tea concentrate in our Traverse City (page 198).
- **Coffee** adds astringency and bitter flavor to balance sweetness in Espresso Tonic (page 104) and Bird in the Hand (page 250).
- **Flavored syrups** add body and layers of flavor, including fruity, tart, herbal, spiced, or nutty. Our Spiced Orange Soda (page 81) uses two types of flavored syrups.
- **Spices and herbs** contribute body, earthy and bitter flavors, and aroma, as in Doctor's Orders (page 103), which has fresh turmeric root, and Tongue Thai'd (page 254), which muddles chile and basil.

Tinctures and Bitters

A tincture is an extremely concentrated infusion made from plant material steeped in a small amount of alcohol or glycerol (vegetable glycerin). Tinctures add concentrated flavor to cocktails when used in tiny amounts.

Not all tinctures are bitter, but in the cocktail world, bitters are the most widely known examples of a tincture. **Potable bitters** are liqueurs intended for sipping, such as aperitivi and digestivi. This broad category includes Campari and similar liqueurs and amari. **Nonpotable bitters** are not meant for sipping on their own; rather, these intensely concentrated elixirs are designed to be added to cocktails in minuscule amounts to contribute nuanced yet complex flavors and aromas.

There are hundreds of types of cocktail bitters. Some have one predominant flavor profile, like orange, mint, or maple, and others are blends of many flavors, like old-fashioned aromatic bitters. Stocking different types is a fun, low-risk way to experiment with different flavor profiles in cocktails. See pages 462–463 for our DIY tinctures and bitters recipes.

- **Vegetable glycerin** adds silky texture and viscosity to our Traverse City (page 198).
- **Effervescence** adds texture, as in Pear-Lavender Punch (page 55) and Bubbly Beet (page 87), which use seltzer, and Sparkling Celery (page 288), for which we carbonate the entire cocktail.
- **Eggs and dairy** add texture and body (especially egg whites) as well as richness (especially whole eggs) to Foggy Day (page 221), Peanut Butter Flip (page 381), and Egg Notnog (page 387).
- **Ice**, when shaken into a zero-proof cocktail, adds texture through emulsification and aeration, as in Smoke and Mirrors (page 223).
- Thoughtful **garnishes** add everything from flavor to aroma to texture. The apple, orange, and cinnamon stick garnish in Mulled Cider (page 420) creates a feast for nose and palate. Edible flowers add aroma to Pear-Lavender Punch (page 55).

CRAFTING A ZERO-PROOF COCKTAIL: TRAVERSE CITY

Flavor
Lapsang souchong tea adds smoky notes like a spirit; cherry juice evokes the dark fruit flavors of sweet vermouth.

Aroma
Rosemary in the tea concentrate adds an herbal scent.

Body and texture
Glycerin adds silky viscosity and tea contributes astringency.

Balance
A sweet cherry garnish offsets the tart cherry juice. Nonalcoholic old-fashioned aromatic bitters tie it all together.

Barware

When it comes to cocktail-making tools and serving glassware, you can certainly get by with a handful of pared-back necessities. To build a more impressive home bar and practice a wider variety of cocktail-making techniques, the sky's the limit in terms of the fun and useful gadgets you can add to your toolkit and the different styles of glassware you can keep at the ready.

Tools

Home-bar equipment essentials include a sturdy cocktail shaker, a mixing glass and bar spoon, a jigger, strainers, and a sharp knife. Additional tools will enhance your cocktail-making experience and help you practice your skills.

SHAKING, STIRRING, MUDDLING, BLENDING

Shakers There are three general styles of shaker: the two-piece Boston shaker, the two-piece tin-on-tin shaker, and the three-piece cobbler shaker.

We used the Boston shaker to develop our recipes. It consists of one larger stainless-steel cup and a second, smaller glass made of tempered (safety) glass. We found the metal-glass seal easier to break than an all-metal seal, and the glass cup allows you to see ingredients as you add them. We like the Houdini by Rabbit 24oz Stainless Steel & Glass Boston Cocktail Shaker.

Two-piece stainless-steel shakers chill your cocktail faster, since stainless steel is a better conductor than glass, transferring heat out of the liquid faster. There's also no risk of breakage with a tin-on-tin shaker.

The cobbler shaker has a bottom mixing cup, a built-in strainer on top, and a cap to seal it. Metal and plastic components will be less likely than glass to break. Our favorite cobbler shaker, the Tovolo Stainless Steel Cocktail Shaker, has a built-in citrus juicer on top. We also like the classic-looking Yukiwa Stainless Steel Jumbo Cobbler Cocktail Shaker. Different brands come in a multitude of sizes, but our preferred size is about 24 ounces.

Mixing Glass A sturdy, straight-sided glass with a pouring spout is our choice for stirring cocktails with ice. These are available in both metal and glass versions. A metal version will obviously never break, but it tends to be less stable at the base than a glass mixing glass. If you buy a glass mixing glass, look for a thick-walled vessel. If you buy a metal mixing glass, look for one that is double walled. Although a metal glass may chill your drink a little faster than a glass one, for many home bartenders, the choice is aesthetic. Whichever type you choose, opt for a 16-ounce mixing glass, which will work for both single cocktails and double batches.

Bar Spoon A long-handled stainless-steel bar spoon is essential to achieve maximum chilling with minimal dilution when stirring drinks with ice. For the greatest ease of use, look for one that has a handle 10½ to 12½ inches long. A twizzled handle will give you greater control than a smooth handle. Medium-size spoon bowls (about 1 inch) provide just enough surface area to push larger pieces of ice confidently while still moving nimbly around the confines of the vessel. These bowls are also big enough to hold olives and cherries and securely transfer them from their jars to finished drinks. We like the Cocktail Kingdom Teardrop Barspoon.

Swizzle Stick A traditional wooden Caribbean swizzle stick, or bois lélé, is the best way to properly froth cocktails such as the Rum Runner (page 249), where the ingredients are mixed together in the serving glass with crushed ice. The bottom of this tool consists of wood prongs forming a fan shape.

Muddler Originally known as toddy sticks and used to crush chunks of sugar into water, muddlers are one of the oldest purpose-built cocktail tools. Nowadays these tools for smashing citrus and herbs can be made of stainless steel, plastic, or wood. Look for one with a long enough handle so that your hand won't be hitting the mixing glass when you use it. We prefer an unvarnished wood muddler at least 9½ inches long with a flat head and a comfortable, indented grip. Our winner is the Fletcher's Mill maple muddler, which is 11 inches long and has two heads, one that's 1.75 inches and a smaller one that's 1.4 inches. If you buy a different wood muddler, make sure it's unvarnished. If you prefer a metal muddler, we recommend the OXO Steel Muddler, which has a nubbly surface head that helps break down citrus and herbs more extensively than a flat head.

Blender This is an essential countertop appliance for frozen and blended drinks. For more information, see page 426.

WHICH SHAKER SHOULD YOU CHOOSE?

Many home bartenders choose the cobbler shaker because it's easy to seal and less likely to leak when you're shaking a drink. Since the built-in strainer is fitted neatly between the cup and the top, when it comes time to serve, there's less juggling of separate strainers, which can take a bit of coordination and has a higher risk of becoming messy. The cobbler shaker has always been the default choice in cocktail bars in Japan, where technique is highly prized, and that has contributed to this shaker's enduring popularity.

Two-piece shakers offer more room for ingredients to move (particularly important when it comes to shaking egg-white cocktails). The two-piece tin-on-tin shaker is the choice of professional bartenders in the United States, who swear by its efficacy. The Boston shaker version with a glass mixing cup is beginner friendly because you can see what's going on in the glass and the seal breaks more easily than the seal on an all-metal shaker (but then again, the glass mixing cup breaks more easily too).

Both styles work, so the choice really is personal. No matter what you use, proper shaking technique (see pages 24–25) will be the factor that earns you cocktail cred in the eyes of your guests.

PREPPING AND MEASURING

Paring Knife A small, sharp paring knife is all you need for slicing or chopping fruit and other fresh ingredients. Our favorite is the Victorinox Swiss Classic Spear Point.

Channel Knife Channel knives have sharp blades and grippy handles for removing pieces of citrus peel from fruit. Many zesters have a built-in channel knife, but these produce citrus pieces that are too thin and wispy for garnishing, so we recommend a dedicated channel knife such as the Victorinox Channel Knife or the Mercer Culinary Channel Knife.

Peeler A Y-shaped peeler cuts thicker strips of citrus peel for expressing citrus oils onto the surface of cocktails. We like the Kuhn Rikon Original Swiss Peeler.

Bar Boards Bar boards are the babies of the cutting board family. Stability, not size, is what counts. We like the OXO Good Grips Prep Cutting Board, which has rubbery grips, is reversible, and has a juice groove on one side. If you prefer a wooden bar board, try the Teakhaus Square Marine Board with Juice Canal, which also is handsome enough to serve cheese or charcuterie on after you've prepped your cocktail ingredients.

Manual Juicer A simple handheld press-style juicer makes quick work of juicing citrus. Our favorite is the Chef'n FreshForce.

Electric Juicer We like the Omega VSJ843QS Pure Press Cold Press Masticating Vegetable and Fruit Extractor, which is easy to use and clean, and the Breville Juice Fountain Cold, which is fast and powerful. See page 12 to learn how to make fresh juice without an electric juicer.

Jigger A read-from-above graduated jigger with ounce and tablespoon markings is best for measuring spirits. Our favorite is the OXO Good Grips Mini Angled Measuring Cup. For something with more pizzazz in the looks department, try the OXO Steel Double Jigger.

Measuring Cup A 1-cup glass liquid measuring cup (our winner is Pyrex) will allow you to measure larger amounts in ounces, our preferred method.

Measuring Spoons For consistent quality and flavor from cocktail to cocktail, we recommend using measuring spoons to measure your bitters (and all amounts less than ¼ ounce). Cuisipro makes our favorites.

Storage Containers For fridge door cocktails, you'll want 1-liter glass bottles or 1-quart Mason jars. For the aged and infused cocktails in chapters 9 and 10 and the bitters recipes in the Backbar, you'll need 1-quart Mason jars. To store homemade simple and flavored syrups, get 8-ounce glass jars. Glass dropper bottles are best for tinctures and are also a good option for storing bitters.

Hawthorne Strainer This strainer is made of a flat circular piece of metal with holes, bordered by a flexible spring. The spring allows the Hawthorne strainer to fit neatly into any shaker or mixing glass. Look for one with a tight spring, which will catch smaller pieces of ice and solids and will make for a better-strained cocktail. Our pick is the Cocktail Kingdom Koriko Cocktail Strainer.

Julep Strainer Developed for mint julep imbibers to hold over their cups to keep from getting a face full of crushed ice and mint as they drink, this perforated bowl-shaped strainer fits well into a standard mixing glass. We use it for stirred cocktails. Any stainless-steel julep strainer will work; just make sure it fits the diameter of your mixing glass. Sets of varying sizes are available.

Small Fine-Mesh Strainer We double-strain cocktails into the serving glass using a small fine-mesh strainer. This provides further insurance against solid ingredients and errant ice shards ending up in your drink. Look for a small strainer with superfine mesh and a straight handle rather than an offset one. Our top picks are the Rösle Stainless Steel Fine Mesh Tea Strainer and the Küchenprofi Heavy Duty Fine Mesh Classic Strainer.

ICE MAKING

Mallet and Lewis Bag Tucking ice for drinks like the Mai Tai (page 240) into a canvas bag and whacking it with a wooden mallet produces fluffier, drier crushed ice than if using a food processor. Plus, it's more fun and makes you look like a cocktail pro in front of guests.

Ice Cube Trays and Molds We recommend ¾- to 1¼-inch silicone or rubber ice cube trays to make ice for shaking cocktails and 2-inch trays to make ice for serving. Trays with lids will keep your cubes from picking up any freezer odors. Our favorite 2-inch cube mold is OXO Good Grips Silicone Ice Cube Tray—Large Cubes. Its interior tray is silicone, but it has a hard plastic frame that keeps the cubes perfectly square.

THE IMPORTANCE OF MEASURING

Though in bars you may be impressed watching a bartender skillfully free-pouring drinks, for cocktails with a perfect balance of flavors every time, measure your ingredients. As little as ¼-ounce difference in lemon juice or simple syrup, for example, can have a significant impact on the outcome of your drink.

We follow this rule even for bitters. Traditionally in cocktail recipes, bitters are called for in "dashes" or "drops." However, we learned in testing that the actual amount in a dash or drop can vary wildly depending on the diameter of the dropper, the size of the dasher, how much liquid is in the bottle, the size of the bottle, and even the force with which you expel the liquid. It's easy and consistent to drop or dash your bitters into a teaspoon measure before adding them to your cocktail. That's what we do, and that's what we recommend you do, too.

Tinctures, on the other hand, are superconcentrated and used in tiny amounts. You need on average 16 drops to equal ⅛ teaspoon, and since you need only 2 or 3 drops of tincture in any given cocktail, we call for drops.

To make sparklingly transparent, perfectly cube-shaped ice cubes, we like True Cubes Clear Ice Maker. Its insulated plastic frame makes it easy to transport to the freezer and helps protect the interior silicone tray from freezer odors. Keep in mind that it does require a larger chunk of freezer space than an ice cube tray, and it can be a bit tricky to pry the silicone ice tray out of its insulated frame.

For even more "wow" factor, consider an ice sphere mold. One large round piece of ice instantly gives your cocktail an elegant, polished look. In addition to the square cube maker, True Cubes sells an ice sphere insert that makes 4 large, clear ice balls. Zoku Ice Ball Molds are more compact, though they don't make clear spheres.

ELEVATED FINISHING TOUCHES

Cocktail Picks and Skewers Whether metal, bamboo, or plastic, cocktail picks allow you to enjoy edible garnishes without having to fish them out with your fingers. A varied collection of picks is a great way to add flair when serving cocktails.

Kitchen Torch Charring garnishes with a kitchen torch is a surefire way to add a professional touch. You can use this for the Cinnamon Old-Fashioned (page 124) or the Caramelized Banana Old-Fashioned (page 132). And generally, torching citrus peel imparts a mellow, caramelized flavor to a citrus garnish. See page 237 to learn how to flame citrus.

Ice Stamps These tools allow you to add an impressive flourish to your ice. Typically made of metal, when pressed against the side of an ice cube, they use thermal properties to impress a pattern into the cube in seconds.

Portable Smoke Infuser Once found only in modernist bars and restaurants, these tools have recently become more accessible to home bartenders. To make cocktails like the Smoked New York Sour (page 312), consider a user-friendly model like the Breville/PolyScience Smoking Gun Pro. For more information on how to smoke cocktails, see page 301.

iSi Cream Whipper To make a carbonated cocktail like Pomme de Champagne (page 286) or Sparkling Celery (page 288), you'll want a 1-quart iSi Gourmet Whip cream whipper, a handheld kitchen tool more typically used for making and piping whipped cream.

Glassware

Beyond looking stylish, particular types of glasses are appropriate for different reasons. A stemmed cocktail glass keeps your hand from warming a drink served up (with no ice) too quickly. A sturdy, thick-bottomed rocks glass allows room for chunky ice cubes and helps insulate your on-the-rocks cocktail. A tall, slender highball glass keeps seltzer bubbles from dissipating too quickly. With every recipe, we recommend a particular style or styles of glassware that we think is best for serving. Having said that, if you have a different preference or want to achieve a different vibe, go for it.

The most important thing, no matter which glass you choose, is to chill it in the freezer for a few minutes. This ensures all the frosty goodness you've created in the shaker or mixing glass won't be lost by serving your carefully made cocktail in a room-temperature glass.

Cocktail Glass This iconic stemmed glass is needed for shaken or stirred cocktails served up. Choose a 5½- or 6-ounce V-shaped martini glass, bowl-shaped coupe , or bell-shaped Nick and Nora.

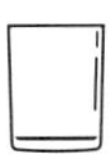

Rocks Glass Rocks glasses are essential for countless stirred or shaken cocktails served usually (but not always) over ice. They have straight sides and a sturdy base. For the most versatility, we recommend an 11-ounce size. Old-fashioned glasses are similar but are traditionally smaller, though the distinctions have blurred (see page 120 for more information).

Highball Glass A tall, narrow 12-ounce highball glass is used for so-called long drinks, which are made with seltzer, juice, or other nonalcoholic mixers and cubed ice. Collins glasses are similar in shape but historically a little smaller in volume.

Wineglass A 10- to 12-ounce wineglass works just as well as a flute glass in any cocktail situation involving wine as a primary ingredient, from the Aperol Spritz (page 49) to Classic Sangria (page 353) to Peach-Strawberry Frosé (page 440). This includes cocktails that use sparkling wine (see page 61 for more information).

Pint Glass A 16-ounce pint glass is the right size for many classic beer-based cocktails like the Michelada (page 366) and for some tropical cocktails.

Mug An 8-ounce heatproof mug is essential for hot drinks like Irish Coffee (page 405) and Mulled Cider (page 420). A glass mug lets you see the cocktail, but any mug you like will do.

Flute Glass A 6-ounce flute glass is a nice option for mimosas (pages 38–41), as well as the Fernet Fizz (page 339). And we do love a classic Champagne Cocktail (page 36) served in a flute.

Punch Cups and Bowl A set of 8-ounce punch cups with a 6-quart punch bowl is great if you have the storage space, and this will let you serve sparkling punches (see pages 54–57) and tropical punches (see pages 256–261) in traditional style. If not, you can use mugs and any 6-quart container.

Hurricane Glass For frozen and tropical drinks (like Frozen Hurricanes, page 438), a 12-ounce version of this hurricane lamp-shaped glass is a nice option. Other tall glasses, such as highballs, work too.

Tropical Glass If you're into tropical drinks, pick up a fun set of glassware in shapes including flamingos, fish, or pineapple. But highball and rocks glasses will work just fine for these cocktails.

Techniques

Cocktail technique is nuanced, so it's easy to lull yourself into thinking that it's not important. Following our guidelines for how to stir, shake, muddle, strain, and make ice will deliver consistently impressive and totally delicious results every time.

Building

With built drinks, the mixing vessel is the serving vessel. We've all had the experience of being served a cocktail that wasn't properly combined; you take a sip through a straw and get just the bottom spirit or sweet juice. A gentle mixing treatment preserves carbonation in spritzes, highballs, and tonics.

How to Build a Cocktail

1. Fill chilled highball glass halfway with ice. Add densest ingredients first (such as spirit, juice, and/or syrup) and, using bar spoon, stir until combined.

2. Add sparkling ingredient and, using bar spoon, gently lift spirit mixture from bottom of glass to top to combine. Top with additional ice.

Swizzling

The technique of swizzling originated in the Caribbean and tends to be used for mixing rum-based tropical drinks. Swizzle sticks are a way to build a drink meant to be served over crushed ice right in the serving glass. We experienced greatest success using this techique with drinks served in highball glasses.

How to Swizzle a Cocktail

1. Fill chilled glass halfway with crushed ice and add cocktail ingredients. Insert swizzle stick prong side down into glass.

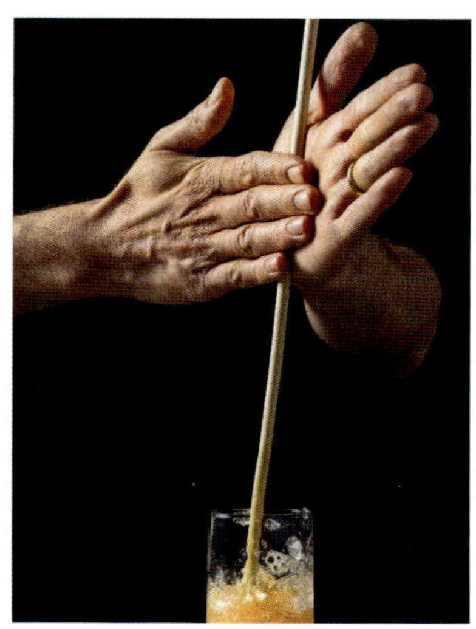

2. Holding swizzle stick between palms of hands, use back-and-forth motion to swizzle cocktail, slowly lifting swizzle stick from bottom of glass to top.

Stirring

Stirring with ice in a mixing glass before straining into a serving glass is the best approach when making spirit-forward cocktails, to gently chill them while avoiding aeration (which would change the texture) and protecting them against excess dilution.

The mixing glass's straight sides and evenly wide circumference allow for optimal ice movement when stirring. As a result, your drink mixes and chills while being diluted just enough to enhance the flavors of the ingredients. The mixing glass's pouring spout makes it easy to transfer your cocktail without losing any precious drops.

The technique of keeping the outer curved side of the spoon against the wall of the glass while stirring takes a little practice, but once you learn it, the spoon will glide around magically, seemingly of its own accord.

For cocktails served up, stir for about 1 minute. Some lower-ABV cocktails served up are stirred for 30 seconds. For cocktails that will be served on the rocks, stir for about 30 seconds. And for drinks that are intended to be stirred together and served over crushed ice, like the Whiskey Smash (page 139), we stir them in the mixing glass with no ice at all.

How to Stir a Cocktail

1. Assemble ingredients in mixing glass, then fill glass three-quarters full with ice.

2. Insert bar spoon into mixing glass with outer curved side positioned against wall of glass. Hold base of mixing glass firmly. Loosely grasp stem of spoon with other hand, between thumb, forefinger, and middle finger (similar to how you would hold a pencil).

3. Pivot wrist of hand holding spoon to guide convex side of spoon around wall of glass, allowing stem of spoon to rotate between your fingers until cocktail is combined and chilled, for time specified in recipe; remove spoon.

4. Fit julep or Hawthorne strainer into mixing glass and decant drink into chilled serving glass.

Shaking

Shaking chills and dilutes cocktails more vigorously than stirring, helping to aerate, emulsify, and integrate ingredients such as juices, cream or milk, or egg whites.

Most shaken cocktails get a single shake with cubed ice before being strained into a serving glass. Drinks containing egg whites or whole eggs benefit from a two-stage shaking process: first an initial "dry" shake (without ice) to break down the egg proteins and develop a light, stable foam, then a second shake with ice to emulsify and aerate the finished cocktail. With no ice to cause the metal to chill and contract around the glass, you must modify the technique to ensure a proper seal. Center the mixing glass in the tin rather than angling it flush. Then unseal, add the ice, and seal and shake a second time as directed.

For cocktails served up, we shake for 15 seconds. For cocktails served over ice, we shake for 5 seconds. For dry-shaking a cocktail containing egg whites or whole eggs, about 45 seconds does the job of emulsifying the ingredients. We recommend a two-piece shaker for dry shaking, as it has more room to allow for expansion of egg whites than a cobbler shaker.

How to Shake Using a Boston Shaker

1. Assemble ingredients in mixing glass or tin, then fill with ice. Invert mixing glass and its contents into shaker tin and angle glass so that one side is flush with tin. Firmly tap base of glass with heel of hand to form tight seal.

2. Hold base of shaker tin firmly with one hand and base of mixing glass firmly with other hand. Using vigorous back-and-forth motion (ice should hit both ends of shaker), shake cocktail for time specified in recipe.

3. To break seal, position shaker on counter with mixing glass on top and angled toward you. Grip side of shaker tin with 1 hand and, using heel of other hand, firmly tap rim of tin on opposite side. (You may have to do this more than once.) Remove mixing glass.

4. Fit Hawthorne strainer onto shaker tin and decant cocktail into chilled serving glass, using fine-mesh strainer to double-strain if directed.

How to Shake Using a Cobbler Shaker

1. Assemble ingredients in base of shaker, then fill with ice.

2. Fit shaker with strainer top and cap to seal.

3. Hold base of shaker firmly with one hand and top of shaker firmly with other hand. Using vigorous back-and-forth motion (ice should hit both ends of shaker), shake cocktail for time specified in recipe.

4. Remove cap (you may need to loosen by gently tapping on counter) and decant cocktail into chilled serving glass, using fine-mesh strainer to double-strain if directed.

THE SCIENCE OF DILUTION

There's a popular notion that it's possible—even desirable—to chill a drink without diluting it. But that's not how ice works. Ice doesn't cool down a cocktail simply by being cold itself; it chills by the process of melting. And the purpose of stirring or shaking a cocktail, or serving it on the rocks, is all about causing the ice to melt in a controlled way.

The cooling power of ice is unleashed only when it undergoes a phase change—that is, when it starts to melt. In order to make that change from solid to liquid, ice needs to draw heat from its surroundings—a lot of heat. When the surroundings are a cocktail, the ice pulls that heat out of the drink, turning it cold.

If you put ½ ounce of ice-cold water (32 degrees Fahrenheit) into 2 ounces of room-temperature liquor (68 degrees Fahrenheit), the mixture will drop to 61 degrees. But if you put ½ ounce of ice (also 32 degrees Fahrenheit) into that same liquor and allow it to melt, the temperature of the whole drink will come down to 30 degrees Fahrenheit. How is this possible?

It's all about that phase change. Any time a substance changes phase—from solid to liquid, liquid to gas, or vice versa—energy is involved. To melt a single ½-ounce ice cube requires 4.7 kilojoules of heat. And pulling 4.7 kilojoules out of 2 ounces of room-temp liquor is enough to chill it to 30 degrees.

The water that melts from the ice dilutes the drink, and cocktail recipes are designed with this in mind. The addition of water helps harmonize and soften the flavors of the drink. In a typical cocktail, 25 to 35 percent of the volume is made up of water that was added by melting ice. And that's no accident.

Muddling

Muddling infuses fresh flavors from solid ingredients directly into a cocktail. This technique creates exciting flavor opportunities because of the range of ingredients that you can muddle. Fresh herbs, spices, fruits, and vegetables are fair game. Try cucumbers, bell or chile peppers, celery, arugula, fresh ginger, or nearly any fruit. Break things down into smaller pieces for ease: Cut citrus into wedges, cut fresh ginger into coins, chop celery, and so on. About 30 seconds is sufficient time to crush any raw ingredients, releasing their juices or expressing their aromatic oils.

A note about muddling herbs: For stirred cocktails and for shaken cocktails served over ice, we muddle delicate herbs such as mint and basil. Adding a little simple syrup when muddling these herbs acts as a lubricant and absorbs the flavors, making for better distribution in the cocktail. For shaken cocktails served up, we add delicate herbs directly to the shaker and shake them along with the other ingredients (which is a means of muddling and effectively consolidates effort).

Because it's easy to overmuddle sturdy herbs like oregano or thyme and end up with a "swampy" flavor, we make syrups with these herbs (see page 459), using heat to extract flavor. Syrups aren't great for delicate herbs because they end up with a cooked flavor.

How to Muddle Fresh Herbs

1. Add herb leaves and simple syrup to base of mixing glass or cocktail shaker.

2. Hold mixing glass or cocktail shaker firmly with one hand. Gripping muddler with other hand, press firmly into herbs, rotating handle slightly as you progress, until herbs are broken down and fragrant, about 30 seconds.

How to Muddle Fresh Fruits and Vegetables

1. Cut fruits or vegetables into small pieces, then add to base of mixing glass or cocktail shaker.

2. Hold mixing glass or cocktail shaker firmly with 1 hand. Gripping muddler with other hand, press firmly into fruit, rotating handle slightly as you progress, until fruit is broken down and all juice has been expressed, about 30 seconds.

Straining

Proper straining prevents large pieces of ice from getting into your cocktail. We use a julep strainer when straining from a mixing glass into a serving glass and a Hawthorne strainer when straining from a Boston shaker into a serving glass.

Double-straining through a small fine-mesh strainer is a great way to take your cocktails to the next level by removing smaller bits of ice and any small solids that may be left over from the mixing process. Double straining may seem fussy, but it's not. While you don't have to double-strain cocktails, we strongly suggest it for the most professional results.

We double-strain all shaken cocktails, including cocktails made with egg whites or whole eggs, and we double-strain muddled stirred cocktails. We single-strain traditional stirred cocktails.

Ice Making

You can learn a lot about ice just by looking at it. A pristinely clear cube tells you it's made from pure water in a perfect crystal lattice. Cloudy ice signals impurities, most commonly trapped gas, which causes irregular crystals. Impurities such as chlorine impart unwanted flavors, while absorbed gases like oxygen and nitrogen and irregular crystals weaken ice cubes, making them more prone to shattering while shaking. This creates unwanted ice shards that will overdilute your cocktail.

For building, stirring, and shaking cocktails, we recommend ¾- to 1¼-inch cubes. This size allows for easy stirring in a serving or mixing glass and roomy shaking in any style of shaker, with just the right amount of melting to ensure proper chilling and dilution.

For serving cocktails, you can use these same cubes. We also love oversize cubes (2 inches), spheres, and hand-carved chunks to add style and pizzazz to a cocktail. If you've chilled your cocktail properly when making it, then both smaller cubes and larger-format ice will work well when presenting it. No matter what you use, we have some tips for making the best ice.

BEST PRACTICES FOR THE CLEAREST ICE

- Use mineral-free distilled water. You can substitute filtered tap water; however, the ice will not be quite as clear due to trace minerals in tap water. We don't suggest unfiltered tap water.
- Boil the water to drive off most of the dissolved air. Trapped air causes ice not only to turn cloudy, but also to melt faster, which dilutes your cocktail more quickly.
- Insulate the bottom of your ice cube trays (see page 28), which will cause the ice to freeze from the top down, pushing any remaining dissolved air to the bottom of the cubes and leaving the bulk of the cubes clear.
- Store your ice in an airtight container to preserve its looks and prevent it from picking up freezer odors.

How to Make Practically Clear Ice

Bartenders may go to time-consuming lengths to achieve perfectly clear ice for craft cocktails—or they may simply purchase it from specialty ice distributors. Our easy technique results in as-close-to-clear ice as is practical for the home bartender. Even using boiled distilled water, you may still get a hazy spot, but it will be much smaller and less noticeable. Insulating the sides and bottom of the ice trays using a baking dish lined with dish towels ensures the ice freezes from the top down, achieving 95 percent perfectly clear cubes. We use this method to make 1-inch cubes for building, stirring, and shaking cocktails and 2-inch cubes for serving. To develop this ice, we used our winning brand of silicone ice trays by Tovolo, which measure about 6½ inches by 4½ inches; rubber ice trays also work. If you have larger trays, you may be able to fit only one in the baking dish. To remove off-odors from silicone ice trays, bake them at 350 degrees for 1 hour. You will get about 7 cups of ice using this method.

1. Fold 3 dish towels in half widthwise, then stack in 13 by 9-inch baking dish, allowing towels to overhang edges.

2. Arrange two 6½ by 4½-inch silicone ice cube trays in center of prepared dish. Roll up additional towels and tuck into sides of dish as needed to ensure trays are packed snugly.

3. Bring 6 cups distilled water to boil in a kettle. Carefully pour water into trays; you may have extra water. Let cool completely, about 30 minutes. Place baking dish in freezer and let sit, uncovered, until ice is completely frozen, at least 8 hours.

4. Remove ice cubes from trays and place in zipper-lock freezer bags for storage. To remove cloudy side of ice cubes, place cloudy side down on overturned sheet pan. (Pan will transfer heat and melt ice.)

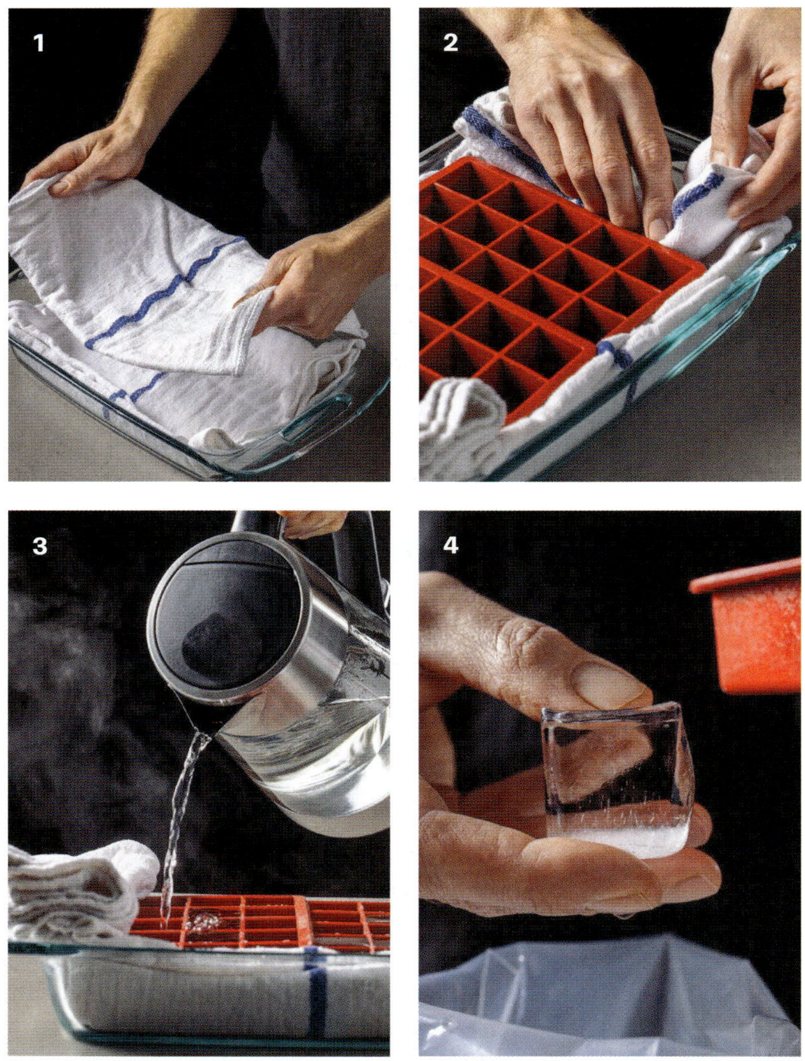

How to Make Block Ice

Elevate your cocktails using a technique seen in craft bars all over the world. Dramatic-looking chunks of hand-carved ice will leave your guests marveling. To make an ice block, you'll need a small, hard insulated drinks cooler (plus enough space in your freezer to store it). A 9-quart cooler approximately 13 inches long by 10 inches wide by 9 inches tall will work, as will a 5-quart cooler about 10 inches long by 8 inches wide by 7 inches tall. You need only the top 2 inches of water to freeze—and knowing when this happens involves trial and error based on your freezer. Since impurities fall to the bottom of the cooler, you don't need distilled water. Tempering is critical to prevent the ice from shattering.

1. Bring large pot of water to boil. Let cool for 1 hour.

2. Pour water into drinks cooler. Do not cover. Freeze until top 2 inches have frozen solid, 36 to 48 hours.

3. Remove from freezer and let sit for 1 hour to temper. Over sink, partially invert cooler to allow excess water to drain. Then, fully invert cooler over rimmed baking sheet to remove ice block.

4. On cutting board, using large serrated knife or ice pick, trim edges of block as needed to create neat 2-inch-thick rectangle. (If not carving right away, transfer to zipper-lock freezer storage bag and store in freezer; let temper for 30 minutes before carving.)

How to Carve Block Ice

1. To make 2-inch cubes, position large serrated knife 2 inches from 1 short end of tempered ice block. Use sawing motion to create ¼-inch-deep groove around block on all sides.

2. Lay block flat and position knife in groove on top of ice block. Firmly tap top side of knife with mallet or meat pounder so ice brick becomes separated from block.

3. Position serrated knife 2 inches from 1 short end of ice brick. Repeat process of scoring and striking ice brick to cleave off pieces measuring 2 inches by 2 inches.

4. If smaller pieces are desired, repeat process of scoring and striking to cleave off smaller cubes or chunks. Repeat entire process as needed to make more ice pieces.

How to Make an Ice Ring

Ice rings are an effective and showstopping way to keep punches cold. To make your ice ring even more decorative, you can add herbs, edible blossoms, or fruits that complement your punch.

1. Arrange 1 to 2 cups herbs, flowers, and/or berries around base of Bundt pan. Nestle 2 to 3 cups sliced citrus, stone fruit, and/or cucumber into pan, ensuring grooves of pan are tightly packed.

2. Slowly pour in water, adding just enough to cover the ingredients. Freeze until solid, at least 8 hours.

3. Let pan sit at room temperature for about 30 minutes, then invert mold onto rimmed baking sheet. Transfer ring to punch bowl or store in freezer.

10 PRO SECRETS TO ELEVATE YOUR COCKTAILS AT HOME

- Understanding cocktail formulas lets you customize cocktails to your palate.
- Stirring or shaking for specified times results in ideal dilution and chilling.
- With good technique, you can muddle nearly anything.
- Splitting the spirit base can increase your cocktail's complexity.
- Flavored simple syrups add a lot more than just sweetness.
- Concentrated tinctures and bitters are an effective way to season cocktails.
- Double-straining most cocktails results in the best texture.
- Investing time in ice makes for a show-stopping presentation.
- Chilling glassware makes a difference in helping to keep cocktails cold.
- Garnishing with intention enhances the entire cocktail experience.

How to Use This Book

The chapters in this book are organized by cocktail family—highballs, martinis, sours, and more—with each family defined based on its fundamental ingredient formula(s) and taking technique into account. Within each chapter, we highlight one or two featured cocktails—titans of their category—by giving them an extended introduction and following them with three or four cocktails that are closely tied to the featured drink. We acknowledge that cocktails cross categories, and different people may define cocktail families in different ways. For example, we placed the Aperol Spritz (page 49) in the sparkling-wine cocktail chapter, though it's often enjoyed as an aperitivo. The Ramos Gin Fizz (page 72) is a sour, but it's also a highball; we've chosen to place it in the highballs chapter. Regardless of whether you agree or disagree with choices like these, our goal is to help you understand both the connections and the divergences between different drinks. Once you understand the fundamental formulas, then you can let your creativity take over to discover new riffs.

A Guide to the Recipes

Each chapter includes one or two "featured recipes" or "parent recipes," which are hallmark recipes for that particular cocktail family. Following those recipes are three or four substantial variations—consider them the offspring of the parent recipes. And there are many additional recipes in each chapter that continue to expand and grow the concept of each cocktail family.

ZERO PROOF

If a cocktail is zero proof, we have noted that in the recipe yield.

SWEETNESS SCALE

Each drink's sweetness level is ranked from zero to three stars, with zero being not sweet at all, as for the Gin Martini (page 155) and three being luscious enough for dessert, as for the Brandy Alexander (page 392).

✧ ✧ ✧ = dry
✦ ✧ ✧ = off-dry
✦ ✦ ✧ = medium-sweet
✦ ✦ ✦ = sweet

FLAVOR PROFILES

When you think about what you're in the mood to drink, you may not always choose a cocktail according to its primary spirit. Maybe you're in the mood for a citrusy cocktail, or a smoky cocktail. The flavor profile we've included with every cocktail lists up to three different descriptors for the primary flavors of that drink, chosen from this list and listed alphabetically. For a list of cocktails grouped by their flavor descriptors, see page 471.

- Bitter
- Citrusy
- Creamy
- Floral
- Fruity (such as berries, stone fruit, apple, melon)
- Herbal
- Nutty
- Savory
- Smoky
- Spiced (think cinnamon, nutmeg, ginger)
- Spicy (chile-spicy)
- Spirit forward
- Tart
- Toasted (imparted by oak aging, such as vanilla, caramel, coffee)
- Tropical (such as pineapple, banana, guava, coconut)

Sparklers, Champagne *and* Otherwise

Cocktails made with Champagne or sparkling wine have been around for a long time. Champagne cocktails specifically were first mentioned in print in the middle of the 1800s. Jerry Thomas's recipe in his 1862 *How to Mix Drinks, or The Bon Vivant's Companion* calls for shaking the cocktail—which seems fairly risky given the tendency for bubbly drinks to become extremely volatile when shaken in a closed environment.

Later, during the pre-Prohibition Golden Age of cocktails, the "cocktail royale" trend emerged, which involved topping stirred, spirit-based cocktails with Champagne, either stirred in or floated on top. The Kir Royale (page 46) is a simplified iteration on this style, in which the white wine in a Kir cocktail is replaced with sparkling wine. There was even a popular version of the Manhattan with a Champagne float, often referred to as the Boothby, named for William Boothby, California congressman and author of the 1908 book *The World's Drinks and How to Mix Them.*

In this chapter, we focus on cocktails with sparkling wine as the star, enhanced by spirits and liqueurs, flavored syrups, juices, and seltzer. We begin with the most iconic sparkling wine cocktail of them all: the Champagne Cocktail (page 36), which is made with simply Champagne and a bitters-soaked sugar cube, adorned with a lemon twist. Then we move into the Mimosa family, in which juices feature prominently—and which counts the Bellini (page 40) as a famous member. Other drinks might substitute liqueur for juice and/or add seltzer for additional carbonation.

Besides individual cocktails, this chapter also highlights sparkling punches to serve a crowd. Their history goes back even further than that of the Champagne cocktail, to 1700s Europe. As you might expect for a drink with such a long history, there are as many recipes as there are stars in the sky. Many are kitchen sink–type recipes, dumping whatever is on hand into a bowl, with predictably amateurish results.

We developed our punch recipes to achieve nuanced, balanced flavors. Certainly when the holiday season rolls around, having a sophisticated, elegant punch recipe that serves a lot of people is key. But why not associate them with conviviality year-round? You can do just that with these punches for all seasons, from Spiced Cranberry-Orange Punch (page 57) to Summer Stone-Fruit Punch (page 54).

Sparklers

Fundamental Formula

sparkling wine + sweetener + bitters

BUILD ON THE FUNDAMENTALS

The Champagne Cocktail (page 36) is an extremely simple formula. Liqueurs and juices are versatile ways to go beyond this when building sparkling wine cocktails. Make a classic Mimosa and variations (page 38–41) by subbing juice and/or liqueur for the sweetener (reducing the amount of sparkling wine accordingly). Or combine sparkling wine with a liqueur and bitters, as in our Royal Berry (page 46). Add seltzer to the wine-liqueur formula to build the spritzes on pages 48–53. For a slightly stronger sparkling wine cocktail, you can incorporate a spirit and juice, as in the French 75 (page 42). Sparkling punches (pages 54–59) can have it all (within reason): sparkling wine, liqueur or spirit, juice, and a sweetener. Our nonalcoholic punches rely on flavorful juices, fresh fruits, seltzer for fizz, and spices and herbs.

Types of Sparkling Wines

CHAMPAGNE is the gold standard. It must be made in the Champagne region of France, using specific grapes and the region's traditional production method (méthode traditionnelle, also called méthode champenoise). The wine must undergo a second fermentation in the bottle, which contributes to its complex flavor and signature bubble. That incredible flavor and texture comes with a higher price tag. Prosecco and cava are often great, more affordable alternatives when making cocktails with sparkling wine.

PROSECCO is also made with specific grapes but tends to use a different method than Champagne (the Charmat process, often called the Martinotti process in Italy). The second fermentation of prosecco takes place in large tanks (usually stainless steel), after which the whole tank of now-sparkling wine is clarified and put into bottles. Wines made in this way typically pick up less of the toasty, yeasty flavors associated with wines that undergo secondary fermentation in the bottle, but they're significantly less expensive to produce. Sparkling wines made in this way also tend to have larger bubbles than those made using méthode traditionnelle.

CAVA, a Spanish sparkler primarily from northeastern Spain, is produced with specific grapes indigenous to Spain (some international grapes are allowed) using the same method used to produce Champagne (called método tradicional in Spain). Its flavor profile tends to be lighter than that of Champagne.

OTHER SPARKLING WINES that are great for cocktail making, including French crémant, Italian metodo classico, and American sparkling wines, are variously made using the méthode traditionnelle, the Charmat process, or other processes.

How to Choose a Sparkler for Cocktails

Champagne is essential in our Champagne Cocktail (page 36). Made by pouring the wine over a sugar cube drenched in Angostura bitters and garnished with a twist of lemon zest, this cocktail evolves from the first sip to the last—but the flavors of the Champagne remain primary until the very end. For the best experience, we think this cocktail's namesake ingredient is a must.

In virtually all other sparkling wine cocktails, it's fine to substitute a less expensive sparkling wine. When we poured an inexpensive prosecco into orange juice and Cointreau to make our classic Mimosa (page 39) and compared them to a batch made with a midpriced Champagne, all tasters could tell the difference, but most found the less expensive bottle entirely acceptable since the juice and liqueur blunted the more subtle nuances of either wine.

Save the Bubbles!

Champagne savers promise to keep sparkling wine fresh after it's been opened. We tested various savers by pouring a glass and a half from each bottle of sparkling wine, sealing them with the savers, and storing them in the refrigerator. We tasted them daily against a freshly opened bottle, one we sealed with a double layer of plastic wrap and an elastic band, and a bottle we left entirely open. Unsurprisingly, the open bottle was barely effervescent after a day. The old plastic-wrap trick, surprisingly, kept the wine reasonably drinkable for two days, so it's not a bad option in a pinch. For the best bubble preservation, we like the Cilio Champagne Bottle Sealer, which has a strong, airtight seal and doesn't add much height to the bottle, making for easy refrigerator storage. This sealer preserved bubbles in our bottle for three days (and for a full week if the bottle is left undisturbed).

No-Fear Uncorking

1. Remove foil and loosen cage, keeping your hand on cork at all times.

2. Tilt bottle to 45-degree angle, pointing it away from people, pets, and fragile objects.

3. Grip cage and cork and slowly twist bottle until cork comes free. It should not foam much, but if it does, continue to hold bottle at angle until foaming subsides.

Mix Sparkling Cocktails Like a Pro

1. Pour how you would a beer: down side of glass that's tilted to 45-degree angle. This shortens distance wine falls so there is less turbulence and therefore less foaming.

2. Mix sparkling cocktails that include liqueurs and juice using single lifting motion with bar spoon. Stirring isn't particularly effective at moving denser liquids up toward top of glass. Using lifting motion is much more efficient, and with less agitation of drink, preserves precious carbonation.

3. For cocktails garnished with citrus twist, be sure to drop twist into drink before sipping. Its essential oils and bitter compounds enhance aroma and flavor of drink.

Champagne Cocktail

Makes 1 cocktail
Sweetness ✦✧✧
Floral, Spiced, Tart

- 1 sugar cube
- ¼ teaspoon old-fashioned aromatic bitters
- 5½ ounces Champagne, chilled
- Lemon twist for garnishing

Customize Your Cocktail

Though we highly recommend Champagne here, you can use another dry sparkling wine. Some versions of Champagne cocktails use brandy: For an extra-celebratory drink, add ½ ounce brandy. Try a brown sugar cube instead of a white one. Instead of old-fashioned aromatic bitters, try Peychaud's bitters; or try orange bitters with an orange twist.

While some wine purists might say it's a shame to add anything at all to Champagne, a long line of cocktail makers would surely disagree. The Champagne cocktail dates all the way back to the mid-1800s. Although some recipes include brandy or Cognac, the first published recipe, which appeared in Jerry Thomas's 1862 *How to Mix Drinks, or The Bon Vivant's Companion*, doesn't include liquor. We start our Champagne cocktail with an old-fashioned aromatic bitters–soaked sugar cube nestled in the bottom of a chilled flute. Then we simply fill the glass with Champagne and garnish it with a lemon twist. These four ingredients interact to form a cocktail that develops from sip to sip. Bursting bubbles aromatize lemon oils from the twist to make the first sip bright and citrusy. Then the Champagne's flavors and aromas take over, with whispers of warm spices and orange hinting at what's to come. The sugar cube provides a rough surface that encourages the formation of bubbles in the glass. As the sugar cube dissolves, it creates a bitters-infused syrup, which stays at the bottom of the glass because it's denser than the wine. The final sips beautifully balance the bitters with the wine's acidity and the sugar's sweetness.

Place sugar cube in small bowl. Add aromatic bitters to sugar cube. Transfer soaked sugar cube to chilled flute glass. Add Champagne and garnish with lemon twist. Serve.

The Mimosa

The mimosa is unfairly maligned. This taken-for-granted standby of brunches, weddings, and business-class airline menus is easy to make poorly, with tepid orange juice from a carton and low-quality sparkling wine. But a well-made mimosa is a thing of beauty. When built with attention to technique and ingredients, there's nothing not to love about this sunny, bubbly, low-alcohol cocktail. Our version is as perfectly suited to cocktail hour as it is to brunchtime.

There's a highly unsubstantiated rumor that Alfred Hitchcock invented the mimosa in the 1940s, though it's more likely that he was just the one to help popularize the drink through his affinity for it. It's believed that earlier, in the 1920s, a bartender at the Paris Ritz riffed off the Buck's fizz cocktail (itself recently invented at the Buck's Club in London), adjusting the ratio of Champagne (using less) to orange juice (adding more) to create a gentler, juicier cocktail. The mimosa supposedly was named for the sunny yellow color of the mimosa flower.

For our classic Mimosa, we banish talk of fruit juice from a carton or bottle, choosing freshly squeezed OJ to bring a not-too-sweet, appealing lightness to the drink. Many mimosas are equal parts wine and juice, but we found that a higher ratio of sparkling wine to juice increased the complexity and firmly-ensconced it as a sparkling wine cocktail, not a juice-with-wine cocktail. A little orange liqueur boosts the flavor in a subtly elegant way.

Because the ingredients are so straightforward, variations have blossomed over the years. The most famous relative is probably the Bellini (page 40), credited to Giuseppe Cipriani, founder and longtime owner of Harry's Bar in Venice. Cipriani said that he named this delicate pink-hued creation (he used white peach puree) after Renaissance painter Giovanni Bellini. Other versions incorporate different juices, fresh fruit, and herbs.

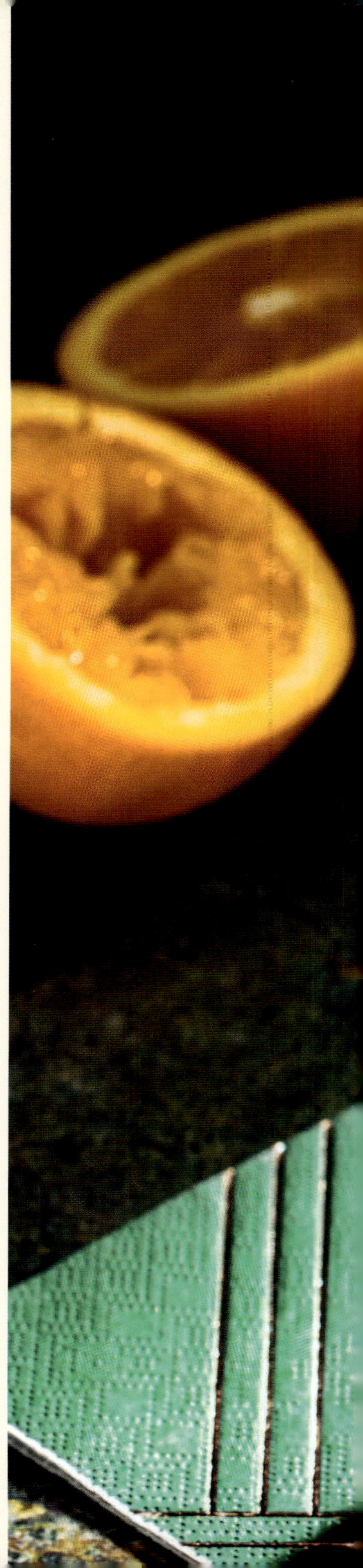

Mimosa

Makes 1 cocktail
Sweetness ✦ ✦ ✧
Citrusy, Tart

- 2½ ounces orange juice, plus orange twist for garnishing
- ¼ ounce orange liqueur
- 3 ounces dry sparkling white wine, chilled

Add orange juice and orange liqueur to chilled flute glass and stir to combine using bar spoon. Slowly add sparkling wine and, using spoon, gently lift juice mixture from bottom of glass to top to combine. Garnish with orange twist and serve.

Customize Your Cocktail

Squeezing your own juice lets you choose your favorite variety of sweet citrus fruit, from blood orange to grapefruit and beyond.

Bellini

Makes 1 cocktail
Sweetness ✦✦✧
Fruity, Tart

The Bellini is a delicious sibling to the mimosa, believed to have been created in the 1940s at the legendary Harry's Bar in Venice, Italy. The original recipe calls for fresh peach puree, but Bellinis made this way are quite pulpy. Peach nectar is readily available and provides great peach flavor. Adding a little peach schnapps intensifies the stone fruit flavor.

- 2½ ounces peach nectar
- ¼ ounce peach schnapps
- 3 ounces dry sparkling white wine, chilled
- Fresh peach slice for garnishing

Add peach nectar and peach schnapps to chilled flute glass and stir to combine using bar spoon. Slowly add sparkling wine and, using spoon, gently lift juice mixture from bottom of glass to top to combine. Garnish with peach slice and serve.

Customize Your Cocktail

A variety of store-bought fruit nectars work in place of the peach nectar. Try mango, guava, or pear nectar, for example, and omit the peach schnapps.

Poinsettia

Makes 1 cocktail
Sweetness ✦✦✧
Citrusy, Fruity, Tart

For a fizzy mimosa alternative for fall and winter holidays, try a Poinsettia, which sports the festive red color of the seasonal plant. Sparkling wine paired with cranberry juice strikes a sweet-tart balance, and a hint of rosemary syrup and orange liqueur adds seasonal flavors and complexity.

- 2½ ounces 100 percent cranberry juice, chilled
- ½ ounce orange liqueur
- ¼ ounce Herb Syrup with rosemary (page 459)
- ⅛ teaspoon orange bitters
- 3 ounces dry sparkling white wine, chilled
- Rosemary sprig for garnishing
- Orange twist for garnishing

Add cranberry juice, orange liqueur, herb syrup, and bitters to chilled flute glass and stir to combine using bar spoon. Slowly add sparkling wine and, using spoon, gently lift juice mixture from bottom of glass to top to combine. Garnish with rosemary sprig and orange twist. Serve.

Jadestone

Makes 1 cocktail
Sweetness ✦ ✦ ✧
Fruity, Herbal

This gorgeously green cocktail is the result of using a fresh puree of honeydew melon (and a little mint) in place of a mimosa's juice. The pour of sparkling wine creates a frothy foam. The refreshing drink is perfect for an outdoor party. Depending on the sweetness of your melon, you may not need to add the simple syrup.

Honeydew Puree

- **1** cup 1-inch honeydew pieces, plus melon balls for garnishing
- **¼** ounce Simple Syrup (page 458) (optional)
- **4** mint leaves, plus mint sprig for garnishing

Cocktail

- **1½** ounces honeydew puree
- **4** ounces dry sparkling white wine, chilled

1. For the honeydew puree: Process honeydew, simple syrup (if using), and mint leaves in blender until smooth, about 30 seconds. Strain honeydew mixture through fine-mesh strainer into small bowl or storage container, pressing on solids to extract as much liquid as possible; discard solids. (You should have about 3 ounces puree, enough for 2 cocktails. Puree can be refrigerated for up to 24 hours.)

2. For the cocktail: Add honeydew puree to chilled flute glass. Slowly add sparkling wine and, using spoon, gently lift puree mixture from bottom of glass to top to combine. Garnish with mint sprig and melon ball. Serve.

French 75

Makes 1 cocktail
Sweetness ✦ ✧ ✧
Citrusy, Tart, Toasted

Named for an early 20th-century French artillery gun famous for its precise and deadly impact, the French 75 cocktail is known for its own potent kick. But its flavor isn't just forceful: When made with brandy, as we enjoy it in our recipe, the cocktail delivers an elegant complexity. However, according to *Difford's Guide*, the first versions of this drink date to 1915 and include gin, apple brandy, grenadine, lemon juice, and sugar, served in a coupe. By the late 1920s, the grenadine and apple brandy were replaced with a pour of Champagne, but to get to the Champagne-topped drink we are most familiar with today, the French 75—also known as the 75 or, in French, the soixante-quinze—evolved significantly.

The version of the French 75 served at the historic Arnaud's Restaurant in New Orleans, famed also for its bar named after the cocktail, reflects the one written in David Embury's 1948 *The Fine Art of Mixing Drinks*: Unlike most versions today, there's no gin, just Cognac to honor the bar's French ties and, in the case of Embury's book, the French in the drink's title. We like how the oaky notes of the brandy add depth and complexity, creating a version of the 75 that for us, clearly hits its target.

- 1 ounce brandy
- ½ ounce lemon juice, plus lemon twist for garnishing
- ½ ounce Simple Syrup (page 458)
- 2 ounces dry sparkling white wine, chilled

Add brandy, lemon juice, and simple syrup to cocktail shaker, then fill with ice. Shake mixture until fully combined and well chilled, about 15 seconds. Double-strain brandy mixture into chilled flute glass. Slowly add sparkling wine and, using bar spoon, gently lift brandy mixture from bottom of glass to top to combine. Garnish with lemon twist and serve.

Customize Your Cocktail

Substitute gin for the brandy to make another common version of the French 75. You can also substitute vodka, bourbon, or rum for the brandy.

ATK 25

Makes 1 cocktail
Sweetness ✦ ✧ ✧
Fruity, Herbal, Tart

America's Test Kitchen co-host Bridget Lancaster developed this cocktail recipe for the 25th anniversary of the TV show. And so, now we have a namesake cocktail. Bridget adores a great gin cocktail, and co-host Julia Collin Davison is a Champagne aficionado; the elegant spin on a French 75 incorporates pomegranate juice and ruby-red grenadine for tart and sweet notes and a gorgeous color that nods to ATK's signature red logo. After shaking the gin, pomegranate and lemon juices, and grenadine together, we top the glass with the sparkling wine float.

- 1 ounce London dry gin
- ½ ounce unsweetened 100 percent pomegranate juice
- ½ ounce lemon juice, plus lemon twist for garnishing
- ½ ounce grenadine
- 2 ounces dry sparkling white wine, chilled

Add gin, pomegranate juice, lemon juice, and grenadine to cocktail shaker, then fill with ice. Shake mixture until fully combined and well chilled, about 15 seconds. Double-strain gin mixture into chilled flute glass. Slowly add sparkling wine and, using bar spoon, gently lift gin mixture from bottom of glass to top to combine. Garnish with lemon twist and serve.

French 75

Lovage or Leave It

Lovage or Leave It

Makes 1 cocktail
Sweetness ✦ ✧ ✧
Citrusy, Herbal, Tart

Lovage leaves look like broad Italian parsley but taste much more intense. Because of its intensity, lovage is very effective at infusing cocktails. We muddle it before shaking the cocktail. Neutral vodka doesn't interfere with the verdant herbal notes, and lemon juice makes this unique cocktail taste bright. If fresh lovage is unavailable, you can substitute an equal amount of celery leaves.

- 2 tablespoons fresh lovage leaves, plus lovage leaf for garnishing
- ½ ounce Simple Syrup (page 458)
- 1 ounce vodka
- ½ ounce lemon juice
- ⅛ teaspoon lemon or grapefruit bitters
- 2 ounces dry sparkling white wine, chilled

Add lovage and simple syrup to base of cocktail shaker and muddle until fragrant, about 30 seconds. Add vodka, lemon juice, and bitters, then fill shaker with ice. Shake mixture until fully combined and well chilled, about 15 seconds. Double-strain vodka mixture into chilled flute glass. Slowly add sparkling wine and, using bar spoon, gently lift vodka mixture from bottom of glass to top to combine. Garnish with lovage leaf and serve.

Bubbles and Blooms

Makes 1 cocktail
Sweetness ✦ ✦ ✧
Floral, Fruity, Tart

The deeply fruity flavor and delicate floral notes combined with the festive fizz and gorgeous blush color of this sparkling wine cocktail make it the life of any party. Adding neutral-tasting vodka as the spirit to the muddled berries enhances rather than competes with the bright berry juice and elderflower liqueur. A small amount of simple syrup and a touch of lemon juice ensure balance. After shaking and straining the cocktail into a cocktail glass, we top it with the sparkling wine float that carries a berry garnish.

- 2 tablespoons blueberries, blackberries, or raspberries, plus extra for garnishing
- ½ teaspoon Simple Syrup (page 458)
- 1 ounce vodka
- 1 ounce elderflower liqueur
- ¼ ounce lemon juice
- 2 ounces dry sparkling white wine, chilled

Add berries and simple syrup to base of cocktail shaker and muddle until berries are broken down and all juice has been expressed, about 30 seconds. Add vodka, elderflower liqueur, and lemon juice, then fill shaker with ice. Shake mixture until fully combined and well chilled, about 15 seconds. Double-strain vodka mixture into chilled flute glass. Slowly add sparkling wine and, using bar spoon, gently lift vodka mixture from bottom of glass to top to combine. Garnish with berries and serve.

Royal Berry

Makes 1 cocktail

Sweetness ✦ ✦ ✧

Fruity, Tart

- 1½ ounces Fruits of the Forest Liqueur (page 466)
- ⅛ teaspoon orange bitters
- 3 ounces dry sparkling white wine, chilled
- Blackberries or raspberries for garnishing

Simple is often sophisticated, and our Royal Berry cocktail is a picture of refinement. It's a sibling to the Kir Royale, which uses sparkling wine and crème de cassis, and a cousin to the Kir, which uses crème de cassis and white wine. Our Fruits of the Forest Liqueur is inspired by berry liqueurs like Chambord, carrying a juicy, intense berry flavor rather than the muskier taste of black currants. We give it the star treatment here, enlivening it with the sparkling wine. The resulting Cognac-colored drink, at once minimal and complex, makes for a brilliant sip. We like to use our Fruits of the Forest Liqueur (page 466); however, a store-bought berry liqueur such as Chambord will also work.

Add fruits of the forest liqueur and bitters to chilled flute glass. Add sparkling wine and, using bar spoon, gently lift liqueur from bottom of glass to top to combine. Garnish with berries and serve.

Customize Your Cocktail

If you would like to try a Kir Royale, substitute crème de cassis for the Fruits of the Forest Liqueur. For a Kir, use crème de cassis and substitute a dry still white wine for the sparkling wine.

The Spritz

The spritz as a concept is believed to have begun in the 1800s, when areas of Italy's northeastern Veneto region were still part of the Austro-Hungarian Empire. German soldiers, it seems, found Italian wines too strong for their tastes, so they took to asking for them to be served with a splash of water (the German verb "spritzen" means "to splash").

A cultural pivot point for the spritz came when the Barbieri brothers invented Aperol in Padua in 1919 and the Pilla brothers invented Select Aperitivo in Venice in 1920. These bittersweet red-orange aperitivi, served on the rocks or mixed with seltzer, became an integral part of Italy's hallowed pre-dinner aperitivo tradition during the period between the world wars. It's not hard to understand why: Aperol's easy-to-love flavor profile includes bitter and sweet oranges, rhubarb, herbs, and roots. Select also includes rhubarb but plays up other botanicals, including juniper. It shares the red hue of the more famous Campari, but its flavor is more herbal and floral, with a softer edge.

The eminently drinkable, delicately fizzy Aperol Spritz cocktail as we know it today was popularized in Italy during the 1950s. Since then, its global popularity has skyrocketed. Considering how ubiquitous the spritz is today, it's hard to believe that Aperol wasn't imported into the United States till 2006. (Select has been available in the United States only since 2016.)

While creating our ideal Aperol Spritz, tasters agreed that the original ratio suggested by the producers of Aperol—3 parts sparkling wine, 2 parts Aperol, 1 part seltzer—achieved the most balanced and complex flavor. The traditional green olive garnish lends an intriguing salty note.

Today it's easy to find members of the spritz family made with other aperitivi, including Lillet, amari (like our Cynar Spritz), or sweeter liqueurs such as limoncello or elderflower liqueur. We've even created an after-dinner version with our Coffee Spritz.

Aperol Spritz

Makes 1 cocktail
Sweetness ✦✦✧
Bitter, Citrusy

- 3 ounces dry sparkling white wine, chilled
- 2 ounces Aperol
- 1 ounce seltzer, chilled
- Orange twist for garnishing
- Brine-cured green olives for garnishing

Fill chilled wineglass halfway with ice. Add sparkling wine, Aperol, and seltzer. Using bar spoon, gently lift mixture from bottom of glass to top to combine. Top with additional ice. Garnish with orange twist and olives. Serve.

Customize Your Cocktail

Replace the Aperol with Campari to make a Campari Spritz or with Select to make a Select Spritz.

Cynar Spritz

Makes 1 cocktail
Sweetness ✦ ✧ ✧
Bitter, Herbal

Aperol gets all the attention but really, a spritz can be made with almost any liqueur. Case in point: The Cynar Spritz is a cocktail with more herbal, almost smoky notes. That's because Cynar is flavored with 13 plants and herbs (the main bittering agent is artichoke, hence the label's decoration).

- 3 ounces dry sparkling white wine, chilled
- 2 ounces Cynar
- 1 ounce seltzer, chilled
- Lemon twist for garnishing
- Brine-cured green olives for garnishing

Fill chilled wineglass halfway with ice. Add sparkling wine, Cynar, and seltzer. Using bar spoon, gently lift mixture from bottom of glass to top to combine. Top with additional ice and garnish with lemon twist and olives. Serve.

Customize Your Cocktail

You can use the other amari here, such as Amaro Averna to make an Averna Spritz or Amaro Nonino to make a Nonino Spritz.

Limoncello Spritz

Makes 1 cocktail
Sweetness ✦ ✦ ✧
Bitter, Citrusy

If you enjoy the celebratory ritual of sharing limoncello after a lovely meal, you'll surely also enjoy the lemony liqueur in a bubbly anytime spritz. Since limoncello is fairly sweet, we use a little less of the liqueur than we would a more bitter aperitivo like Aperol, and we balance the flavors with a dash of citrus bitters.

- 3 ounces dry sparkling white wine, chilled
- 1½ ounces limoncello
- 1 ounce seltzer, chilled
- ⅛ teaspoon lemon or grapefruit bitters
- Lemon twist for garnishing

Fill chilled wineglass halfway with ice. Add sparkling wine, limoncello, seltzer, and bitters. Using bar spoon, gently lift mixture from bottom of glass to top to combine. Top with additional ice and garnish with lemon twist. Serve.

Customize Your Cocktail

Swap in another citrus liqueur, such as Grand Marnier to make a Grand Marnier Spritz or Italicus to make an Italicus Spritz.

Spring Blossom Spritz

Makes 1 cocktail
Sweetness ✦ ✦ ✧
Floral, Fruity

Elderflower liqueur is a common spritz ingredient. We found a cocktail made with just sparkling wine, elderflower liqueur, and seltzer (a Hugo Spritz) to be one-note sweet. A little orange liqueur and a dash of orange bitters create a cocktail with dimension and just enough balancing bitterness. Every floral sip reminds us of spring.

- **3 ounces dry sparkling white wine, chilled**
- **1¼ ounces elderflower liqueur**
- **¼ ounce orange liqueur**
- **1 ounce seltzer, chilled**
- **⅛ teaspoon orange bitters**
- **Orange twist for garnishing**
- **Edible flowers for garnishing**

Fill chilled wineglass halfway with ice. Add sparkling wine, elderflower liqueur, orange liqueur, seltzer, and bitters. Using bar spoon, gently lift mixture from bottom of glass to top to combine. Top with additional ice and garnish with orange twist and flowers. Serve.

Coffee Spritz

Makes 1 cocktail
Sweetness ✦ ✦ ✧
Bitter, Fruity, Nutty

A spritz is typically served as an aperitivo, but who's to say you can't enjoy one after dinner? For an evening-appropriate cocktail that's lighter and less dessert-like than an Espresso Martini (page 343), we concocted a Coffee Spritz. Since Aperol has bitter and fruity notes, it makes sense to reach for coffee liqueur, and we pair it with a touch of maraschino liqueur.

- **3 ounces dry sparkling white wine, chilled**
- **1½ ounces coffee liqueur**
- **¼ ounce maraschino liqueur**
- **1 ounce seltzer, chilled**
- **⅛ teaspoon Peychaud's bitters**
- **Cocktail cherries for garnishing**
- **Lemon twist for garnishing**

Fill chilled wineglass halfway with ice. Add sparkling wine, coffee liqueur, maraschino liqueur, seltzer, and bitters. Using bar spoon, gently lift mixture from bottom of glass to top to combine. Top with additional ice and garnish with cherries and lemon twist. Serve.

Customize Your Cocktail

More of a tea drinker? Substitute black tea liqueur (see page 468) for the coffee liqueur to make a Tea Spritz.

From left: Coffee Spritz, Limoncello Spritz, Cynar Spritz, Spring Blossom Spritz

PAIR WITH A SNACK

Crunchy Kettle Potato Chips

Serves 6
Total Time: 35 minutes

In Italy, salty potato chips are a frequent offering with lightly sweet spritzes. We recommend using a mandoline to slice the potatoes. A heavy 7-quart Dutch oven accommodates the full batch of chips and helps the oil retain heat, leading to crunchy chips. Don't use a smaller, lighter pot.

- 2 quarts vegetable oil, for frying
- 1 pound russet potatoes, unpeeled
- ½ teaspoon table salt

1. Set wire rack in rimmed baking sheet and line with double layer of paper towels. Heat oil in large Dutch oven over medium heat to 375 degrees. While oil heats, slice potatoes crosswise 1/16 inch (1½ millimeters) thick. Carefully add all potatoes to oil, 1 small handful at a time, separating slices as much as possible (oil will bubble vigorously). Cook, stirring constantly with wooden spoon, until bubbling has calmed (it will not completely stop) and slices begin to stiffen, 2 to 4 minutes.

2. Continue to cook, stirring frequently, until shape of chips is set and slices are rigid at edges (chips will make rustling sound when stirred), about 5 minutes longer, adjusting heat as needed to maintain oil temperature between 240 and 250 degrees.

3. Continue to cook, stirring and flipping potatoes frequently with spider skimmer or slotted spoon, until all bubbling ceases and chips are crisp and lightly browned, 6 to 8 minutes longer, adjusting heat as needed during final minutes of cooking to maintain oil temperature between 280 and 300 degrees. Using spider skimmer or slotted spoon, transfer chips to prepared rack. Sprinkle with salt. Serve. (Chips can be stored in zipper-lock bag at room temperature for up to 5 days.)

Frutti di Bosco Punch

Makes 16 cocktails
Sweetness ✦ ✦ ✧
Citrusy, Fruity, Tart

Oftentimes, a successful punch is about restraint. This mixed berry one looks idyllic—bright red and filled with fruit. But it manages to avoid the kitchen-sink (or rather fruit-bowl) mentality associated with these big-batch drinks; it's clean and simple, with some sweetness. White grape juice is a neutral juice base alongside the sparkling wine. If you'd like, you can use our homemade Fruits of the Forest Liqueur (page 466) for the berry liqueur here. An ice ring does the best job of keeping the punch chilled for several hours without overdiluting. If necessary, 8 large ice cubes can be used instead.

- 3 (750-ml) bottles dry sparkling white wine, chilled
- 12 ounces 100 percent white grape juice, chilled
- 6 ounces berry liqueur
- 6 ounces orange liqueur
- 5 ounces (1 cup) blackberries, blueberries, and/or raspberries
- 5 ounces strawberries, hulled and quartered (1 cup)
- 1 Ice Ring (page 30)
- Mint leaves for garnishing

Combine all ingredients in large punch bowl. Add ice ring and garnish with mint leaves. Serve in chilled punch cups.

Summer Stone-Fruit Punch

Makes 16 cocktails
Sweetness ✦ ✦ ✧
Floral, Fruity, Tart

The height of summer is the perfect time for a bright, refreshing punch. Beat the late-season heat with one that celebrates its fruit. For that celebration, we combine sparkling white wine, peach nectar, elderflower liqueur, and stone fruits, punched up (so to speak) with bright lemon slices. You can substitute apricot nectar for the peach nectar if you'd like. An ice ring does the best job of keeping the punch chilled for several hours without overdiluting. If necessary, 8 large ice cubes can be used instead.

- 3 (750-ml) bottles dry sparkling white wine, chilled
- 12 ounces peach nectar, chilled
- 12 ounces elderflower liqueur
- 1 Ice Ring (page 30)
- Lemon slices for garnishing
- Sliced peaches and/or apricots for garnishing

Combine all ingredients in large punch bowl. Add ice ring and garnish with sliced lemons and peaches. Serve in chilled punch cups.

Pear-Lavender Punch

Makes 16 zero-proof cocktails
Sweetness ✦✦✧
Citrusy, Floral, Fruity

Honeyed pears and lavender marry in this celebratory spring punch. An ice ring does the best job of keeping the punch chilled for several hours without overdiluting. If necessary, 8 large ice cubes can be used instead.

- 3 ounces water
- ½ cup sugar
- ¼ cup dried lavender flowers
- 2 liters (68 ounces) seltzer, chilled
- 32 ounces unsweetened 100 percent pear juice, chilled
- 6 ounces lemon juice, chilled, plus lemon slices for garnishing
- 1 Ice Ring (page 30)
- Sliced Bartlett or Bosc pears for garnishing
- Edible flowers for garnishing

1. Heat water, sugar, and lavender in small saucepan over medium heat, stirring often, until sugar has dissolved, about 5 minutes; do not boil. Off heat, let syrup cool completely, about 30 minutes. Strain syrup through fine-mesh strainer into bowl or storage container, cover, and refrigerate until well chilled, about 1 hour. (Syrup can be refrigerated for up to 1 month.)

2. Combine lavender syrup, seltzer, pear juice, and lemon juice in large punch bowl. Add ice ring and garnish with lemon slices, pear slices, and flowers. Serve in chilled punch cups.

Pear-Lavender Punch

Spiced Cranberry-Orange Punch

Makes 16 zero-proof cocktails
Sweetness ✦ ✧ ✧
Citrusy, Fruity, Spiced

This is the ultimate holiday party punch, flavored with the stars of the season, red and green from festive garnishes. It's deliciously zero proof, so you can serve it at every party you attend. Cranberry and orange juices are the base flavors of this punch, and they're heightened with an infusion of spicy ginger, piney rosemary, and warm cinnamon and anise. Lightly cooking the cranberry garnish in this syrup makes them pleasant to eat. An ice ring does the best job of keeping the punch chilled for several hours without overdiluting. If necessary, 8 large ice cubes can be used instead.

- 7 ounces water
- 1 cup sugar
- 1 (3-inch) piece ginger, sliced
- 1 sprig fresh rosemary, plus rosemary sprigs for garnishing
- 1 cinnamon stick, halved
- 2 whole star anise
- 12 ounces (3 cups) fresh or thawed frozen cranberries
- 2 liters (68 ounces) seltzer, chilled
- 12 ounces 100 percent cranberry juice, chilled
- 12 ounces orange juice, chilled, plus orange slices for garnishing
- 1 Ice Ring (page 30)

1. Heat water, sugar, ginger, rosemary sprig, cinnamon stick, and star anise in large saucepan over medium heat, stirring often, until sugar has dissolved, about 5 minutes; do not boil. Stir in cranberries and cook, stirring often, until cranberries just begin to pop open, about 3 minutes. Off heat, let cranberry mixture cool completely, about 30 minutes. Transfer to bowl or storage container, cover, and refrigerate until well chilled, at least 1 hour or up to 4 days.

2. Combine cranberry mixture, seltzer, cranberry juice, and orange juice in large punch bowl. Add ice ring and garnish with rosemary sprigs and orange slices. Serve in chilled punch cups.

Sparkling Mulled Wine

Makes 16 cocktails
Sweetness ✦✦✧
Fruity, Herbal, Spiced

This celebratory drink is modeled after glögg, Swedish mulled wine. Although that name derives from the word "glödga," which means "to heat," we thought it would be fun to make a chilly counterpart beverage with sparkling red wine. To mull without heating the punch, we steep just 12 ounces of sweet Madeira wine with a host of warm spices on the stovetop until it becomes a deep garnet spiced syrup. We strain this potent syrup, chill it, and then combine it with the other ingredients, including aquavit (a common glögg choice) for a nice kick and orange slices for the requisite citrus. We developed this recipe using a medium-dry Madeira, though an extra-dry Madeira will also work; avoid using sweet varieties of Madeira here. We prefer this with aquavit, but you can substitute London dry gin or another style of gin with strong botanicals. An ice ring does the best job of keeping the punch chilled for several hours without overdiluting. If necessary, 8 large ice cubes can be used instead.

- **3** cinnamon sticks, broken into pieces
- **12** green cardamom pods, cracked
- **8** allspice berries, cracked
- **4** whole star anise, broken into pieces
- **½** teaspoon whole cloves
- **¼** teaspoon black peppercorns, cracked
- **12** ounces Madeira wine
- **1** cup sugar
- **8** (3-inch) strips orange zest, plus orange slices for garnishing
- **1** (2-inch) piece ginger, peeled and sliced ¼ inch thick
- **3** (750-ml) bottles dry sparkling red wine, chilled
- **16** ounces aquavit
- **1** Ice Ring (page 30)

1. Toast cinnamon stick pieces, cardamom pods, allspice berries, star anise, cloves, and peppercorns in small saucepan over medium heat, shaking saucepan occasionally, until fragrant, 1 to 3 minutes. Remove saucepan from heat and add Madeira, sugar, orange zest, and ginger. Once bubbling subsides, return saucepan to medium heat and bring to simmer. Off heat, cover and let steep for 30 minutes. Strain syrup through fine-mesh strainer into bowl or storage container, cover, and refrigerate until well chilled, at least 1 hour or up to 4 days.

2. Combine sparkling wine, aquavit, and Madeira syrup in large punch bowl. Add ice ring and garnish with orange slices. Serve in chilled punch cups.

PAIR WITH A SNACK

Goat Cheese Log with Herbes de Provence

Serves 12 to 16
Total Time: 15 minutes, plus 1½ hours freezing and 1 hour resting

This herbes de Provence and olive oil–dressed cheese log is ideal for any larger gathering. A simple mixture of goat cheese and cream cheese (with an addition of olive oil) creates a spreadable log that holds its shape throughout the party.

- **6 ounces goat cheese, crumbled (1½ cups)**
- **6 ounces cream cheese**
- **¼ cup extra-virgin olive oil, divided**
- **1 small garlic clove, minced**
- **½ teaspoon pepper**
- **3 tablespoons herbes de Provence**

1. Process goat cheese, cream cheese, 2 tablespoons oil, garlic, and pepper in food processor until smooth, scraping down sides of bowl as needed, about 1 minute. Lay 18 by 11-inch sheet of plastic wrap on counter with long side parallel to counter edge. Transfer cheese mixture to center of plastic and shape into 9-inch log with long side parallel to counter edge. Fold plastic over log and roll up. Pinch plastic at ends of log and roll log to form tight cylinder. Tuck ends of plastic underneath. Freeze until firm, 1½ to 2 hours.

2. Spread herbes de Provence on large plate. Unwrap cheese log and roll in herbes de Provence. (Coated log can be wrapped in plastic and refrigerated for up to 2 days.) Transfer to serving dish and let sit at room temperature for 1 hour. Drizzle with remaining 2 tablespoons oil and serve.

The Physics of Fizz

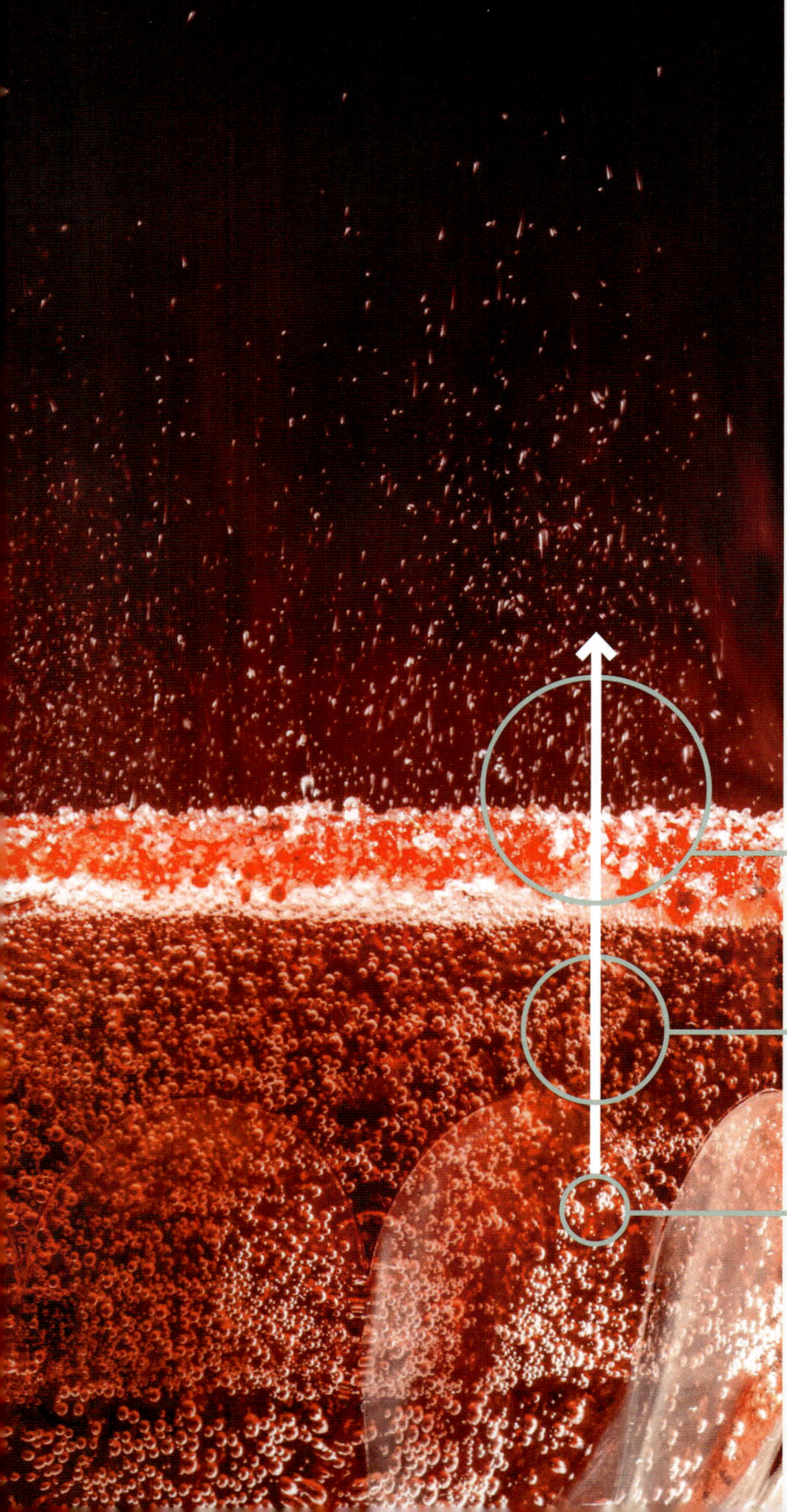

Carbonation doesn't just give sparkling wine a pretty appearance and create a sharp bite on your tongue. The bubbles convey aromatic compounds to the surface of the wine and deliver fragrance to your nose when they burst. But how do the bubbles form in the first place?

They start with dissolved carbon dioxide that stays in the pressurized wine until the bottle is opened. For a bubble to form, the carbon dioxide needs a trigger, or an interruption in the otherwise homogeneous liquid, called a nucleation site: a microscopic gas pocket that's already in the glass, on a fleck of dust, a cloth fiber left behind when you wiped the glass clean, or a scratch or etching in the glass (or, in a Champagne cocktail, a sugar cube).

The gas pocket is all that's needed to incite some carbon dioxide to come out of the wine, forming a bubble. The bubble grows as it rises through the liquid and carbon dioxide enters the bubble. This process repeats itself over and over, creating a trail of effervescence from the nucleation site up to the surface of the wine.

BUBBLES BLAST OFF CO_2 bubbles reach the surface of the liquid and blast aroma compounds into the air in the space above the liquid.

BUBBLES GROW UP CO_2 bubbles rise through the liquid in the glass, growing in diameter as more CO_2 diffuses into them.

BUBBLES ARE BORN Microscopic gas pockets attached to fibers or dust or a scratch in the glass are called nucleation sites, and they trigger a bubble of CO_2 to form.

Keep Everything Chilly

Sparkling wine is best served at about 40 degrees. Cold suppresses the sensation of sweetness on the tongue, so wine will taste sweeter at warmer temperatures. Higher temperatures also make sparkling wine lose its carbonation more quickly. While this makes it initially fizzier and more aromatic, the trade-off is that it becomes flat and loses its aroma faster. That's why it's critical to chill not only sparkling wine for cocktails, but your mixers and glassware as well. Wine poured into an unchilled flute shot from 38 to 48 degrees. But poured into a chilled flute, it rose to only 43 degrees.

WHEN CORKS FLY

While flavor might be your primary consideration when deciding what kind of sparkling wine to buy for different applications, you may also want to factor in the fizz. Traditional-method sparkling wines usually contain about 12 grams of carbon dioxide per liter, which is a lot of pressure. It's also why you want to be sure you open the bottle properly; any CO_2 that sends the cork flying is CO_2 that won't be making bubbles in your drink. Standard proseccos commonly have half that amount, 6 grams of CO_2 per liter—these are considered spumante (in Italian). Some prosecco styles are less fizzy and considered frizzante; they may have just 2 grams of CO_2 per liter. In French, those lightly effervescent wines are called pétillant.

Coupe or Flute?

Champagne is a complex beverage traditionally served in specialty glasses. But the two styles of glasses are very different in shape and cause the sparkling wine to behave in different ways. Does this matter in a cocktail?

In a flute, bubbles have to rise through several inches of wine to get to the surface, growing in size as they ascend. They take longer to dissipate, and when they hit the surface, their aroma and CO_2 is released into the flute's narrow headspace. When you stick your nose in to inhale or sip, the sensation can be quite prickly.

A coupe is wide and shallow, so a rising bubble travels less distance and is still quite tiny when it reaches the top. And a coupe has a lot of surface area at the top of the liquid, leading to faster dissipation of bubbles. When the bubbles hit the surface, they disperse into the air so quickly that some tasters find that Champagne served in a coupe loses some vividness of flavor.

When it comes to sparkling-wine cocktails, you can use either glass, depending on your preferences for aesthetics and nose-tickling bubbles. If you seek a compromise that will deliver the best of the sparkling wine's nuances to your nose, many professional bartenders recommend a white wine glass. This has less height than a flute but more than a coupe and a taper at the top to effectively deliver the wine's aroma.

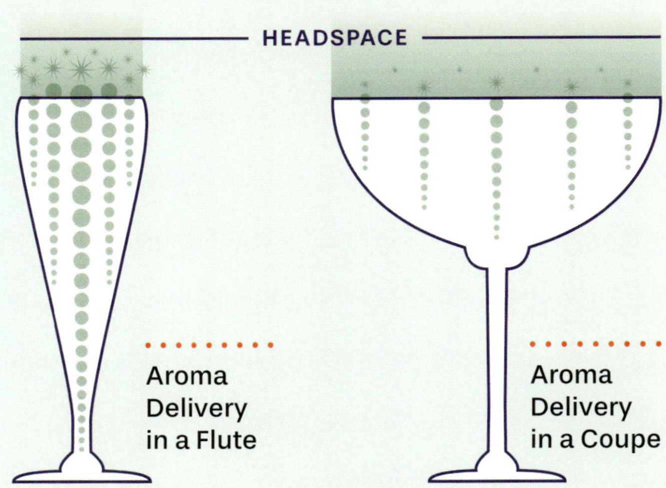

Highballs

A long, frosty, refreshing drink, the highball can trace its origins all the way back to the mid-17th century. The first manmade sparkling liquid was actually wine, produced by some British innovators who added yeast and sugar to imported French wine. (The French, of course, adopted this idea and ran with it, but that's another story.)

It was also the British who first produced glass bottles strong enough to hold artificially carbonated beverages to begin with—and it was a Brit who first successfully artificially carbonated water (a crucial highball ingredient), in the 1760s. The Schweppes company (also British!) got its start before the end of the century.

In England, brandy was initially the spirit of choice to mix with this new carbonated water, although these highball prototypes were ice-free. By the 19th century, other spirits began to be used, most notably Scotch whisky, and the tall, narrow highball or Collins glass came to be the default glassware.

By the turn of the 20th century, it started to become popular to add commercial soda to lengthen spirits; the Cuba Libre (page 70), which uses cola, was invented in Cuba at the turn of the 20th century. Highballs entered a roaring popularity during the Roaring Twenties, as a way to dilute and lengthen spirits (which were both less than optimal and hard to come by, thanks to Prohibition). Contemporary highball culture really took off in Japan in the 1950s and '60s.

While at heart the highball is as simple as a spirit (traditionally whiskey) lengthened with a fizzy liquid and chilled with ice, in today's cocktail environment, it has evolved in all sorts of creative directions to include practically any spirit (or no spirit at all), as well as juices, flavored syrups, muddled fruits (and vegetables), and more. In this chapter, you'll find highballs made with Scotch, Tennessee whiskey, bourbon, rum, tequila, gin, vodka, and soju.

Because the nonalcoholic component is already so important to highballs, the highball formula lends itself especially well to completely nonalcoholic versions, so you'll find a bounty of zero-proof options here. Think about grown-up "sodas" with fresh, fun, not-too-sweet flavors, like Strawberry-Thyme Soda (page 80), and spritzers that skip the (stereo)typical white wine in favor of inspired flavor combinations such as Grapefruit-Rosemary Spritzer (page 83) and Lychee-Rose Spritzer (page 84).

Highballs

Fundamental Formula

base spirit(s) + sparkling water

BUILD ON THE FUNDAMENTALS

Seltzer is not the only way to lengthen a classic highball; you can substitute another sparkling liquid, as in the sparkling black tea in the High Tea (page 68), sparkling cider in the Orchard Stroll (page 69), or cola in the Cuba Libre (page 70). You can also add juice plus a sweetener to the fundamental formula, as in the Tom Collins (page 71), Paloma (page 74), or New Englander (page 75). To make a zero-proof highball, swap out the spirits for a flavored syrup, as in Spiced Orange Soda (page 81), or for juice plus a sweetener to make a spritzer, as in the Grapefruit-Rosemary Spritzer and variations (pages 83–85).

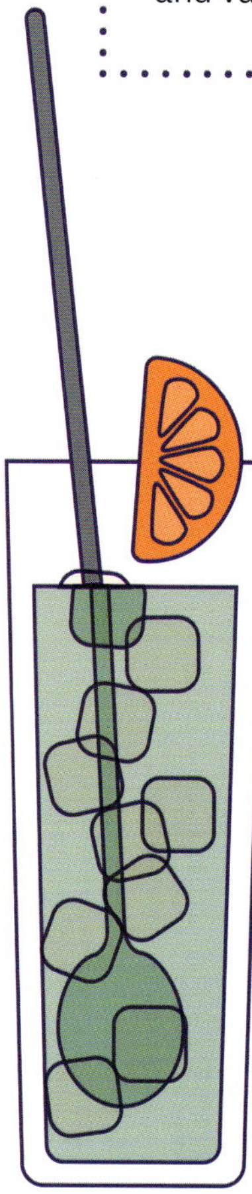

HIGHBALL CONSTRUCTION

- Tall 12-ounce glass
- Plenty of ice, added in two parts
- Noncarbonated ingredients: added directly to the glass, or shaken or muddled first
- Long-handled bar spoon: the best tool for incorporating seltzer
- Gently lift spirits from bottom of glass to top to prevent loss of fizz.
- Garnish: never an afterthought!

Highball Ice

When building highballs, we use ¾-inch to 1¼-inch cubes—an ideal size for easy, gentle stirring in the glass. To ensure they don't melt too quickly, we like the cubes to be as clear as possible (see page 28 for our best ice-making practices).

We first fill the empty highball glass halfway with ice, then top the finished mixed drink with additional ice. You might think that all that ice would dilute the drink too much, but it's the opposite: More ice keeps the drink colder while you enjoy it, leading to more controlled dilution.

Our Favorite Seltzer Water

Our favorite store-bought seltzer water for cocktails is Polar Original Seltzer, which has a strong but balanced fizz and a clean, neutral flavor that's free of any bitterness or acidity. We also like Schweppes Sparkling Water, which is slightly less fizzy with a faint sweet aftertaste, and La Croix Sparkling Water, Pure, which has comparable fizz to Schweppes and a hint of tartness. If you want something super bubbly, try Topo Chico Mineral Water. Because it's a mineral water, it has a slightly more pronounced flavor, with a salty, dry aftertaste.

Bitters & Soda

You can skip the spirits altogether without losing the ritual of enjoying a sophisticated cocktail. While you can simply add your bitters of choice to seltzer, we like to boost the complex flavors of this style of drink by adding a bit of flavored syrup. Simply mix ⅛ teaspoon bitters and ½ to ¾ ounce Simple Syrup (page 458) in a highball glass, then add ice and top with seltzer. If you use plain simple syrup and plain seltzer, you can use any type of bitters you like. Or get inspired to start experimenting with flavor combinations using these suggestions:

- Herb Syrup with sage (page 459), lemon bitters, plain seltzer
- Spice Syrup with cinnamon (page 459), orange bitters, orange seltzer
- Spice Syrup with star anise (page 459), Peychaud's bitters, black cherry seltzer
- Citrus Syrup with lime (page 458), old-fashioned aromatic bitters, watermelon seltzer
- Herb Syrup with rosemary (page 459), orange bitters, cranberry seltzer

Taking Sodas Out of Sweet Territory

This chapter includes a section of nonalcoholic highball sodas and spritzers. Developing these recipes caused us to rethink the concept of soda. It doesn't have to be like most commercial sodas, with their over-the-top sweetness and artificial flavors. It's easy to make elevated homemade sodas and spritzers that are barely sweet and that highlight subtle, natural flavors. Using a small blend of high-impact ingredients and minimal sweeteners gives you more control over the ingredients you consume. We like those ingredients to include fresh fruit juices, small amounts of intensely flavored syrups, bitters, and fresh fruits and herbs for garnishing.

Get started with these recipes:

- Strawberry-Thyme Soda (page 80)
- Spiced Orange Soda (page 81)
- Raspberry Lime Rickey (page 81)
- Cucumber-Dill Spritzer (page 85)
- Bubbly Beet (page 87)

Bubbly Beet

The Whiskey Highball

The whiskey highball is the first true modern highball, meaning it's made with sparkling water and served over plenty of ice. It's thought to have evolved from the ice-free sparkling brandy prototype of 18th-century England. During the 19th century, thanks to geopolitics and the phylloxera scourge that decimated European grapevines, there was a shift from French brandy to Scotch whisky, and Scotch and soda became the intermediary between that original brandy drink and the modern highball as we know it.

Some stories say the whiskey highball was first served in the United States in Boston, in either the former Adams House Hotel or the still-existing Parker House Hotel. However, a bartender by the pen name of Patrick Gavin Duffy claimed to have served it in his New York City café earlier than anyone, back in the 1890s. Duffy (real name: Joseph Gavin Duffy) was a cocktail legend in his own right, an important historical link between pre-Prohibition and post-Prohibition cocktail culture. He wrote *The Official Mixer's Manual* in 1934, a 900-recipe book that was later updated by James Beard as *The Standard Bartender's Guide.* Duffy called the whiskey highball "the high priest of tall drinks."

Fast-forward to the present day. Thanks in large part to its popularity in Japan, highball culture has gone global. Whiskey highballs have reached iconic status there, where there are many rituals surrounding the ratio of whiskey to seltzer, handmade ice in particular sizes and shapes (sometimes it's even tempered before use to smooth any rough edges), and varying ways to precisely stir the drink before serving it. We've found that the golden ratio for a whiskey highball is one part whiskey to two parts seltzer. As for the choice of whiskey—American bourbon, Canadian rye, Scotch, Irish, Japanese—that really all depends on your personal preferences. Think of the whiskey highball as your favorite whiskey turned into a session cocktail: lightened up, chilled, and thirst-quenching.

Whiskey Highball

Makes 1 cocktail
Sweetness ✧ ✧ ✧
Toasted

- 2 ounces whiskey
- 4 ounces seltzer, chilled
- Lemon twist for garnishing

Fill chilled highball glass halfway with ice, then add whiskey. Add seltzer and, using bar spoon, gently lift whiskey from bottom of glass to top to combine. Top with additional ice. Garnish with lemon twist and serve.

Customize Your Cocktail

The highball is adaptable to your taste in spirits. Make a Brandy Highball with brandy, make a Rum Highball with aged rum and an orange twist, or make a Tequila Highball with tequila and a lime twist.

Tartan Tipple

Makes 1 cocktail
Sweetness ✧ ✧ ✧
Toasted

Scotch can have a woodsy, peaty profile, but in a highball its boldness is tamed just enough by sparkling water. Floral, zesty Amaro Montenegro creates even more layers in this drink, while a grapefruit peel adds an unexpected bit of balancing brightness.

- **2 ounces Scotch**
- **½ ounce Amaro Montenegro**
- **4 ounces seltzer, chilled**
- **Grapefruit twist for garnishing**

Fill chilled highball glass halfway with ice. Add Scotch and amaro and stir to combine using bar spoon. Add seltzer and, using spoon, gently lift Scotch mixture from bottom of glass to top to combine. Top with additional ice. Garnish with grapefruit twist and serve.

Customize Your Cocktail

Try another amaro, such as Amaro Averna or Amaro Ramazzotti.

High Tea

Makes 1 cocktail
Sweetness ✦ ✧ ✧
Bitter, Toasted

Nothing is better suited for hot summer days than a tall glass of iced tea—except maybe this sparkling tea highball with a good splash of whiskey. This cocktail is refreshing, familiar-yet-different, and perfect for savoring under a sunbeam. We like Spindrift Unsweetened Half Tea & Half Lemon for its bright notes and balanced flavor, but any unsweetened sparkling iced tea will do.

- **2 ounces Tennessee whiskey**
- **¼ ounce Simple Syrup (page 458)**
- **4 ounces unsweetened sparkling black tea, chilled**
- **Lemon wedge for garnishing**

Fill chilled highball glass halfway with ice. Add whiskey and simple syrup and stir to combine using bar spoon. Add sparkling tea and, using spoon, gently lift whiskey mixture from bottom of glass to top to combine. Top with additional ice. Garnish with lemon wedge and serve.

Customize Your Cocktail

If you're more of a sweet tea drinker, increase the syrup to up to ¾ ounce. Besides Simple Syrup, try Herb Syrup (page 459), any Citrus Syrup (page 458), any Spice Syrup (page 459), or Ginger Syrup (page 93).

Orchard Stroll

Makes 1 cocktail
Sweetness ✦✦✧
Fruity, Toasted

You don't need a whole mélange of warm spices to conjure the vibe of a cozy autumn day. Sometimes all it takes is a bit of apple—that season's star fruit—and some oaky bourbon, with all its vanilla and caramel undertones, to get into the spirit of fall. Sparkling apple cider replaces the seltzer for this simple highball. Any sweet, nonalcoholic sparkling cider will work.

- 2 ounces bourbon
- 4 ounces nonalcoholic sparkling apple cider, chilled
- Apple slice for garnishing

Fill chilled highball glass halfway with ice, then add bourbon. Add sparkling cider and, using bar spoon, gently lift bourbon from bottom of glass to top to combine. Top with additional ice. Garnish with apple slice and serve.

Customize Your Cocktail

Bourbon is our favorite choice, but you could experiment with other styles of whiskey, or even brandy or aged rum.

Cuba Libre

Makes 1 cocktail
Sweetness ✦ ✧ ✧
Citrusy, Spiced, Toasted

This rum and Coke toast to an independent Cuba focuses intently on the spirit, while also muddling to make the most of the drink's awakening lime. According to Bacardí's marketing material, the combo was first enjoyed with Bacardí, when a U.S. Army captain added Coca-Cola and lime to his rum and cheered, "Por Cuba Libre!" in a Havana bar a couple years after the Spanish-American War. This idea, however, was popularized by the Bacardí family, so it's hard to know its veracity; it's likely that rum, cola, and lime were already being enjoyed in Cuba. With so few ingredients, we prefer this refresher with an aged rum, whose complex caramelly notes sing through the cola and lime.

- ½ lime, cut into 4 pieces, plus lime slice for garnishing
- 2 ounces aged rum
- 4 ounces cola, chilled

Add lime pieces to chilled highball glass and muddle until broken down and all juice has been expressed, about 30 seconds. Add rum and stir to combine using bar spoon. Add cola and, using spoon, gently lift rum mixture from bottom of glass to top to combine. Top with additional ice. Garnish with lime slice and serve.

Tom Collins

Makes 1 cocktail
Sweetness ✦✦✧
Citrusy, Herbal, Tart

The Tom Collins is an excellent go-to if you like a straightforward, well-balanced cocktail. But its origin story isn't straightforward at all. It's possible that the drink was originally called the John Collins after the charming headwaiter of London's Limmer's Hotel in the early 1800s. Among other gin punches that his patrons loved, Collins made this long drink but with genever, or Holland gin. Despite the Collins name and its popularity among John Collins's fans, others believe the cocktail's invention is actually owed to an anecdotally less agreeable American bartender, Stephen Price of London's Garrick Club. Eventually the John Collins cocktail came to be known as the Tom Collins cocktail when the drink was increasingly made with Old Tom gin (although London dry gin is also popular and our choice). And today, some consider the John Collins a Collins made with whiskey.

Still others hold that this drink's name actually comes from the Great Tom Collins Hoax of 1874. Mischievous New Yorkers would tell a friend that a man by the name of Tom Collins was speaking ill of them and that Mr. Collins was hanging around a certain bar. This would send the friend to find the fabricated mystery man. The hoax was widespread and even captured in a song of the era. A clever bartender, it's said, capitalized on the hoax and created the drink.

We can't say which tale is responsible for this shaken drink's name, but we can say that this version is light and bright, and carries just the perfect amount of sweetness.

- **2 ounces London dry gin**
- **1 ounce lemon juice, plus lemon wedge for garnishing**
- **1 ounce Simple Syrup (page 458)**
- **4 ounces seltzer, chilled**
- **Cocktail cherries for garnishing**

Add gin, lemon juice, and simple syrup to cocktail shaker, then fill with ice. Shake mixture until just combined and chilled, about 5 seconds. Double-strain gin mixture into chilled highball glass half-filled with ice. Add seltzer and, using bar spoon, gently lift gin mixture from bottom of glass to top to combine. Top with additional ice and garnish with lemon wedge and cocktail cherries. Serve.

Customize Your Cocktail

You can make a Vodka Collins or a Whiskey Collins by using those spirits.

Ramos Gin Fizz

Makes 1 cocktail

Sweetness ✦ ✧ ✧

Citrusy, Creamy, Floral

- 2 ounces London dry gin
- 1 ounce Simple Syrup (page 458)
- 1 ounce egg white
- ½ ounce lemon juice
- ½ ounce lime juice
- ⅛ teaspoon orange blossom water
- 1½ ounces heavy cream
- 5 ounces seltzer, chilled, divided
- Orange twist for garnishing

Our Ramos Gin Fizz wows with its good looks as much as it does with its flavor—which is showstoppingly delicious. A New Orleans original, this cocktail includes gin, simple syrup, lemon juice, lime juice, and orange blossom water, and adds egg white and heavy cream, which, when shaken and topped with seltzer, create a luscious levitating layer of foam that is like a meringue crossed with an ice cream soda. There's a romantic notion that making this cocktail is a thing of legend, requiring fleets of bartenders to pass the cocktail shaker from one to the next for the 10 minutes of shaking purportedly required. We found that extended shaking actually results in foam with a curdled, overwhipped texture; however, we do have best practices for the most dramatically fizzy-foamy result. We turn to dry-shaking everything except the ice, cream, and seltzer to maximize the aeration before adding ice and cream and shaking again to chill and emulsify the drink. Pouring the cocktail over some of the chilled seltzer gently creates the signature top layer of foam, and allowing the cocktail to rest before slowly topping it with the remaining seltzer creates a sturdier, denser foam that rises above the edge of the glass.

1. Add gin, simple syrup, egg white, lemon juice, lime juice, and orange blossom water to cocktail shaker and vigorously shake until foamy, about 45 seconds.

2. Add cream to shaker, then fill with ice. Shake mixture until fully combined and well chilled, about 30 seconds.

3. Pour 3 ounces seltzer into chilled highball glass. Double-strain gin mixture into glass and refrigerate for at least 2 minutes or up to 10 minutes. Using straw, poke hole in center of foam, then slowly pour remaining 2 ounces seltzer into glass through hole (foam will rise above rim). Garnish with orange twist and serve.

Paloma

Paloma

Makes 1 cocktail

Sweetness ✦✦✧

Bitter, Citrusy

"Paloma" means "dove" in Spanish, and it's hard not to feel at peace when this refreshing Mexican cocktail is in hand. Citrus and tequila's agave notes dovetail in this fizzy lengthened drink. In Mexico, the paloma is frequently made with grapefruit Jarritos or Squirt soda. For a consistent drink with unmistakable grapefruit flavor, we like to use fresh juice.

- 2 ounces blanco or reposado tequila
- 1½ ounces grapefruit juice, plus grapefruit twist for garnishing
- ¾ ounce Simple Syrup (page 458)
- ½ ounce lime juice
- ⅛ teaspoon grapefruit or lemon bitters
- 2 ounces seltzer, chilled

Add tequila, grapefruit juice, simple syrup, lime juice, and bitters to cocktail shaker, then fill with ice. Shake mixture until just combined and chilled, about 5 seconds. Double-strain tequila mixture into chilled highball glass half-filled with ice. Add seltzer and, using bar spoon, gently lift tequila mixture from bottom of glass to top to combine. Top with additional ice. Garnish with grapefruit twist and serve.

Customize Your Cocktail

Make a Smoky Paloma with a split base of 1½ ounces of tequila and ½ ounce of mezcal.

PAIR WITH A SNACK

Jalapeño Poppers

Serves 8 to 10 (makes 24 poppers)
Total Time: 45 minutes

This cocktail bite comes together fast and easy because you simply bake the jalapeños instead of breading and deep-frying them. The cream cheese filling base is boosted with a dose of shredded cheddar and minced ham. Just 20 minutes in the oven softens the chiles and ensures the filling is nice and melty. To soften cream cheese quickly, microwave it for 20 to 30 seconds. You can use red and green jalapeños interchangeably, as you like.

- 8 ounces cream cheese, softened
- 2 ounces cheddar cheese, shredded (½ cup)
- 2 ounces deli ham, minced
- 2 scallions, minced
- 1 tablespoon lime juice
- 1 teaspoon chili powder
- ½ teaspoon table salt
- 12 jalapeño chiles, halved and seeded

Adjust oven rack to middle position and heat oven to 350 degrees. Line rimmed baking sheet with parchment paper. Combine cream cheese, cheddar, ham, scallions, lime juice, chili powder, and salt in bowl. Spoon cream cheese mixture into jalapeño halves and arrange on prepared baking sheet. Bake until cheese is hot, about 20 minutes. Serve warm.

New Englander

Makes 1 cocktail
Sweetness ✦ ✦ ✧
Fruity, Tart

Our inspiration here is the Cape Codder, a venerable mid-century cocktail made of vodka mixed with cranberry juice and lime, which was invented by Ocean Spray to help market the company's Cranberry Juice Cocktail beverage. To bring it into the 21st century, we turn to an even older recipe: a shrub, and we use our Cranberry Shrub Syrup (page 460). Shrubs are acidulated fruit syrups that evolved from the fruit-and-vinegar preserves made in colonial America. (The term "shrub" actually refers to both the syrup and the drink made from the syrup.) Sweet-tart cranberries are a perfect fruit to receive the shrub treatment. The bright flavor of the cranberry shines when mixed with seltzer and a splash of tangy lime juice, making this a beverage that's equally appropriate to serve at a winter holiday gathering or a summertime beach party.

- 2 ounces vodka
- 2 ounces Cranberry Shrub Syrup (page 460)
- ¼ ounce lime juice, plus lime twist for garnishing
- 5 ounces seltzer, chilled

Add vodka, shrub syrup, and lime juice to cocktail shaker, then fill with ice. Shake mixture until just combined and chilled, about 5 seconds. Double-strain vodka mixture into chilled highball glass half-filled with ice. Add seltzer and, using bar spoon, gently lift vodka mixture from bottom of glass to top to combine. Top with additional ice. Garnish with lime twist and serve.

Hole in One

Makes 1 cocktail
Sweetness ✦ ✧ ✧
Bitter, Citrusy

Muddling fruit adds complexity to a simple highball, and we think this shaken summer drink is best in its league. Inspired by a spiked Arnold Palmer (equal parts iced tea and lemonade), our Hole in One is made with fresh lemons and tea liqueur. Adding plain vodka along with the liqueur smooths out the tannins and astringency of the tea and citrus. Pouring the contents of the shaker into the glass and topping off with seltzer results in a tart, refreshing cocktail for sipping after your activity of choice. You can use our homemade Tea Liqueur (page 468) or store-bought tea liqueur in this recipe.

- ¼ lemon, cut into 4 pieces, plus lemon slice for garnishing
- 1½ ounces black tea liqueur
- 1 ounce vodka
- ¾ ounce Citrus Syrup with lemon (page 458)
- 2 ounces seltzer, chilled

1. Add lemon pieces to base of cocktail shaker and muddle until broken down and all juice has been expressed, about 30 seconds. Add tea liqueur, vodka, and citrus syrup, then fill shaker with ice. Shake mixture until just combined and chilled, about 5 seconds.

2. Pour contents of shaker into chilled highball glass (do not strain). Add seltzer and, using bar spoon, gently lift tea mixture from bottom of glass to top to combine. Top with additional ice and garnish with lemon slice. Serve.

Mojito

Makes 1 cocktail
Sweetness ✦ ✦ ✧
Citrusy, Herbal

Origin stories for the mojito range from it being invented during Sir Francis Drake's attempted plunder of Cuba in 1586 to it being concocted in a Havana bar that Ernest Hemingway frequented in the 1950s. What is clear: The mojito is the king of muddled drinks. Fresh and herbaceous from muddled mint, sweet yet tart from fresh lime juice and sugar, and with a kick of white rum and a fizzy splash of seltzer, the mojito is perennially popular. Yet there are some versions of a mojito that we'd rather not drink again: those with a crunchy layer of undissolved sugar at the bottom, and those where we have to strain out shreds of muddled mint with our teeth. To solve these problems, we muddle a generous amount of mint with simple syrup instead of granulated sugar to ensure that the sweetener is fully dissolved in the cocktail. Muddling the mint for a full 30 seconds, until it is fragrant, extracts maximum mint flavor even without the help of abrasive granulated sugar. We do all the muddling in a cocktail shaker, add the remaining ingredients and ice to shake, and then double-strain it all into a chilled glass over ice.

- ⅓ cup fresh mint leaves, plus mint sprig for garnishing
- 1 ounce Simple Syrup (page 458)
- 2 ounces white rum
- ¾ ounce lime juice
- 4 ounces seltzer, chilled

1. Add mint leaves and simple syrup to base of cocktail shaker and muddle until fragrant, about 30 seconds. Add rum and lime juice, then fill shaker with ice. Shake mixture until just combined and chilled, about 5 seconds.

2. Double-strain rum mixture into chilled highball glass half-filled with ice. Add seltzer and, using bar spoon, gently lift rum mixture from bottom of glass to top to combine. Top with additional ice and garnish with mint sprig. Serve.

Customize Your Cocktail

Muddle ¼ cup chopped berries of your choice with the mint to make a Berry Mojito.

Kiwi Blossom

Makes 1 cocktail
Sweetness ✦ ✦ ✧
Floral, Fruity

Sweet-tart kiwifruit evokes a kind of tropical melon. Intensely fresh cucumber similarly echoes flavors of melon, to which it's related botanically. The pairing makes a lot of sense in this refreshing cocktail. We showcase jasmine liqueur here: Its heady, deeply fragrant aroma perks up the delicate cucumber and kiwi. You can use our homemade Floral Liqueur (page 467) made with jasmine or store-bought jasmine liqueur in this recipe.

- **½ kiwi, quartered, plus kiwi slice for garnishing**
- **1 (1-inch) piece English cucumber, quartered**
- **1½ ounces jasmine liqueur**
- **1 ounce vodka**
- **½ ounce Simple Syrup (page 458)**
- **¼ ounce lemon juice**
- **3 ounces seltzer, chilled**

1. Add kiwi and cucumber to base of cocktail shaker and muddle until broken down and all juice has been expressed, about 30 seconds. Add jasmine liqueur, vodka, simple syrup, and lemon juice, then fill shaker with ice. Shake mixture until just combined and chilled, about 5 seconds.

2. Double-strain jasmine mixture into chilled highball glass half-filled with ice. Add seltzer and, using bar spoon, gently lift jasmine mixture from bottom of glass to top to combine. Top with additional ice and garnish with kiwi slice. Serve.

Just Peachy

Makes 1 cocktail
Sweetness ✦ ✦ ✧
Fruity, Herbal

Soju, the Korean rice-based spirit, is versatile in cocktails thanks to its smooth, clean taste. This joyful, bubbly drink is inspired by peach soju, a popular variation. We found we could make our cocktail taste most forwardly peachy by using regular soju and an equal part of peach nectar. To add complexity, we muddle a generous amount of herbaceous perilla leaves (a relative of shiso), used in Korean cuisine. Their notes of warm anise and mint pair well with the peach. You can garnish with a peach slice in addition to the perilla leaf, if desired.

- **4 perilla leaves, plus perilla leaf for garnishing**
- **½ ounce Simple Syrup (page 458)**
- **2 ounces soju**
- **2 ounces peach nectar**
- **1 teaspoon lime juice**
- **4 ounces seltzer, chilled**

1. Add perilla leaves and simple syrup to base of cocktail shaker and muddle until fragrant, about 30 seconds. Add soju, peach nectar, and lime juice, then fill shaker with ice. Shake mixture until just combined and chilled, about 5 seconds.

2. Double-strain soju mixture into chilled highball glass half-filled with ice. Add seltzer and, using bar spoon, gently lift soju mixture from bottom of glass to top to combine. Top with additional ice. Garnish with perilla leaf and serve.

참이슬

Spiced Orange Soda

Strawberry-Thyme Soda

Makes 1 zero-proof cocktail
Sweetness ✦ ✦ ✧
Fruity, Herbal

Making your own soda is a really cool party trick. We love to keep our home bars stocked with lots of homemade syrups for fun drinks that will wow anyone you serve, or simply make your own day more special. You can create a number of blends at home. This combo of thyme and strawberries is one of our favorites.

- ½ ounce Herb Syrup with thyme (page 459)
- ½ ounce Berry Syrup with strawberries (page 458)
- 6 ounces seltzer, chilled
- Thyme sprig for garnishing
- Fresh strawberry slices for garnishing

Fill chilled highball glass halfway with ice, then add herb syrup and berry syrup. Add seltzer and, using bar spoon, gently lift syrups from bottom of glass to top to combine. Top with additional ice. Garnish with thyme sprig and strawberry slices and serve.

Customize Your Cocktail

Switch up the syrup pairings to try Ginger Syrup (page 93) in place of the Herb Syrup, and Citrus Syrup (page 458) made with lime instead of the Berry Syrup.

Spiced Orange Soda

Makes 1 zero-proof cocktail
Sweetness ✦✦✧
Citrusy, Spiced

We can't imagine you'd find a match for this orange soda from any canned or bottled version. It has a mature flavor profile that tastes worthy of a holiday or special occasion. Equal parts spiced and citrus syrups make it both warm and bright, and a touch of orange bitters fortifies the flavor. The clear soda is stunning with an orange slice and cinnamon stick garnish. You can use traditional orange bitters in this recipe.

- ½ ounce Spice Syrup (page 459)
- ½ ounce Citrus Syrup with orange (page 458)
- ⅛ teaspoon nonalcoholic orange bitters
- 6 ounces seltzer, chilled
- Orange slice for garnishing
- Cinnamon stick for garnishing

Fill chilled highball glass halfway with ice, then add spiced syrup, citrus syrup, and bitters. Add seltzer and, using bar spoon, gently lift syrups from bottom of glass to top to combine. Top with additional ice. Garnish with orange slice and cinnamon stick. Serve.

Raspberry Lime Rickey

Makes 1 zero-proof cocktail
Sweetness ✦✦✧
Citrusy, Fruity, Tart

The raspberry lime rickey is a classic holdover from the soda fountains of the Prohibition era, and it stands as one of the OG zero-proof cocktails. Taking inspiration from its antecedent, the gin rickey, the original nonalcoholic rickey was a tart mixture of lime juice, simple syrup, and seltzer. In New England, raspberry flavor became a common addition. These days it can be hard to find one that doesn't taste artificial. Easy fix: our homemade raspberry syrup.

- 1½ ounces Berry Syrup with raspberries (page 458)
- ½ ounce lime juice, plus lime wedge for garnishing
- 6 ounces seltzer, chilled

Fill chilled highball glass halfway with ice. Add berry syrup and lime juice and stir to combine using bar spoon. Add seltzer and, using spoon, gently lift raspberry mixture from bottom of glass to top to combine. Top with additional ice. Garnish with lime wedge and serve.

The Zero-Proof Spritzer

Spritzers are different from *spritzes*. Contemporary Italian spritzes (see page 48) combine white wine (usually sparkling) with liqueur and seltzer and could be considered an evolution of the traditional spritzer, which at its simplest is just still white wine and seltzer. The two share the same origin legend: traveling soldiers of the 19th-century Austro-Hungarian empire wanting to lighten up what they perceived as too-strong local wines.

Like the spritz, the spritzer has evolved over time. Spritzers had a bit of a low point in the 1980s, when they became eclipsed and subsumed by wine coolers. A wine cooler is made of wine mixed with sweetened soda—which can be a very good thing, as you'll see in our Kalimotxo (page 358). But it's often quite the opposite. Throughout the 1980s, large commercial brands mass-produced headache-inducingly sweet (but mind-bogglingly popular) bottled products using industrial wine of questionable quality. In the '90s, when excise taxes on wine rose dramatically, it became prohibitively expensive for most companies to continue to produce these wine coolers.

Spritzers are now in a golden age—and they are being reborn as sophisticated zero-proof cocktails. Thanks to current bartending trends, including the growing desire for nonalcoholic cocktails, a greater focus on fresh ingredients in cocktails, and more, the spritzer has rebounded to become a craft cocktail option with plenty of room for experimentation. We think the spritzer is an ideal canvas for creative nonalcoholic options. Our zero-proof spritzers start with juices—freshly made or 100 percent pure bottled products—combined with plain or flavored simple syrups, bitters or fresh herbs, seltzer, and plenty of ice to make a decidedly grown-up bubbly beverage.

Grapefruit-Rosemary Spritzer

Makes 1 zero-proof cocktail
Sweetness ✦ ✧ ✧
Bitter, Citrusy, Herbal

Garnish with a rosemary sprig in addition to the grapefruit twist, if desired.

- **4 ounces grapefruit juice, plus grapefruit twist for garnishing**
- **½ ounce Herb Syrup with rosemary (page 459)**
- **4 ounces seltzer, chilled**

Fill chilled highball glass halfway with ice. Add grapefruit juice and herb syrup and stir to combine using bar spoon. Add seltzer and, using spoon, gently lift grapefruit mixture from bottom of glass to top to combine. Top with additional ice. Garnish with grapefruit twist and serve.

Pomegranate Spritzer

Makes 1 zero-proof cocktail
Sweetness ✦ ✦ ✧
Fruity, Spiced

There are some juices that plead to be mixed with other ingredients to bring out their best. Ruby-hued pure pomegranate juice isn't one of them—its full-bodied flavor and perfect balance of sweet and tart is brilliant alone. Here we simply add old-fashioned bitters, along with just enough syrup and seltzer, to turn the juice into an elegant zero-proof cocktail. The initial sip delivers a vibrant sweetness, similar to ripe berries, balanced by a tangy, slightly astringent edge reminiscent of cranberries or red wine. You can also use traditional old-fashioned bitters in this recipe.

- **4 ounces unsweetened 100 percent pomegranate juice**
- **½ ounce Simple Syrup (page 458)**
- **¼ teaspoon nonalcoholic old-fashioned bitters**
- **4 ounces seltzer, chilled**
- **Pomegranate seeds for garnishing**

Fill chilled highball glass halfway with ice. Add pomegranate juice, simple syrup, and bitters and stir to combine using bar spoon. Add seltzer and, using spoon, gently lift pomegranate mixture from bottom of glass to top to combine. Top with additional ice. Garnish with pomegranate seeds and serve.

Lychee-Rose Spritzer

Makes 1 zero-proof cocktail
Sweetness ✦ ✧ ✧
Floral, Fruity, Tropical

Perfumed and richly sweet, lychee is a perfect base for a sparkling cocktail. Its delicate flavor is often compared to Asian pears and white jasmine. Adding a couple of dashes of rose water emphasizes that floral quality, and lime juice keeps the sweetness in check. We developed this recipe using canned lychees in syrup; if using unsweetened lychees, we recommend adding ½ ounce Simple Syrup (page 458) with the lychee puree in step 2.

- **8 ounces canned lychees, drained, plus extra canned lychee for garnishing**
- **½ ounce lime juice**
- **¼ teaspoon rose water**
- **4 ounces seltzer, chilled**

1. Process lychees in blender until smooth, about 1 minute. Strain mixture through fine-mesh strainer into storage container, pressing on solids to extract as much puree as possible. (You should have about 5 ounces lychee puree enough for 2 cocktails. Puree can be refrigerated for up to 3 days.)

2. Fill chilled highball glass halfway with ice. Add 2½ ounces lychee puree, lime juice, and rose water and stir to combine using bar spoon. Add seltzer and, using spoon, gently lift lychee mixture from bottom of glass to top to combine. Top with additional ice. Garnish with reserved lychee and serve.

Cucumber-Dill Spritzer

Makes 1 zero-proof cocktail
Sweetness ✦✧✧
Citrusy, Herbal

Think of this as spa water that's actually as delicious as it is refreshing. Cucumber juice tastes like freshness itself and pairs beautifully with the subtle savory notes of fresh dill. A splash of lemon juice brightens the drink, and seltzer gives it a bubbly lift, making it a great choice for afternoons by the pool or elegant evening gatherings. For information on making fresh cucumber juice, see page 12. You can garnish with a cucumber spear in addition to the lemon slice and dill, if desired.

- 4 ounces fresh cucumber juice
- ½ ounce Simple Syrup (page 458)
- ¼ ounce lemon juice, plus lemon slice for garnishing
- 2 tablespoons fresh dill, plus extra dill sprig for garnishing
- 4 ounces seltzer, chilled

1. Add cucumber juice, simple syrup, lemon juice, and dill to cocktail shaker, then fill with ice. Shake mixture until just combined and chilled, about 5 seconds.

2. Double-strain cocktail into chilled highball glass half-filled with ice. Add seltzer and, using bar spoon, gently lift juice mixture from bottom of glass to top to combine. Top with additional ice. Garnish with lemon slice and dill. Serve.

Sicilian Sojourn

Makes 1 zero-proof cocktail
Sweetness ✦✦✧
Citrusy, Herbal

Blood oranges make for a striking dark magenta drink with flavor notes of raspberries and just a touch of grapefruit-esque bitterness. Muddling in anise-y fresh tarragon creates a classic Mediterranean flavor pairing. This beautiful citrusy cocktail has a unique herbal note that will transport you to vacation anytime.

- 3½ ounces blood orange juice
- 1 ounce Simple Syrup (page 458)
- ¼ ounce lemon juice
- 2 tablespoons fresh tarragon leaves, plus tarragon sprig for garnishing
- 4 ounces seltzer, chilled

1. Add orange juice, simple syrup, lemon juice, and tarragon leaves to cocktail shaker, then fill with ice. Shake mixture until just combined and chilled, about 5 seconds.

2. Double-strain cocktail into chilled highball glass half-filled with ice. Add seltzer and, using bar spoon, gently lift juice mixture from bottom of glass to top to combine. Top with additional ice. Garnish with tarragon sprig and serve.

Customize Your Cocktail

Substitute fresh basil for the tarragon.

PAIR WITH A SNACK

Marinated Olives with Pearl Mozzarella

Serves 8 to 10 (makes about 2½ cups)
Total Time: 15 minutes, plus 4 hours chilling

A briny, savory, salty snack is often the most satisfying cocktail pairing. These elegant olives have way more flavor and freshness than anything store-bought. The most important step is to start with good olives and good olive oil. We use olives with pits (pitted olives tend to have less flavor), packed in brine. Along with aromatics—garlic, thyme, and red pepper flakes—we use shallot, fresh basil, and grated lemon zest for a bright citrus note.

- ½ cup brine-cured green olives with pits
- ½ cup brine-cured black olives with pits
- 8 ounces (2 cups) fresh pearl mozzarella balls (perlini)
- ¾ cup extra-virgin olive oil
- 1 shallot, minced
- 2 teaspoons grated lemon zest
- 2 teaspoons minced fresh thyme
- 2 teaspoons shredded fresh basil
- 1 garlic clove, minced
- ½ teaspoon red pepper flakes
- ½ teaspoon table salt

Pat olives dry with paper towels. Toss with cheese, oil, shallot, lemon zest, thyme, basil, garlic, pepper flakes, and salt in bowl. Cover and refrigerate for at least 4 hours before serving. (Olives can be refrigerated for up to 4 days.)

Bubbly Beet

Makes 1 zero-proof cocktail
Sweetness ✦ ✦ ✧
Floral, Spiced

This drink's name is quite literal. We found that the bubbles from the seltzer amplify the foam from fresh beet juice, creating a massive head of pink foam on top of the glass for an incredibly fun zero-proof drink. Building this drink in a narrow highball glass helps emphasize the foamy head. The profound depth of flavor and rich color of earthy beet juice pairs beautifully with the spicy heat of ginger and the sweet acidity of orange. We use a lower ratio of juice to seltzer because the taste of the beets is so potent; it doesn't require much to flavor the water and make an enjoyable drink. For information on making fresh beet juice, see page 12. We prefer to use our homemade Ginger Syrup (page 93), but store-bought versions will also work.

- 1½ ounces fresh beet juice
- ½ ounce orange juice
- ½ ounce ginger syrup
- 6 ounces seltzer, chilled, divided

Fill chilled highball glass halfway with ice. Add beet juice, orange juice, and ginger syrup and stir to combine using bar spoon. Add 4 ounces seltzer and, using spoon, gently lift beet mixture from bottom of glass to top to combine. Top with additional ice and let sit for 30 seconds. Slowly pour remaining 2 ounces seltzer into glass (foam will rise above rim). Serve.

Ways with Water

A cool thing about water is that it's a powerful solvent, and indeed almost always has stuff dissolved in it. All those bottles at the supermarket differ from each other in terms of what's dissolved in the H_2O. Soda waters—the fizzy waters used for cocktail-making (or sipping)—have a generous amount of carbon dioxide gas dissolved into them, which gives them the bite and tang that effervescence lovers love. (When it enters your mouth, the dissolved gas diffuses through the skin of your tongue, stimulating the same nerves that horseradish does.)

Studying Soda Waters

Fizzy waters originated with sparkling mineral water, which was first discovered occurring in nature, bubbling from underground springs where volcanic activity introduced CO_2 into the water under pressure. The waters were popular for bathing since prehistory, and people started bottling and distributing them centuries ago. The famous water called Selterser, from fizzy springs in the town of Selters, near Frankfurt, lent its name to seltzer.

Seltzer has become a generic term for sparkling water that's artificially carbonated with CO_2; there's also soda water and club soda. There's no regulation about the differences among them, but in practice, soda water is a general term for this category of fizzy waters; sparkling water, seltzer, and club soda do have distinct properties.

SELTZER

Seltzer is simply water that gets carbonated, with no added ingredients, so it has a clean taste. It's particularly indispensable in highball-style cocktails that are built right in the glass. It's also frequently used in zero-proof cocktails for sparkling interest.

CLUB SODA

Differing slightly from seltzer, club soda has added dissolved minerals like salt, sodium bicarbonate, and potassium sulfate (inspired by the naturally dissolved minerals in water from springs), which affect its flavor—from the subtle softness that calcium gives a Schweppes to the salt- and sulfur-tinged bite of Mineragua. Club soda can be used as a substitute for seltzer in recipes, but it is often less carbonated than seltzer and commands a higher price; in our opinion, it's not worth it.

WHAT ABOUT SPARKLING WATERS?

These waters are often labeled "mineral water," "well water," or "spring water," and any minerals and carbonation they contain must come from the same source. They trend less fizzy than seltzer but can be used in cocktails. Note that mineral waters carry a distinct taste.

Finessing the Most Fizz

Some people like a gentle fizz in their soda. Some like a fierce carbonation that bursts and tingles as it goes down. When you carbonate your own seltzer in a soda maker, you can decide: the more carbon dioxide dissolved into the water, the fizzier the seltzer. Learn how to fine-tune your carbonation so every cocktail is made to your taste.

WEIGH IT

You can quantify how much fizz is in your seltzer—or, the amount of CO_2 gas dissolved in water—easily and objectively by weighing it. Place your noncarbonated bottle of water on a kitchen scale and record the weight in grams. Then, carbonate it to the best of your ability and weigh it again. It will be a few grams heavier. The difference is a measure of how much gas was added. A liter of gently carbonated water contains maybe 3 grams of CO_2. We aim for 9 grams per liter, for powerful fizz, which is comparable to some Champagnes.

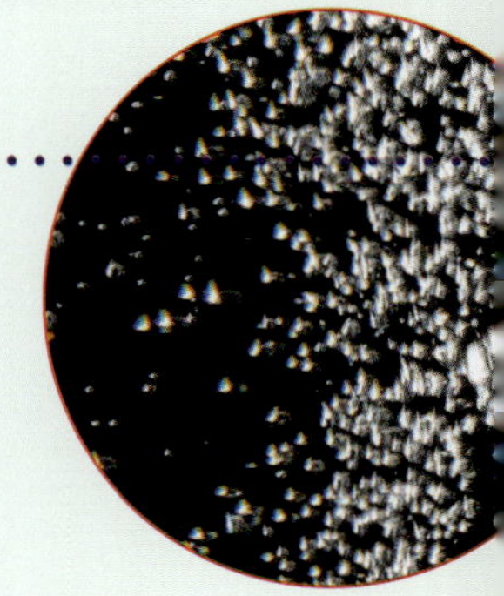

Seltzer made from refrigerated water (40°)

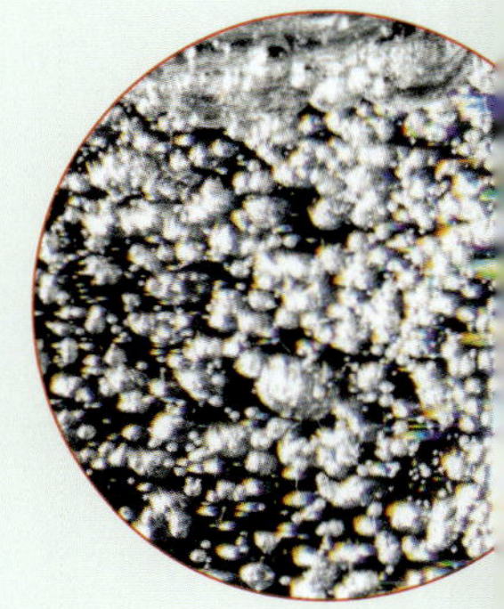

Seltzer made from chilled water (32°)

CHILL IT

Gases are more soluble in colder water. So the simplest way to increase the amount of fizz in your seltzer is to chill it before you begin. Keeping water in the fridge pre-carbonation will bring it down to about 40 degrees Fahrenheit—a start. If you instead set the bottle in ice beforehand, you can chill the water to 32 degrees, which will allow for even more fizz. You can also place ice cubes in the bottle of water, seal, and shake vigorously to chill. Or, fill the bottle about one-fifth with water, keep it in the freezer between uses and shake to chill when you fill it the rest of the way. Your scale will tell you that the colder water holds quite a bit more CO_2.

SPARGE IT

Sparging is the process of bubbling gas through a liquid to purify the liquid and remove other dissolved materials. Usually, the water you start with when making seltzer has a lot of air dissolved in it. That air limits the amount of CO_2 you can dissolve in the water. But there's a step you can take to remove that initial air. After carbonating water, open the bottle and wait 15 seconds while bubbles rise to the surface. Those bubbles are mostly CO_2 coming out of solution, and they bring dissolved air with them. Carbonate the water again, and you'll find you can dissolve more gas.

DIY WATER

If you own a soda maker, use it for seltzer. Homemade seltzer will taste best to you because you can use your favorite water. Not to mention, if you are making cocktails often—or if you just love to drink seltzer every day—making your own seltzer is a smart financial decision.

Tonics *and* Bucks

Tonics and bucks are generally considered to be subcategories of highballs. Because these members of the family are each so established and famous in their own right, we have devoted a separate chapter to them, taking a good look at beloved stalwarts as well as some fresh new faces.

A distinction of each subcategory is that tonics and bucks are made with specific flavored carbonated liquids, rather than plain seltzer or carbonated sodas. Tonics, unsurprisingly, use tonic water, while bucks use ginger ale or ginger beer.

The original "tonic cocktail" was made with simply a spirit and tonic water. Tonic water was patented in 1858 in London, and the gin and tonic cocktail was first referred to in print in the 1860s as something that British colonialists in India were drinking, although Brits in India and other tropical climates had begun to mix gin (or whatever spirit happened to be available) into their daily ration of antimalarial quinine "tonic" several decades earlier. There was also an 1860s reference to a brandy tonic being consumed in Hong Kong, but clearly that version lost the popularity contest.

While the highball is, at its core, a spirit mixed with a carbonated beverage and served over ice (like the G&T), it's the introduction of ginger and citrus specifically that makes the drink a buck. One origin story for the name goes back to the early 20th century, when adding ginger ale or beer to a cocktail was referred to as "adding a buck."

If you're not familiar with the term "buck," you almost certainly are familiar with two of the most famous members of the buck family: the Moscow Mule (page 107) and the Dark and Stormy (page 112). In fact, buck cocktails are more popularly called "mules" because of the popularity of the Moscow mule, a specific type of vodka buck.

Both the tonic and the buck are canvases that are easy to layer additional flavors onto while still preserving the integrity of the drink. You can temper the bitterness of tonics by adding elderflower, strawberries, or carrot juice—or lean into it by adding Campari or espresso. With the bucks, focusing on the ginger will help illuminate the way into different flavors, using ingredients such as apples, black tea, hibiscus, or pineapple.

Tonics & Bucks

Fundamental Formula

liquor + tonic or ginger syrup + seltzer

BUILD ON THE FUNDAMENTALS

Add a liqueur along with the spirit, as in the Elderflower Gin and Tonic (page 96) or Bourbon Mint Tea Mule (page 109), and/or a muddled fruit or vegetable, as in the Sweet Pea Gin and Tonic (page 97) or Once in a Blue Mule (page 109) for additional flavor. You can remove the seltzer to make our spirit-forward New-Fashioned Gin and Tonic (page 99). Or make a nonalcoholic tonic or buck by using fresh juice, tea, or espresso in place of the spirit, as in our Espresso Tonic (page 104).

A Little About Quinine

Tonic water's characteristic bitterness comes from quinine, an alkaloid usually extracted from the bark of the tropical cinchona tree. Quinine has been used for centuries for medicinal purposes, most famously in the treatment of malaria. British colonialists in Southeast Asia made their daily doses of quinine water more palatable by mixing them with alcohol and/or fruit. Eventually, because of its flavor, quinine found its way into liqueurs, including Lillet and Campari.

Store-Bought Tonic Water

Our homemade Tonic Syrup makes superior tonic water when combined with seltzer, but we get it: Sometimes you just want to open a bottle or can and be done with it. Our overall favorite store-bought tonic water is Polar Premium Tonic Water, which has a clean, bright, balanced flavor. There are several other good brands on the market, including Schweppes and Fever-Tree, so do your own taste tests to see which one you prefer, tasting them both on their own and in our Gin and Tonic (page 95). You might find that you have different preferences for zero-proof cocktails versus cocktails containing spirits.

Tonic Syrup

You can purchase premade tonic syrup, but it's not hard to make a superior version in your kitchen. Our homemade syrup strikes an ideal balance between bitter and sweet and has bright citrus notes from lemon and lime zest and juice; lemongrass rounds it out. The citric acid provides more tartness and increases the syrup's shelf life. Tonic water made from this syrup has an amber color from the quinine (unless you set it under ultraviolet light, in which case the quinine will fluoresce and appear bright blue!). Purchase cinchona bark chips online or in specialty spice shops; look for ¼-inch chips. Purchase food-grade citric acid online or in grocery stores that sell canning supplies.

Makes about 16 ounces

- 16 ounces water
- 2 tablespoons (½ ounce) cinchona bark chips
- 5 (3-inch) strips lemon zest plus ½ ounce juice
- 4 (2-inch) strips lime zest plus ¼ ounce juice
- 1 lemongrass stalk, trimmed to bottom 6 inches and chopped coarse
- Pinch table salt
- 1 cup sugar
- 2 tablespoons citric acid

1. Bring water, cinchona bark chips, lemon zest and juice, lime zest and juice, lemongrass, and salt to simmer in medium saucepan over medium-high heat. Reduce heat to low, cover, and cook, stirring occasionally, for 30 minutes.

2. Off heat, stir in sugar and citric acid until dissolved. Cover and let sit for at least 12 hours or up to 24 hours.

3. Set fine-mesh strainer over medium bowl and line with triple layer of cheesecloth. Strain syrup through prepared strainer, pressing on solids to extract as much syrup as possible; discard solids. (Tonic Syrup can be refrigerated in airtight container for up to 2 months. Shake gently before using.)

Beyond Gin

Try tonic with other spirits, including vodka, blanco tequila, or aged rum, as well as dry or sweet vermouth and aperitivi, including Lillet Blanc and Cocchi Americano. Custom blend your own nonalcoholic tonic cocktails, mixing tonic syrup and seltzer with other flavors, such as cranberry juice, grenadine and lime juice, or even lemonade.

Ginger: Ale or Beer?

Ginger ale and ginger beer used to be synonymous, referring to an effervescent fermented beverage with a moderate alcohol content. During the temperance movement that began in the late 19th century, ginger ale evolved to become a nonalcoholic, artificially carbonated soda with a milder flavor (ironically, within a few decades it had become a popular mixer in whiskey highballs). Commercially produced ginger beer eventually followed a similar route, losing the alcohol while keeping a more pungent ginger flavor and being less sweet than ginger ale. Today most (but not all) commercial brands are alcohol-free. We suggest you avoid uncertainty and make our potent homemade Ginger Syrup.

Ginger Syrup

This vibrant syrup can be used in combination with seltzer to make a homemade ginger beer and as a mixer on its own by using it in place of simple syrup. A lot of chopped fresh ginger plus a touch of ground ginger results in plenty of "buck." Lemon juice brightens the flavor and, thanks to its citric acid, increases the syrup's shelf life.

Makes about 8 ounces

- 8 ounces fresh ginger, unpeeled, chopped coarse
- ¾ cup sugar
- 5 ounces water
- ½ teaspoon ground ginger
- 2 teaspoons lemon juice

Ginger Syrup

1. Process ginger in food processor until finely chopped, about 30 seconds, scraping down sides of bowl as needed.

2. Heat sugar and water in small saucepan over medium heat, whisking often, until sugar has dissolved, about 5 minutes; do not boil. Off heat, stir in chopped ginger and ground ginger and let cool to room temperature, about 30 minutes. Cover and refrigerate for at least 12 hours or up to 24 hours.

3. Set fine-mesh strainer over medium bowl and line with triple layer of cheesecloth that overhangs edges. Transfer ginger mixture to prepared strainer and let drain until liquid no longer runs freely, about 10 minutes. Pull edges of cheesecloth together to form pouch, then firmly squeeze pouch to extract as much syrup from pulp as possible; discard pulp. Stir in lemon juice. (Ginger Syrup can be refrigerated in airtight container for up to 1 month. Shake gently before using.)

The Gin and Tonic

The ultimate tonic cocktail, the gin and tonic is very much about the sum of its parts. You can use a bottom-shelf gin and any tonic water you grab off the supermarket shelf, but paying more attention to ingredients will result in a significant flavor payoff in your G&T. There are multitudes of good gins to choose from. We tasted our way through them (someone had to do it) and agreed on London dry as our favorite gin style for this cocktail, thanks to its crisp, juniper-forward character, with a touch of citrus and a hint of earthy aroma.

To craft a truly superior gin and tonic, worthy of being designated our favorite, we developed a Tonic Syrup (page 92) that was more flavorful than any of the commercial tonic waters, with all the desirable qualities we wanted—bracing, bittersweet, and boldly perfumed with citrus and grassy notes. Then we stirred together the gin and syrup directly in the glass with some ice, topping that mixture with seltzer and just barely combining to ensure the bubbliest G&T before finishing it with more ice. We recommend that you make the homemade syrup, but you can substitute a store-bought tonic syrup or 6 ounces store-bought tonic water for the syrup and seltzer, if you like.

Even if you're making your own syrup, the gin and tonic remains a very simple drink to build. This makes it supereasy to riff off of to create other versions that are more than the sum of their parts, keeping the gin, tonic syrup, and seltzer while adding complementary flavors. The herbal quality of the classic gin and tonic inspired us to incorporate fresh flavors based on fruits, flowers, herbs, and even spring vegetables like sugar snap peas. We even infuse gin with makrut lime leaves to make a gin and tonic that's intensely citrusy without being tart (see page 303).

Gin and Tonic

Makes 1 cocktail
Sweetness ✦ ✧ ✧
Bitter, Citrusy, Herbal

2	ounces London dry gin
1¼	ounces tonic syrup
5	ounces seltzer, chilled
	Lime wedge for garnishing

Fill chilled highball glass halfway with ice. Add gin and tonic syrup and stir, using bar spoon, until combined. Add seltzer and, using spoon, gently lift gin mixture from bottom of glass to top to combine. Top with additional ice and garnish with lime wedge. Serve.

Customize Your Cocktail

For a slightly less botanical-forward G&T, you can use Plymouth Gin; for a sweeter one, you can use Old Tom gin. This build also works with other clear spirits, such as white rum, blanco tequila, and vodka.

Elderflower Gin and Tonic

Makes 1 cocktail

Sweetness ✦ ✧ ✧

Bitter, Citrusy, Floral

The gin and tonic is a blank canvas, and liqueurs offer quick flavor upgrades. We tried a variety of liqueurs and, honestly, they all worked great, but we were especially enamored with the floral flavor of elderflower liqueur paired with the bitter and citrus notes of tonic.

- 2 ounces London dry gin
- 1¼ ounces tonic syrup
- ½ ounce elderflower liqueur
- 5 ounces seltzer, chilled
- Lime wedge for garnishing

Fill chilled highball glass halfway with ice. Add gin, tonic syrup, and elderflower liqueur and stir, using bar spoon, until combined. Add seltzer and, using spoon, gently lift gin mixture from bottom of glass to top to combine. Top with additional ice and garnish with lime wedge. Serve.

Customize Your Cocktail

Have fun trying other liqueurs, such as orange liqueur, berry liqueurs, and coffee liqueur.

Strawberry Gin and Tonic

Makes 1 cocktail

Sweetness ✦ ✧ ✧

Bitter, Citrusy, Fruity

Strawberry puree is so easy to make—just blend fresh or frozen berries and simple syrup, then strain. And with that, it's so easy to add complementary fruitiness to an herbal gin cocktail.

- 2 ounces London dry gin
- 1½ ounces Strawberry Puree (page 461)
- 1¼ ounces tonic syrup
- 5 ounces seltzer, chilled
- Fresh strawberry for garnishing

Fill chilled highball glass halfway with ice. Add gin, strawberry puree, and tonic syrup and stir, using bar spoon, until combined. Add seltzer and, using spoon, gently lift gin mixture from bottom of glass to top to combine. Top with additional ice and garnish with strawberry. Serve.

Customize Your Cocktail

Make Blackberry Puree (page 461) to stir up a Blackberry Gin and Tonic or Raspberry Puree (page 461) for a Raspberry Gin and Tonic.

Sweet Pea Gin and Tonic

Makes 1 cocktail
Sweetness ✦ ✦ ✧
Bitter, Citrusy, Herbal

This is a superlatively fresh-tasting cocktail for spring. To blanch the peas, simply submerge them in boiling water for 1 minute, then quickly transfer them to a bowl of ice water to prevent further cooking. If lemon verbena is unavailable, substitute basil, mint, or tarragon.

- **1 ounce sugar snap peas, blanched and coarsely chopped, plus blanched sugar snap peas for garnishing**
- **¼ cup fresh lemon verbena leaves**
- **1¼ ounces tonic syrup**
- **2 ounces London dry gin**
- **5 ounces seltzer, chilled**

1. Add peas, lemon verbena, and tonic syrup to base of cocktail shaker and muddle until lemon verbena is fragrant and peas have broken down and all juice has been expressed, about 30 seconds. Add gin, then fill shaker with ice. Shake mixture until just combined and chilled, about 5 seconds.

2. Double-strain gin mixture into chilled highball glass half-filled with ice. Add seltzer and, using bar spoon, gently lift gin mixture from bottom of glass to top to combine. Top with additional ice and garnish with blanched peas. Serve.

Gin Camp

Makes 1 cocktail
Sweetness ✦ ✧ ✧
Bitter, Citrusy, Herbal

The Gin Camp introduces bittersweet Campari (hence the name) and a measured amount of lime juice (for pitch-perfect acidity) to a classic gin and tonic. The Campari adds bitter citrus and spice notes and turns the cocktail a beautiful blush hue. We prefer to make our own tonic water here using our homemade Tonic Syrup (page 92); however, you can substitute 4 ounces store-bought tonic water for the syrup and seltzer.

- 1½ ounces London dry gin
- ¾ ounce tonic syrup
- ½ ounce Campari
- ½ ounce lime juice, plus lime twist for garnishing
- 3 ounces seltzer, chilled

Fill chilled highball glass halfway with ice. Add gin, tonic syrup, Campari, and lime juice and stir, using bar spoon, until combined. Add seltzer and, using spoon, gently lift gin mixture from bottom of glass to top to combine. Top with additional ice and garnish with lime twist. Serve.

New-Fashioned Gin and Tonic

Makes 1 cocktail
Sweetness ✧ ✧ ✧
Bitter, Spirit Forward

Creating our tonic syrup caused a spark of cocktail inspiration: a gin and tonic in the style of an old-fashioned (see page 122). Here we skip the carbonation (and the accompanying dilution) of a tonic water and present a stirred cocktail in a rocks glass. The cocktail has all the character of the original gin and tonic, but with a little more concentrated flavor and—dare we say—panache. A few drops of old-fashioned aromatic bitters provide just the right amount of seasoning. We prefer to use our homemade Tonic Syrup (page 92); however, store-bought tonic syrup will work.

- 2 ounces London dry gin
- ¼ ounce tonic syrup
- ⅛ teaspoon old-fashioned aromatic bitters
- Strip of lime peel for garnishing

Add gin, tonic syrup, and bitters to mixing glass, then fill three-quarters full with ice. Using bar spoon, stir until mixture is just combined and chilled, about 30 seconds. Strain cocktail into chilled rocks glass half-filled with ice or containing 1 large ice cube. Pinch lime peel over drink and rub outer edge of glass with peel, then garnish with lime peel. Serve.

PAIR WITH A SNACK

Tuna Crudo with Furikake

Serves 4 to 6
Total Time: 15 minutes

The botanical notes of gin and the crispness of a tonic cocktail work really well with raw seafood. We add flavor and texture to our recipe by finishing the dish with the Japanese seaweed–sesame seed spice blend furikake. Freshness is key when serving fish raw. Speak with your fishmonger to make sure you are purchasing high-quality, sushi-grade fish. You can try other sushi-grade fish such as fluke, sea bass, or scallops in this recipe. Inspect the fillets for bones and remove before slicing. Freeze the fish for about 15 minutes to make slicing easier.

- 12 ounces skinless sushi-grade tuna fillets
- 1½ tablespoons extra-virgin olive oil
- 1 tablespoon lemon juice
- 1 tablespoon soy sauce
- 2 teaspoons furikake

1. Using sharp knife, cut tuna lengthwise into 2- to 3-inch-wide strips. Working with 1 strip at a time, slice tuna crosswise on bias into ⅛-inch-thick slices. Arrange tuna attractively on individual chilled plates.

2. Whisk oil, lemon juice, and soy sauce together in small bowl. Drizzle sauce over tuna and sprinkle with furikake. Serve immediately.

Lillet Tonique

Makes 1 cocktail
Sweetness ✦ ✧ ✧
Citrusy, Floral, Herbal

- 3 ounces Lillet Blanc
- ¾ ounce tonic syrup
- 3 ounces seltzer, chilled
- Lemon slice for garnishing

Customize Your Cocktail

If you want a tonique cocktail that's a little more full-bodied and nutty, make a White Port Tonique, swapping out the floral-herbal Lillet for white port and garnishing with an orange slice.

The original formula for Lillet Blanc, dating to the 1870s, contained quinine (the ingredient that wards off malaria and makes tonic water bitter), but that was removed in the 1980s, making the current iteration of Lillet lighter and more citrus-forward. To make a playful cocktail while maintaining the aromatized wine's air of sophistication, we decided to put the quinine back in. Incorporating ¾ ounce of tonic syrup in addition to the seltzer provides a lovely, balanced mix of citrus, herbal, and floral flavors. Cocchi Americano Bianco or vermouth bianco (also sometimes labeled blanc or blanco) can be used in place of the Lillet Blanc. We prefer to make our own tonic water here using our homemade Tonic Syrup (page 92); however, you can substitute 4 ounces store-bought tonic water for the syrup and seltzer.

Fill chilled wineglass halfway with ice. Add Lillet and tonic syrup and stir, using bar spoon, until combined. Add seltzer and, using bar spoon, gently lift Lillet mixture from bottom of glass to top to combine. Top with additional ice and garnish with lemon slice. Serve.

Doctor's Orders

Doctor's Orders

Makes 1 zero-proof cocktail
Sweetness ✦ ✧ ✧
Fruity, Savory, Tart

The striking orange color is a clue that this drink is nothing short of energizing, featuring sweet, earthy carrot juice; punchy turmeric; a crackle of black pepper; and, of course, our bold tonic syrup. And with all of those beneficial ingredients, you can consider this satisfying sipper good for your health as well. Now that's refreshing. We prefer to use our homemade Tonic Syrup (page 92); however, store-bought tonic syrup will work. For more information on making fresh carrot juice, see page 12.

- 1 (3-inch) piece turmeric root, sliced thin
- 1 ounce tonic syrup
- ½ cup fresh carrot juice
- 4 ounces seltzer, chilled
- Black pepper for garnishing

1. Add turmeric and tonic syrup to base of cocktail shaker and muddle until turmeric is broken down and fragrant, about 30 seconds. Add carrot juice, then fill shaker with ice. Shake mixture until just combined and chilled, about 5 seconds.

2. Double-strain carrot mixture into chilled highball glass half-filled with ice. Add seltzer and, using bar spoon, gently lift carrot mixture from bottom of glass to top to combine. Top with additional ice. Sprinkle with pepper and serve.

Tamarind and Tonic

Makes 1 zero-proof cocktail
Sweetness ✦ ✧ ✧
Fruity, Tart, Tropical

Tamarind is an increasingly popular cocktail ingredient, and its earthy, caramelly flavor works really well with tonic syrup. While mixologists might introduce the tamarind through labor-intensive housemade purees and syrups, we found that store-bought tamarind nectar works great. Lime juice brings the right brightness to this fruity drink. We prefer to make our own tonic water here using our homemade Tonic Syrup (page 92); however, you can substitute 6 ounces store-bought tonic water for the syrup and seltzer.

- 2 ounces tamarind nectar
- 1¼ ounces tonic syrup
- ½ ounce lime juice, plus lime slice for garnishing
- ¼ ounce Simple Syrup (page 458)
- 5 ounces seltzer, chilled

Fill chilled highball glass halfway with ice. Add tamarind nectar, tonic syrup, lime juice, and simple syrup and stir, using bar spoon, until combined. Add seltzer and, using spoon, gently lift tamarind mixture from bottom of glass to top to combine. Top with additional ice and garnish with lime slice. Serve.

Espresso Tonic

Makes 1 zero-proof cocktail

Sweetness ✦ ✧ ✧

Bitter, Citrusy

- **6 ounces tonic water**
- **2 ounces brewed espresso, chilled**
- **Strip of orange peel for garnishing**

You might think that bitter espresso and bitter tonic, when combined, would be, well, too bitter. But their marriage is actually a beautifully complementary pairing and makes a complex-tasting drink. The fruitiness of the espresso brings out the fruitier notes in the tonic water and vice versa. The expression of orange peel encourages that relationship to flourish. This is a simple recipe: Layer espresso over tonic water. So we suggest store-bought tonic water here for ease, but you can also make this cocktail using our homemade Tonic Syrup (page 92); combine 5 ounces chilled seltzer and 1¼ ounces syrup in an ice-filled glass before topping with espresso. This cocktail tastes best with freshly made and chilled espresso, but you can substitute an equal amount of strong cold brew coffee.

Fill chilled rocks glass three-quarters full with ice, then add tonic water. Arrange bar spoon concave side down near surface of ice. Gently pour espresso onto back of spoon and into cocktail. Pinch orange peel over drink and rub outer edge of glass with peel, then garnish with orange peel. Serve.

The Mule

One of the superstars of the buck cocktail family is the Moscow mule. While its origins may be up for debate, the likelihood that this drink was born out of necessity in the 1940s is strong. As the most famous story goes, an overabundance of product triggered a brainstorming meeting between a vodka distributor (John G. Martin) and a friend (Jack Morgan) who owned the Cock'n Bull pub in Los Angeles and who also happened to produce ginger beer. One night, Cock'n Bull bartender Wes Price decided to experiment with these two ingredients that his boss was trying to push, adding lime juice to brighten the flavor.

The story continues that Morgan and Martin teamed up with Sophie Berezinski, a recent Russian émigré who had arrived in America with thousands of copper mugs from her father's factory in need of a buyer. In a bit of marketing brilliance, these three supposedly decided that a copper mug should be the signature vessel for the new cocktail—the Moscow mule. And while a solid copper mug is an excellent temperature conductor to keep the cocktail icy, most copper mugs these days are copper veneer, which is less effective. A highball glass will also work just fine.

Origin legends aside, one truth is that this cocktail was at least partially responsible for greatly increasing the popularity of vodka in the United States in the mid-20th century. We think the key to a great Moscow mule is adding enough potent ginger flavor to temper the vodka. Our homemade Ginger Syrup (page 93) offers that perfectly, but you can use a store-bought syrup or sub 6 ounces high-quality ginger beer for the syrup and seltzer.

It's easy to play with the fundamental formula to create all kinds of mule relatives. Other clear spirits like tequila, or dark spirits like bourbon, can work just as well as vodka, in conjunction with the additions of fruit and juice. And don't forget about the ice—while crushed ice is often used, we favor slower-melting larger cubes to keep our mule mugs (or glasses) frosty.

Moscow Mule

Makes 1 cocktail
Sweetness ✦✦✧
Citrusy, Spicy

Garnish with a mint sprig in addition to the lime slice, if desired.

- **2 ounces vodka**
- **1½ ounces ginger syrup**
- **½ ounce lime juice, plus lime slice for garnishing**
- **5 ounces seltzer, chilled**

Fill chilled mule mug halfway with ice. Add vodka, ginger syrup, and lime juice and stir, using bar spoon, until combined. Add seltzer and, using spoon, gently lift vodka mixture from bottom of mug to top to combine. Top with additional ice and garnish with lime slice. Serve.

Customize Your Cocktail

You can substitute other spirits for the vodka and make a London Mule using London dry gin, a French Mule using brandy, or a Kentucky Mule using bourbon.

Mexican Mule

Makes 1 cocktail
Sweetness ✦ ✦ ✧
Citrusy, Smoky, Spicy

If it pairs well with ginger, it belongs in an easily riffable mule. Here we replace the neutral-flavored vodka with two agave-based spirits, as tied to Mexico as vodka (once) was to Russia: crisp blanco tequila and earthy, smoky mezcal. A 3:1 ratio of tequila to mezcal provides enough smokiness without overwhelming the drink, allowing the lime and ginger to come through for a sweet, spicy, smoky sip.

- 1½ ounces blanco tequila
- 1½ ounces ginger syrup
- ½ ounce mezcal
- ½ ounce lime juice, plus lime slice for garnishing
- 5 ounces seltzer, chilled

Fill chilled mule mug halfway with ice. Add tequila, ginger syrup, mezcal, and lime juice and stir, using bar spoon, until combined. Add seltzer and, using spoon, gently lift tequila mixture from bottom of mug to top to combine. Top with additional ice and garnish with lime slice. Serve.

Orchard Mule

Makes 1 cocktail
Sweetness ✦ ✦ ✧
Fruity, Spicy

"A mule walked into an apple orchard" could be the start of a bad joke—or inspiration for a great cocktail. This drink has a full range of orchard flavors—fresh, tart, juicy muddled Granny Smith apple rounded out by sweet, earthy, ripe-tasting apple cider. Vodka's neutral flavor allows the apple and spice to shine through.

- ½ cup peeled and chopped Granny Smith apple, plus apple slice for garnishing
- 1¼ ounces ginger syrup
- 2½ ounces apple cider, chilled
- 2 ounces vodka
- ½ ounce lemon juice
- 2¾ ounces seltzer, chilled

1. Add apple and ginger syrup to base of cocktail shaker and muddle until broken down and all juice is expressed, about 30 seconds. Add apple cider, vodka, and lemon juice, then fill shaker with ice. Shake mixture until just combined and chilled, about 5 seconds.

2. Double-strain cider mixture into chilled mule mug half-filled with ice. Add seltzer and, using bar spoon, gently lift cider mixture from bottom of mug to top to combine. Top with additional ice and garnish with apple slice. Serve.

Once in a Blue Mule

Makes 1 cocktail
Sweetness ✦ ✦ ✧
Fruity, Spicy

Despite its name, this cocktail is decidedly not blue: Blueberry juice runs shockingly pink, painting this mule a beautiful rosy hue. For enough fresh berry flavor to rival the intensity and spice of our ginger syrup, we muddle a generous handful of blueberries and use neutral vodka for our spirit. Complementary lemon juice keeps the syrup's sweetness in check.

- ¼ cup blueberries, plus extra blueberries for garnishing
- 2 ounces ginger syrup
- 2 ounces vodka
- ½ ounce lemon juice
- 5 ounces seltzer, chilled

1. Add blueberries and ginger syrup to base of cocktail shaker and muddle until broken down and all juice is expressed, about 30 seconds. Add vodka and lemon juice, then fill shaker with ice. Shake mixture until just combined and chilled, about 5 seconds.

2. Double-strain cider mixture into chilled mule mug half-filled with ice. Add seltzer and, using bar spoon, gently lift blueberry mixture from bottom of mug to top to combine. Top with additional ice and garnish with extra blueberries. Serve.

Bourbon Mint Tea Mule

Makes 1 cocktail
Sweetness ✦ ✦ ✧
Herbal, Spicy

We use the classic pairing of bourbon and mint to delicious effect in this iced tea–inspired spin on a mule. The tea here comes from black tea liqueur, which provides sweetness and just a hint of tea's tannic profile, without being harsh. It's complemented by bourbon's oak and vanilla notes. A generous ⅓ cup of mint leaves, muddled, gives plenty of flavor in addition to the requisite ginger syrup. You can use our homemade Tea Liqueur (page 468) or store-bought black tea liqueur in this recipe.

- ⅓ cup fresh mint leaves, plus mint sprig for garnishing
- 1½ ounces ginger syrup
- 1½ ounces bourbon
- 1 ounce black tea liqueur
- ½ ounce lemon juice
- 4 ounces seltzer, chilled

1. Add mint and ginger syrup to base of cocktail shaker and muddle until fragrant, about 30 seconds. Add bourbon, tea liqueur, and lemon juice, then fill shaker with ice. Shake mixture until just combined and chilled, about 5 seconds.

2. Double-strain bourbon mixture into chilled mule mug half-filled with ice. Add seltzer and, using bar spoon, gently lift bourbon mixture from bottom of mug to top to combine. Top with additional ice and garnish with mint sprig. Serve.

From left to right: Once in a Blue Mule, Orchard Mule, Bourbon Mint Tea Mule, Mexican Mule

PAIR WITH A SNACK

BBQ Party Mix

Serves 6
Total Time: 1 hour

This party mix is a genius way to turn a few cups of cereal, chips, pretzels, and/or nuts—whatever's on hand—into a crunchy, salty, and irresistible cocktail snack. Bold seasonings such as chili powder, cayenne, and dried oregano hold their flavor through baking (unlike subtler spices like paprika and onion powder). A blend of tangy, spicy bottled barbecue sauce and sweet, nutty melted butter ties it all together.

- 5 **cups combination of Corn or Rice Chex cereal, corn chips, Melba toast rounds, pretzels, and/or smoked almonds**
- 3 **tablespoons unsalted butter, melted**
- 2 **tablespoons barbecue sauce**
- ½ **teaspoon chili powder**
- ¼ **teaspoon dried oregano**
- ⅛ **teaspoon cayenne pepper**

1. Adjust oven rack to middle position and heat oven to 250 degrees. Toss cereal, corn chips, Melba toast, pretzels, and/or almonds together in large bowl. Whisk melted butter and barbecue sauce together in separate bowl, then drizzle over cereal mixture. Sprinkle with chili powder, oregano, and cayenne and toss until well combined.

2. Spread mixture over rimmed baking sheet and bake, stirring every 15 minutes, until golden and crisp, about 45 minutes. Let cool to room temperature. Serve. (Mix can be stored at room temperature for up to 1 week.)

Dark and Stormy

Makes 1 cocktail
Sweetness ✦✦✧
Citrusy, Herbal, Spiced

The story goes that this sweet-spicy cocktail was born in Bermuda just after World War I, the love child of Goslings Black Seal Rum and some ginger beer brewed by furloughed British sailors. A sailor commented that the combination of the black rum (the "dark") and the ginger beer (the "stormy") looked like "the colour of a cloud that only a fool or a dead man would sail under." According to certificates on file with the United States Patent and Trademark Office, Goslings holds the trademark on "Dark 'n Stormy." We like the deep, burnt sugar–like flavors of Black Seal Rum here. Floating the rum on top makes for a dramatic layered presentation. We prefer to make our own ginger beer here using our homemade Ginger Syrup (page 93); however, you can substitute 6 ounces store-bought ginger beer for the syrup and seltzer.

1½ ounces ginger syrup
½ ounce lime juice, plus lime wedge for garnishing
5 ounces seltzer, chilled
2 ounces black rum, such as Goslings

1. Fill chilled highball glass halfway with ice. Add ginger syrup and lime juice and stir, using bar spoon, until combined. Add seltzer and, using spoon, gently lift ginger mixture from bottom of glass to top to combine. Top with additional ice, allowing room for rum.

2. Arrange spoon concave side down near surface of ice. Gently pour rum onto back of spoon and into cocktail. Garnish with lime wedge and serve.

Hibiscus-Lime Buck

Makes 1 zero-proof cocktail
Sweetness ✦✦✧
Citrusy, Spicy, Tart

Beautifully showy hibiscus flowers show off in cocktails as well. When soaked in hot water, dried hibiscus flowers create a very tart liquid with fruit and berry flavors. This deep fuchsia liquid forms the basis of teas and other drinks in many countries across Africa, Latin America and the Caribbean, South Asia, and in the United States as well. Hibiscus's assertive flavor works well with ginger, so for a zero-proof buck, we make a sweetened concentrated tea. We balance the sweet and tart flavors with a bit of lime juice. Use whole dried hibiscus flowers, not ones that have been cut and sifted. If you can find only ones that have been cut and sifted, use the weight listed (¾ ounce), not the volume. We prefer to make our own ginger beer here using our homemade Ginger Syrup (page 93); however, you can substitute 6 ounces store-bought ginger beer for the syrup and seltzer.

Hibiscus Tea Concentrate

- 12 ounces water
- ¾ ounce whole dried hibiscus flowers (about ¾ cup)
- 3 tablespoons sugar

Cocktail

- 2 ounces hibiscus tea concentrate, chilled
- 1½ ounces ginger syrup
- ½ ounce lime juice, plus lime slice for garnishing
- 5 ounces seltzer, chilled

1. **For the hibiscus tea concentrate:** Combine water and hibiscus flowers in small saucepan and bring to simmer over medium heat. Off heat, cover and let steep for 15 minutes. Strain mixture through fine-mesh strainer into bowl, pressing on solids to extract as much liquid as possible; discard solids. Whisk in sugar until dissolved. Let concentrate cool to room temperature, then transfer to airtight container and refrigerate until chilled, about 30 minutes. (You should have about 8 ounces tea concentrate, enough for 4 cocktails. Concentrate can be refrigerated for up to 1 week.)

2. **For the cocktail:** Fill chilled highball glass halfway with ice. Add hibiscus tea concentrate, ginger syrup, and lime juice and stir, using bar spoon, until combined. Add seltzer and, using spoon, gently lift tea mixture from bottom of glass to top to combine. Top with additional ice and garnish with lime slice. Serve.

Pineapple-Makrut Buck

Makes 1 zero-proof cocktail
Sweetness ✦ ✦ ✦
Citrusy, Fruity, Tropical

Makrut limes are a citrus fruit native to Southeast Asia, and their intensely aromatic leaves are used in curry pastes, soups, and other dishes. They also add bright citrus-floral aroma to the tropical trio of pineapple, coconut, and ginger in this zero-proof buck. To impart their unique flavor to a drink, we infuse sugar syrup with torn leaves, along with grated fresh ginger. We combine the lime syrup with pineapple juice and cream of coconut for a drink that is frothy and creamy, reminiscent of an ice cream soda. If you cannot find makrut lime leaves, you can substitute 3 (2-inch) strips of lime zest and 3 (2-inch) strips of lemon zest. You can garnish with a slice of pineapple in addition to the makrut lime leaf, if desired.

Ginger-Makrut Syrup

- 6 tablespoons sugar
- 2½ ounces water
- 2 tablespoons grated fresh ginger
- 12 makrut lime leaves (¼ ounce), chopped, plus extra lime leaf for garnishing

Cocktail

- 2 ounces pineapple juice, chilled
- 1 ounce ginger-makrut syrup
- ¾ ounce lime juice
- 1 tablespoon cream of coconut
- 4 ounces seltzer, chilled

1. For the ginger-makrut syrup: Heat sugar, water, and ginger in small saucepan over medium heat, whisking often, until sugar has dissolved, about 5 minutes; do not boil. Stir in lime leaves and let cool completely, about 30 minutes. Strain syrup through fine-mesh strainer into airtight container; discard solids. (You should have about ½ cup syrup, enough for 4 cocktails. Syrup can be refrigerated for up to 1 month.)

2. For the cocktail: Add pineapple juice, ginger-makrut syrup, lime juice, and cream of coconut to cocktail shaker, then fill with ice. Shake mixture until just combined and chilled, about 5 seconds. Strain cocktail into chilled highball glass half-filled with ice. Add seltzer and, using bar spoon, gently lift juice mixture from bottom of glass to top to combine. Top with additional ice and garnish with extra lime leaf. Serve.

Bitter and Bubbly

Makes 1 zero-proof cocktail
Sweetness ✦✦✧
Bitter, Spiced, Spicy

- 1½ ounces nonalcoholic amaro
- 1 ounce ginger syrup
- 4 ounces tonic water, chilled
- Lime slice for garnishing

Amaro brings the buck to Italy. Amaro and ginger are both complex-tasting ingredients, but they live harmoniously in this bitter, spicy, nose-tingling quaff that's refreshing to drink thanks to the carbonation. Among the growing number of nonalcoholic spirits on the market , we find that amari are some of the most successful—able to achieve the same body and bitterness as their alcoholic counterparts. We developed this recipe using Amaro Lucano Zero, but other brands of nonalcoholic (as well as traditional) amari will also work. We prefer to use our homemade Ginger Syrup (page 93), but store-bought versions will also work. You can also make this cocktail using our homemade Tonic Syrup (page 92); combine 1 ounce tonic syrup with the amaro and ginger syrup before topping with the chilled seltzer.

Fill chilled highball glass halfway with ice. Add amaro and ginger syrup and stir, using bar spoon, until combined. Add tonic water and, using spoon, gently lift amaro mixture from bottom of glass to top to combine. Top with additional ice and garnish with lime slice. Serve.

Old-Fashioneds

The origins of the old-fashioned take us to the primordial beginnings of modern cocktail history. The style of stirred cocktail employing simply spirit, sugar, bitters, and water was being served all the way back in the early 1800s. In fact, it's so classic that some sources simply call it "cocktail."

As the 19th century progressed, cocktails became more complicated, thanks to commercially available ice and the introduction of imported liqueurs. "Improved whiskey cocktails" of the 1870s and 1880s added maraschino liqueur and absinthe to the basic template. In a backlash, bar patrons began requesting what they referred to as the "old-fashioned" style of cocktail: spirit, sugar, bitters, and water. (Nowadays water is included in this drink through the act of stirring it with ice.)

Fruit came along during Prohibition as an attempt to mimic the flavors of the old-fashioned cocktails people enjoyed while softening the bootleg spirits of the day. Initially fruit was muddled into the drink, and eventually a nonmuddled fruit garnish emerged. These days, you may still encounter versions made with muddled fruit, as in our Fond du Lac Old-Fashioned (page 126).

So how do the Whiskey Smash (page 139) and its siblings fit into this story? Like the old-fashioned, the smash possibly evolved from the julep, which involves a spirit, sugar, and herbs served over crushed or shaved ice. People in America were making types of juleps in the 1700s, and cocktail historian David Wondrich mentions centuries-earlier references to medicinal juleps in the Middle East. An early distinction from the julep may have been how the herbs were incorporated at that time ("smashed" rather than stirred), although that line has disappeared. Modern smashes are distinguished from juleps by their inclusion of fruit.

Old-fashioneds fell out of fashion in the 1970s and '80s, with the rise of disco-era cocktails. Legendary bartender Dale DeGroff helped to repopularize the whiskey smash during his time at the Rainbow Room in New York City in the 1990s. Thanks to the efforts of many contemporary bartenders, the old-fashioned hasn't been relegated to antiquity.

These recipes showcase the modern potential of old-fashioned cocktails. Although it's a simple template, experimenting with the ingredients allows for a wide and creative range of flavors. Old-fashioneds make ideal sipping drinks to savor slowly, enjoying the changing taste profile from beginning to end as the ice in the drink slowly melts and dilutes the cocktail.

COCKTAIL KNOWLEDGE

Old-Fashioneds

Fundamental Formula

spirit + sweetener + bitters

BUILD ON THE FUNDAMENTALS

Adding fruit—as a garnish or muddled in—is a classic way to augment the fundamental old-fashioned formula. Instead of plain simple syrup, use flavored syrup, as in the Fireside (page 130). Add a liqueur in addition to or in place of the sweet syrup, as in the Berry Old-Fashioned (page 124), Old Poblano (page 134), or Irish Godfather (page 135). Expand the formulas further by switching up the spirits, bitters, fruits, and herbs and adding spices or concentrated flavor tinctures. Make a smash by muddling in fruit or herbs and adding plenty of crushed ice.

Go Beyond Bourbon

We use bourbon in our Old-Fashioned (page 123) and offer recipes that build on that formula using brandy, rye, tequila, and rum. Here are a few other spirits to try, along with flavor-pairing suggestions:

- Canadian whisky + Citrus Syrup with lime (page 458) + smoked cherry bitters
- Japanese whisky + Ginger Syrup (page 93) + plum bitters
- Scotch + honey + tea bitters
- Applejack + Spice Tincture with cinnamon (page 464) + lemon bitters

Raise Your Spirits

The recipes in this chapter are strongly spirit-forward drinks, without juices and with relatively small amounts of flavored syrups or additional liqueurs or flavoring ingredients. This makes the spirits you use extra important. Consider these drinks an opportunity to use your best aged, sipping-quality spirits.

Old-Fashioned Glass or Rocks Glass?

Although these two terms are often used interchangeably and there is overlap in their style, technically and traditionally there are differences between an old-fashioned glass and a rocks glass. Old-fashioned glasses are on the smaller side, holding 6 to 8 ounces; these glasses were originally designed with a wide diameter and a thick base to have the drink built directly in the glass. Then there are rocks glasses, which are typically larger, holding anywhere from 7 to 14 ounces. For building your old-fashioned and smash cocktails, you want to look for a glass that holds at least 11 ounces (a common size), with a wide mouth for easy muddling and a sturdy base to withstand the force of the muddler.

Speaking of Muddling...

One common way to incorporate sugar into an old fashioned is by muddling granulated sugar with fruit in the bottom of the glass. For the best consistency of flavor and the smoothest texture in our recipes, we use sweetened syrup instead of a sugar cube, sometimes stirring it with the spirit, as in our Old-Fashioned (page 123), sometimes muddling it with fruit, as in the Fond du Lac Old-Fashioned (page 126), and sometimes muddling it with fruit and herbs, as in the Whiskey Smash (page 139).

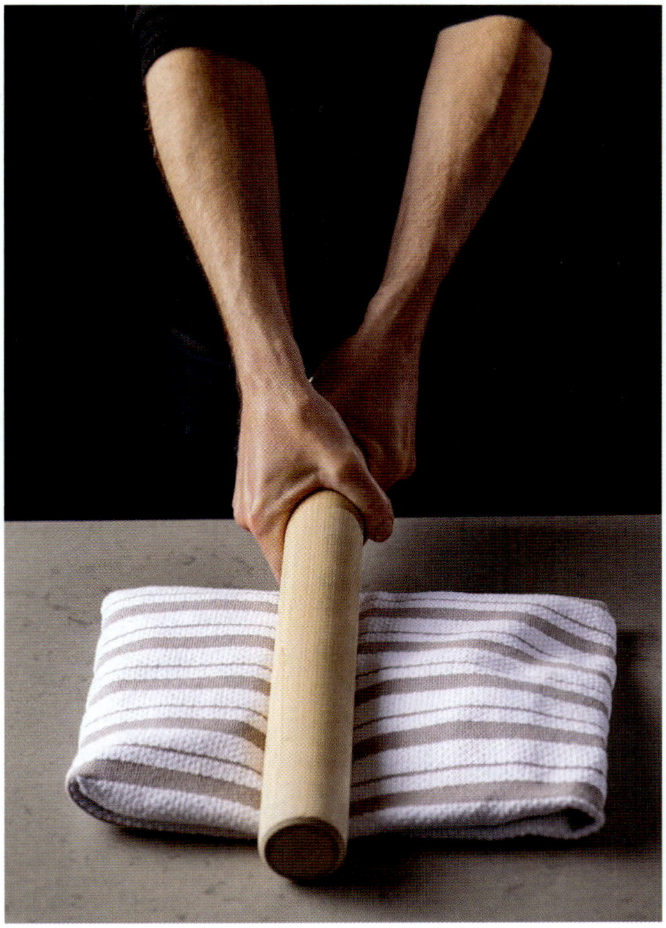

Cocktail Cherries

The cocktail cherry and orange twist are more contemporary additions to the old-fashioned. There's some debate about whether the cherry should be included or not, but we think it adds an element of playfulness. And if you use the right type of cherry, it can be a great way to subtly alter the experience of the drink. (We usually avoid those bright red, artificially colored and flavored "maraschino" cherries.) We love our homemade Cocktail Cherries (page 456), which are sour Morello dark red cherries in a syrup made from unsweetened cherry juice and sugar. If you choose to buy cocktail cherries, there are several good brands worth trying.

LUXARDO ORIGINAL MARASCHINO CHERRIES
Marasca dark red–black cherries in a sweet syrup

AMARENA TOSCHI
Amarena black cherries in a tart-sweet syrup

AMARENA FABBRI
Amarena black cherries in a bittersweet syrup

WOODFORD RESERVE BOURBON CHERRIES
cherries macerated in a sweet syrup enhanced with bourbon

ST. AGRESTIS AMARO SOAKED CHERRIES
sour Balaton cherries macerated in St. Agrestis Amaro

Crushed Ice for Smashes

The best way to crush ice is by hand, with a Lewis bag and wooden mallet (see page 19 for more information). If you don't own these items, you can still make homemade crushed ice, controlling the water quality in a way that you can't if you purchase a bag of crushed ice (or used crushed ice from your freezer's ice maker). Here's how:

Fill a heavy-duty 1-gallon zipper-lock freezer bag about three-quarters full with ice cubes and press out as much air as possible before sealing. Wrap the bag tightly with a large dish towel. Strike the wrapped bag with a rolling pin, skillet, or mallet to break the ice to the desired size. Don't use a pin made of softwood or one with ball bearings, as it could be damaged by the ice.

The Old-Fashioned

The old-fashioned's place on contemporary cocktail menus owes more than a little something to TV's *Mad Men*, which premiered in 2007. The drink had already come into its renaissance, but Don Draper's oft-displayed preference for it made its popularity skyrocket. Asking for one at the bar made you simultaneously modern-cool and old-soul wise, just like Don Draper.

It may have been Draper's cocktail of choice in the 1960s, but this American classic has been around since the early 1800s, made variously with brandy, rum, and eventually bourbon and rye. More variations quickly followed. Versions with gin were being made in the mid-1800s. Wisconsin has a particular and famous take on the drink that calls for brandy as the base spirit, with the addition of lemon-lime soda.

Despite the modern renaissance of old-fashioneds, it's still distressingly common to be served simply awful renditions in many bars, made with low-quality whiskey and with far too much sugar added. Our recipes use small amounts of simple syrup or flavored syrups to ensure that the finished drink is always well balanced and never too sweet—a cocktail worthy of your best spirits. Having said that, it's not unreasonable to expect that old-fashioneds may trend sweeter than other spirit-forward cocktails like Manhattans. We lean into that just a bit, with bourbon as our first choice for the spirit.

For this classic recipe and its relatives, we love incorporating bitters and a fruit garnish, both of which offer nuanced flavor. (We do play around with muddling citrus elsewhere in the chapter.) Because the bitters play such a prominent role, we especially enjoy our homemade Orange Bitters (page 463) and Old-Fashioned Aromatic Bitters (page 462), though you can use store-bought.

Old-Fashioned

Makes 1 cocktail

Sweetness ✦ ✧ ✧

Spirit Forward, Toasted

- 2 ounces bourbon
- 1 teaspoon Simple Syrup (page 458)
- ⅛ teaspoon old-fashioned aromatic bitters
- ⅛ teaspoon orange bitters
- Strip of orange peel for garnishing
- Cocktail cherries for garnishing

Add bourbon, simple syrup, aromatic bitters, and orange bitters to mixing glass, then fill three-quarters full with ice. Using bar spoon, stir until mixture is just combined and chilled, about 30 seconds. Strain cocktail into chilled rocks glass half-filled with ice or containing 1 large ice cube. Pinch orange peel over drink and rub outer edge of glass with peel, then garnish with orange peel and cocktail cherries. Serve.

Customize Your Cocktail

You can feature any aged spirit in an old-fashioned, such as brandy, rye, rum, or tequila.

Cinnamon Old-Fashioned

Makes 1 cocktail
Sweetness ✦ ✧ ✧
Spiced, Spirit Forward, Toasted

As old-fashioneds are all about the spirit, small tweaks make a notable difference. Here we focus on the spiced angle by introducing cinnamon. Our super-concentrated cinnamon tincture shows what just a few drops can do. A fun trick, charring the cinnamon stick garnish, adds extra aroma and, of course, visual appeal to this cocktail. If you don't have a kitchen torch, the burner of a gas stove will also work.

- **2 ounces bourbon**
- **1 teaspoon Simple Syrup (page 458)**
- **10 drops Spice Tincture with cinnamon (page 464)**
- **Cinnamon stick for garnishing**

Add bourbon, simple syrup, and spice tincture to mixing glass, then fill three-quarters full with ice. Using bar spoon, stir until mixture is just combined and chilled, about 30 seconds. Strain cocktail into chilled rocks glass half-filled with ice or containing 1 large ice cube. Using kitchen torch, lightly char 1 end of cinnamon stick until smoking. Garnish cocktail with smoking cinnamon stick and serve.

Customize Your Cocktail

Spice up your old-fashioned in other ways. Make a Cardamom Old-Fashioned with cardamom tincture, or make a Star Anise Old-Fashioned with star anise tincture and a star anise garnish (do not char it).

Berry Old-Fashioned

Makes 1 cocktail
Sweetness ✦ ✧ ✧
Fruity, Spirit Forward, Toasted

We like how dark berry flavor melds with caramelly bourbon in this old-fashioned. A bit of berry liqueur provided more present fruit flavor than berry syrup did. Orange bitters and expressed orange peel reinforce the fruitiness.

- **2 ounces bourbon**
- **½ ounce berry liqueur**
- **¼ teaspoon orange bitters**
- **Strip of orange peel for garnishing**
- **Blackberries for garnishing**

Add bourbon, berry liqueur, and bitters to mixing glass, then fill three-quarters full with ice. Using bar spoon, stir until mixture is just combined and chilled, about 30 seconds. Strain cocktail into chilled rocks glass half-filled with ice or containing 1 large ice cube. Pinch orange peel over drink and rub outer edge of glass with peel, then garnish with orange peel and blackberries. Serve.

Fridge Door Old-Fashioneds

Makes 8 cocktails
Sweetness ✦ ✧ ✧
Spirit Forward, Toasted

What better way to make guests feel at home at a gathering than to pour out a round of old-fashioneds? Add ice to your glasses, grab your premade cocktail from the freezer, express your citrus, garnish—and enjoy. You can store the cocktail in a 1-quart Mason jar instead of a bottle if you'd like.

- 16 ounces bourbon
- 8 ounces water
- 1¼ ounces Simple Syrup (page 458)
- ½ teaspoon old-fashioned aromatic bitters
- ½ teaspoon orange bitters
- Strips of orange peel for garnishing
- Cocktail cherries for garnishing

1. Combine bourbon, water, simple syrup, aromatic bitters, and orange bitters in 1-liter glass bottle. Cover and freeze until well chilled, about 2 hours. Prepare cocktails immediately or transfer to refrigerator and store for up to 1 month; return to freezer and chill for 30 minutes before preparing cocktails.

2. Gently shake bottle to recombine, then serve cocktails in chilled rocks glasses half-filled with ice or containing 1 large ice cube. Pinch orange peels over individual drinks and rub outer edges of glasses with peels. Garnish with orange peels and cocktail cherries.

Fond du Lac Old-Fashioned

Makes 1 cocktail
Sweetness ✦ ✦ ✧
Spiced, Spirit Forward, Toasted

1 teaspoon cocktail cherry syrup, plus cocktail cherries for garnishing
Strip of orange peel, plus orange slice for garnishing
2 ounces brandy
¼ teaspoon old-fashioned aromatic bitters

Consider the brandy old-fashioned, the state drink of Wisconsin, where fruit is often muddled before the cocktail is built. It's usually made with American brandy. There's one theory that Wisconsinites took to domestic brandies after the spirits were featured at the Chicago World's Fair of 1893. The muddling came from Prohibition, when the fruit was meant to approximate the flavor of liqueurs folks could no longer get (the cherry and orange for maraschino liqueur and curaçao, respectively). Today, you can order your brandy old-fashioned in Wisconsin "sweet" (with lemon-lime soda), "sour" (with Squirt or sour mix), or "soda" (with club soda).

We wanted to develop a Wisconsin-inspired brandy old-fashioned, and we've named it after Wisconsin's lakeside city. To respect the old-fashioned's roots as simple and spirit forward (and with plenty of good brandy to choose from), we take a subtle approach and simply muddle a strip of orange peel with syrup from our cherry garnish rather than whole fruits. However, we do endorse following the lead of Wisconsinites by adding a splash of chilled club soda (pictured) or lemon-lime soda. Choose high-quality cocktail cherries in syrup for this recipe (see page 121).

1. Add cherry syrup and orange peel to mixing glass and muddle until fragrant, about 10 seconds. Add brandy and bitters, then fill three-quarters full with ice. Using bar spoon, stir until mixture is just combined and chilled, about 30 seconds.

2. Strain cocktail into chilled rocks glass half-filled with ice or containing 1 large ice cube. Garnish with cocktail cherries and orange slice. Serve.

Sazerac

Makes 1 cocktail
Sweetness ✦ ✧ ✧
Herbal, Spirit Forward

The New Orleans–born Sazerac cocktail gets its name from the Cognac—Sazerac de Forge et Fils—likely used in the earliest versions of the drink. The origin story claims that in 1838, an apothecary named Antoine Peychaud (a Creole immigrant with a pharmacy in the French Quarter) combined Cognac with absinthe and a dash of his secret-recipe bitters for his friends. The drink grew in popularity, and in 1850 a bar known as the Sazerac Coffeehouse became an importer of the Sazerac de Forge et Fils Cognac and promoted the cocktail it featured. In 1869, an entrepreneur purchased the bar and eventually founded the Sazerac Company to market spirits, liqueurs, and mixers (including Peychaud's bitters and a bottled version of the Sazerac cocktail) that built upon the iconic cocktail's fame. Eventually, as others tried their hands at crafting the Sazerac, the Cognac was replaced by whiskey, but the overall formula—brown liquor with an absinthe wash and a hit of Peychaud's bitters—endured. In our version, we opt for simple syrup rather than a sugar cube, which is difficult to dissolve. We developed our Sazerac with absinthe, an intensely aromatic spirit made with anise, fennel, and wormwood. Herbsaint (developed by the Sazerac Company when absinthe was banned) or another dry anise-forward liqueur (such as Ricard or dry anisette) can be used.

- ½ **teaspoon absinthe**
- 2 **ounces rye**
- 1 **teaspoon Simple Syrup (page 458)**
- ⅛ **teaspoon Peychaud's bitters**
- **Strip of lemon peel for garnishing**

1. Pour absinthe into chilled rocks glass, then tilt and rotate glass to coat interior wall; pour off excess absinthe.

2. Add rye, simple syrup, and bitters to mixing glass, then fill three-quarters full with ice. Using bar spoon, stir until mixture is fully combined and well chilled, about 1 minute. Strain cocktail into prepared glass. Pinch lemon peel over drink and rub outer edge of glass with peel, then garnish with lemon peel. Serve.

Tequila Old-Fashioned

Makes 1 cocktail
Sweetness ✦ ✧ ✧
Spirit Forward, Toasted

An old-fashioned is a great way to showcase a high-quality spirit in all of its glory. Many early tequila cocktails in the United States aimed to do the opposite, to mask low-quality tequilas that were widely available in the mid- to late 1900s. Now, tequila is the fastest growing spirit category in the USA. There are plenty of high-quality products—honor your favorite here. Generally speaking, old-fashioneds feature barrel-aged spirits, but we found that some añejo tequilas had heavy barrel notes that overpowered the agave notes, so we opted for a reposado.

- 2 ounces reposado tequila
- 1 teaspoon agave syrup
- ¼ teaspoon mole bitters
- Strip of lime peel for garnishing

Add tequila, agave syrup, and bitters to mixing glass, then fill three-quarters full with ice. Using bar spoon, stir until mixture is just combined and chilled, about 30 seconds. Strain cocktail into chilled rocks glass half-filled with ice or containing 1 large ice cube. Pinch lime peel over drink and rub outer edge of glass with peel, then garnish with lime peel. Serve.

Customize Your Cocktail

Try this with old-fashioned aromatic bitters, lime bitters, or grapefruit bitters.

Tequila Old-Fashioned

Fireside

Makes 1 cocktail
Sweetness ✦✦✧
Spiced, Spirit Forward, Toasted

Sip on this soul-warming drink on a cozy night in. Our spiced syrup injects a brandy old-fashioned with notes of cinnamon, cloves, and allspice, all of which bring out the fruit and spice in the spirit. (You could even use Cognac for a luxe version of this cocktail.) Orange bitters provide the right amount of brightness—just as citrus juice does in the best apple pie fillings. We garnish with an apple slice, too. The optional rim sugar further bumps up the sweet and warmly spiced elements.

- ¼ cup Pumpkin Spice Rim Sugar (page 454) (optional)
- Orange wedge (if using sugar)
- 2 ounces brandy
- 1 teaspoon Spice Syrup (page 459)
- ⅛ teaspoon orange bitters
- Apple slice for garnishing

1. Spread sugar, if using, into even layer on small saucer. Moisten about ½ inch of chilled rocks glass rim by running orange wedge around outer edge; blot any excess juice with paper towel. Roll moistened rim in sugar to coat. Remove any excess sugar that falls into glass; set aside.

2. Add brandy, spice syrup, and bitters to mixing glass, then fill three-quarters full with ice. Using bar spoon, stir until mixture is just combined and chilled, about 30 seconds. Strain cocktail into prepared rocks glass half-filled with ice or containing 1 large ice cube. Garnish with apple slice and serve.

PAIR WITH A SNACK

Toasted Five-Spice Almonds

Serves 6 to 8
Total Time: 15 minutes, plus 30 minutes cooling

Toasting raw almonds for just 8 minutes in hot oil gives them a rounder, more complex flavor and makes them a worthy accompaniment to a nice cocktail. The five-spice powder makes them stand out.

- 1 teaspoon extra-virgin olive oil
- 2 cups skin-on raw almonds
- 1 teaspoon table salt
- 1 teaspoon five-spice powder
- ¼ teaspoon pepper

Heat oil in 12-inch nonstick skillet over medium-high heat until just shimmering. Add almonds, salt, five-spice powder, and pepper and reduce heat to medium-low. Cook, stirring often, until fragrant and color deepens slightly, about 8 minutes. Transfer almonds to paper towel–lined plate and let cool before serving.

Customize Your Cocktail

Bourbon, Scotch, or aged rum would all taste great in this cocktail. Not a fan of pumpkin spice? Adorn the glass with our Vanilla Rim Sugar (page 454) or simply with demerara sugar instead.

Ti' Punch

Makes 1 cocktail
Sweetness ✦ ✧ ✧
Citrusy, Spirit Forward

The ti' punch (ti' being short for "petit") is a classic cocktail from the French Caribbean, specifically Martinique and Guadeloupe, which are known for their highly flavorful agricole rhums made from fresh pressed sugarcane juice. Similar to how everyone has their own martini order, in Martinique, everyone has their own ti' punch preferences. It's common for a bartender to give you a tray containing a bottle of rhum, a bottle of sirop de canne, a glass of lime coins, and a swizzle stick, with the instructions, "Chacun prépare sa propre mort" (each prepares their own death). Note the lime coin (not slice, wheel, or wedge) is not muddled to a pulp as in other cocktails; it's agitated just long enough to release mostly its oils rather than its juice. See page 450 for information on how to make a lime coin for ti' punch. This cocktail is traditionally served at room temperature, but it can also be enjoyed chilled by filling the glass with ice before serving (pictured). Rhum J.M. Sirop de Canne and Steen's are popular brands of cane syrup, though the latter is much darker and has a pronounced molasses-like flavor.

- Lime coin
- 1 teaspoon cane syrup
- 2 ounces white rhum agricole

Place lime coin and syrup in rocks glass and muddle until fragrant and small amount of juice has been released, about 10 seconds. Add rhum agricole and stir until combined using bar spoon, about 15 seconds. Serve.

Ti' Punch

Caramelized Banana Old-Fashioned

Makes 1 cocktail

Sweetness ✦ ✦ ✧

Spirit Forward, Toasted, Tropical

- 1 (½-inch-thick) slice banana for garnishing
- ½ teaspoon sugar
- 2 ounces bourbon
- ¾ ounce banana liqueur
- ⅛ teaspoon old-fashioned aromatic bitters

While you might not instantly associate banana with bourbon, the two surprisingly share a number of flavor compounds (namely isoamyl acetate and ethyl hexanoate). We further enhance the banana flavor by substituting a banana liqueur for the simple syrup. But what takes this cocktail over the top is our garnish of a caramelized banana slice, which, together with the spirit, evokes freshly flambéed bananas Foster. Caramelizing the banana adds visual appeal and aroma to this cocktail, but you can skip this step, if desired. Dehydrated banana chips can also be used as a garnish. Using a high-quality banana liqueur makes a big difference here; we had success with Tempus Fugit Spirits Crème de Banane.

1. Place banana on aluminum foil–lined plate and sprinkle with sugar. Ignite kitchen torch and, holding flame 2 to 4 inches from banana, sweep flame over surface to caramelize sugar, about 1 minute.

2. Add bourbon, banana liqueur, and bitters to mixing glass, then fill three-quarters full with ice. Using bar spoon, stir until mixture is just combined and chilled, about 30 seconds. Strain cocktail into chilled rocks glass half-filled with ice or containing 1 large ice cube. Garnish with caramelized banana slice and serve.

Old Poblano

Makes 1 cocktail
Sweetness ✦ ✦ ✧
Spicy, Spirit Forward, Toasted

Pairing a dark chile (such as ancho) liqueur with aged rum creates an old-fashioned that is warm and raisiny. When infused into a spirit, ancho chiles, which are dried poblano chiles, bring a subtle, smoky, slow-burning spiciness (as compared with green chiles like jalapeños, which give a grassier, slap-your-face heat). Orange bitters and a lime peel expressed over the top add a welcome bright element to the finish. You can use our homemade Ancho Chile Liqueur (page 468) or store-bought ancho liqueur in this recipe.

- **1½ ounces aged rum**
- **1 ounce ancho chile liqueur**
- **⅛ teaspoon orange bitters**
- **Strip of lime peel for garnishing**

Add rum, chile liqueur, and bitters to mixing glass, then fill three-quarters full with ice. Using bar spoon, stir until mixture is just combined and chilled, about 30 seconds. Strain cocktail into chilled rocks glass half-filled with ice or containing 1 large ice cube. Pinch lime peel over drink and rub outer edge of glass with peel, then garnish with lime peel. Serve.

Fly by Night

Makes 1 cocktail
Sweetness ✦ ✦ ✧
Smoky, Spirit Forward, Toasted

Slightly woody reposado tequila mellows out the smokiness of mezcal in this cocktail with a hint of coffee. The coffee liqueur adds complexity, and the warmth of the spice syrup pairs well with the rich coffee flavor, resulting in a toasty, smoky, and comforting drink—a perfect nightcap.

- **1½ ounces reposado tequila**
- **½ ounce mezcal**
- **1 teaspoon Spice Syrup (page 459)**
- **1 teaspoon coffee liqueur**
- **⅛ teaspoon old-fashioned aromatic bitters**
- **Strip of orange peel for garnishing**
- **Coffee beans for garnishing**

Add tequila, mezcal, spice syrup, coffee liqueur, and bitters to mixing glass, then fill three-quarters full with ice. Using bar spoon, stir until mixture is just combined and chilled, about 30 seconds. Strain cocktail into chilled rocks glass half-filled with ice or containing 1 large ice cube. Pinch orange peel over drink and rub outer edge of glass with peel, then garnish with orange peel and coffee beans. Serve.

Irish Godfather

Makes 1 cocktail
Sweetness ✦ ✧ ✧
Citrusy, Spirit Forward, Toasted

The Godfather cocktail has its roots in the 1970s and the eponymous movie. It is a two-ingredient drink of Scotch and amaretto. There is no definitive build, just the intention of taking the edge off the whiskey with the marzipan- and cherry-fragranced liqueur. We riff on this classic by introducing some Irish—in the form of smooth Irish whiskey. Godfather proportions can vary wildly, from equal parts to the 8:1 ratio of whiskey to amaretto that we favor. Our goal here is simply to smooth out the whiskey without masking the subtleties of the triple-distilled spirit. While it's not traditional, we love the minor adjustments of adding orange bitters and an orange twist, as a nod to the memorable scene between Marlon Brando and his grandson in the film. Think of these as simply seasoning a beautiful spirit.

- 2 ounces Irish whiskey
- ¼ ounce amaretto
- ⅛ teaspoon orange bitters
- Orange twist for garnishing

Add whiskey, amaretto, and bitters to mixing glass, then fill three-quarters full with ice. Using bar spoon, stir until mixture is just combined and chilled, about 30 seconds. Strain cocktail into chilled rocks glass half-filled with ice or containing 1 large ice cube. Garnish with orange twist and serve.

Promise Us Paradise

Makes 1 cocktail
Sweetness ✦✦✧
Bitter, Nutty, Spirit Forward

- 2 ounces aged rum
- ½ ounce Amaro Averna Siciliano
- 1 teaspoon orgeat syrup
- ⅛ teaspoon old-fashioned aromatic bitters
- Strip of orange peel for garnishing
- Cocktail cherries for garnishing

Customize Your Cocktail

We developed this recipe with Amaro Averna, but you can also try other styles of medium-bitter amari such as Amaro Montenegro or Cynar.

This full-flavored rum old-fashioned is as rich in taste as it is in its gorgeous color. Voluptuous, bittersweet Amaro Averna is the perfect amaro to pair with aged rum to complement its notes of spice, vanilla, and dried fruit. A teaspoon of nutty orgeat syrup creates an even more sumptuous drink, one to linger over. The classic expression of orange awakens all of the deep flavors.

Add rum, Amaro Averna, orgeat syrup, and bitters to mixing glass, then fill three-quarters full with ice. Using bar spoon, stir until mixture is just combined and chilled, about 30 seconds. Strain cocktail into chilled rocks glass half-filled with ice or containing 1 large ice cube. Pinch orange peel over drink and rub outer edge of glass with peel, then garnish with orange peel and cherries. Serve.

The Whiskey Smash

The whiskey smash is a great way to enjoy a lightened-up, chilled, refreshing whiskey cocktail. Unlike with the equally refreshing whiskey highballs (see pages 67–69), there is usually no seltzer in the smash; rather, it relies on plenty of crushed or shaved ice to both dilute and chill the drink.

The whiskey smash is a more relaxed, citrusy cousin of the Mint Julep (page 145), with the difference being that a smash requires muddled fruit, whereas a julep doesn't. Calling it a "smash," as you might expect, comes from the satisfying action of muddling the fruit and herbs at the start of the build.

Many sources credit Jerry Thomas with the invention of the whiskey smash. It seems likely that it was invented before his time, but he was the first to mention it by name in print, in his 1887 revised version of *How to Mix Drinks, or The Bon Vivant's Companion*. In its early years, it was considered simply as a variation on the already long-established mint julep, but it wasn't long before the smash began to be treated as an individual cocktail in its own right, with distinct variations. As with the old-fashioned, one of the earliest versions used brandy as the base spirit.

The whiskey smash (like the julep) is indelibly associated with the American South. In the 19th century, large amounts of whiskey were produced in Kentucky, and Southerners loved to serve up icy, thirst-quenching whiskey cocktails on a hot summer day. In a nod to this enduring popularity in the South, we use bourbon in our smashes. You could try it with a different dark spirit, though, such as rye, Canadian whisky, or aged rum. The basic formula we use of spirit-herb-citrus is fun to experiment with. For different takes, we swap the mint and lemon of the classic smash for thyme and grapefruit, or ginger and peach, or basil and blood orange.

Whiskey Smash

Makes 1 cocktail
Sweetness ✦✦✧
Citrusy, Herbal, Toasted

- 1 (¼-inch) slice lemon, quartered, plus lemon slice for garnishing
- 4 fresh mint leaves, plus mint sprig for garnishing
- ¾ ounce Simple Syrup (page 458)
- 2 ounces bourbon

1. Add lemon pieces, mint leaves, and simple syrup to mixing glass and muddle until mint is fragrant and lemon has broken down and all juice has been expressed, about 30 seconds. Add bourbon and stir, using bar spoon, until mixture is combined.

2. Double-strain cocktail into chilled rocks glass half-filled with crushed ice. Top with additional crushed ice to form mound above rim of glass. Garnish with mint sprig and lemon slice. Serve.

Customize Your Cocktail

You can make a Rum Smash with aged rum or a Tequila Smash with reposado tequila—or try your favorite spirit.

Grapefruit-Thyme Smash

Makes 1 cocktail
Sweetness ✦ ✦ ✧
Citrusy, Herbal, Toasted

We love how the earthy notes of thyme pair with the zesty freshness of grapefruit. Muddling half of the grapefruit wheel in the cocktail and using half as a garnish gives the drink the perfect amount of sour and sweet to keep it easy to sip.

- 1 (¼-inch) slice grapefruit, cut into quarters, divided
- 4 fresh thyme sprigs, plus thyme sprig for garnishing
- ¾ ounce Simple Syrup (page 458)
- 2 ounces bourbon

1. Add 2 grapefruit quarters, thyme sprigs, and simple syrup to mixing glass and muddle until thyme is fragrant and grapefruit has broken down and all juice has been expressed, about 30 seconds. Add bourbon and stir, using bar spoon, until mixture is combined.

2. Double-strain cocktail into chilled rocks glass half-filled with crushed ice. Top with additional crushed ice to form mound above rim of glass. Garnish with thyme sprig and remaining 2 grapefruit quarters. Serve.

Ginger-Peach Smash

Makes 1 cocktail
Sweetness ✦ ✦ ✧
Fruity, Spiced, Toasted

This drink is meant for leisurely sipping on a hot summer afternoon. The sweet jamminess of muddled peach pairs splendidly with the spicy bite of fresh ginger. This drink was built with bourbon in mind, but Tennessee whiskey or rye would work as well. The success of this drink relies on using fresh, in-season peaches.

- ⅓ cup chopped fresh peaches, plus peach slice for garnishing
- 1 (½-inch) piece ginger, peeled and sliced thin, plus ginger slice for garnishing
- ¾ ounce Simple Syrup (page 458)
- 2 ounces bourbon

1. Add peach, ginger, and simple syrup to mixing glass and muddle until ginger is fragrant and peach has broken down and all juice has been expressed, about 30 seconds. Add bourbon and stir, using bar spoon, until mixture is combined.

2. Double-strain cocktail into chilled rocks glass half-filled with crushed ice. Top with additional crushed ice to form mound above rim of glass. Garnish with peach slice and ginger slice and serve.

Blood and Basil Smash

Makes 1 cocktail
Sweetness ✦✦✧
Citrusy, Herbal, Toasted

The citrus-herb combo in this drink will deliver a much-needed taste of freshness in the winter, when blood oranges are in season. The basil makes the smash a bold sip, and the blood orange offers its gorgeous color.

- 1 (¼-inch) slice blood orange, quartered, plus blood orange slice for garnishing
- ⅓ cup fresh basil leaves, plus basil sprig for garnishing
- ¾ ounce Simple Syrup (page 458)
- 2 ounces bourbon

1. Add orange, basil, and simple syrup to mixing glass and muddle until basil is fragrant and orange has broken down and all juice has been expressed, about 30 seconds. Add bourbon and stir, using bar spoon, until mixture is combined.

2. Double-strain cocktail into chilled rocks glass half-filled with crushed ice. Top with additional crushed ice to form mound above rim of glass. Garnish with basil sprig and orange slice and serve.

From Beirut with Love

Makes 1 cocktail
Sweetness ✦✦✧
Citrusy, Herbal, Spirit Forward

- 1 (¼-inch) slice lemon, quartered, plus strip of lemon peel for garnishing
- ¼ cup fresh mint leaves, plus mint sprig for garnishing
- ¾ ounce honey
- 2 ounces arak

One of the world's most ancient spirits, arak is made from grapes and anise seeds, which impart its defining licorice flavor. Favored across the Levant, arak is traditionally prepared simply, diluted with some water to mellow out its bold flavors and then topped with ice. For a cocktail using arak, we borrow inspiration from another iconic drink enjoyed in Levantine cafés, mint lemonade (limonana). We muddle the lemon pieces and mint together with honey to release their flavorful oils. Arak is meant to be served at convivial gatherings, savored slowly over lively conversations at a table full of mezzes. Its boldness makes this cocktail perfect for unhurried evenings, since gradual dilution from ice melt opens it up further and further over time. We encourage you to seek out arak for this cocktail, but if it's unavailable, ouzo is a good substitute. Do not confuse arak for Batavia arrack.

1. Add lemon pieces, mint leaves, and honey to mixing glass and muddle until mint is fragrant and lemon has broken down and all juice has been expressed, about 30 seconds. Add arak, then fill glass three-quarters full with ice. Using bar spoon, stir until mixture is just combined and chilled, about 30 seconds.

2. Double-strain cocktail into chilled rocks glass half-filled with ice or containing 1 large ice cube. Pinch lemon peel over drink and rub outer edge of glass with peel, then garnish with lemon peel and mint sprig. Serve.

عرق رزوق
ARAK

Mint Julep

Makes 1 cocktail
Sweetness ✦✦✧
Herbal, Spirit Forward

Served in a frosted silver julep cup and topped with a mound of crushed ice and a fragrant, bountiful bouquet of mint, the mint julep became the official drink of the Kentucky Derby in 1938. But while mint juleps are inexorably tied to Kentucky, they may go back more than a century earlier to Virginia, where mint was mixed with brandy or rum as a medicinal morning pick-me-up. This three-ingredient cocktail (four counting the ice) is elegant in its simplicity and is meant to be sipped, the flavors and intensity of the drink evolving as the crushed ice melts. We don't stray far from the classic composition, muddling plenty of fresh mint leaves with simple syrup to release the aromatic oils, and stirring in bourbon before straining the cocktail into a serving vessel and topping with a mound of crushed ice and a generous sprig of fresh mint.

- ⅓ cup fresh mint leaves, plus mint sprig for garnishing
- ½ ounce Simple Syrup (page 458)
- 2 ounces bourbon

1. Add mint leaves and simple syrup to mixing glass and muddle until fragrant, about 30 seconds. Add bourbon and stir, using bar spoon, until mixture is combined.

2. Double-strain cocktail into chilled julep cup half-filled with crushed ice. Top with additional crushed ice to form mound above rim of cup. Garnish with mint sprig and serve.

PAIR WITH A SNACK

Pimento Cheese Spread

Serves 12 (makes about 3 cups)
Total Time: 15 minutes

A quintessential Southern cocktail deserves a quintessential Southern snack. Although pimento cheese spread is sacred for most Southerners (some call it the pâté of the South), this iconic snack was actually created in the North. The recipe emerged around the turn of the 20th century and showed off the benefits of a new invention: canning. But this rosy-tinted cheese spread made with canned pimentos was quickly adopted by Southern cooks. Some recipes call for a combination of extra-sharp cheddar cheese and a milder cheddar or Monterey Jack, but we prefer the bolder flavor that comes from using all extra-sharp cheddar. Don't substitute preshredded cheese here; it includes added starches (meant to prevent the shreds from sticking together) that will result in a dry spread. Serve with crackers.

- **½ cup jarred pimentos, drained and patted dry**
- **6 tablespoons mayonnaise**
- **2 garlic cloves, minced**
- **1½ teaspoons Worcestershire sauce**
- **1 teaspoon hot sauce, plus extra for seasoning**
- **1 pound extra-sharp cheddar cheese, shredded (4 cups)**

Process pimentos, mayonnaise, garlic, Worcestershire, and hot sauce in food processor until smooth, about 20 seconds. Add cheddar and pulse until uniformly blended, with fine bits of cheese throughout, about 20 pulses. Season with salt, pepper, and extra hot sauce to taste, and serve.

Makes 1 cocktail
Sweetness ✦ ✦ ✧
Citrusy, Floral, Tart

- 1 lime, halved crosswise, each half quartered, plus lime slice for garnish
- 2 ounces cachaça
- ¾ ounce Simple Syrup (page 458)

Caipirinha

The caipirinha is sometimes, though somewhat inaccurately, known as the daiquiri of Brazil. While it's true that the cocktail is made simply from sugarcane spirit, limes, and sugar, the nuance of the ingredients and the methodology set it apart. The main ingredient, cachaça, is often thought of as a type of rum, since both are made from sugarcane. However, whereas rum is made from molasses (a product of sugarcane), cachaça is made by distilling fermented sugarcane juice, which makes it more similar to French Caribbean rum, rhum agricole (for more information on cane spirits, see page 236). Cachaça has a grassy flavor, and the caipirinha balances it with lots of lime and sweetness. The first step is muddling lime pieces, often with granulated sugar. After muddling the limes, we shake them with ice, cachaça, and simple syrup to fully and easily incorporate the citrus and sweetener. Then, for the best of both worlds, we dump it all straight into a glass without straining: This gives a few pleasantly crunchy nuggets of cracked ice with some whole ice cubes that won't overdilute the drink.

Add lime pieces to base of cocktail shaker and muddle until broken down and all juice has been expressed, about 30 seconds. Add cachaça and simple syrup, then fill shaker with ice. Shake mixture until just combined and chilled, about 5 seconds. Pour contents of shaker into chilled rocks glass (do not strain) and garnish with lime slice. Serve.

What Happens When Whiskey Ages?

Freshly distilled whiskey is as clear as water, can have a harsh bite, and lacks much of the flavor that whiskeys are known for. In order to become a smooth, golden-amber beverage, it needs to age in an oak barrel. But what exactly happens during those years in a barrel? There are a few different processes going on at the same time.

Extraction

Just as when you steep a vanilla bean in alcohol to make vanilla extract, the alcohol and water in the whiskey steadily extract a wealth of chemical compounds from the wood of the barrel. Vanilla extract is an especially pertinent analogy because one of the main flavor compounds extracted from the wood is vanillin (the same compound found in vanilla beans), which forms when lignin—a structural molecule in wood—breaks down. Sugars and astringent tannins also migrate from the wood to the liquor, as well as the red and brown pigments that give whiskey its color.

Before a barrel is ready for use, its wood is aged and dried—sometimes for years—and the interior of the barrel is sometimes charred with fire. These steps break down some of the wood's chemical components, paving the way for extraction. Some compounds also pass out of the liquor and into the charred wood (subtraction), which helps mellow the harsh taste of young whiskey. Bourbon is aged in unused barrels, which contribute a lot of wood flavor in a few years. Scotch is often aged in barrels that have been used previously and already given up a fair amount of their flavor.

Reaction

Whether a spirit is aged in wood or another material, its chemical components react with each other over time to change the nature of the drink. Esterification is a process in which acids and alcohols react to create flavorful esters, which contribute fruity and floral complexity to the aged spirit. As oxygen slowly enters the barrel through pores in the wood, other reactions take place. Some add new flavors, and some remove unwanted flavors, such as those from sulfur compounds.

Evaporation

A certain amount of liquor evaporates out of the barrel during the aging process. Depending on whether the ambient humidity is more favorable for evaporation of ethanol or water, this can cause either a net increase or decrease in the proof of the aging spirit. Evaporation is also responsible for some flavor transformations as volatile compounds slowly make their way out of the barrel.

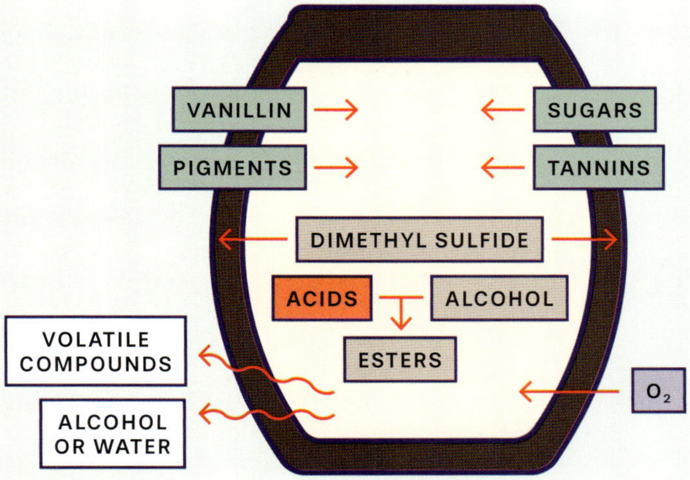

Opening Up Whiskey's Flavor

Want to taste all those subtle flavors that barrel-aging imparts into your whiskey? The burning, pungent qualities contributed by the high proportion of alcohol in whiskey can make it hard to evaluate nuances. So, many aficionados add a splash of water or an ice cube to the glass to "open up" the spirit's flavor and aroma. That's because most of the flavor in whiskey is in the form of ethanol-soluble molecules. The higher the proof of the whiskey, the more flavor molecules are dissolved in the alcohol portion. Adding water frees up more of the aroma molecules to evaporate into the taster's nose. Since appreciation of flavors happens at least as much in the nose as on the tongue, "watered-down" spirits actually seem more flavorful. Dilution also reduces the burn and bite of the alcohol when sipped so that you can sense more of the flavor nuances.

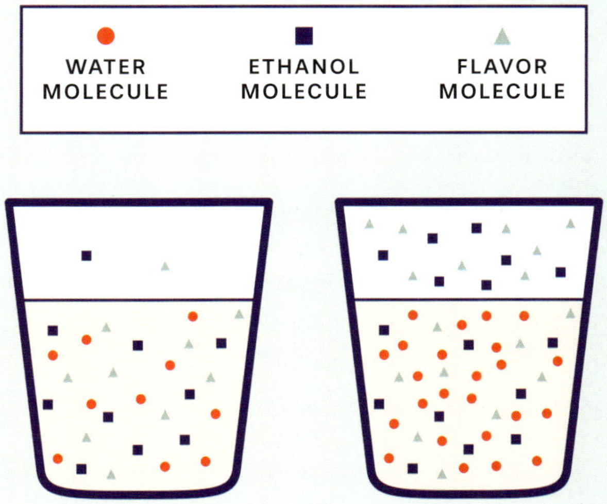

LEFT: Whiskey, neat: All the molecules are evenly mixed together and a small amount of ethanol and flavor molecules evaporate.

RIGHT: Whiskey, cut with a splash of water: Water molecules cluster together, and the ethanol and flavor molecules are pushed toward the surface, where more of them evaporate.

Taste-Off: Tap Water Versus Distilled Water

We wondered if whiskey's flavor could be further amplified by using distilled water. We held a tasting of anonymized samples, diluting whiskey with liquid and ice forms of both tap water and distilled water.

There was a clear consensus that distilled water was better, though the preferred amount of dilution varied among tasters (from 1 teaspoon to 1 tablespoon of water added to a 2-ounce pour of 100-proof spirits). Tasters found that samples cut with distilled water and ice both were smoother sips and exhibited more robust aroma and flavor notes.

WHY? Water is a powerful solvent, so tap (and spring) water is full of dissolved minerals from the earth, water pipes, and the container it is stored in, which can muddy the flavor of the drink. Distilled water has had all its minerals removed, so not only is it neutral in flavor, but it is chemically very eager to dissolve whatever it can. When it is added to whiskey, the ethanol bonds readily with the water, which frees more flavor compounds, making the whiskey much more vivid.

What It Means for Your Old-Fashioned

Stirring up a cocktail with ice doesn't just make your drink refreshingly cold. It also dilutes it a bit—and, in a whiskey-forward cocktail such as the old-fashioned, brings out all those subtle flavors in the spirit. That's why we prefer to use ice cubes made with distilled water (see How to Make Practically Clear Ice, page 28). When stirred, the ice melts into approximately one-third of the old-fashioned's total volume, so you want to make sure you're using water that will let your spirit shine.

Martinis

The martini is often posited to have its origins in the California town of Martinez, north of San Francisco, during the 1860s Gold Rush, when a prospector went into a bar looking to celebrate his success with a strong and tasty libation.

This original iteration was actually quite different from the martini that we know today. It was called a Martinez (naturally) and was rather sweet, since it was made with Old Tom gin (a sweetened gin), sweet vermouth, and maraschino liqueur (plus bitters). There's a lot to say about that important cocktail on its own; see page 164 to learn more. But the basic template of unaged spirit combined with aromatized wine and bitters was born.

At some point in the late 1800s, the drink began being referred to as a "martini," although the ingredients hadn't changed. The rise of the London dry gin style and the prevalent marketing by the Martini & Rossi company around the turn of the 20th century may have nudged the cocktail toward a drier style; print versions around this time started omitting the liqueur and calling for less-sweet styles of gin and dry vermouth instead of sweet.

Versions with vodka (unjustly maligned, in our opinion) came along decades later, with the first printed reference in a 1952 cocktail book. The following year they started gaining in popularity thanks to the publication of the first James Bond novel, *Casino Royale*, which featured the Vesper (page 160), with its blend of gin and vodka.

With a cocktail like the martini that uses so few ingredients, even small changes make a big impact. The choice of spirit is paramount; we like the juniper-forward botanical qualities of London dry gin in our Gin Martini (page 155), but other gin styles with less pronounced juniper also work well. Swapping in sherry or vermouth makes the flavors more warmly nutty. Muddling in herbs adds a prominent freshness. Using cocktail onions as the garnish instead of the traditional olives changes the flavor profile such that the drink warrants a whole new name: the Gibson (page 156).

This chapter takes you through all these martini iterations and more before transitioning to the Martinez branch of the family, which incorporates liqueurs, including Chartreuse and the corn liqueur Nixta, into the formula.

Like the cocktails in the Old-Fashioneds chapter (page 119), these are stirred, spirit-forward drinks to be sipped. Unlike those drinks, these are served up (not over ice). While it's always best practice to start with a chilled cocktail glass, that's especially true for drinks served up. And although there's room for creative license, it's also a good idea to use stemware for martinis, so your warm hands don't diminish the delicate chill prematurely. The iconic V-shaped martini glass or bowl-shape coupe isn't just for elegance and style—it can also enhance the bracing experience of enjoying these iconic cocktails.

Fundamental Formulas

- Martini = non-aged base spirit + fortified wine
- Martinez = non-aged base spirit + fortified wine + liqueur + bitters

BUILD ON THE FUNDAMENTALS

To build on the classic Gin Martini (page 155), start by adding bitters of your choice or olive brine. There are any number of additional ways to dirty your martini or add flavor (see opposite). Replace the vermouth with a fortified wine, as in the Sherry Martini (page 157), or an aromatized wine such as Lillet Blanc or Cocchi Americano (or even split the base with sherry and Cocchi, as in the Jabberwocky on page 163). To build on the Martinez, swap the maraschino liqueur to vary flavor and sweetness—or add bitterness, as the Fernet-Branca does in the Hanky Panky (page 168). Split the spirit base between gin and another spirit, as we do with rhum agricole in the Las Palmas (page 170).

Dry Vermouth

The vermouth is just as important a player as the gin or vodka, so choose one you would drink on its own, on the rocks. We love our Dry Vermouth (page 469), which will really shine in martini recipes, but we understand that it's a bit of a commitment to make. Our favorite store-bought dry vermouth is Dolin Dry Vermouth de Chambéry, which has a crispness and flavor notes of citrus and mint. We also like Noilly Prat Extra Dry Vermouth, which is smooth and light, and Martini & Rossi Extra Dry Vermouth, which has more fruit-forward flavors.

Dry Versus Wet

The "proper" way to make a martini is subject to much debate. To make a cocktail to your liking, you're allowed to tinker with the ratios—just as pro bartenders do. Here are general guidelines for some common styles.

Extra-dry martini

Swirl vermouth in the glass and then dump it out.

Dry martini

5–7:1 spirit to dry vermouth

ATK martini

4:1 spirit to dry vermouth

Wet martini

2:1 spirit to dry vermouth

50/50 martini

1:1 spirit to dry vermouth

Reverse martini

1:2 spirit to dry vermouth

Dirty martini

Brine is added (usually olive brine); can be made wet or dry.

The Dirty Lowdown

According to cocktail historian David Wondrich, the original dirty martini was invented in 1901 at New York's Waldorf Astoria, where bartender John O'Connor "sullied" the cocktail with muddled olives. Many were appalled (some still are), but the drink took off. At some point, brine replaced the muddled olives. The brine contributes saltiness, umami, and a bit of additional body and texture, plus a touch of cloudiness. Dirty martinis often omit the vermouth, although we find that its floral, fruity, and herbal notes keep the cocktail well balanced.

WAYS TO MAKE YOUR MARTINI DIRTY BEYOND OLIVE BRINE

We taste-tested a variety of ingredients to amp up the savory qualities of a martini. The standout winners among tasters were pickled banana pepper brine and pickled jalapeño brine, each of which added pronounced chile flavor and a warming capsaicin kick, in addition to a nice level of salinity. We loved the unexpected twist that some other brines brought: The lactic acid in feta brine added appealing smoothness; preserved lemon brine contributed mellow lemon flavor; and cornichon brine brought pleasing herbal notes. Tasters rejected caper brine, which added fruity flavors, and weren't fans of pickled onion brine, which was too acidic without enough salinity. Try a different brine instead of olive brine in a Dirtiest Martini (page 156).

ALTERNATIVE BRINES	
Pickled Banana Pepper	✓+
Pickled Jalapeño	✓+
Feta	✓
Preserved Lemon	✓
Cornichon	✓
Caper	✗
Pickled Onion	✗

Martini Misappropriation

Thanks to the martini menus of the 1980s and '90s, "martini" is still sometimes used to define practically anything that's served in a conical glass, no matter the ingredients. Such cocktails, often made with fruit or flavored sweet syrups, can be delicious in their own right when well made, but please don't call them martinis.

Clean It Up

If you're not in the dirty martini camp, there are other creative ways to add something flavorful to your martini that isn't a salty brine.

- Lemon, lime, orange, or grapefruit twist or strip
- Cucumber coin
- Fresh herb sprig, such as thyme, rosemary, or basil
- Thinly sliced or shaved celery
- Food-grade fresh flower blossoms or petals, such as lavender, cherry, or rose

The Martini

Since it evolved from the Martinez (page 164), the martini started out as a sweet drink, with early transitional versions sometimes even calling for simple syrup or cocktail cherries. That seems hard to believe now, since modern conversations are so focused on the drink's qualities of dryness. But drier isn't in and of itself better—give a 50/50 martini with a high-quality vermouth a try.

The character of a classic martini is defined by a delicate balance of botanical flavors and aromas imparted by both gin and dry vermouth. Having said that, what's considered the best martini preparation is the one that you like best.

Over the course of decades and across countless cocktail books, the ratio of gin to vermouth recommended for a "classic" martini has varied significantly. In older recipes, martinis approached a nearly equal ratio of gin to vermouth. Current trends for "classic" dry martinis suggest ranges from 5:1 to 7:1. Julia Child's favorite was the reverse martini, also called the upside-down martini, with 1 part gin to 2 parts vermouth. On the other hand, Winston Churchill supposedly said, "I would like to observe the vermouth from across the room while I drink my martini."

Through our testing, we settled on a ratio of 4:1 for our recipe, which allows for appreciation of the distinct flavor notes of both the gin and the vermouth. We favor London dry gin here, with its bracing dryness and juniper-forward flavor. When creating variations, this ratio isn't so hard and fast; for example, we love the round, nutty flavors that a larger pour of sherry brings to our Sherry Martini.

And now to the big question: shaken or stirred? As with all our cocktails that are made up of just spirits, we stir our martini with ice before straining it into a chilled glass. Stirring creates a silky texture in the finished drink. But truth be told, it really won't ruin a martini to lightly shake it, which has the effect of aerating the drink. Some people even like their martinis to have tiny ice chips on the surface. Give it a try yourself sometime and see what you think.

Gin Martini

Makes 1 cocktail
Sweetness ✧ ✧ ✧
Herbal, Savory, Spirit Forward

- 2 ounces London dry gin
- ½ ounce dry vermouth
- Brine-cured green olives for garnishing

Add gin and vermouth to mixing glass, then fill three-quarters full with ice. Using bar spoon, stir until mixture is fully combined and well chilled, about 1 minute. Strain cocktail into chilled cocktail glass. Garnish with olives and serve.

Customize Your Cocktail

Not a gin drinker? Make a Vodka Martini by substituting vodka for the gin. To make a drier martini, reduce the vermouth to ¼ ounce; to make a wetter martini, increase it to up to 1 ounce. Or, try an Upside-Down Martini, with 2 ounces of vermouth and 1 ounce of gin. If you prefer, for the olive garnish you can substitute (or add) a lemon twist.

Dirtiest Martini

Makes 1 cocktail
Sweetness ✧ ✧ ✧
Savory, Spirit Forward

A martini made "dirty" with olive brine has tantalizing salinity and a savory bite. In addition to stirring in a generous 1 ounce of olive brine, we've discovered that adding a pinch of umami-boosting monosodium glutamate makes a dirty martini taste even dirtier. We didn't invent adding MSG to cocktails, and we have seen bartenders around the globe utilizing this ingredient. You'll find MSG in the spice aisle under the brand name Ac'cent.

- 2 ounces London dry gin
- 1 ounce olive brine, plus brine-cured olives for garnishing
- ½ ounce dry vermouth
- Pinch monosodium glutamate (optional)

Add gin, olive brine, vermouth, and monosodium glutamate, if using, to mixing glass, then fill three-quarters full with ice. Using bar spoon, stir until mixture is fully combined and well chilled, about 1 minute. Strain cocktail into chilled cocktail glass. Garnish with olives and serve.

Customize Your Cocktail

You can create interesting dirty martinis with a variety of brine-cured pantry items; see page 153 for suggestions.

Gibson

Makes 1 cocktail
Sweetness ✧ ✧ ✧
Savory, Spirit Forward

Today, a Gibson is distinguished from a martini by its cocktail-onion garnish. But some believe that the Gibson arose in the late 1800s as a way to ask for a martini without bitters at a time when the de facto martini included them. The intentional omission of bitters from a martini is thought to have been first made at San Francisco's Bohemia Club by socialite Walter D. K. Gibson, so he is credited for the drink (and its name). That said, there's another Gibson, illustrator Charles Dana Gibson, who may have first drunk a dry martini with an onion garnish, when he asked a bartender to level up a martini. Today, we'll toast to both Mr. Gibsons.

- 2 ounces London dry gin
- ¼ ounce dry vermouth
- Cocktail onions for garnishing

Add gin and vermouth to mixing glass, then fill three-quarters full with ice. Using bar spoon, stir until mixture is fully combined and well chilled, about 45 seconds. Strain cocktail into chilled cocktail glass. Garnish with onions and serve.

Customize Your Cocktail

You can make a Dirty Gibson by adding 1 ounce of cocktail onion brine.

Sherry Martini

Makes 1 cocktail
Sweetness ✧ ✧ ✧
Savory, Spirit Forward

Use fino sherry in place of the vermouth in a martini and you have, simply, a sherry (or fino) martini. Sherry isn't infused with botanicals, so while it lacks the herbal and floral notes of vermouth, it brings dryness and savor, with savory, oxidized flavors on the finish. The result is a rounder cocktail that can handle both a lemon twist and olive garnish.

- 2 ounces London dry gin
- 1 ounce fino sherry
- Lemon twist for garnishing
- Brine-cured green olives for garnishing

Add gin and sherry to mixing glass, then fill three-quarters full with ice. Using bar spoon, stir until mixture is fully combined and well chilled, about 1 minute. Strain cocktail into chilled cocktail glass. Garnish with lemon twist and olives and serve.

Customize Your Cocktail

We like making this drink with fino sherry, but you can explore different flavor profiles by using a dry amontillado, oloroso, or palo cortado sherry.

Fridge Door Martinis

Makes 8 cocktails
Sweetness ✧ ✧ ✧
Savory, Spirit Forward

As a spirit-only cocktail, served ice cold, martinis are the perfect recipe to serve after a deep chill. Pour one out to unwind or to entertain—just make sure to have olives on hand to garnish when the time comes! A measured amount of water in the mix adds the perfect amount of dilution, so you can serve the martinis straight from the bottle. You can store the cocktail in a 1-quart Mason jar instead of a bottle if you'd like.

- 16 ounces London dry gin
- 10 ounces water
- 4 ounces dry vermouth
- Brine-cured green olives for garnishing

1. Combine gin, water, and vermouth in 1-liter glass bottle. Cover and freeze until well chilled, about 2 hours. Prepare cocktails immediately or transfer to refrigerator and store for up to 1 month; return to freezer and chill for 30 minutes before preparing cocktails.

2. Gently shake bottle to recombine, then serve cocktails in chilled cocktail glasses, garnishing with olives.

Customize Your Cocktail

You can make Fridge Door Gibsons by reducing the dry vermouth to 2 ounces and garnishing with cocktail onions.

From left: Fridge Door Martinis, Gibson, Dirtiest Martini, Sherry Martini

PAIR WITH A SNACK

Smoked Trout Pâté

Serves 6
Total Time: 25 minutes

Salty, smoky trout pâté pairs well with the sharp flavor of clear, spirit-forward cocktails. This one also packs a punch with some complementary grassy heat from minced jalapeño in addition to the common Tabasco sauce. The trout combined with the creamy cream cheese is a perfectly rich counterpoint to your cocktail. You'll need one jalapeño and one lemon here. We suggest using a good-quality refrigerated prepared horseradish, such as Woeber's Pure Horseradish. We developed this recipe using Ducktrap Smoked Trout. To quickly soften the cream cheese, microwave it in a large bowl for about 20 seconds. This pâté tastes even better as it sits; we recommend making it at least 1 hour before serving and refrigerating. Serve with crostini or crackers.

- 8 ounces smoked trout
- 4 ounces cream cheese, cut into 4 pieces and softened
- ¼ cup sour cream
- 2 tablespoons mayonnaise
- 1 scallion, sliced thin
- 4 teaspoons minced jalapeño chile
- 4 teaspoons lemon juice
- 1 tablespoon prepared horseradish
- ¾ teaspoon pepper
- ½ teaspoon Tabasco sauce
- ¼ teaspoon table salt

Using your hands, finely shred trout in medium bowl, discarding skin and bones. Add cream cheese, sour cream, mayonnaise, scallion, jalapeño, lemon juice, horseradish, pepper, Tabasco, and salt. Stir and mash vigorously with fork until thoroughly combined. Transfer to shallow bowl and serve.

Vesper

Makes 1 cocktail
Sweetness ✧ ✧ ✧
Floral, Herbal, Spirit Forward

Crisp, botanical, lemony, and strong, the Vesper was initially brought to life on the pages of Ian Fleming's first James Bond novel, *Casino Royale*. Named after 007's ill-fated girlfriend, Vesper Lynd, this cocktail (originally 3 parts gin, 1 part vodka, and 1 part Kina Lillet) saw a resurgence in the aughts largely because of the big-screen remake of *Casino Royale* and its follow-up, *Quantum of Solace*. This gin-based drink uses the addition of more neutral-flavored vodka to help lengthen the botanical gin flavor while allowing the delicate, fruity Lillet to come through. Kina Lillet, which is no longer commercially produced, was an aromatized wine that contained quinine. Lillet Blanc, a similar product that is slightly more citrusy and less bitter, makes an excellent substitute.

We started with the original recipe ratios for this iconic Bond cocktail, which pours out a drink that's very strong and gin-forward. For a more nuanced cocktail, we found balance in 2 parts gin to 1 part vodka and 1 part Lillet. Though it's originally ordered shaken by Bond (naturally), we stir our version to avoid too much dilution given the reduced amount of gin. Cocchi Americano or vermouth bianco (also sometimes labeled blanc or blanco) can be used in place of the Lillet Blanc.

1½ ounces London dry gin
¾ ounce vodka
¾ ounce Lillet Blanc
Lemon twist for garnishing

Add gin, vodka, and Lillet to mixing glass, then fill three-quarters full with ice. Using bar spoon, stir until mixture is fully combined and well chilled, about 1 minute. Strain cocktail into chilled cocktail glass. Garnish with lemon twist and serve.

Herb Martini

Makes 1 cocktail
Sweetness ✧ ✧ ✧
Herbal, Savory, Spirit Forward

Martinis are savory cocktails. To up the savor more, we muddle a variety of herbs—grassy parsley, cooling mint, and citrusy dill. Using vodka instead of gin allows the fresh flavors to come through without having to compete with gin's botanicals. Increasing the amount of dry vermouth from our standard martini ratio creates a slightly wetter martini that makes this drink more refreshing. You can garnish the martini with extra herbs if desired.

- 2 tablespoons fresh dill fronds
- 2 tablespoons fresh parsley leaves
- 2 tablespoons fresh mint leaves
- 2 ounces vodka
- 1 ounce dry vermouth
- Lemon twist for garnish

1. Add herbs to mixing glass and muddle until fragrant, about 30 seconds. Add vodka and vermouth, then fill three-quarters full with ice. Using bar spoon, stir until mixture is fully combined and well chilled, about 1 minute.

2. Double-strain cocktail into chilled cocktail glass. Garnish with lemon twist and serve.

Customize Your Cocktail

We've listed our favorite combination of herbs in this martini, but feel free to experiment with others, such as basil, celery leaves, chervil, lovage, and tarragon.

El Capitán

El Capitán

Makes 1 cocktail
Sweetness ✦ ✧ ✧
Floral, Spirit Forward

While the exact origins of el capitán remain unknown, the Peruvian cocktail is the marriage of sweet vermouth and Peru's own national spirit, pisco. Some think el capitán is named as such because it was popular among army captains in the southern city of Puno in the 1920s, a period of change and unrest for the country. Pisco is distilled from grapes, and can be made in either Chile or Peru (both claim the spirit); as a result, it can vary widely in taste. We tested this cocktail using a pisco made from 100 percent Quebranta grapes—grapes indigenous to Peru. It tastes dry and has fruity notes. You can also use Acholado pisco, which is made from a blend of grape varietals, adding complexity to the spirit and therefore your cocktail.

- 2 ounces pisco
- ¾ ounce sweet vermouth
- ⅛ teaspoon old-fashioned aromatic bitters
- Brine-cured green olives for garnishing

Add pisco, vermouth, and bitters to mixing glass, then fill three-quarters full with ice. Using bar spoon, stir until mixture is fully combined and well chilled, about 1 minute. Strain cocktail into chilled cocktail glass. Garnish with olives and serve.

Jabberwocky

Makes 1 cocktail
Sweetness ✦ ✧ ✧
Herbal, Savory, Spirit Forward

This drink can be called either the Jabberwocky or Jabberwock. Both names are inspired by the 1871 Lewis Carroll poem—the poem itself or the iconic character therein. The cocktail first appeared in Harry Craddock's 1930 book, *The Savoy Cocktail Book*, and it even calls out some of the iconic nonsensical words in Carroll's poem. Craddock's recipe includes a product called Caperitif. This is what some call a "ghost ingredient"—one that may show up in an old cocktail book but is not available today. Caperitif was an aperitif-style wine made near Cape Town, South Africa. Most agree that this was a fortified wine in the style of Cocchi Americano or Lillet Blanc; just about everyone agrees that it hasn't been available since the mid-20th century. Lillet Blanc or vermouth bianco (also sometimes labeled blanc or blanco) can be used in place of the Cocchi Americano.

- 1 ounce London dry gin
- 1 ounce fino sherry
- 1 ounce Cocchi Americano
- ⅛ teaspoon lemon or grapefruit bitters
- Lemon twist for garnishing

Add gin, sherry, Cocchi Americano, and bitters to mixing glass, then fill three-quarters full with ice. Using bar spoon, stir until mixture is fully combined and well chilled, about 1 minute. Strain cocktail into chilled cocktail glass. Garnish with lemon twist and serve.

The Martinez

The Martinez is one of the more overlooked canonical cocktails. Popular in its early days (the late 1800s and early 1900s), it got swallowed up in the juggernaut rise of the martini. It has in recent times regained its level of respect, at least, if not its level of popularity.

There's a powerful reason why it deserves such respect. Simply and boldly put, the Martinez is the direct link between the Manhattan and the martini. The first printed recipes for the Martinez positioned it essentially as a gin Manhattan, substituting gin for whiskey. The first print mention of the Martinez, in 1884's *Modern Bartender's Guide* by O. H. Byron, called for the addition of curaçao. However, the 1887 edition of Jerry Thomas's *How to Mix Drinks, or The Bon Vivant's Companion*, includes the version that is widely recognized today: Old Tom gin, sweet vermouth, maraschino liqueur, and bitters.

The Martinez was intended to be on the sweeter side. It gradually started to evolve to become drier with versions that swapped in dry vermouth for sweet. Eventually, versions emerged that skipped the liqueur and used higher proportions of gin to vermouth. The sweeter style of Old Tom gin went out of fashion in favor of the drier London dry gin. And voilà: the martini.

The ratios in a Martinez have always varied wildly (and maybe that's why martini ratios vary so much), and some recipes also split the vermouth between sweet and dry. So even though it holds an important place in cocktail history and evolution, you might say that it is a chameleon, changing and evolving throughout history according to its context.

We take that as an opportunity to explore options. Our Martinez uses London dry gin, sweet vermouth, and maraschino liqueur. A citrusy version subs orange liqueur for the maraschino, and another version "improves" the cocktail by adding absinthe along with the maraschino.

Martinez

Makes 1 cocktail
Sweetness ✦✦✧
Floral, Spirit Forward, Toasted

- 1¾ ounces London dry gin
- 1¼ ounces sweet vermouth
- ¼ ounce maraschino liqueur
- ⅛ teaspoon old-fashioned aromatic bitters
- Strip of orange peel for garnishing

Add gin, vermouth, maraschino liqueur, and bitters to mixing glass, then fill three-quarters full with ice. Using bar spoon, stir until mixture is fully combined and well chilled, about 1 minute. Strain cocktail into chilled cocktail glass. Pinch orange peel over drink and rub outer edge of glass with peel, then garnish with orange peel. Serve.

Customize Your Cocktail

If you'd like to try the original Martinez, use Old Tom gin, which makes the cocktail slightly sweeter.

Martinez, but Make It Citrusy

Makes 1 cocktail
Sweetness ✦ ✦ ✧
Citrusy, Herbal, Spirit Forward

It's common to play off of the Martinez by substituting other liqueurs for the maraschino liqueur. Orange liqueur is often the choice, so we lean in to a citrus-flavored cocktail with orange liqueur, orange bitters, and an orange twist.

- **1¾ ounces London dry gin**
- **1 ounce sweet vermouth**
- **½ ounce orange liqueur**
- **⅛ teaspoon orange bitters**
- **Strip of orange peel for garnishing**

Add gin, vermouth, orange liqueur, and bitters to mixing glass, then fill three-quarters full with ice. Using bar spoon, stir until mixture is fully combined and well chilled, about 1 minute. Strain cocktail into chilled cocktail glass. Pinch orange peel over drink and rub outer edge of glass with peel, then garnish with orange peel. Serve.

Tuxedo

Makes 1 cocktail
Sweetness ✦ ✦ ✧
Herbal, Savory, Spirit Forward

What do you get when you dress a martini in elegant evening wear? The aromatic tuxedo first appeared in print in Harry Johnson's *Bartenders' Manual* in 1900. While for some, an "improved" cocktail can mean simply the addition of a liqueur or absinthe, for many, it is this magical combination of maraschino liqueur, absinthe, and old-fashioned bitters. Other dry anise-flavored spirits (such as Herbsaint, pastis, or dry anisette) can be substituted for the absinthe.

- **1¾ ounces London dry gin**
- **1 ounce dry vermouth**
- **¼ ounce maraschino liqueur**
- **⅛ teaspoon absinthe**
- **⅛ teaspoon old-fashioned aromatic bitters**
- **Strip of lemon peel for garnishing**

Add gin, vermouth, maraschino liqueur, absinthe, and bitters to mixing glass, then fill three-quarters full with ice. Using bar spoon, stir until mixture is fully combined and well chilled, about 1 minute. Strain cocktail into chilled cocktail glass. Pinch lemon peel over drink and rub outer edge of glass with peel, then garnish with lemon peel. Serve.

Fridge Door Martinez

Makes 8 cocktails
Sweetness ✦✦✧
Floral, Spirit Forward, Toasted

Sweeter than a martini and thus, for many people, more drinkable, the Martinez is a good bet if you're serving company—dressed-up and universally palatable. You can store the cocktail in a 1-quart Mason jar instead of a bottle if you'd like.

- 14 ounces London dry gin
- 10 ounces sweet vermouth
- 6 ounces water
- 2 ounces maraschino liqueur
- ½ teaspoon old-fashioned aromatic bitters
- Strip of orange peel for garnishing

1. Combine gin, vermouth, and water in 1-liter bottle. Cover and freeze until well chilled, about 2 hours. Prepare cocktails immediately or transfer to refrigerator and store for up to 1 month; return to freezer and chill for 30 minutes before preparing cocktails.

2. Gently shake bottle to recombine, then serve cocktails in chilled cocktail glasses. Pinch orange peels over individual drinks and rub outer edges of glasses with peels. Garnish with orange peels.

Hanky Panky

Makes 1 cocktail
Sweetness ✦ ✧ ✧
Bitter, Herbal, Spirit Forward

The hanky panky is a 100-year-old cocktail that feels unbelievably current. We love this drink (among other delicious reasons) because it clearly places its creator, Ada Coleman, among the pantheon of iconic, otherwise all men bartenders of the pre-Prohibition era. Coleman ran perhaps the most prestigious bar in the world—the American Bar in London—for more than 20 years. While there were countless bartending women who made discoveries that built cocktail history, much of their labor has been erased, and we don't know many of their names.

Coleman first mixed up the cocktail for actor Charles Hawtrey. He arrived at the bar late one night and requested "something with a bit of punch in it." When served the creation, he exclaimed, "By Jove, that is the real hanky panky!" This cocktail that was made for someone famous is on the list of reasons why Coleman herself is one of the most famous bartenders of all time. Fernet is a subcategory of amari, intensely flavored with roots, barks, herbs, and fruit; here it adds complexity, a clear savoriness, and a bit of bitterness to what could otherwise be a sweet spirit-forward cocktail. Fernet is generally full proof (40% ABV). There are many fernets, including standout examples from Italy, Mexico, and the United States. We like Fernet-Branca here, but you may try out another fernet or an amaro such as Cynar, if you like.

- 1½ ounces London dry gin
- 1½ ounces sweet vermouth
- ¼ ounce Fernet-Branca
- Strip of orange peel for garnishing

Add gin, vermouth, and Fernet-Branca to mixing glass, then fill three-quarters full with ice. Using bar spoon, stir until mixture is fully combined and well chilled, about 1 minute. Strain cocktail into chilled cocktail glass. Pinch orange peel over drink and rub outer edge of glass with peel, then garnish with orange peel. Serve.

Customize Your Cocktail

For a delicious variation, try replacing the vermouth with Punt e Mes, a more bitter sweet vermouth made by the same company as Fernet-Branca.

PAIR WITH A SNACK

Ricotta Crostini with Asparagus and Radish

Serves 6
Total Time: 45 minutes, plus 30 minutes cooling

Silky ricotta and crisp raw vegetables make a perfect crostini bite. Day-old bread is easier to slice. A 12-inch demi-baguette yields the 24 slices.

- 24 (¼-inch-thick) slices baguette
- 6 tablespoons extra-virgin olive oil, divided
- 2 ounces asparagus, trimmed and sliced thin on bias
- 4 radishes, trimmed and sliced thin
- ¼ cup minced fresh chives
- 1 tablespoon lemon juice
- 1 small garlic clove, minced
- 1 anchovy fillet, minced
- ½ teaspoon table salt, divided
- ½ teaspoon black pepper, divided
- 6 ounces (¾ cup) whole-milk ricotta cheese

1. Adjust oven rack to middle position and heat oven to 400 degrees. Arrange baguette slices in single layer on rimmed baking sheet. Brush tops of slices with 2 tablespoons oil. Bake until golden brown and crispy, 8 to 10 minutes. Let cool completely on sheet, about 30 minutes.

2. Combine asparagus, radishes, chives, lemon juice, garlic, anchovy, ¼ teaspoon salt, ¼ teaspoon pepper, and 2 tablespoons oil in bowl; set aside.

3. Process ricotta, remaining ¼ teaspoon salt, and remaining ¼ teaspoon pepper in food processor until smooth, about 10 seconds. With processor running, slowly add remaining 2 tablespoons oil until incorporated; transfer to bowl. Spread ricotta mixture evenly on baguette slices. Spoon asparagus mixture over ricotta. Serve.

Makes 1 cocktail
Sweetness ✦ ✧ ✧
Bitter, Herbal, Spirit Forward

- 1 ounce rhum agricole
- 1 ounce London dry gin
- ¾ ounce Cocchi Americano
- ¼ ounce orange liqueur
- ⅛ teaspoon orange bitters
- Strip of orange peel for garnishing

Customize Your Cocktail

We like the rhum agricole in this recipe, but you can try another rum made from fresh sugarcane, like cachaça or Haitian clairin.

Las Palmas

Our las palmas cocktail stirs together classic and contemporary inspirations: a Martinez and a martini variation called the Air-Conditioned Eden (named after a UK documentary about the so-called tiki culture of post–World War II America) created by bartender Ryan Lotz at Shore Leave, a bar and restaurant in Boston. Lotz's cocktail is a creative solution to making a stirred, martini-style drink that fits in with the tropical, rum-forward theme of the restaurant. We follow his lead by using a split base of 1 ounce of gin and 1 ounce of rum—specifically grassy, intensely flavored rhum agricole, which adds a refreshing complexity, while pulling a martini into the land of tropical drinks. While Lotz makes his martini fruity with pineapple-infused vermouth, we go a citrusy route, adding orange liqueur and bitters. Cocchi Americano stands in for the vermouth to provide complexity. Lillet Blanc or vermouth bianco (also sometimes labeled blanc or blanco) can be used in place of the Cocchi Americano.

Add rhum, gin, Cocchi Americano, orange liqueur, and bitters to mixing glass, then fill three-quarters full with ice. Using bar spoon, stir until mixture is fully combined and well chilled, about 1 minute. Strain cocktail into chilled cocktail glass. Pinch orange peel over drink and rub outer edge of glass with peel, then garnish with orange peel. Serve.

Arroyo

Arroyo

Makes 1 cocktail
Sweetness ✦✧✧
Bitter, Citrusy, Spirit Forward

Based on the Martinez but inspired by Mexican spirits and flavors, this intriguing cocktail swaps out the gin for tequila, and the maraschino liqueur for a Mexican corn liqueur to create something undeniably different. The corn liqueur balances the tequila and bitters with round, buttery flavor. Arroyo also serves as a nod to the Rio Grande cocktail, a martini with a split base of gin and tequila that shows up in the 1937 *Café Royal Cocktail Book*.

- 2 ounces blanco tequila
- ¾ ounce dry vermouth
- ½ ounce Nixta Licor de Elote
- ⅛ teaspoon grapefruit or lemon bitters
- Strip of grapefruit peel for garnishing

Add tequila, vermouth, Nixta Licor de Elote, and bitters to mixing glass, then fill three-quarters full with ice. Using bar spoon, stir until mixture is fully combined and well chilled, about 1 minute. Strain cocktail into chilled cocktail glass. Pinch grapefruit peel over drink and rub outer edge of glass with peel, then garnish with grapefruit peel. Serve.

Bijou

Makes 1 cocktail
Sweetness ✦✦✧
Bitter, Herbal, Spirit Forward

A brilliant jewel tone hints at just how special this drink tastes—and explains the naming of this cocktail in Cincinnati bartender C. F. Lawlor's 1895 book *The Mixicologist*. That drink is equal parts gin, vermouth, and Grand Marnier—fine, but not nearly as interesting as a drink made with Chartreuse, as introduced by Harry Johnson in 1900 in his *Bartenders' Manual*. A bijou made with the herbal green liqueur defines the cocktail today. This sweet drink is perfect for a date—Chartreuse is always a brilliant conversation starter. Orange comes from a dash of bitters.

- 1 ounce London dry gin
- 1 ounce green Chartreuse
- 1 ounce sweet vermouth
- ⅛ teaspoon orange bitters

Add gin, Chartreuse, vermouth, and bitters to mixing glass, then fill three-quarters full with ice. Using bar spoon, stir until mixture is fully combined and well chilled, about 1 minute. Strain cocktail into chilled cocktail glass and serve.

Mixing-ology

Stirring or shaking a cocktail with ice affects not just temperature but also dilution, flavor, and aroma. This is due to the chemistry of how the alcohol interacts with the water in the ice and the other ingredients. Dilution and chilling make harsh ethanol less volatile and assertive, allowing the pleasant, subtle flavors of the spirit to come through. (The rules don't apply the same way for zero-proof cocktails.) Here's why mixing correctly matters.

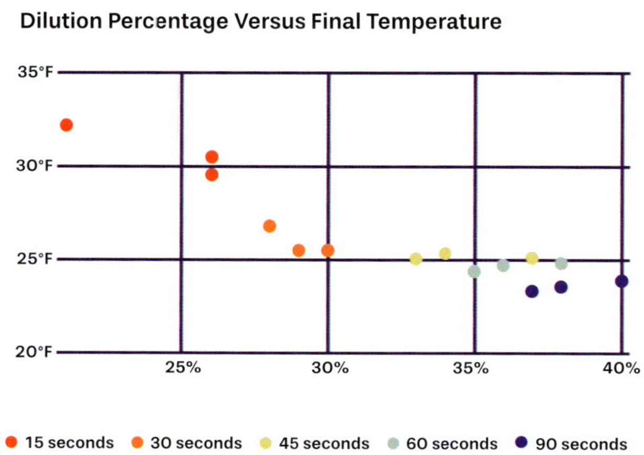

The Science of Stirring

Is how long you stir a cocktail really of any consequence? To find out, we made our Gin Martini (page 155) over and over again, measuring the dilution after five different stirring times: 15 seconds, 30 seconds, 45 seconds, 60 seconds, and 90 seconds. We weighed each sample before and after stirring it (straining out the remaining ice) to determine how much water the melting ice added to the drink. After a 15-second stir, the martini was only about 20 percent water. By 90 seconds, the water content had increased to about 40 percent.

We also took the temperature of the drink at each interval to determine how quickly the drink chilled and whether we could use that as a benchmark for dilution. We found that the temperature of the drink dropped steeply for the first 45 seconds, then began to plateau as we continued to stir. The 15-second stir had a high temperature of 32 degrees Fahrenheit, the 45-second stir hit an average of 25 degrees, and the 90-second stir bottomed out around 23 degrees. This is because the added ice continues to melt and chill the drink the more you stir it (see The Science of Dilution on page 25). Since alcohol has a much lower freezing point than water, it's possible for a martini to reach temperatures colder than the freezing point of water—just how we like it.

How Much Dilution Is Too Much?

Some dilution is necessary to make a good martini. The ethanol in gin (and other spirits) dissolves some of the water-insoluble aroma compounds. Diluting the spirit with water from the ice drives these molecules (and their aromas) out of the solution and into the air, resulting in a more intense, purer-tasting martini. But what is the ideal amount of dilution? To find out, we held a tasting of martinis stirred for different amounts of time.

Most tasters thought the martini stirred for 15 seconds was too strong, with ethanol overwhelming the more subtle notes of the gin and the aromatic flavors of the vermouth. The martini stirred for 30 seconds was no one's favorite, though no one hated it either. The clear winner was the martini stirred for 1 minute, which had the most prevalent aromatic notes and complex flavor.

We also tasted a martini stirred for 2 full minutes to emulate the most enthusiastic of stirrers. Though not as favored as the 1-minute martini, it still had its fans among tasters.

The takeaway? For the best flavor, err on the longer side of stirring. We recommend a 60-second stir to achieve the coldest martini with the best flavor. The amount of dilution that occurs after that is negligible for up to 2 minutes, so if you go a little too long, don't sweat it. This applies to other stirred cocktails, too.

TEMP YOUR COCKTAIL

Not everyone stirs at the same rate; as a result, the time it takes to properly chill and dilute a stirred cocktail is difficult to perfectly standardize. Though our suggested stir time is likely to get you good results, the most precise way to know if your cocktail is ready is the same way to know if your chicken or side of beef is done: Temp it.

When you feel like you've finished stirring, use an instant-read thermometer to check if you should keep going. When the temperature drops below 25 degrees, your cocktail has reached the on-target amount of dilution. Try timing yourself to get a sense of how vigorous your stir is compared to ours.

The Science of Shaking

We tried a similar experiment using a shaken cocktail, our Daiquiri (page 205), with different (and interesting) results. The drink chilled quickly for the first 15 seconds of shaking, with the temperature dropping by over 42 degrees. But as we continued shaking, the temperature began to rise again—likely because heat stored in our cocktail shaker began to transfer into the drink.

Overdilution was more of an issue in the daiquiris, too. Tasters were more sensitive to a higher proportion of water in the final cocktail, perceiving it as weaker and less flavorful. Since the drink only gets warmer and more diluted after 15 seconds, we recommend you stop there. And for precision's sake, you can temp shaken cocktails, too; we find that the ideal dilution of a shaken cocktail is achieved at a final temperature of 28 degrees or less.

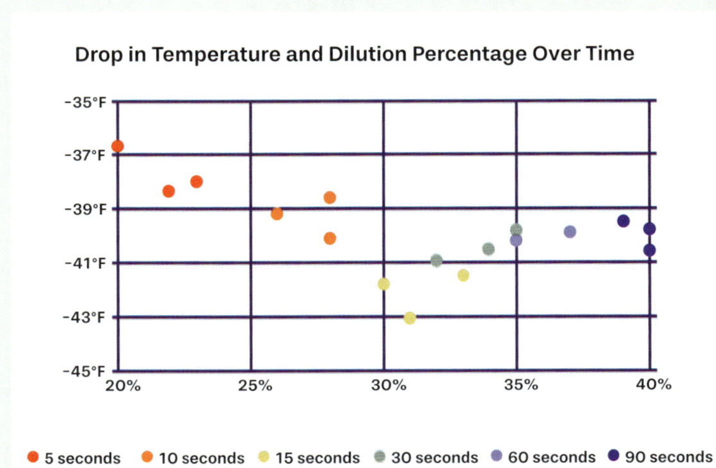

Manhattans

Major-league and spirit forward, the Manhattan is a cocktail—and cultural—icon. Gary "gaz" Regan, legendary bartender and author of 18 books, including *The Joy of Mixology*, called the Manhattan "the drink that changed the face of cocktails." It's considered by many to be the cocktail of choice for whiskey aficionados.

The Manhattan family was born sometime during the mid-19th century, and the first written recipe for the Manhattan appeared in O. H. Byron's 1884 *The Modern Bartenders' Guide*. "Recipes" is more accurate, actually, since the book included two versions of the Manhattan; both used whiskey, vermouth, and Angostura bitters, with one version adding curaçao and the other adding gum syrup (a type of simple syrup made from gum arabic, the crystallized sap of the acacia tree). That same year, several other bar books also included recipes for the Manhattan, and different versions began to emerge as the years passed.

As with so many cocktails, Prohibition exerted a major influence. During this time, when American rye and bourbon were hard to come by, imported whiskey, such as Canadian rye and Scotch, began to be used more frequently.

In terms of its cultural status and shared tales of lore and legend, the Manhattan is right up there with the martini. Maybe more so, for two reasons. First, the Manhattan is generally believed to be older and the progenitor of the martini. Second, there's arguably a healthier debate to be had about presentation: Though most agree that a Manhattan should be stirred rather than shaken, when you order one at a bar, you are much more likely to be asked whether you want it up or on the rocks. Discuss.

Like the martini, there are nearly infinite variations substituting in different ingredients for the three core components. Building from a base formula of whiskey, vermouth, and bitters, this chapter takes you through the old and modern classics using rye, bourbon, and even Cognac. We also share recipes that use rum, reposado tequila, and sherry, supplementing or replacing the vermouth with liqueurs including Bénédictine, Amaro Montenegro, crème de cacao, and more. These possibilities and more ensure that the Manhattan family will continue to propagate and prosper.

Manhattans

Fundamental Formula

aged base spirit + aromatized wine + bitters

BUILD ON THE FUNDAMENTALS

Simply swap out whiskey for a different spirit, such as the aged rum or reposado tequila in the Palmetto (page 183). Swap out the classic sweet vermouth for a liqueur, as we do with amaro in the Black Manhattan (page 182) and Bénédictine in the Monte Carlo (page 186). Change the sweet vermouth to dry vermouth and add a liqueur, as in the Little Baloney (page 191). Split the base spirit, plus add a liqueur in addition to vermouth, to make the Vieux Carré (page 196) and the Smoky Peat (page 196). You can even make a nonalcoholic homage to the spirit-forward Manhattan by using a smoky brewed tea concentrate in our Traverse City (page 198).

Which Whiskey?

The great Manhattan debate is usually between rye and bourbon, but there are other whiskeys to consider in addition to those.

- **Rye** offers a dry, spicy brashness.
- **Bourbon** can bring a fuller body and subtle sweetness.
- **Tennessee whiskey** is lighter bodied than bourbon, with a smooth texture thanks to its charcoal filtering.
- **Canadian blended whisky** generally brings a light, smooth quality.
- Make a Manhattan with **Scotch** and you have a Rob Roy (page 181).
- **Split the base**, as in the Smoky Peat (page 196), which uses bourbon and Scotch.

Sweet Vermouth

Sweet vermouth is a much broader category than dry vermouth, and these aromatized wines can vary dramatically in color, body, and flavor. The best one for a Manhattan is one that you like on its own. Also take into account the whiskey you are planning to use for your Manhattan: Richer whiskeys, like bourbon, benefit from being paired with a richer style of vermouth so that neither overwhelms the other. Likewise, lighter whiskeys pair well with a lighter-bodied vermouth. There is variation within vermouth styles, but here are some general guidelines.

ITALIAN VERMOUTH often tends to be on the sweeter side, darker in color with a fuller body, with flavor notes of burnt sugar and warm spices. A bitter finish is often a hallmark of Italian vermouth. Try Cinzano Rosso Vermouth, Martini & Rossi Rosso Vermouth, Cocchi Storico Vermouth di Torino, or for greater richness, Carpano Antica Formula.

FRENCH VERMOUTH tends to be slightly less sweet, lighter in body and color, and floral and herbal in flavor—of all sweet vermouths, these tend to taste the most like the wines from which they are made. Try Dolin Rouge Vermouth de Chambéry or Noilly Prat Rouge Vermouth.

SPANISH VERMOUTH falls between French and Italian in body; its color may be similarly dark to Italian vermouth or a bit lighter. These vermouths are fairly sweet but balanced through good acidity and bright fruit flavor, making them particularly excellent to drink on their own—which is an extremely popular choice in Spain. Try Yzaguirre Vermouth Rojo or Lustau Vermut Rojo.

AMERICAN VERMOUTH is a bit of a wild card, having fewer defining legal standards than European vermouths. Try Gallo Sweet Vermouth, which is light bodied, with an herbaceous, orangey flavor and a tea-like bitter finish, or Vya, which is richer, with warm spices and herbal bitterness.

Or Skip the Sweet Vermouth

Sweet vermouth is the classic and most often used choice for the Manhattan, but there's a wide range of aromatized wines to experiment with, including Cocchi Americano (Bianco or Rosa), Cocchi Barolo Chinato, and Lillet (Blanc or Rouge). You can also substitute a fortified wine such as port or sherry for the vermouth, or even a wine-based amaro such as Pasubio Vino Amaro.

Improved? Try Perfect!

In the Old-Fashioneds chapter, we introduce the concept of the "improved" cocktail, which adds measured amounts of a liqueur such as maraschino or absinthe to an existing recipe formula. There's also something called the "perfect" cocktail, which uses equal parts sweet and dry vermouth instead of just one type. If you want to try a "perfect" version of our Manhattan, increase the vermouth to 1 ounce and split it equally between dry and sweet. Also in this chapter, the Bamboo (page 188) uses fino sherry in place of sweet vermouth, and the Chancellor (page 195) uses tawny port; both add a measure of dry vermouth.

Balance the Bitter and the Sweet

If you were ever in doubt about the value that bitters bring to a cocktail, try a side-by-side taste test of Manhattans with and without them. A Manhattan just isn't a Manhattan without bitters. The default choice is old-fashioned aromatic bitters, but there are many excellent alternatives to subtly alter the flavor profile, including:

- citrus bitters
- orange bitters
- cherry bitters
- fig bitters
- Peychaud's bitters
- walnut bitters
- cardamom bitters
- tea bitters
- chocolate bitters
- whiskey barrel–aged bitters

The Manhattan

Replace the nonalcoholic sweetener of the old-fashioned with vermouth and ditch the ice, and you're on your way to a Manhattan. Along with the old-fashioned and the martini, it's one of the most recognizable cocktails of all time, with its balance of subtle bitterness, hints of sweetness, herbal-floral undertones, and whiskey spice.

Created sometime in the 1800s, somewhere in Manhattan (possibly at the Manhattan Club, near the current site of the Empire State Building, or at the Manhattan Inn, in the neighborhood that's now SoHo), the Manhattan is a touchstone and an important drink to learn.

It's also simple to learn, traditionally made from rye, sweet vermouth, and old-fashioned aromatic bitters and garnished with a cocktail cherry. And it's infinitely customizable according to preference. We love how the dry, spicy qualities of rye offset the fruitier sweetness of sweet vermouth. However, nowadays bourbon is an equally popular choice, and this makes a richer cocktail with softer flavor notes. There's also a rum version here. Whatever you choose, the flavor of the spirit will be prominent, so choose one you love.

Like its sibling the martini, some recipes specify equal parts rye and vermouth. (We also offer a "reverse" version with more vermouth than rye, and another that swaps in amaro for the vermouth.) Bitters marry the ingredients for an ultimately strong but smooth cocktail. Because the sweet vermouth is also so prominent, it's a great opportunity to make and use homemade Sweet Vermouth (page 470).

The classic way to serve the Manhattan is up in a chilled cocktail glass, and that is our preference. However, there is an established—and respected—alternative practice of serving it on the rocks or with one oversized rock. We won't judge if you choose that route.

Manhattan

Makes 1 cocktail

Sweetness ✦ ✧ ✧

Herbal, Spirit Forward, Toasted

- 2 ounces rye
- ¾ ounce sweet vermouth
- ⅛ teaspoon old-fashioned aromatic bitters
- Cocktail cherries for garnishing

Add rye, vermouth, and bitters to mixing glass, then fill three-quarters full with ice. Using bar spoon, stir until mixture is fully combined and well chilled, about 1 minute. Strain cocktail into chilled cocktail glass. Garnish with cherries and serve.

Customize Your Cocktail

Have fun trying your favorite whiskeys or bourbons in this recipe. Using Scotch makes the drink a Rob Roy.

Reverse Manhattan

Makes 1 cocktail
Sweetness ✦ ✦ ✧
Bitter, Herbal, Toasted

Just as the name suggests, the reverse Manhattan takes our classic formula for a Manhattan and flips the base ratio, similar to the reverse martini. The result is a lighter, sweeter cocktail that is full of more fruit and herb notes. The emphasis on lower-ABV vermouth makes this a good option for those looking to pace themselves. You can garnish with an orange twist in addition to the cocktail cherries, if desired.

- 2 ounces sweet vermouth
- ¾ ounce rye
- ⅛ teaspoon old-fashioned aromatic bitters
- Cocktail cherries for garnishing

Add vermouth, rye, and bitters to mixing glass, then fill three-quarters full with ice. Using bar spoon, stir until mixture is fully combined and well chilled, about 1 minute. Strain cocktail into chilled cocktail glass. Garnish with cherries and serve.

Black Manhattan

Makes 1 cocktail
Sweetness ✦ ✦ ✧
Bitter, Spirit Forward, Toasted

This twist on the classic Manhattan substitutes Amaro Averna for the vermouth. This one small change makes a grand impact on the profile, which becomes rich, deep, and complex. The Manhattan's history is long (pre-Prohibition), while the black Manhattan's is short; it was developed in 2005 by bartender Todd Smith of San Francisco's Bourbon & Branch. You can garnish with an orange twist in addition to the cocktail cherries, if desired.

- 2 ounces rye
- ¾ ounce Amaro Averna Siciliano
- ⅛ teaspoon old-fashioned aromatic bitters
- Cocktail cherries for garnishing

Add rye, amaro, and bitters to mixing glass, then fill three-quarters full with ice. Using bar spoon, stir until mixture is fully combined and well chilled, about 1 minute. Strain cocktail into chilled cocktail glass. Garnish with cherries and serve.

Customize Your Cocktail

A Black Manhattan is traditionally made with Amaro Averna, but you can experiment with other amari. For a sweeter cocktail, try a sweeter amaro like Montenegro; for a drier cocktail, try a drier amaro like Cynar.

Palmetto

Makes 1 cocktail
Sweetness ✦ ✧ ✧
Spiced, Spirit Forward, Toasted

The Manhattan formula lets aged spirits shine, and whiskey isn't the only one that deserves the spotlight. The palmetto features aged rum and balances the equation with citrus: Orange bitters and a strip of orange peel add fresh notes that help lighten the otherwise deep, aged flavors of classic Manhattan builds.

- 2 ounces aged rum
- ¾ ounce sweet vermouth
- ⅛ teaspoon orange bitters
- Strip of orange peel for garnishing

Add rum, vermouth, and bitters to mixing glass, then fill three-quarters full with ice. Using bar spoon, stir until mixture is fully combined and well chilled, about 1 minute. Strain cocktail into chilled cocktail glass. Pinch orange peel over drink and rub outer edge of glass with peel, then garnish with orange peel. Serve.

Customize Your Cocktail

If you want to try a different spirit, reposado tequila pairs well with the orange in the palmetto.

Fridge Door Manhattans

Makes 8 cocktails
Sweetness ✦ ✧ ✧
Herbal, Spirit Forward, Toasted

Next time you invite over big-city whiskey connoisseurs, be prepared with cold Manhattans in storage. You can store the cocktail in a 1-quart Mason jar instead of a bottle if you like.

- 16 ounces rye
- 8 ounces water
- 6 ounces sweet vermouth
- ½ teaspoon old-fashioned aromatic bitters
- Cocktail cherries for garnishing

1. Combine rye, water, vermouth, and bitters in 1-liter glass bottle. Cover and freeze until well chilled, about 2 hours. Prepare cocktails immediately or transfer to refrigerator and store for up to 1 month; return to freezer and chill for 30 minutes before preparing cocktails.

2. Gently shake bottle to recombine, then serve cocktails in chilled cocktail glasses, garnishing with cherries.

From left: Reverse Manhattan, Black Manhattan, Palmetto, Fridge Door Manhattans

PAIR WITH A SNACK

Cinnamon-Ginger Spiced Cashews

Serves 8 to 10
Total Time: 1 hour 10 minutes, plus 30 minutes cooling

The warm, spiced sweetness of these cashews complements the flavors of spirits like whiskey. The base coating of egg white, water, and salt covers the nuts evenly, helping the sugar and spices cling tightly to each nut. Superfine sugar ensures a crunchy, not gritty, candied coating; if you can't find it, process granulated sugar in a food processor for 1 minute.

- ⅔ cup superfine sugar
- 2 teaspoons ground cinnamon
- 1 teaspoon ground ginger
- 1 teaspoon ground coriander
- 1 large egg white
- 1 tablespoon water
- 1 teaspoon table salt
- 1 pound raw cashews

1. Adjust oven racks to upper-middle and lower-middle positions and heat oven to 275 degrees. Line 2 rimmed baking sheets with parchment paper. Mix sugar, cinnamon, ginger, and coriander in small bowl.

2. Whisk egg white, water, and salt together in large bowl. Add cashews and toss to coat. Sprinkle spices over cashews, toss to coat, then spread evenly over prepared sheets. Bake until cashews are dry and crisp, about 50 minutes, stirring occasionally. Let cashews cool completely on sheets, about 30 minutes. Break cashews apart and serve. (Cashews can be refrigerated for up to 3 weeks.)

Monte Carlo

Makes 1 cocktail
Sweetness ✦✦✧
Spiced, Spirit Forward, Toasted

For some visitors, Manhattan can feel a bit in-your-face—and the namesake cocktail is similarly bold. A trip to Monte Carlo, on the other hand, might be luxurious and easy, like this cocktail made with Bénédictine and Peychaud's bitters instead of sweet vermouth and old-fashioned bitters. The swaps soften the edges of a classic Manhattan, so it becomes more approachable. Bénédictine makes the drink sweeter and more spice-forward, dialing back on the herbal, bitter notes of sweet vermouth. Old-fashioned aromatic bitters can be substituted for the Peychaud's bitters.

- 2 ounces rye
- ¾ ounce Bénédictine
- ⅛ teaspoon Peychaud's bitters
- Cocktail cherries for garnishing

Add rye, Bénédictine, and bitters to mixing glass, then fill three-quarters full with ice. Using bar spoon, stir until mixture is fully combined and well chilled, about 1 minute. Strain cocktail into chilled cocktail glass. Garnish with cherries and serve.

PAIR WITH A SNACK

Prosciutto-Wrapped Figs with Gorgonzola

Serves 8 to 10
Total Time: 15 minutes

We pair sweet, ripe figs with savory, salty prosciutto and bold, pungent blue cheese for a delectable cocktail bite. We halve the figs so they are easy to eat, then wrap them in thin slices of the ham. A little honey brings out the sticky-sweet qualities of the figs. The Gorgonzola offers a rich, bold counterpoint to the fig's tender flesh and sweet flavor. To guarantee the prosciutto stays put, we stick a toothpick through the center of each bundle.

- 2 ounces Gorgonzola cheese
- 16 figs, stemmed and halved lengthwise
- 1 tablespoon honey
- 16 thin slices prosciutto (8 ounces), halved lengthwise

Mound 1 teaspoon Gorgonzola into center of each fig half. Microwave honey in bowl to loosen, about 10 seconds, then drizzle over cheese. Wrap prosciutto securely around figs, leaving fig ends uncovered. Secure prosciutto with toothpick and serve.

Bamboo

Makes 1 cocktail
Sweetness ✦ ✧ ✧
Fruity, Savory, Toasted

- 1½ ounces fino sherry
- 1½ ounces dry vermouth
- 1 teaspoon Simple Syrup (page 458) (optional)
- ⅛ teaspoon old-fashioned aromatic bitters
- ⅛ teaspoon orange bitters
- Lemon twist for garnishing

Customize Your Cocktail

You can make an Adonis cocktail by swapping the dry vermouth for sweet vermouth.

The bamboo is, perhaps, the world's first classic low-ABV cocktail. While it's not clear who mixed the first bamboo, bartender Louis Eppinger certainly popularized the cocktail in the late 1800s. First working in San Francisco and Pacific Northwest bars, Eppinger—and the bamboo—made his way to Japan, where he managed the bar at the Grand Hotel in Yokohama. Eppinger had been recruited by some American naval officers stationed there who sought to bring U.S. cocktail culture to Japan via this hotel in 1889.

The cocktail gets a double dose of savory, aromatic flavors through the pairing of sherry and dry vermouth, while a touch of simple syrup rounds it out with a bit of body and barely perceptible sweetness. As cocktail historian David Wondrich says, "The Bamboo looks like a cocktail, tastes like a cocktail, and punches like a six-year-old."

Add sherry; vermouth; simple syrup, if using; old-fashioned bitters; and orange bitters to mixing glass, then fill three-quarters full with ice. Using bar spoon, stir until mixture is just combined and chilled, about 30 seconds. Strain cocktail into chilled cocktail glass. Garnish with lemon twist and serve.

Little Baloney

Little Baloney

Makes 1 cocktail
Sweetness ✦ ✦ ✧
Floral, Spirit Forward, Toasted

Whereas the Manhattan is taut, brown, and concentrated, the Little Baloney is soft, golden, and generous. Our cocktail is a play on the modern classic, the Little Italy, mixed by Audrey Saunders at the Pegu Club in the mid-2000s. She split the vermouth in a Manhattan with Cynar to add some bittering complexity. This led to a whole host of Manhattan variations named for New York locations (see Customize Your Cocktail). Here we pair the spiciness of rye with floral Amaro Montenegro and round Cocchi Americano for an approachable aperitif. Lillet Blanc or vermouth bianco (also sometimes labeled blanc or blanco) can be used in place of the Cocchi Americano.

- 1½ **ounces rye**
- ½ **ounce Amaro Montenegro**
- ½ **ounce Cocchi Americano Bianco**
- **Cocktail cherries for garnishing**

Add rye, amaro, and Cocchi Americano to mixing glass, then fill three-quarters full with ice. Using bar spoon, stir until mixture is fully combined and well chilled, about 1 minute. Strain cocktail into chilled cocktail glass. Garnish with cherries and serve.

Customize Your Cocktail

Consider replacing half of the Cocchi Americano with yellow Chartreuse for a Greenpoint, or with maraschino liqueur to get a Red Hook.

Helia Bravo

Makes 1 cocktail
Sweetness ✦ ✧ ✧
Bitter, Spirit Forward, Toasted

This drink gets its distinctiveness from the beloved Italian amaro Cynar, whose herbal, vegetal, woodsy notes pair well with anything from Scotch to orange juice to seltzer. We love how it combines with tequila, especially with reposado tequila and sweet vermouth in this cocktail. Using just ¼ ounce of vermouth ensures a balanced cocktail, with a strong tequila backbone and a clean hit of Cynar. The chile rim sugar adds some fitting (but optional) sweet spice.

- ¼ **cup Smoky Chile Rim Sugar (page 454) (optional)**
- **Lemon wedge (if using sugar), plus strip of lemon peel for garnishing**
- 2 **ounces reposado tequila**
- ¾ **ounce Cynar**
- ¼ **ounce sweet vermouth**

1. Spread sugar, if using, into even layer on small saucer. Moisten about ½ inch of chilled cocktail glass rim by running lemon wedge around outer edge; dry any excess juice with paper towel. Roll moistened rim in sugar to coat. Remove any excess sugar that falls into glass; set aside.

2. Add tequila, Cynar, and vermouth to mixing glass, then fill three-quarters full with ice. Using bar spoon, stir until mixture is fully combined and well chilled, about 1 minute. Strain cocktail into prepared glass. Pinch lemon peel over drink and, if rim is unsugared, rub outer edge of glass with peel. Garnish with lemon peel and serve.

Rosita

Makes 1 cocktail

Sweetness ✦✦✧

Bitter, Spirit Forward, Toasted

- 1½ ounces reposado tequila
- 1 ounce sweet vermouth
- ½ ounce Campari
- ⅛ teaspoon old-fashioned aromatic bitters
- Strip of orange peel for garnishing

This cocktail with vermouth and Campari is no aperitif—a good dose of tequila is responsible for that. The rosita tells us more about bartender, hospitality professional, and drinks expert, British-born, American-aged Gary "gaz" Regan, whom the *New York Times* called a "maestro of mixology and cocktail culture." Regan didn't invent the cocktail, but his version from his 1991 book *The Bartender's Bible* adds a dash of bitters and more tequila (we're not complaining) than other published versions. Funny enough, the prolific cocktail concocter and writer, who studied thousands of cocktails over his career, forgot he penned this version of the recipe. He had read about the rosita and made it for a party after seeing it in a piece authored by colleague Terry Sullivan. Regan enjoyed the drink and on a couple of occasions asked about the recipe's origin, but Sullivan couldn't recall. Finally, Sullivan remembered that he found it in *The Bartender's Bible*—Regan's very own book! We know we'll never forget this bitter but balanced cocktail. Instead of both dry and sweet vermouths, we opt for only sweet vermouth to balance the spirit-forward flavor and the bitterness of the Campari and old-fashioned bitters.

Add tequila, vermouth, Campari, and bitters to mixing glass, then fill three-quarters full with ice. Using bar spoon, stir until mixture is just combined and chilled, about 30 seconds. Strain cocktail into chilled rocks glass half-filled with ice or containing 1 large ice cube. Pinch orange peel over drink and rub outer edge of glass with peel, then garnish with orange peel. Serve.

Chancellor

Rumsicle

Makes 1 cocktail
Sweetness ✦ ✦ ✧
Bitter, Spirit Forward, Toasted

Ask a bartender what their favorite spirit to mix is and they just might proclaim "rum!" It's equally at home blended into tropical drinks or stirred into complex, spirit-forward cocktails, and it's great simply sipped alone. Here we play up rum's darker, chocolaty side with the luscious chocolate liqueur crème de cacao for sweetness, plus chocolate bitters for a hit of concentrated flavor. We also turn to a secret ingredient we often add to chocolate desserts—instant espresso powder. It really makes the flavor pop, bringing out the fruitier, richer notes of chocolate without any discernible taste of coffee.

- 1½ ounces aged rum
- ½ ounce crème de cacao
- ½ ounce sweet vermouth
- ⅛ teaspoon chocolate bitters
- ⅛ teaspoon instant espresso powder
- Chocolate curl for garnishing

Add rum, crème de cacao, vermouth, bitters, and espresso powder to mixing glass, then fill three-quarters full with ice. Using bar spoon, stir until mixture is fully combined and well chilled, about 1 minute. Strain cocktail into chilled cocktail glass. Garnish with chocolate curl and serve.

Chancellor

Makes 1 cocktail
Sweetness ✦ ✧ ✧
Smoky, Spirit Forward, Toasted

We think that a modern revival couldn't happen to a better drink than this magnificent, somewhat forgotten Prohibition-era cocktail. The name hints at its sophistication and richly delicious profile. Following the basic template of a "perfect" Manhattan (a variation on the Manhattan made with both sweet and dry vermouths), the chancellor uses tawny port instead of sweet vermouth and, more significantly, uses Scotch for the whiskey of choice. An assertive blended Scotch could dominate a cocktail, but the dried-fruit and caramel flavors of tawny port pair beautifully with it. A final touch of orange bitters and an orange twist add bright seasoning to this complex, impressively delicious libation.

- 2 ounces Scotch
- 1 ounce tawny port
- ½ ounce dry vermouth
- 1 teaspoon Simple Syrup (page 458)
- ⅛ teaspoon orange bitters
- Orange twist for garnishing

Add Scotch, port, vermouth, simple syrup, and bitters to mixing glass, then fill three-quarters full with ice. Using bar spoon, stir until mixture is fully combined and well chilled, about 1 minute. Strain cocktail into chilled cocktail glass. Garnish with orange twist and serve.

Vieux Carré

Makes 1 cocktail

Sweetness ✦ ✧ ✧

Herbal, Spirit Forward, Toasted

Along with the Sazerac (page 128) and Ramos Gin Fizz (page 72), the Vieux Carré is an iconic New Orleans cocktail. The Vieux Carré, another name for the French Quarter, essentially stretches the Manhattan formula of rye and vermouth, by cutting each with another ingredient—rye gets brandy, and vermouth the French liqueur Bénédictine. And the old-fashioned bitters are split with anise-inflected Peychaud's. The result is stunning: The dryness of the rye is overlaid with the fruit and honey of the brandy, while the aromatics of the vermouth are bolstered by the sweet spices of Bénédictine. The bitters plus a lemon twist give this cocktail a dry finish.

- ¾ ounce rye
- ¾ ounce brandy
- ¾ ounce sweet vermouth
- ¼ ounce Bénédictine
- ⅛ teaspoon old-fashioned aromatic bitters
- ⅛ teaspoon Peychaud's bitters
- Lemon peel for garnishing

Add rye, brandy, vermouth, Bénédictine, old-fashioned bitters, and Peychaud's bitters to mixing glass, then fill three-quarters full with ice. Using bar spoon, stir until mixture is just combined and chilled, about 30 seconds. Strain cocktail into chilled rocks glass half filled with ice or containing 1 large ice cube. Pinch lemon peel over drink and rub outer edge of glass with peel, then garnish with lemon peel. Serve.

Smoky Peat

Makes 1 cocktail

Sweetness ✦ ✦ ✧

Smoky, Spirit Forward, Toasted

The right amount of smoke can elevate and season a cocktail in the same way that salt can complete a dish. Here we blend the mellow, caramelly, charred notes of bourbon with an assertively smoky Scotch. We prefer blended Islay Scotch here; it's generally on the smokier side thanks to the burning peat used to dry barley in its malting process. The maraschino liqueur and the sweet vermouth combine to form a complex, rounded profile. While we like Islay Scotch to reinforce the smoky flavor, the cocktail is still tasty, if less smoky, using other styles of Scotch.

- 1½ ounces bourbon
- ½ ounce Scotch
- ½ ounce sweet vermouth
- ½ ounce maraschino liqueur

Add bourbon, Scotch, vermouth, and maraschino liqueur to mixing glass, then fill three-quarters full with ice. Using bar spoon, stir until mixture is just combined and chilled, about 30 seconds. Strain cocktail into chilled rocks glass half filled with ice or containing 1 large ice cube. Serve.

Traverse City

Makes 1 zero-proof cocktail
Sweetness ✦✧✧
Fruity, Herbal, Smoky

Traverse City, Michigan (the "Cherry Capital of the World"), produces much of the country's tart cherries, a key ingredient in this elegant, nonalcoholic Manhattan-style cocktail. To capture the rich, dark fruit notes typically found in sweet vermouth, we use tart cherry juice as a flavorful substitute. For the base, we brew a concentrated tea using smoky Lapsang souchong and fresh rosemary, which adds subtle piney, herbal notes. A touch of vegetable glycerin brings the sweetness of simple syrup to balance the bold flavors, while providing extra body in this nonalcoholic drink. Finally, aromatic bitters provide the classic Manhattan complexity. Through layers of smoky, herbal, and fruity flavors, we've delivered a sophisticated, spirit-free sipper. The smoky flavor of Lapsang souchong tea is important to the success of this drink; you can try other black teas, but you will get very different results. See page 15 for more information on vegetable glycerin in zero-proof cocktails. If unavailable, an equal amount of Simple Syrup (page 458) can be used. You can use traditional old-fashioned aromatic bitters in this recipe.

Tea Concentrate

- 9 ounces boiling water
- 1½ teaspoons Lapsang souchong tea leaves
- 1 fresh rosemary sprig

Cocktail

- 2 ounces tea concentrate
- 1 ounce tart cherry juice
- ¼ ounce vegetable glycerin
- ⅛ teaspoon nonalcoholic old-fashioned aromatic bitters
- Cocktail cherries for garnishing

1. **For the tea concentrate:** Combine boiling water, tea, and rosemary sprig in 2-cup liquid measuring cup. Cover and let steep for 5 minutes. Strain tea through fine-mesh strainer into liquid measuring cup or storage container, gently pressing on solids to extract as much liquid as possible; discard solids. Let tea cool to room temperature, then refrigerate until chilled, about 30 minutes. (You should have about 8 ounces tea concentrate, enough for 4 cocktails. Tea concentrate can be refrigerated for up to 1 week.)

2. **For the cocktail:** Add tea concentrate, cherry juice, vegetable glycerin, and bitters to mixing glass, then fill three-quarters with ice. Using bar spoon, stir until mixture is just combined and chilled, about 30 seconds. Strain cocktail into chilled cocktail glass. Garnish with cherries and serve.

Sours

The resourceful Brits, who are credited with inventing the gin and tonic, can also take some credit for creating the sour—or at least for helping to spread it around the world. Sailors in the British Navy received a spirit ration—and in the Caribbean in the 17th century, that was rum, since rum was so plentiful on the island nations they were conquering. By the mid-1700s, sailors liked their rum so much that it was becoming a bit of a problem. Vice Admiral Edward Vernon ruled that rum rations were to be mixed with water, and that sailors would be allowed to mix in lime juice and sugar, when possible, to make their rations more palatable (and as a bonus, this helped stave off scurvy).

So the story goes, the vice admiral had a predilection for wearing a cloak made of grogram, a coarse, wool-based fabric. Thus he developed the nickname "Old Grog"—and so "grog" became synonymous with the tart-sweet rum libation, which eventually came to be thought of as a sort of rudimentary rum punch.

While the first recorded mention of a sour cocktail dates to an 1856 Toronto saloon menu, the first written recipes for the sour, which included a rum sour, a gin sour, and a brandy sour, were in Jerry Thomas's 1862 *How to Mix Drinks, or The Bon Vivant's Companion.* According to cocktail historian David Wondrich, from the 1860s to the 1960s, the sour, and particularly the whiskey sour, was one of the cornerstones of American drinking culture. After an unfortunate stretch starting in the 1970s when prepackaged sour mix was in vogue, resulting in unbalanced, too-sweet drinks, the cocktail renaissance of the late 20th century revived sours made with fresh, balanced ingredients.

This is the first chapter we devote to shaking cocktails rather than building them in the glass or stirring them with ice and straining. Shaking sours, in addition to mixing the spirit and juice thoroughly, creates a frothy, palate-pleasing texture and helps release the citrus aromas that are so important to these cocktails.

Speaking of citrus, the key to a sour is fresh juice. Lemon or lime is classic, but grapefruit, pomelo, yuzu, or any variety of orange can be used. The sweetening balance can involve sugar, simple syrup, or other sweet syrups, including those from honey or agave. Orange liqueur can be added to enhance the sour flavor while tempering it with a touch of sweetness. Achieving the right balance of all these elements makes for an intensely flavorful, perfectly puckery cocktail—and is what takes a sour from good to great.

Sours

Fundamental Formula

spirit + citrus juice + sweetener

BUILD ON THE FUNDAMENTALS

The Daiquiri (page 204) is the classic rum sour, which is easily built upon by splitting the rums (see page 237) or by muddling in herbs or berries to augment the flavor. Make it a Gimlet (page 205) by using gin (or vodka) instead of rum; you can also muddle in flavoring ingredients, as we do in our Celery Gimlet (page 208). Use whiskey or amaretto plus an egg white to make sours with a fuller, silkier texture (see pages 208 and 211). Change the souring ingredient from citrus to apple, as we do in Autumn Remedy (page 212). Adding a liqueur to the fundamental formula creates a daisy—the most famous of which is the tequila-based Margarita and its variations (pages 214–219). Another famous daisy is the brandy-based Sidecar (page 225). We reimagined a pisco sour as a daisy in our Yellowlegs (page 230). Swapping in a flavored syrup for the spirit lets you easily make nonalcoholic cocktails like Smoke and Mirrors (page 223).

Family Ties

The extended sours family tree has many branches and includes many celebrity members. In addition to daiquiris, gimlets, and daisies, all of which are in this chapter, here are some other stars you'll find elsewhere.

- **Cobblers:** typically made with fortified wine, often muddled, served over crushed ice (see Sherry Cobbler, page 340)
- **Collinses**: lengthened with seltzer or soda to make a highball and served over cubed ice (see Tom Collins, page 71)
- **Fizzes**: often lengthened with seltzer and typically served without ice (see Ramos Gin Fizz, page 72, and Fernet Fizz, page 339)

Mix-and-Match Sours

With a starting basic ratio of 2 parts (2 ounces) spirit to 0.75 part (¾ ounce) citrus juice and 0.75 part (¾ ounce) sweetener, you can experiment and still be confident that you'll make a great cocktail. Just as the recipes in this chapter don't always match this ratio exactly, you should feel free to tweak amounts to suit your palate.

- **Gimlet** = gin or vodka + lime juice + simple syrup
- **Limontini** = vodka + lemon juice + simple syrup or limoncello
- **Whiskey sour** = whiskey + lemon juice + simple syrup
- **Greyhound** = vodka + grapefruit + simple syrup
- **Sidecar** = brandy + lemon juice + orange liqueur
- **Cosmopolitan** = vodka + lime and cranberry + orange liqueur

MIX-AND-MATCH CITRUS

Beyond lemon, lime, and grapefruit, try pomelo, yuzu, or varieties of orange. If you choose one of these, taste and consider adding a touch of lemon juice to enhance their softer acidity.

MIX-AND-MATCH SWEETENER

Try a flavored simple syrup (see pages 458–459), a shrub syrup (see pages 460–461) , maple syrup, agave syrup, honey, or grenadine.

Egg White Cocktails

This chapter features several cocktails, including the Whiskey Sour (page 208) and Yellowlegs (page 230), that contain egg whites. Bartenders began incorporating egg whites into sours as a way to soften their citric acidity in the 19th century. Egg whites contribute a smooth, silky body and a foamy head, making for visual appeal as well as a rich mouthfeel.

Our egg white cocktails call for 1 ounce egg white. To achieve an accurate measurement, lightly beat an egg white in a bowl and then measure out the desired amount.

We use a two-step shaking technique for the smoothest, foamiest cocktails. First, dry shaking the ingredients (without ice) uncoils the egg proteins and develops a stable, light foam. Then, adding ice and shaking again chills and dilutes the cocktail and increases the foam. Double-straining ensures that any small shards of ice or tiny egg solids are removed, leading to a velvety foam texture in the finished drink. See pages 372 and 396–397 for more information on using eggs in cocktails.

The Aquafaba Option

If you'd prefer not to use egg whites but still want the experience of an egg white cocktail, try aquafaba. This starchy liquid in canned chickpeas shakes up just like egg whites to trap air and create a foam that brings texture and body to cocktails—without adding beany flavor.

To get started, shake an unopened can of no-salt-added chickpeas well. The starches in the liquid settle in the can, so to take full advantage of them, you need them evenly distributed throughout the liquid. Drain the beans through a fine-mesh strainer over a bowl and reserve for another use. Then, simply substitute an equal amount of aquafaba for the egg white. For the best aquafaba foam, we recommend dry shaking, as we do with egg whites.

Also as with egg whites (see page 372), you can freeze leftover aquafaba in 1-ounce portions in ice cube trays for future cocktails. Once the cubes are frozen, pop them into a zipper-lock freezer bag for storage. Add a frozen cube directly to the shaker for the dry-shake step, adjusting the shaking time to 1 minute.

Friend or Foam

We made our Whiskey Sour (page 208) with seven different foaming agents to see how well they all worked.

Fresh egg white	Egg white in any form creates great foam and perfectly emulsified texture. We noticed a slightly reduced volume of foam from frozen egg whites and pasteurized eggs, but the difference was small.
Frozen egg white (see page 372)	
Pasteurized egg white	
Fresh aquafaba	Aquafaba makes good foam and emulsifies well, though the emulsification eventually separates.
Frozen aquafaba	
Artificial cocktail foamer	We tested Fee Foam, one of several brands of egg-free products marketed as able to create the same foam as an egg white with just a few drops. It does make impressive foam but does not emulsify the cocktail at all. We also did not like the resulting mouthfeel.

The Daiquiri

Banish the thought of slushy, supersweet, candy-colored daiquiris cranked out of frozen slushie machines. In its traditional and purest form, the daiquiri is a thing of simple beauty: lime juice, sugar, and rum, served ice-cold.

The daiquiri is a classic sour made with rum, and so it's nearly certain that people were mixing this drink before it got its now-popular name. But the honor of coming up with that name, according to some stories, goes to Jennings Cox, an American engineer working in a Cuban mining and beach village at the turn of the 20th century. The name of that village? Daiquirí.

The story goes that supplies were limited in Daiquirí, so the cocktail was born of necessity. "On the sideboard in the dining room in the mines, there was neither gin nor vermouth," wrote Francesco Domenico Pagliuchi, a colleague of Cox's, in a 1948 letter to *El País* newspaper. "There was only Bacardi [sic], lemons, sugar, and ice." It's possible that the "lemons" referred to were in fact limes, with the term being incorrectly translated into English.

The engineers took the name with them up the coast to bars in Santiago de Cuba, where it then spread to Havana, and from there to the United States. The drink caught on even more in America during Prohibition, when rum from the Caribbean islands was easier to procure than European spirits. Plus, a version of the daiquiri called the Papa Doble was a favorite of author Ernest Hemingway's, enhancing its reputation further.

Though granulated or powdered sugar is traditional and still frequently used to make a daiquiri, we prefer our Simple Syrup (page 458) for sweetening the cocktail and ensuring a smooth texture—no risk of undissolved granules. We like the harmonious and classic combination of equal parts lime juice and simple syrup added to a larger amount of white rum, but this formulation is easily adaptable to your preferred levels of sour and sweet. (Hemingway liked his daiquiris heavier on the rum and lighter on the sugar.) It's also easy to jazz up the flavors with fresh herbs or fruit, as you'll see here.

Daiquiri

Makes 1 cocktail
Sweetness ✦✦✧
Citrusy, Tart

- 2 ounces white rum
- ¾ ounce lime juice, plus lime slice for garnishing
- ¾ ounce Simple Syrup (page 458)

Add rum, lime juice, and simple syrup to cocktail shaker, then fill with ice. Shake mixture until fully combined and well chilled, about 15 seconds. Double-strain cocktail into chilled cocktail glass. Garnish with lime slice and serve.

Customize Your Cocktail

Make a Gimlet by substituting London dry gin for the rum. Vodka is also a good substitute for the rum. For a richer, more full-bodied cocktail, substitute aged rum for the white rum. You can also add more complexity by utilizing two distinct styles of rum; see page 237 for more information on splitting rum. Try any of the flavored syrups on pages 458–459 in this simple cocktail.

Basil Daiquiri

Makes 1 cocktail
Sweetness ✦✦✧
Citrusy, Herbal, Tart

Shaking basil leaves with standard daiquiri ingredients gives just the right amount of refreshing basil flavor to elevate this simple drink.

- 2 ounces white rum
- ¾ ounce lime juice
- ¾ ounce Simple Syrup (page 458)
- ¼ cup fresh Italian or Thai basil leaves, plus extra basil sprig for garnishing

Add rum, lime juice, simple syrup, and basil leaves to cocktail shaker, then fill shaker with ice. Shake mixture until fully combined and well chilled, about 15 seconds. Double-strain cocktail into chilled cocktail glass. Garnish with basil sprig and serve.

Customize Your Cocktail

Substitute an equal amount of fresh mint or tarragon for the basil. If you use vodka in place of the rum, the herb flavor will shine even brighter. Consider splitting the rum by reducing the white rum to 1¾ ounces and adding ¼ ounce of rhum agricole, which will accentuate the herbal notes.

Strawberry Daiquiri

Makes 1 cocktail
Sweetness ✦✦✧
Citrusy, Fruity, Tart

If you offer someone a strawberry daiquiri, they may imagine a pink frozen blender drink with one-note sweetness. Surprise them with this sophisticated cocktail, served up, bursting with berry flavor and without any artificial taste or sickly sweetness. Muddled strawberries impart a ton of flavor to this sweet-sour rum cocktail—no blender required!

- ¼ cup chopped strawberries, plus sliced strawberry for garnishing
- ¾ ounce Simple Syrup (page 458)
- 2 ounces white rum
- ¾ ounce lime juice

Add strawberries and simple syrup to base of cocktail shaker and muddle until berries are broken down and all juice has been expressed, about 30 seconds. Add rum and lime juice, then fill shaker with ice. Shake mixture until fully combined and well chilled, about 15 seconds. Double-strain cocktail into chilled cocktail glass. Garnish with sliced strawberry and serve.

Customize Your Cocktail

You can make other fruit-flavored daiquiris by substituting an equal amount of other chopped fruit for the strawberries. We've had success with raspberries, pineapple, banana, and watermelon.

Fridge Door Daiquiris

Makes 6 cocktails
Sweetness ✦✦✧
Citrusy, Tart

We love a world where there's an easy-sipping rum cocktail in our fridge at all times. Make it a reality with this stir-together special. You can store the cocktail in a 1-quart Mason jar instead of a bottle if you'd like.

- 12 ounces white rum
- 9 ounces water
- 4½ ounces lime juice, plus lime slices for garnishing
- 4½ ounces Simple Syrup (page 458)

1. Combine rum, water, lime juice, and simple syrup in 1-liter glass bottle. Cover and freeze until well chilled, about 2 hours. Prepare cocktails immediately or transfer to refrigerator and store for up to 1 week; return to freezer and chill for 30 minutes before preparing cocktails.

2. Shake vigorously to recombine and aerate, then serve cocktails in chilled cocktail glasses, garnishing individual portions with lime slices.

Celery Gimlet

Makes 1 cocktail
Sweetness ✦ ✧ ✧
Citrusy, Herbal, Tart

You may have never incorporated celery into a drink (beyond a celery stalk in a Bloody Mary), but mixologists have used it at least since 1917 when a recipe for a celery sour appeared in Tom Bullock's 1917 *The Ideal Bartender* (this was a nonalcoholic shaved ice drink). Muddled celery adds refreshing grassy notes and a pale green color to a cocktail. We think the classic gimlet—made with gin and lime—is the perfect place for celery: The vegetal celery complements gin's botanical notes, and the lime perks everything up. We prefer the flavor of fresh lime juice and simple syrup to bottled cordial.

- ⅓ **cup chopped celery, plus celery leaf for garnishing**
- ¾ **ounce Simple Syrup (page 458)**
- 2 **ounces London dry gin**
- ¾ **ounce lime juice**

Add celery and simple syrup to base of cocktail shaker and muddle until celery is broken down and all juice has been expressed, about 30 seconds. Add gin and lime juice, then fill shaker with ice. Shake mixture until fully combined and well chilled, about 15 seconds. Double-strain cocktail into chilled cocktail glass. Garnish with celery leaf and serve.

Customize Your Cocktail

Try substituting arugula (yes!) or cucumber for the celery and vodka for the gin to make an Arugula Gimlet or a Cucumber Gimlet.

Whiskey Sour

Makes 1 cocktail
Sweetness ✦ ✦ ✧
Citrusy, Tart, Toasted

At its simplest, a whiskey sour is whiskey, lemon juice, and sugar, shaken with ice. We think an egg white, a traditional addition that has gone in and out of style over the years, elevates a whiskey sour from good to great. It adds rich, silky body and frothiness while mellowing the dark spirit. You can garnish with old-fashioned aromatic bitters if desired.

- 2 **ounces rye**
- 1 **ounce egg white**
- ¾ **ounce Simple Syrup (page 458)**
- ½ **ounce lemon juice**
- **Cocktail cherries for garnishing**

1. Add rye, egg white, simple syrup, and lemon juice to cocktail shaker and vigorously shake until mixture is foamy, about 45 seconds.

2. Fill shaker with ice, then shake mixture until fully combined and well chilled, about 15 seconds. Double-strain cocktail into chilled cocktail glass. Garnish with cherries and serve.

Customize Your Cocktail

We prefer the spiciness of rye, but bourbon, Scotch, or Irish whiskey all work. If using one of those, decrease the simple syrup to ½ ounce. Use aged rum instead of rye for a Rum Sour or reposado tequila for a Tequila Sour.

Whiskey Sour

Amaretto Sour

Makes 1 cocktail
Sweetness ✦✦✧
Citrusy, Nutty, Tart

The amaretto sour is a cocktail of the 1970s, possibly created to promote the nutty liqueur in the United States. But this drink shouldn't stay in the disco era—a well-made amaretto sour is shockingly delicious. Because the amaretto is so sweet, there's no need for simple syrup, just liqueur, lemon juice, and the fun and frothy egg white. Old-fashioned aromatic bitters give this pleasant cocktail dimension. Cocktail cherries also make a nice garnish.

- 2 ounces amaretto
- 1 ounce egg white
- 1 ounce lemon juice
- ⅛ teaspoon old-fashioned aromatic bitters, plus extra for garnishing

1. Add amaretto, egg white, lemon juice, and bitters to cocktail shaker and vigorously shake until mixture is foamy, 30 to 45 seconds.

2. Fill shaker with ice, then shake mixture until fully combined and well chilled, about 15 seconds. Double-strain cocktail into chilled cocktail glass. Garnish with a few drops of bitters and serve.

Customize Your Cocktail

Try cutting the amaretto back to 1½ ounces and add ½ ounce of whiskey for more depth and less sweetness.

PAIR WITH A SNACK

Spicy Caramel Corn

Serves 12 (makes about 3½ quarts)
Total Time: 45 minutes

This bittersweet, crisp-but-not-hard caramel corn is perked up with heat and smoke. If you're using salted popcorn, decrease the salt to ¼ teaspoon.

- 10 cups popped popcorn
- 1¼ cups (8 ounces) sugar
- ½ cup water
- ⅓ cup light corn syrup
- 6 tablespoons unsalted butter
- ½ teaspoon table salt
- ⅛ teaspoon cayenne pepper
- ½ teaspoon baking soda
- ⅔ cup salted smoked almonds, chopped coarse

1. Lightly spray large bowl and rimmed baking sheet with vegetable oil spray. Place popcorn in prepared bowl. Bring sugar, water, and corn syrup to boil in medium heavy-bottomed saucepan over medium-high heat. Cook, without stirring, until mixture is straw-colored, 6 to 8 minutes. Reduce heat to medium-low and continue to cook, swirling saucepan occasionally, until mixture is dark amber and registers between 365 and 375 degrees, 2 to 5 minutes longer.

2. Off heat, quickly but carefully add butter, salt, and cayenne; stir until fully combined (mixture will bubble and steam). Return saucepan to low heat; stir in baking soda; and cook, stirring constantly, until mixture is uniform in color. Pour caramel over popcorn and, working quickly, stir until well coated. (Use dish towel or oven mitt to hold bowl, and avoid touching hot caramel.) Stir in almonds. Spread mixture into even layer on prepared sheet. Let cool for 15 minutes. Break popcorn into pieces of desired size. Serve. (Caramel corn can be stored in airtight containers for up to 2 months.)

Autumn Remedy

Makes 1 cocktail
Sweetness ✦ ✧ ✧
Fruity, Herbal, Toasted

- 2–4 fresh sage leaves, plus extra sage sprig for garnishing
- ¼ ounce maple syrup
- 2 ounces bourbon
- 1 ounce apple cider
- ¼ ounce cider vinegar

Piney sage is the perfect perfume for the caramelly bourbon and bright, sweet apple cider in this autumnal recipe. The slightly astringent herb packs a punch: We muddle just a couple of its hardy leaves in maple syrup (whereas we would need a decent ⅓ cup of leaves from a delicate herb, like tarragon). To counterbalance the sweetness, cider vinegar is the sour component; it further clarifies the apple flavor, and its clean, bracing acidity adds another touch of savoriness to this round, juicy cocktail. If your sage leaves are longer than 2 inches, use the lesser amount.

Add sage leaves and syrup to base of cocktail shaker and muddle until fragrant, about 30 seconds. Add bourbon, apple cider, and vinegar, then fill shaker with ice. Shake mixture until just combined and chilled, about 5 seconds. Double-strain cocktail into chilled rocks glass half-filled with ice or containing 1 large ice cube. Garnish with extra sage sprig and serve.

Customize Your Cocktail

Brandy is a nice change from bourbon in this cocktail.

The Margarita

A contender for the title of the most beloved sour of them all, the margarita consistently ranks as one of the most popular cocktails in the United States. The name of the drink most likely comes from the Spanish word for daisy—probably because it evolved from a type of cocktail that was quite popular in the early 20th century called the daisy, which combined a spirit (usually brandy at that time) with a liqueur (usually orange) or flavored syrup instead of sugar, plus lemon and/or lime juice. In fact, the margarita as we know it may have started as a tequila daisy, which first appeared in print in 1936.

There are many apocryphal stories regarding the margarita's place of origin, from a racetrack in Tijuana to a bar in Ciudad Juárez to a Christmas party in Acapulco. But despite its apparently Mexican roots, for much of its history the margarita was rarely the drink of choice south of the border. It first gained traction at Tail o' the Cock restaurant in Los Angeles, where certain tequila brands had begun local distribution in the 1930s. By the 1950s, U.S. national distribution and interest in both tequila and margaritas had ballooned, which was further helped along by pop culture presence (see the Champs' "Tequila" and the Eagles' "Tequila Sunrise") and increased American tourism to Mexican resorts from the '60s onwards. And thanks to Jimmy Buffet, Americans have been wasting away in Margaritavilles across the country since 1977.

Over the decades, there have been countless margarita riffs of varying style and quality—including frozen (see page 437), artificially flavored and neon colored, and even shelf-stable premixed. We believe that the best margaritas are made with real, fresh ingredients. We start by making our own sour mix with sugar, water, a pinch of salt, and both lemons and limes. For our flavored margaritas, we add the necessary fresh ingredients to this sour mix, rather than when shaking the cocktail. Equal parts of sour mix and tequila plus a splash of orange liqueur is all you need. A salted rim and lime slice are optional—but, of course, highly recommended.

Fresh Margarita

Makes 1 cocktail
Sweetness ✦ ✦ ✧
Citrusy, Tart

Sour Mix

- 6 tablespoons sugar
- 3 ounces water
- Pinch table salt
- 1 teaspoon grated lime zest plus 2 ounces juice
- 1 teaspoon grated lemon zest plus 2 ounces juice

Cocktail

- ¼ cup kosher salt (optional)
- Lime wedge (if using salt), plus lime slice for garnishing
- 2 ounces blanco or reposado tequila
- 2 ounces sour mix
- ¾ ounce orange liqueur

1. For the sour mix: Heat sugar, water, and salt in small saucepan over medium heat, stirring often, until sugar has dissolved, about 2 minutes; do not boil. Off heat, stir in lime zest and lemon zest and let cool completely, about 30 minutes. Stir in lime juice and lemon juice. Strain sour mix through fine-mesh strainer into airtight container, pressing on solids to extract as much liquid as possible. (You should have about 8 ounces sour mix, enough for 4 cocktails. Sour mix can be refrigerated for up to 1 week.)

2. For the cocktail: Spread salt, if using, into even layer on small saucer. Moisten about ½ inch of chilled rocks glass rim by running lime wedge around outer edge; dry any excess juice with paper towel. Roll moistened rim in salt to coat. Remove any excess salt that falls into glass; set aside.

3. Add tequila, sour mix, and orange liqueur to cocktail shaker, then fill with ice. Shake mixture until just combined and chilled, about 5 seconds. Double-strain cocktail into prepared glass half-filled with ice. Top with additional ice and garnish with lime slice. Serve.

Spicy Margarita

Makes 1 cocktail
Sweetness ✦✦✧
Citrusy, Spicy, Tart

Spicy margaritas are the most popular variation of the classic—crowd-pleasers but still a bit adventurous. To achieve the fresh, grassy heat we want here, we kick up our sour mix with jalapeño. We adorn the glass with our Sriracha Rim Salt to hint at the infused heat within and add some smokiness. For a spicier margarita, use the greater amount of jalapeños.

Sour Mix

- 6 tablespoons sugar
- 3 ounces water
- Pinch table salt
- 1–2 jalapeños, stemmed and chopped fine
- 1 teaspoon grated lime zest plus 2 ounces juice
- 1 teaspoon grated lemon zest plus 2 ounces juice

Cocktail

- ¼ cup Sriracha Rim Salt (page 453) (optional)
- Lime wedge (if using salt)
- 2 ounces blanco or reposado tequila
- 2 ounces sour mix
- ¾ ounce orange liqueur
- Sliced jalapeño for garnishing

1. For the sour mix: Heat sugar, water, and salt in small saucepan over medium heat, stirring often, until sugar has dissolved, about 2 minutes; do not boil. Off heat, stir in jalapeño, lime zest, and lemon zest and let cool completely, about 30 minutes. Stir in lime juice and lemon juice. Strain sour mix through fine-mesh strainer into airtight container, pressing on solids to extract as much liquid as possible. (You should have about 8 ounces sour mix, enough for 4 cocktails. Sour mix can be refrigerated for up to 1 week.)

2. For the cocktail: Spread rim salt, if using, into even layer on small saucer. Moisten about ½ inch of chilled rocks glass rim by running lime wedge around outer edge; dry any excess juice with paper towel. Roll moistened rim in salt to coat. Remove any excess salt that falls into glass; set aside.

3. Add tequila, sour mix, and orange liqueur to cocktail shaker, then fill with ice. Shake mixture until just combined and chilled, about 5 seconds. Double-strain cocktail into prepared glass half-filled with ice. Top with additional ice and garnish with jalapeño slices. Serve.

Watermelon Margarita

Makes 1 cocktail
Sweetness ✦✦✧
Citrusy, Fruity, Tart

There are a lot of different ways to enhance the flavor of margaritas, but adding watermelon makes the most refreshing marg of all. While we usually offer a choice, we like to make this with blanco tequila so we don't overshadow the watermelon flavor. For more information on making fresh watermelon juice, see page 12.

Sour Mix

- 6 tablespoons sugar
- 3 ounces water
- Pinch table salt
- 1 teaspoon grated lime zest plus 3 ounces juice
- 5 ounces fresh watermelon juice

Cocktail

- ¼ cup kosher salt (optional)
- Lime wedge (if using salt), plus wedge for garnishing
- 3 ounces sour mix
- 2 ounces blanco tequila
- ¾ ounce orange liqueur
- Watermelon ball for garnishing

1. For the sour mix: Heat sugar, water, and salt in small saucepan over medium heat, stirring often, until sugar has dissolved, about 2 minutes; do not boil. Off heat, stir in lime zest and let cool completely, about 30 minutes. Stir in watermelon juice and lime juice. Strain sour mix through fine-mesh strainer into airtight container, pressing on solids to extract as much liquid as possible. (You should have about 12 ounces sour mix, enough for 4 cocktails. Sour mix can be refrigerated for up to 1 week.)

2. For the cocktail: Spread salt, if using, into even layer on small saucer. Moisten about ½ inch of chilled rocks glass rim by running lime wedge around outer edge; dry any excess juice with paper towel. Roll moistened rim in salt to coat. Remove any excess salt that falls into glass; set aside.

3. Add sour mix, tequila, and orange liqueur to cocktail shaker, then fill with ice. Shake mixture until just combined and chilled, about 5 seconds. Double-strain cocktail into prepared glass half-filled with ice. Top with additional ice and garnish with lime slice and watermelon ball. Serve.

Big-Batch Margaritas

Makes 12 cocktails
Sweetness ✦ ✦ ✧
Citrusy, Tart

Everyone loves a pitcher of margaritas. What we don't love? A big mess to clean up right before guests arrive. These big-batch margaritas use the same sour mix method as in our individual margarita recipe, and they can be stored in the fridge for up to 24 hours while you get everything else in order—maybe homemade Classic Guacamole (page 222)? When you're ready to serve, just grab a few glasses with ice.

- 14 ounces water
- 1 cup plus 2 tablespoons sugar
- ⅛ teaspoon table salt
- 1 tablespoon grated lime zest plus 6 ounces juice, plus lime wedge (if using rim salt) and lime slices for garnishing
- 1 tablespoon grated lemon zest plus 6 ounces juice
- 24 ounces blanco or reposado tequila
- 9 ounces orange liqueur
- ½ cup kosher salt (optional)

1. Heat water, sugar, and table salt in medium saucepan over medium heat, stirring often, until sugar has dissolved, about 2 minutes; do not boil. Off heat, stir in lime zest and lemon zest and let cool completely, about 30 minutes. Strain citrus syrup through fine-mesh strainer into bowl, pressing on solids to extract as much liquid as possible.

2. Combine citrus syrup, tequila, orange liqueur, lime juice, and lemon juice in serving pitcher or large container. Cover and refrigerate until well chilled, at least 2 hours or up to 24 hours.

3. Stir cocktail to recombine. Spread kosher salt, if using, into even layer on small saucer. Moisten about ½ inch of chilled rocks glass rims by running lime wedge around outer edge; dry any excess juice with paper towel. Roll moistened rims in salt to coat. Remove any excess salt that falls into glasses. Serve in prepared glasses filled with ice, garnishing individual portions with lime slices.

From front to back:
Spicy Margarita,
Watermelon Margarita,
Big-Batch Margaritas

Bitter with the Sweet

Foggy Day

Makes 1 zero-proof cocktail
Sweetness ✦✦✦
Citrusy, Creamy, Floral

This tea-awakened zero-proof sour, with its fluffy egg foam, is reminiscent of both the London fog latte that inspired it and an actual foggy day. In the absence of spirit, and with the tea flavor beautifully flavoring our syrup, this cocktail has really nice body. The bitters on top make the egg foam add great aroma. You can use traditional old-fashioned aromatic bitters in this recipe.

- 2 ounces Tea Syrup with Earl Grey tea (page 459)
- 1 ounce lemon juice
- 1 ounce egg white
- Nonalcoholic old-fashioned aromatic bitters for garnishing

1. Add tea syrup, lemon juice, and egg white to cocktail shaker and vigorously shake until mixture is foamy, about 45 seconds.

2. Fill shaker with ice, then shake mixture until fully combined and well chilled, about 30 seconds. Double-strain cocktail into chilled cocktail glass. Garnish with a few drops of bitters and serve.

Bitter with the Sweet

Makes 1 zero-proof cocktail
Sweetness ✦✦✧
Bitter, Citrusy, Spiced

A more complete name would be Bitter with the Sweet, Sour, and Spiced; the complex flavors here make a sophisticated zero-proof cocktail. We developed this recipe using Wilfred's Non-Alcoholic Aperitif, but other brands of nonalcoholic (as well as traditional) aperitifs will also work. Nonalcoholic aperitif syrup can be used as well; reduce spice syrup to ¾ ounce.

- 1 ounce egg white
- 1 ounce Spice Syrup with cinnamon (page 459)
- ¾ ounce nonalcoholic aperitif
- ¾ ounce grapefruit juice
- ¾ ounce lemon juice
- Freshly grated cinnamon for garnishing

1. Add egg white, spice syrup, aperitif, grapefruit juice, and lemon juice to cocktail shaker and vigorously shake until mixture is foamy, about 45 seconds.

2. Fill shaker with ice, then shake mixture until fully combined and well chilled, about 15 seconds. Double-strain cocktail into chilled cocktail glass. Garnish with cinnamon and serve.

Tumbleweed

Makes 1 cocktail
Sweetness ✦ ✦ ✧
Spicy, Tropical

Infused into a liqueur, ancho chiles add unexpected dimension to a cocktail—a mild, earthy heat that lingers at the end of each sip. To meet the liqueur's match in this brand-new marg, we add fruity guava nectar. The tumbleweed drinks tart at the start and spicy at the finish. To assist, we coat the glass with chile sugar. You can use our homemade Ancho Chile Liqueur (page 468) or store-bought liqueur in this recipe.

- **¼ cup Smoky Chile Rim Sugar (page 454) (optional)**
- **Lime wedge (if using sugar)**
- **1½ ounces guava nectar**
- **1 ounce blanco or reposado tequila**
- **½ ounce ancho chile liqueur**
- **½ ounce Simple Syrup (page 458)**
- **¼ ounce lime juice, plus lime slice for garnishing**

1. Spread rim sugar, if using, into even layer on small saucer. Moisten about ½ inch of chilled cocktail glass rim by running lime wedge around outer edge; dry any excess juice with paper towel. Roll moistened rim in sugar to coat. Remove any excess sugar that falls into glass; set aside.

2. Add guava nectar, tequila, chile liqueur, simple syrup, and lime juice to cocktail shaker, then fill with ice. Shake mixture until fully combined and well chilled, about 15 seconds. Double-strain cocktail into prepared glass. Garnish with lime slice and serve.

PAIR WITH A SNACK

Classic Guacamole

Makes 2 cups
Total Time: 15 minutes

An invigorating tequila cocktail (or two or three) and rich, creamy guacamole are a beloved pairing. This guacamole comes together without relying on the coarse surface of a molcajete, a three-legged Mexican mortar made of volcanic rock. We mince the onion and chile by hand with kosher salt; the coarse crystals break down the aromatics, releasing their juices and flavors and transforming them into a paste that is easy to combine with the avocado and other ingredients. We then use a whisk to mix and mash the avocado into the paste, creating a creamy but still chunky dip. For a spicier version, mince and add the serrano ribs and seeds to the onion mixture. Be sure to use Hass avocados here; Florida, or "skinny," avocados are too watery for dips. Serve with tortilla chips.

- **2 tablespoons finely chopped onion**
- **1 serrano chile, stemmed, seeded, and minced**
- **1 teaspoon kosher salt**
- **¼ teaspoon grated lime zest plus 1½–2 tablespoons juice**
- **3 ripe avocados, halved, pitted, and cut into ½-inch pieces**
- **1 plum tomato, cored, seeded, and cut into ⅛-inch dice**
- **2 tablespoons chopped fresh cilantro**

Place onion, serrano, salt, and lime zest on cutting board and chop until very finely minced. Transfer onion mixture to medium bowl and stir in 1½ tablespoons lime juice. Add avocados and, using sturdy whisk, mash and stir mixture until well combined, with some ¼- to ½-inch chunks of avocado remaining. Stir in tomato and cilantro. Season with salt and up to 1½ teaspoons additional lime juice to taste. Serve.

Smoke and Mirrors

Makes 1 zero-proof cocktail
Sweetness ✦✦✦
Citrusy, Smoky, Spicy

This tea creation reminds us of a mezcal margarita—the Lapsang souchong tea used to infuse the syrup boasts a smokiness and a savory profile that hold their own when the syrup is mixed with lime juice. A little more smolder comes from our homemade tincture made with dried chile. And a sprinkle of tangy, spicy Tajín—the Mexican chile, salt, and dehydrated lime blend—on the cocktail amplifies all of those flavors within. Chile bitters can be used in place of the spice tincture, though they often contain adjunct flavors.

- 2 ounces Tea Syrup with Lapsang souchong tea (page 459)
- 1 ounce lime juice, plus lime slice for garnishing
- ⅛ teaspoon Spice Tincture with chiles (page 464)
- Pinch table salt
- Tajín Clásico Seasoning for garnishing

Add tea syrup, lime juice, chile tincture, and salt to cocktail shaker, then fill with ice. Shake mixture until fully combined and well chilled, about 15 seconds. Double-strain cocktail into chilled rocks glass half-filled with ice or containing 1 large ice cube. Sprinkle with Tajín and garnish with lime slice. Serve.

Aperol Sour

Makes 1 cocktail
Sweetness ✦✦✧
Bitter, Citrusy, Tart

Make this cocktail and you'll see why Aperol is the perfect liqueur for receiving the sour treatment. The beloved Italian aperitif features a beguiling mix of the flavors of sweet and bitter oranges, bitter roots and herbs, and a touch of rhubarb. It reminds us of the flavor of grapefruit, minus the acidity. Here we give the drink a base of aromatic gin, add acid with lemon juice, and turn it creamy and smooth with the addition of a shaken egg white. You can garnish with extra orange bitters, if desired.

- 1½ ounces London dry gin
- 1 ounce egg white
- ¾ ounce lemon juice
- ¾ ounce Simple Syrup (page 458)
- ½ ounce Aperol
- ⅛ teaspoon orange bitters

1. Add gin, egg white, lemon juice, simple syrup, Aperol, and bitters to cocktail shaker and vigorously shake until mixture is foamy, about 45 seconds.

2. Fill shaker with ice, then shake mixture until fully combined and well chilled, about 15 seconds. Double-strain cocktail into chilled cocktail glass. Serve.

Sidecar

Makes 1 cocktail
Sweetness ✦✧✧
Citrusy, Spirit Forward

The story most often proffered regarding the sidecar's origin is that it was created at Harry's New York Bar in Paris during the First World War for an eccentric American captain who used to arrive at the bar in a chauffeur-driven sidecar. A rival version has it that bar owner Harry MacElhone learned the cocktail at Buck's Club in London post–World War I and imported it to Paris, where it fast became a local favorite. Debatable history aside, the sidecar, like the margarita, is a member of the daisy family of cocktails: a strong spirit, balanced by citrus and a flavored liquid sweetener, most often in the form of orange liqueur. In our sidecar, the warm, aromatic notes of the orange liqueur smooth out the edges of the stronger brandy to make a cohesive and mellow whole. The sugared rim is the traditional garnish for this cocktail. It has fallen out of fashion, but we include it because we love its celebratory nod to the roaring twenties.

- ¼ cup sugar (optional)
- Lemon wedge (if using sugar)
- 1½ ounces brandy
- 1 ounce orange liqueur
- ¾ ounce lemon juice, plus lemon twist for garnishing
- 1 teaspoon Simple Syrup (page 458)

1. Spread sugar, if using, into even layer on small saucer. Moisten about ½ inch of chilled cocktail glass rim by running lemon wedge around outer edge; dry any excess juice with paper towel. Roll moistened rim in sugar to coat. Remove any excess sugar that falls into glass; set aside.

2. Add brandy, orange liqueur, lemon juice, and simple syrup to cocktail shaker, then fill with ice. Shake mixture until fully combined and well chilled, about 15 seconds. Double-strain cocktail into prepared glass. Garnish with lemon twist and serve.

Corpse Reviver No. 2

Makes 1 cocktail
Sweetness ✦✦✧
Citrusy, Herbal, Tart

- 1 ounce London dry gin
- 1 ounce Lillet Blanc
- ¾ ounce orange liqueur
- ¾ ounce lemon juice
- ¼ ounce Simple Syrup (page 458)
- ⅛ teaspoon absinthe
- Orange twist for garnishing

The corpse reviver no. 2 may be the best brunch cocktail you've never heard of. Originally "hair of the dog" drinks designed to cure a hangover, corpse reviver cocktails (there are a few) were developed "to be taken before 11 a.m., or whenever steam and energy are needed," according to *The Savoy Cocktail Book* by Harry Craddock. While cocktails do have a long history of being used for medicinal purposes—the original form of Lillet Blanc, one of this drink's main components, was developed as a more appealing way to consume quinine for malaria treatment—we make no claims as to the restorative (or reviving) properties of this (or any other) cocktail. But we do think its bright, citrusy, herbal, and anise flavors make this a refreshing and unique drink to add to your brunch cocktail rotation. Many recipes use equal parts gin, Lillet Blanc, and orange liqueur; we prefer a slightly reduced amount of orange liqueur to avoid a pithy, bitter flavor, replacing the lost sweetness with simple syrup. The anise notes of the absinthe pair well with the citrus and botanical flavors of this drink. Other dry anise-flavored spirits (such as Herbsaint, pastis, or dry anisette) can be substituted for the absinthe. Cocchi Americano Bianco or vermouth bianco (also sometimes labeled blanc or blanco) can be used in place of the Lillet Blanc.

Add gin, Lillet, orange liqueur, lemon juice, simple syrup, and absinthe to cocktail shaker, then fill with ice. Shake mixture until fully combined and well chilled, about 15 seconds. Double-strain cocktail into chilled cocktail glass. Garnish with orange twist and serve.

Aviation

Makes 1 cocktail
Sweetness ✦✦✧
Citrusy, Floral, Tart

The aviation traces its origin at least as far back as 1916. This cocktail brings to mind the turn-of-the-century spirit of possibility and fascination with luxury air travel by the (very) leisured classes. Sleek and sophisticated, and with a touch of the unknown, it's a gin sour that has been softened by maraschino liqueur, with crème de violette adding a floral undertone (and a sky-shaded hue). The cocktail in its original form vanished mid-century, as crème de violette was no longer available in the United States. Its fortunes shifted during the cocktail renaissance of the 1990s, when drinkers clamored for pre-Prohibition drinks, and the forgotten liqueur was once again imported from Europe. The key to balance in this cocktail is the interplay between its alcoholic strength and its delicate floral quality. For perceptible floral (but not hand-soap) flavor, we add ½ ounce of crème de violette, a generous amount compared with other recipes; we found that we could balance additional liqueur with slightly less sweetener and more lemon juice. You can substitute ¼ ounce of Floral Liqueur with lavender (page 467) for the crème de violette if desired; increase the Simple Syrup in the cocktail to ½ ounce.

- **2 ounces London dry gin**
- **¾ ounce lemon juice, plus lemon twist for garnishing**
- **½ ounce crème de violette**
- **¼ ounce maraschino liqueur**
- **¼ ounce Simple Syrup (page 458)**
- **Cocktail cherries for garnishing**

Add gin, lemon juice, crème de violette, maraschino liqueur, and simple syrup to cocktail shaker, then fill with ice. Shake mixture until fully combined and well chilled, about 15 seconds. Double-strain cocktail into chilled cocktail glass. Garnish with lemon twist and cocktail cherries. Serve.

Yellowlegs

Makes 1 cocktail
Sweetness ✦ ✧ ✧
Citrusy, Herbal, Spirit Forward

The foundation of this sunny yellow drink is built from the well-known pisco sour, the national cocktail of both Chile and Peru; the latter has celebrated Pisco Sour Day on the first Saturday in February for more than 20 years. In addition to the pisco and lemon juice, we add a little more complexity to the classic by incorporating Italian Strega. Strega, which translates to "witch," is made with more than 70 herbs and spices. Its juniper and mint notes balance out the earthiness of the pisco in this cocktail. An egg white is a classic addition to any pisco sour, giving the drink a creamy mouthfeel.

- 2 **ounces pisco**
- 1 **ounce egg white**
- ¼ **ounce Strega**
- ½ **ounce lemon juice, plus lemon coin for garnishing**
- ½ **ounce Simple Syrup (page 458)**

1. Add pisco, egg white, Strega, lemon juice, and simple syrup to cocktail shaker and vigorously shake until mixture is foamy, about 45 seconds.

2. Fill shaker with ice, then shake mixture until fully combined and well chilled, about 15 seconds. Double-strain cocktail into chilled cocktail glass. Pinch lemon coin over drink and rub outer edge of glass with peel, then garnish with lemon coin. Serve.

Bichon Frise

Makes 1 cocktail
Sweetness ✦ ✦ ✧
Citrusy, Floral

For this celebration of elderflower, we pair the delicate floral liqueur with neutral vodka to let its flavors shine through. Grapefruit juice adds a pleasing bitterness, tempered by a touch of brightening lemon. Why name this elegant drink after a dog (albeit a cute, white, fluffy one)? A simple cocktail of vodka and grapefruit juice is a greyhound; add elderflower liqueur, lemon, and a vanilla sugar–rimmed glass, and it becomes our primped and pampered Bichon Frise.

- ¼ **cup Vanilla Rim Sugar (page 454) (optional)**
  Grapefruit wedge (if using sugar)
- 1½ **ounces vodka**
- 1 **ounce red grapefruit juice, plus grapefruit twist for garnishing**
- ¾ **ounce elderflower liqueur**
- ¼ **ounce lemon juice**

1. Spread sugar, if using, into even layer on small saucer. Moisten about ½ inch of chilled cocktail glass rim by running grapefruit wedge around outer edge; dry any excess juice with paper towel. Roll moistened rim in sugar to coat. Remove any excess sugar that falls into glass; set aside.

2. Add vodka, grapefruit juice, liqueur, and lemon juice to cocktail shaker, then fill with ice. Shake mixture until fully combined and well chilled, about 15 seconds. Double-strain cocktail into prepared glass. Garnish with grapefruit twist and serve.

Yellowlegs

Dream Tree

Seelie Sipper

Makes 1 cocktail
Sweetness ✦ ✧ ✧
Citrusy, Floral, Smoky

For its balance and connection to place, this cocktail tastes like a classic at first sip. Scotch whisky is shaken with our chamomile liqueur and sweetened with a touch of herb syrup made with thyme. The floral, faintly earthy chamomile picks up the grassy, herbal quality of the thyme, suggesting heather-laden Scottish Highlands. We veer away from smokier Islay-type whiskies to preserve the freshness of the drink; a lighter blended Scotch from the Lowlands will make a more balanced counterpoint. We generally serve our shaken drinks straight up, as shaking dilutes the cocktail sufficiently. Here, however, we like how the cocktail evolves over ice, with the drink starting off powerful and unwinding in the glass over time. We've named this magic cocktail the Seelie Sipper after the fairies prominent in Scottish folklore.

- 1½ ounces Scotch
- ¾ ounce Floral Liqueur with chamomile (page 467)
- ½ ounce lemon juice, plus strip of lemon peel for garnishing
- ¼ ounce Herb Syrup with thyme (page 459)

Add Scotch, floral liqueur, lemon juice, and herb syrup to cocktail shaker, then fill with ice. Shake mixture until just combined and chilled, about 5 seconds. Double-strain cocktail into chilled rocks glass half-filled with ice or with 1 large ice cube. Pinch lemon peel over drink and rub outer edge of glass with peel, then garnish with lemon peel and serve.

Dream Tree

Makes 1 cocktail
Sweetness ✦ ✧ ✧
Citrusy, Floral, Tropical

This cocktail, developed by test cook Kelly Song to celebrate the Lunar New Year, centers on Chinese baijiu, the most-consumed spirit in the world, surpassing whiskey, vodka, gin, rum, and tequila. In China, it is often sipped with meals. Baijiu is typically distilled from grains such as sorghum, using a fermentation starter called qu in Mandarin, which is derived from pulverized grains. The recipe for qu is unique to each distillery, leading to vastly different flavors of baijiu. The cocktail here marries a strong-aroma baijiu with vibrant pomelo. This style of baijiu has notes of tropical fruit and anise, and the citrus provides a sweet-tart, thirst-quenching, and slightly bitter base. To offset the pungency of the spirit, we include an equal amount of elderflower liqueur, which adds complementary floral notes and subtle sweetness. An addition of lime juice also helps brighten and balance the drink. This cocktail both tastes like a dream and inspires dreams for a fortuitous year ahead.

- 2 ounces pomelo juice, plus pomelo slice for garnishing
- 1 ounce strong-aroma baijiu
- 1 ounce elderflower liqueur
- ½ ounce lime juice

Add pomelo juice, baijiu, elderflower liqueur, and lime juice to cocktail shaker, then fill with ice. Shake mixture until just combined and chilled, about 5 seconds. Strain cocktail into chilled rocks glass half-filled with ice or with 1 large ice cube. Garnish with pomelo slice. Serve.

Tropical

Tropical cocktails radiate carefree, sun-splashed vibes. Although the mood may be relaxed, the tropical branch of the cocktail family tree is complex. Legendary bartenders working in this area have made invaluable contributions to cocktail culture.

The history of this cocktail movement goes back to 1930s California and two bars: Don's Beachcomber (which was renamed Don the Beachcomber) in Hollywood, owned by Donn Beach, and Hinky Dinks in Oakland, which had a back room called the Bamboo Room. The owner of the latter, Victor Bergeron, went on to open Trader Vic's in San Francisco in the 1950s.

With World War II vets returning from the Pacific theater, Hawaii moving toward statehood, and surf culture on the rise (not to mention the smash Rodgers and Hammerstein musical *South Pacific*), Americans' curiosity about the South Pacific swelled. So-called tiki bars with over-the-top decor helped slake their thirst, while menus offering Americanized Chinese and Polynesian food sated their hunger. By the 1970s, tiki iconography was widely regarded as kitschy, and the trend faded. (The rise of premixed cocktail ingredients and the move away from fresh, complex mixed drinks during this decade didn't help.) As the craft cocktail movement began around the turn of the 21st century, this category experienced a parallel revival, rebranded as nostalgic mid-century American pop culture.

In recent years, many bartending professionals have moved away from using the term "tiki" in favor of the term "tropical." Tiki actually refers to the Maori name for the first human and is also a sacred symbol of creation and life. Many in the professional community and beyond find the term "tiki" used to describe cocktails to be culturally inappropriate.

The key to appreciating these tropical drinks lies in understanding the spirits (frequently rum, which has many different styles) and fresh ingredients that go into them. The mai tai, jet pilot, and various punches are classic and festive examples, but you'll also discover some creative new takes in this chapter, including Monkey of the Mind (page 248).

So embrace the tropical escapism ethos. You don't need any specialty glassware to serve these drinks, but if you want something with an island vibe, by all means seek out glasses or ceramic cups shaped like pineapples, coconuts, or flamingos. Fun in the sun awaits.

A World of Rum

Although sugarcane-growing Asian countries were producing fermented spirits from the stalks thousands of years ago, rum as we know it began to emerge in the Caribbean in the 17th century. Molasses, a product of sugar refining, can ferment into alcohol in the tropical heat, and enslaved people consumed it. Eventually, people started distilling it into rum, and soon molasses was being exported to colonial New England for distillation. By the 18th century, rum had become a valuable trading commodity that was distributed around the world. Entire books have been written about rum; here's some basic guidance on primary styles of rum to get you started.

	White Rum	Aged Rum	Cane Spirits
Production	◊ Fermentation base: largely molasses ◊ Distillation: Continuous distillation/column still is most common, although pot distillation is sometimes used. ◊ Aging: Unaged or lightly aged (in stainless-steel tanks or in oak barrels, then filtered to remove color). We include any rum aged less than 5 years in this category. ◊ Produced worldwide	◊ Fermentation base: largely molasses ◊ Distillation: Column and pot distillation are both common. ◊ Aging: At its simplest, rested in oak barrels. We include any rum aged at least 5 years in this category. ◊ Produced worldwide	◊ Fermentation base: sugarcane juice ◊ Distillation: Pot still is more common than column still. ◊ Aging: Aged 0 to 10 years or longer (average is 2 to 5 years); if aged, commonly in oak barrels ◊ Produced worldwide, with unique names based on country of origin: cachaça from Brazil; rhum agricole from Martinique and Guadaloupe; clairin from Haiti
Color	Colorless to light straw	Light gold to dark amber	Colorless to straw gold
Body, Flavors, Aromas	◊ Comparatively lighter in character and body ◊ Light caramel, spices, tropical fruit, nuts, grassy	◊ Comparatively bolder in character and body ◊ Spices, tropical fruit, dark caramel, wood, roasted notes ◊ This category includes "aged Jamaican rum," which can have additional notes of forest floor, wet hay, or compost, sometimes referred to as "funk" or "hogo."	◊ A broad spectrum of character and body since this category contains both unaged and aged spirits ◊ Grass, fresh sugarcane, flowers, tropical fruit, anise, rubber; plus wood and caramel when aged
Words on Label	Silver, white, blanca	Aged for [5 or greater] years (just "aged" with no number, or just a number with no "years," doesn't mean much)	Cane, sugarcane, rhum agricole, clairin, cachaça, arrack
Examples	Mount Gay Silver; Planteray 3 Stars; Bacardí Superior; El Dorado 3 Year; Havana Club Original Añejo 3 Años; Don Q Cristal	Bacardí Reserva Ocho; El Dorado Rum 5, 8, or 12; Mount Gay; Doorly's; Plantation Barbados 5; Appleton Estate Signature; Pusser's	Clément Rhum Blanc; Clairin Communal; Batavia-Arrack van Oosten; Rhum Barbancourt; Ypioca Reserva; Paranubes

Splitting Rums

Because rum styles are so diverse, it's common practice to craft drinks using multiple styles of rum to take advantage of their different flavors. Splitting rums is an easy way to add a pro touch to your tropical drinks at home, allowing you to create more complex flavors. If a recipe calls for 2 ounces aged rum or 2 ounces white rum, you can try any combination of aged and/or white rums to get to that 2 ounces. Start with a 50/50 split between aged and white, and experiment further from there. If you'd like to incorporate rhum agricole, which has a grassier flavor profile, start by swapping in 25 percent rhum agricole (i.e., 1½ ounces rum to ½ ounce rhum agricole), then adjust according to your preference.

Big-Batch Tropical Fun

Tropical drinks lend themselves well to doubling without changing the ingredient ratios; our Scorpion Cup (page 243) is a classic example of a drink we love to share. A double batch of a tropical drink fits easily in a standard shaker, and it's even easy enough to shake two double batches to serve four people. When we want to serve a bigger crowd, we turn to one of our punches (pages 256–261).

Tropical Ice

Tropical cocktails often call for crushed ice for serving. The fast cooling and dilution that come from crushed ice work wonders for both integrating and properly diluting the layers of bold flavors from the strongly flavored rums and liqueurs and the sweet juices, syrups, and coconut products often used in tropical drinks. Whereas in an Old-Fashioned (page 123), for example, you add cubed ice with the intention of slowly sipping the drink, tropical cocktails are designed for refreshment and cooling yourself off. They're too easy to slurp right down, so the crushed ice truly is important. We like to make crushed ice using a Lewis bag and mallet (see page 19); or use our rolling-pin hack (see page 121).

Play with Fire

Increase the wow factor of tropical drinks by garnishing them with a flaming rum shot in a lime cup.

1. Turn spent lime half inside out to create a cup. Omit any additional ice for topping drink and nestle lime cup in filled glass.

2. Microwave ½ ounce rum in small bowl until just beginning to bubble, 10 to 20 seconds. Pour hot rum into lime half.

3. Ignite rum carefully with match. Be sure to blow out flames before drinking!

Seaport Sling

Makes 1 cocktail
Sweetness ✦ ✦ ✧
Herbal, Spiced, Tropical

The sling was one of the earliest categories of cocktails, consisting of a strong spirit, sweetened and diluted in some way. While the original sling was basically an old fashioned, the Singapore sling couldn't be more different. Singapore's stately colonial-era Raffles Hotel lays claim to the origin of the well-known cocktail in 1915, although some drinks experts suggest a longer history.

Today, this sling conjures up thoughts of bright cherry-red, insipidly sweet, supersize cocktails; in fact, many modern sling recipes contain up to five different sweeteners (such as cherry liqueur, Bénédictine, grenadine, orange liqueur, and pineapple juice). We developed a pared-back Seaport Sling, named for the neighborhood in Boston where the Test Kitchen offices reside. Sling nonnegotiables are gin for the spirit and cherry liqueur. The honeyed, lightly herbal sweetness of Bénédictine adds an intriguing complexity. Pineapple juice rounds out the main ingredients with its tropical acidity. We found it unnecessary to add other typical ingredients like grenadine and orange liqueur, as their nuance gets lost.

- **1½ ounces unsweetened 100 percent pineapple juice**
- **1½ ounces London dry gin**
- **1 ounce Bénédictine**
- **½ ounce cherry liqueur**
- **½ ounce lime juice**
- **⅛ teaspoon old-fashioned aromatic bitters**
- **2 ounces seltzer, chilled**
- **Pineapple slice for garnishing**
- **Cocktail cherries for garnishing**

Add pineapple juice, gin, Bénédictine, cherry liqueur, lime juice, and bitters to cocktail shaker, then fill with ice. Shake mixture until just combined and chilled, about 5 seconds. Double-strain cocktail into chilled highball glass half-filled with ice. Add seltzer and, using bar spoon, gently lift pineapple mixture from bottom of glass to top to combine. Top with additional ice and garnish with pineapple slice and cherries. Serve.

Ombré Sling

Makes 1 zero-proof cocktail
Sweetness ✦✦✦
Citrusy, Tropical

With its fruity flavors, a sling is a strong candidate for making zero-proof with juices. We like equal parts orange juice and pineapple juice for sweetness, with just a touch of balancing tart lime juice. For a wow factor, we top the drink with a pour of grenadine. The syrup diffuses its sweet-tart pomegranate flavor and ruby color throughout the drink as it settles to the bottom, creating an ombré effect. If you don't have crushed ice, you can shake the cocktail with ice until just combined and chilled, about 5 seconds, then strain into a highball glass half-filled with cube ice. Top with additional ice and garnish as directed.

- 2½ ounces orange juice
- 2½ ounces unsweetened 100 percent pineapple juice
- ½ ounce lime juice
- ½ ounce grenadine
- Mint sprig for garnishing

Fill chilled highball glass halfway with crushed ice. Add orange juice, pineapple juice, and lime juice to glass and swizzle until just combined and chilled, about 10 seconds. Top with additional ice, then pour grenadine over top, allowing it to settle to bottom of glass. Garnish with mint sprig and serve.

Customize Your Cocktail

Make a Spiked Ombré Sling by adding 1 ounce of your favorite rum with the orange juice.

Seaport Sling

Mai Tai

Makes 1 cocktail
Sweetness ✦✦✧
Citrusy, Floral, Toasted

- 2 ounces aged rum
- 1 ounce lime juice, plus lime slice for garnishing
- ¾ ounce orgeat syrup
- ½ ounce Simple Syrup (page 458)
- ½ ounce orange liqueur
- Mint sprig for garnishing

Customize Your Cocktail

Add more complexity to the cocktail by utilizing two distinct styles of aged and/or white rum; see page 237 for more information on splitting rums.

Many mai tais served in bars are a far cry from the original drink, which Victor Bergeron (Trader Vic) claims he created in his restaurant Hinky Dinks in Oakland, California, in 1944. It was based on just five ingredients: a singular 17-year-old Jamaican rum, simple syrup, orgeat, orange liqueur, and lime juice. The name "mai tai" derives from the Tahitian phrase for "out of this world—the best." But with the passage of time and changing rum production methods and availability, the mai tai metamorphosed into something less than the best: A variety of inferior rums were substituted, and canned pineapple and bottled orange juices frequently made appearances. The abundant garnishes, like umbrellas, neon cherries, and pineapple wedges, were also absent from the original mai tai. For our version, we use an aged rum and pare down the ingredients to the original list for a result we think lives up to its name. If you don't have crushed ice, you can shake the cocktail with ice until just combined and chilled, about 5 seconds, then strain into a rocks glass half-filled with cube ice. Top with additional ice and garnish as directed.

Add rum, lime juice, orgeat syrup, simple syrup, and orange liqueur to cocktail shaker and shake until combined, about 5 seconds. Pour cocktail into chilled rocks glass half-filled with crushed ice, then top with additional ice. Garnish with lime slice and mint sprig. Serve.

Scorpion Cup

Makes 1 cocktail
Sweetness ✦ ✦ ✧
Citrusy, Floral, Toasted

A scorpion bowl usually suggests a giant vessel for a thirsty straw-wielding crowd. But relegating this cocktail only to large gatherings seems like a shame to us. We wanted to create a personal-size cocktail, and we also wanted to ramp up its quality while maintaining the fun. Scorpion bowls are often found in Chinese American restaurants. Since the so-called tiki bars of the 1950s borrowed Cantonese-style cooking for their menus, Chinese restaurants capitalized on the trend by borrowing the tiki drinks. They can feature a mash-up of liquors, canned fruit juices, and sugary syrups, with various garnishes that sometimes include a "volcano" in the middle—but they sure are fun. We limit the number of spirits in our Scorpion Cup to an essential two, with aged rum providing smooth caramel notes and brandy adding a touch of slightly fruity warmth. We prefer fresh orange juice as the primary fruit juice, with a small amount of lime juice for zingy acidity, grenadine for color and tang, and orgeat for floral nuttiness. Whether garnished simply with cocktail cherries, or with the added bonus of a spectacular flaming lime half (see page 237), our personal-size scorpion bowl is a drink worthy of being part of your regular cocktail rotation—or of doubling to share. You can garnish with pineapple and citrus slices in addition to the cocktail cherries, if desired.

2 ounces orange juice
1½ ounces aged rum
½ ounce brandy
¼ ounce grenadine
¼ ounce lime juice
¼ ounce orgeat syrup
Cocktail cherries for garnishing

Add orange juice, rum, brandy, grenadine, lime juice, and orgeat syrup to cocktail shaker, then fill with ice. Shake mixture until just combined and chilled, about 5 seconds. Double-strain cocktail into chilled rocks glass half-filled with ice. Top with additional ice and garnish with cocktail cherries. Serve.

Customize Your Cocktail

Add more complexity to the cocktail by utilizing two distinct styles of aged and/or white rum; see page 237 for more information on splitting rums.

Jet Pilot

Makes 1 cocktail
Sweetness ✦✦✧
Citrusy, Spiced, Toasted

The jet pilot is a classic tropical cocktail born from another pilot, the test pilot cocktail, developed by the infamous Donn Beach, a Hollywood-by-way-of-Louisiana nomad and rum guzzler who introduced the faux-Polynesian bar phenomenon to Americans post-Prohibition. The jet pilot was developed by Steven Crane in his own similarly themed restaurant, also in Hollywood. Fittingly, both drinks center on rum dressed up with citrus and liqueurs. The jet pilot is the more complex cocktail, with equal parts grapefruit and lime juices, sweetened with cinnamon simple syrup. Velvet Falernum liqueur, a very sweet tropical rum–based liqueur with notes of spice, almond, and lime, enhances all the flavors of this cocktail; however, an equal amount of Simple Syrup (page 458) can be used in its place. Other dry anise-flavored spirits (such as Herbsaint, pastis, or dry anisette) can be substituted for the absinthe. If you don't have crushed ice, you can shake the cocktail with ice until just combined and chilled, about 5 seconds, then strain into a highball glass half-filled with cube ice. Top with additional ice. Garnish with citrus slices, if desired.

2 ounces aged rum
¾ ounce grapefruit juice
¾ ounce lime juice
¾ ounce Spice Syrup with cinnamon (page 459)
½ ounce Velvet Falernum liqueur
¼ teaspoon absinthe
⅛ teaspoon old-fashioned aromatic bitters

Fill chilled highball glass halfway with crushed ice. Add rum, grapefruit juice, lime juice, spice syrup, Velvet Falernum liqueur, absinthe, and bitters to glass and swizzle until just combined and chilled, about 10 seconds. Top with additional ice and serve.

Customize Your Cocktail

Add more complexity to the cocktail by utilizing two distinct styles of aged and/or white rum; see page 237 for more information on splitting rums.

PAIR WITH A SNACK

Crispy Crab Cups

Serves 4 to 6
Total Time: 30 minutes

The fried dumplings known as crab rangoon first became famous at Trader Vic's in San Francisco, and they remain a staple on many Chinese American takeout menus. This easy open-faced take is packed with sweet, delicate crabmeat; the wrappers are crisped up in a muffin tin in the oven rather than deep-fried. To soften cream cheese quickly, microwave it for 20 to 30 seconds.

- Vegetable oil spray
- 16 wonton wrappers
- 4 ounces lump crabmeat, picked over for shells
- 3 ounces cream cheese, softened
- 1 scallion, white part sliced thin, green part sliced thin on bias
- 1 teaspoon grated fresh ginger
- ¾ teaspoon soy sauce

1. Adjust oven rack to middle position and heat oven to 350 degrees. Spray mini muffin tin with oil spray. Gently press wonton wrappers into tin cups, making sure bottoms and sides are flush with tin; let edges of wrappers extend out of cups. Lightly spray wrappers with oil spray and bake until lightly browned, 6 to 9 minutes; let cool slightly.

2. Combine crabmeat, cream cheese, scallion whites, ginger, and soy sauce in bowl. Using small spoon, fill each wonton cup with 2 teaspoons filling. Bake until filling is heated through, 6 to 8 minutes. Sprinkle with scallion greens. Serve warm.

Jungle Bird

Jungle Bird

Makes 1 cocktail
Sweetness ✦ ✦ ✧
Bitter, Tropical

Created in 1973 by Jeffrey Ong at the Aviary Bar in the Hilton Kuala Lumpur, the jungle bird was originally served in a porcelain bird-shaped vessel—until patrons kept stealing the birds, resulting in the move to wine goblets. The jungle bird is Malaysia's best-known cocktail, enjoying a resurgence in popularity in 2003 with the publishing of *Beachbum Berry's Intoxica!*, which aimed to revisit recipes from the tropical-escapism cocktail bar boom. Like so many tropical cocktails, the jungle bird is a refreshing mix of rum and juices, but with an alluring bitter twist achieved through the addition of Campari. If you don't have crushed ice, you can shake the cocktail with ice until just combined and chilled, about 5 seconds, then strain into a highball glass half-filled with cube ice. Top with additional ice and garnish as directed.

2 ounces unsweetened 100 percent pineapple juice
1¼ ounces aged rum
¾ ounce Campari
½ ounce lime juice
½ ounce Simple Syrup (page 458)
Mint sprig for garnishing
Pineapple slice for garnishing

Fill chilled highball glass halfway with crushed ice. Add pineapple juice, rum, Campari, lime juice, and simple syrup to glass and swizzle until just combined and chilled, about 10 seconds. Top with additional ice and garnish with mint sprig and pineapple slice. Serve.

Painkiller

Makes 1 cocktail
Sweetness ✦ ✦ ✦
Creamy, Toasted, Tropical

The painkiller is an iteration of a piña colada so delicious we thought it deserved its own spotlight. The Soggy Dollar Bar on Jost Van Dyke, British Virgin Islands (BVI)—named for the wet cash patrons used after swimming from their boats to the bar—claims to have invented the drink in the 1970s. The painkiller adds orange juice and a bit more pineapple juice. The result is a BVI specialty that transports you to the Caribbean from the first sip. If you don't have crushed ice, you can shake the cocktail with ice until just combined and chilled, about 5 seconds, then strain into a rocks glass half-filled with cube ice. Top with additional ice and garnish as directed.

2 ounces aged rum
1½ ounces unsweetened 100 percent pineapple juice
¾ ounce orange juice
¾ ounce cream of coconut
Pineapple slice for garnishing
Mint sprig for garnishing
Freshly grated nutmeg for garnishing

Add rum, pineapple juice, orange juice, and cream of coconut to cocktail shaker and shake until combined, about 5 seconds. Pour cocktail into chilled rocks glass half-filled with crushed ice, then top with additional ice. Garnish with pineapple slice, mint sprig, and grated nutmeg. Serve.

Monkey of the Mind

Monkey of the Mind

Makes 1 cocktail
Sweetness ✦✦✦
Creamy, Spiced, Tropical

The Monkey King from the Chinese novel *Journey to the West* inspired the name of this baijiu cocktail. To balance the potent, distinct taste of the baijiu, we mix it with coconut milk and orange juice and build complexity with aged rum. Velvet Falernum liqueur enhances the flavor of this cocktail; however, an equal amount of Simple Syrup (page 458) can be used in its place. If you don't have crushed ice, you can shake the cocktail until just combined and chilled, about 5 seconds, then strain into a rocks glass half-filled with cube ice. Top with additional ice and garnish as directed. You can garnish with citrus slices in addition to the mint sprig, if desired.

- 1¼ ounces aged rum
- ¾ ounce strong-aroma baijiu
- ¾ ounce lime juice
- ¾ ounce orange juice
- ½ ounce Velvet Falernum liqueur
- 1 tablespoon cream of coconut
- Mint sprig for garnishing

Add rum, baijiu, lime juice, orange juice, Velvet Falernum liqueur, and cream of coconut to cocktail shaker and shake until combined, about 5 seconds. Pour cocktail into chilled rocks glass half-filled with crushed ice, then top with additional ice. Garnish with mint sprig and serve.

Rum Runner

Makes 1 cocktail
Sweetness ✦ ✦ ✧
Citrusy, Fruity, Tropical

According to local folklore, the rum runner was first served at a bar in the Florida Keys that needed to clear shelf space for a new liquor order. Into the cocktail everything went. Made of both light and dark rums, pineapple and orange juices, banana and blackberry liqueurs, and grenadine, the potent punch has a name that holds weight despite the fluffy backstory, alluding to the history of liquor smugglers who brought rum from Caribbean sugar plantations to South Florida speakeasies during Prohibition. We love the blackberry liqueur here, but it can be hard to find at liquor stores. If that is the case, you can substitute black raspberry liqueur or Chambord, but the drink will be a little sweeter and have a less vibrant hue. If you don't have crushed ice, you can shake the cocktail with ice until just combined and chilled, about 5 seconds, then strain into a hurricane glass half-filled with cube ice. Top with additional ice and garnish as directed.

- 2 ounces aged rum
- 1½ ounces lime juice
- 1 ounce orange juice, plus orange slice for garnishing
- 1 ounce unsweetened 100 percent pineapple juice
- 1 ounce banana liqueur
- ½ ounce blackberry liqueur
- ½ ounce grenadine
- Pineapple slice for garnishing
- Cocktail cherries for garnishing
- Blackberries for garnishing

Fill chilled hurricane glass halfway with crushed ice. Add rum, lime juice, orange juice, pineapple juice, banana liqueur, blackberry liqueur, and grenadine to glass and swizzle until just combined and chilled, about 10 seconds. Top with additional ice and garnish with orange slice, pineapple slice, cocktail cherries, and blackberries. Serve.

Customize Your Cocktail

Add more complexity to the cocktail by utilizing two distinct styles of aged and/or white rum; see page 237 for more information on splitting rums.

Bird in the Hand

Makes 1 zero-proof cocktail

Sweetness ✦✦✧

Bitter, Spiced, Tropical

- 2 ounces brewed espresso, chilled
- 1 ounce nonalcoholic aperitivo
- 1 ounce unsweetened 100 percent pineapple juice
- ¾ ounce Spice Syrup (page 459)
- ½ ounce lime juice, plus lime slice for garnishing
- Mint sprig for garnishing

Tropical drinks are fun but far from frivolous. Take this zero-proof one that's full of complex flavor to satisfy even the most discerning cocktail drinker. It's vaguely tropical while also bitter and tart. We love drinks whose flavor journey starts one way and ends another (even better if there are more twists and turns in the middle), so that each sip gets us excited for the next one. That's the Bird in the Hand. Texturally intriguing, too, the drink's head is frothy and decadent—and will stay for a long time without dissipating. It's a result of the double play of frothy emulsifiers found in the coffee and pineapple juice. This cocktail tastes best with freshly made and chilled espresso, but you can substitute an equal amount of strong cold brew coffee. We developed this recipe using Wilfred's Non-Alcoholic Aperitif, but other brands of nonalcoholic aperitivi (as well as traditional bitter aperitivi) will also work. Nonalcoholic aperitivo syrup can be used as well; reduce the spice syrup to ½ ounce. If you don't have crushed ice, you can shake the cocktail with ice until just combined and chilled, about 5 seconds, then strain into a rocks glass half-filled with cube ice. Top with additional ice and garnish as directed.

Add espresso, aperitivo, pineapple juice, spice syrup, and lime juice to cocktail shaker and shake until well combined and frothy, about 20 seconds. Pour cocktail into chilled rocks glass about three-quarters full with crushed ice. Garnish with lime slice and mint sprig. Serve.

The Sun Also Rises

The Sun Also Rises

Makes 1 zero-proof cocktail
Sweetness ✦ ✦ ✦
Fruity, Tropical

Inspired by a classic tropical cocktail called the missionary's downfall, which features rum and peach liqueur, this drink certainly won't lead to anyone's downfall. The peach, here in the form of peach nectar, is a nice addition to familiar tropical ingredients, pineapple and lime juices. Mint complements all of the fruit flavors within, and the drink's smooth texture makes it incredibly pleasing and sippable. You can garnish with fresh, dried, or dehydrated pineapple slices in addition to the mint, if desired.

- 3 ounces unsweetened 100 percent pineapple juice
- 1 ounce peach nectar
- 1 ounce lime juice
- 1 ounce Simple Syrup (page 458)
- ⅓ cup fresh mint leaves, plus mint sprig for garnishing

Add pineapple juice, peach nectar, lime juice, simple syrup, and mint to cocktail shaker, then fill with ice. Shake mixture until just combined and chilled, about 5 seconds. Double-strain cocktail into chilled rocks glass half-filled with ice. Top with additional ice and garnish with mint sprig. Serve.

Stormy Seas

Makes 1 cocktail
Sweetness ✦ ✦ ✧
Bitter, Creamy, Tropical

We love a piña colada as much as the next person, but sometimes we're in the mood for something less sweet. Stormy Seas is essentially what you get if a piña colada ditched the rum and replaced it with a lower-alcohol, bitter amaro, Cynar. This is a fine example of a drink that liberates amari from the land of stirred cocktails—and, as in the Jungle Bird (page 247), the amaro gets along quite well with the flavors of tropical drinks.

- 2 ounces unsweetened 100 percent pineapple juice
- 1 ounce Cynar
- 1 tablespoon cream of coconut
- ¼ ounce Simple Syrup (page 458)

Add pineapple juice, Cynar, cream of coconut, and simple syrup to cocktail shaker, then fill with ice. Shake mixture until fully combined and well chilled, about 15 seconds. Double-strain cocktail into chilled cocktail glass and serve.

Customize Your Cocktail

Try other bitter aperitivi such as Campari, Punt e Mes, or Select Aperitivo in place of the Cynar.

Tongue Thai'd

Makes 1 zero-proof cocktail
Sweetness ✦✦✧
Citrusy, Nutty, Spicy

As with many delicious creations inspired by Thai cuisine, this cocktail features sour, spicy, and sweet flavors. We muddle fragrant Thai basil with lime-based citrus syrup for a fresh aromatic base with just a hint of anise. Muddling half a seeded Thai chile with the basil swathes the cocktail in spiciness. Coconut water imparts a sweet, nutty-yet-fresh flavor. A good slug of lime juice lends brightness. Italian basil can be used instead of Thai basil.

- 4 fresh Thai basil leaves
- 1 Thai chile, halved and seeded, divided
- ¼ ounce Citrus Syrup with lime (page 458)
- 3 ounces coconut water
- ½ ounce lime juice

Add basil leaves, half of chile, and citrus syrup to base of cocktail shaker and muddle until fragrant, about 30 seconds. Add coconut water and lime juice, then fill shaker with ice. Shake mixture until just combined and chilled, about 5 seconds. Double-strain cocktail into chilled cocktail glass. Garnish with remaining chile half and serve.

Customize Your Cocktail

Not a fan of heat? The chile can be omitted; skip muddling and shake basil and citrus syrup with coconut water and lime juice as directed.

PAIR WITH A SNACK

Pigs in a Blanket

Serves 8 to 10
Total Time: 1¼ hours

For a sophisticated version of this retro snack, we use puff pastry, which has a flakier texture than the more typical crescent roll dough. To thaw frozen puff pastry, let it sit either in the refrigerator for 24 hours or on the counter for 30 minutes to 1 hour. One 10- to 13-ounce package of cocktail franks usually contains 32 franks. Serve with mustard.

- 1 sheet puff pastry, thawed
- 1 large egg, beaten with 1 tablespoon water
- 32 cocktail franks, patted dry
- ¼ cup grated Parmesan cheese
- ½ teaspoon pepper

1. Adjust oven rack to middle position and heat oven to 400 degrees. Line rimmed baking sheet with parchment paper. Unfold puff pastry on lightly floured counter and roll into 12 by 9-inch rectangle with short side parallel to edge of counter, flouring top of dough as needed to prevent sticking.

2. Using pizza wheel or chef's knife, trim dough to 12 by 8-inch rectangle. Cut dough lengthwise into eight 1-inch strips. Cut dough crosswise at three 3-inch intervals. (You should have thirty-two 3 by 1-inch dough strips.) Lightly brush 1 row of dough strips with egg wash. Roll 1 frank in each dough strip and transfer bundle, seam side down, to prepared sheet. Repeat with remaining dough strips and franks, spacing bundles ½ inch apart.

3. Combine Parmesan and pepper in bowl. Working with a few bundles at a time, brush tops with egg wash and sprinkle with Parmesan mixture. Bake until pastry is golden brown, about 23 minutes. Let pigs cool on sheet for 10 minutes. Serve.

The Punches

Punch is considered by many to be the world's oldest cocktail. Sailors traversing oceans in the 1600s combined citrus, spice, and sugar with South Asian cane spirits, adding water for dilution. Known as arrack, these spirits were made from sugarcane, molasses, coconut, or rice. The sailors called their concoction punch, possibly after the style of wood storage cask known as a puncheon or the Hindi or Urdu word for "five" (referencing the five traditional components).

Arrack and punch were crucial to sailors: The spirit took up less space belowdecks than wine or beer and had a longer shelf life. The punch helped prevent scurvy and got them a little drunk (but not *too* drunk) on monotonously long voyages. Ashore, sailors shared their punch with passersby for a few pence a cup, forever classifying punch as a convivial social beverage.

There are five key components for any punch: sour (citrus juice), spice (ingredients from nutmeg to bitters to rose water), sweet (sugar), strong (spirit), and weak (juice, tea, water, or wine). The "weak" adds appeal by putting punches into a category of lower-ABV cocktails that you can enjoy over the course of an evening with friends. The weak component is intended to dilute the spirit without diluting flavor. Our "sweet," a simplified version of oleosaccharum (a type of syrup made by macerating citrus peels in sugar until they express their aromatic, flavorful oils) also adds big flavor.

Our Bowl-o-Punch, bursting with citrusy, floral sweetness, is a celebration of everything we love about a great bowl of punch. Regent Punch is luxurious, using green tea and sparkling wine, splitting the spirits, and finishing with nutmeg (which once was worth more than gold). Planter's Punch has two rums and embraces tropical fruits. Redcoat's Revenge uses gin, going in a different spirited direction.

An ice ring (see page 30) keeps punches cold in style, without overdiluting. If necessary, use 8 large ice cubes instead.

Bowl-o-Punch

Makes 16 cocktails
Sweetness ✦✦✧
Citrusy, Floral, Toasted

- 12 limes, divided, plus lime slices for garnishing
- 1¾ cups sugar
- 12 ounces boiling water, plus 16 ounces chilled water
- 20 ounces aged rum
- 20 ounces Batavia arrack
- 2 teaspoons rose water
- 2 pounds (8 cups) ice cubes
- 1 Ice Ring (page 30)

1. Using vegetable peeler, remove zest from 6 limes in strips, removing as little white pith as possible. Toss zest with sugar in large bowl. Using potato masher, mash zest and sugar vigorously until mixture is damp, clumpy, and very fragrant, about 2 minutes. Add boiling water and stir until sugar has dissolved, about

2 minutes. Let cool completely, about 30 minutes. Meanwhile, juice enough limes to yield 12 ounces juice.

2. Stir lime juice, rum, Batavia arrack, and rose water into zest mixture until combined. Strain through fine-mesh strainer set over large container; discard zest. Stir ice cubes and chilled water into punch until fully melted. Cover and refrigerate until well chilled, about 1 hour. (Punch can be refrigerated for up to 3 days.) Stir punch to recombine, then transfer to punch bowl. Add ice ring and garnish with lime slices. Serve in chilled punch cups.

Customize Your Cocktail

The combination of aged rum and Batavia arrack adds complexity to this punch, but feel free to use aged rum entirely or substitute another unique style of aged and/or white rum for the Batavia arrack. Lime slices are really just the start for garnishing a punch bowl. Consider sliced tropical fruit, edible flowers, mint sprigs, candied or dried citrus and ginger, whole cinnamon sticks or star anise pods, and/or other decorative flair.

Regent Punch

Makes 16 cocktails
Sweetness ✦✦✧
Citrusy, Floral, Toasted

This luxurious punch—with its sparkling wine, brandy, and nutmeg—is in a style that would be served during the European upper crust's parties in the late 18th century, emphasizing the wealth and social standing of the host. Luckily for us, whole nutmeg and tea no longer break the bank, and this delicious punch can be enjoyed by us commoners. We prefer the higher quality of loose-leaf tea here; however, 4 tea bags can be substituted.

- 4 oranges, plus orange slices for garnishing
- 4 lemons, plus lemon slices for garnishing
- 1 cup sugar
- 4 teaspoons green tea leaves
- 16 ounces boiling water, plus 12 ounces chilled water
- 12 ounces brandy
- 3 ounces aged rum
- 3 ounces Batavia arrack
- 2 ounces maraschino liqueur
- 12 ounces (3 cups) ice cubes
- 1 (750-ml) bottle sparkling white wine, chilled
- 1 Ice Ring (page 30)
- Freshly grated nutmeg for garnishing

1. Using vegetable peeler, remove zest from oranges and lemons in strips, removing as little white pith as possible. Toss zest with sugar in large bowl. Using potato masher, mash zest and sugar vigorously until mixture is damp, clumpy, and very fragrant, about 2 minutes.

2. Place tea in 2-cup liquid measuring cup. Add boiling water and let steep for 4 minutes. Strain tea through fine-mesh strainer into zest mixture and stir until sugar has dissolved, about 2 minutes. Set aside until cool, about 30 minutes. Meanwhile, juice enough oranges to yield 10 ounces juice and lemons to yield 4 ounces.

3. Stir orange juice, lemon juice, brandy, rum, Batavia arrack, and maraschino liqueur into zest mixture until combined. Strain through fine-mesh strainer set over large container; discard zest. Stir ice cubes and chilled water into punch until fully melted. Cover and refrigerate until well chilled, about 1 hour. (Punch can be refrigerated for up to 3 days.) Just before serving, transfer punch to punch bowl and gently stir in sparkling wine. Add ice ring and garnish with orange slices and lemon slices. Serve in chilled punch cups, garnishing individual portions with grated nutmeg.

Customize Your Cocktail

The combination of aged rum and Batavia arrack adds complexity to this punch, but you can use aged rum entirely or substitute another aged and/or white rum for the Batavia arrack. Orange and lemon slices are excellent garnishes here, but you can add others like sliced tropical fruit, edible flowers, mint sprigs, candied or dried citrus and ginger, whole cinnamon sticks or star anise pods, and/or other baubles you might like.

Planter's Punch

Makes 16 cocktails
Sweetness ✦✦✧
Citrusy, Toasted, Tropical

It can be hard to nail down a definitive origin story for planter's punch. Some legends say the Planters Hotel in Charleston, South Carolina, a 19-century retreat for wealthy rice planters, served the first citrus-rum libation. Other stories claim the sweet tropical drink was first served by Caribbean plantation owners. Today, most cocktail historians agree planter's punch was probably invented in Jamaica, with some sources connecting it to Myers's brand rum. The combination of aged and white rums in this recipe strikes a good balance of caramel flavor and booziness. A citrus syrup, plus pineapple, orange, and lime juices, give this punch balanced fruitiness.

- 6 oranges, plus orange slices for garnish
- 8 limes, plus lime slices for garnish
- ⅔ cup sugar
- 4 ounces boiling water
- 24 ounces unsweetened 100 percent pineapple juice, chilled
- 16 ounces aged rum
- 16 ounces white rum
- 2 teaspoons old-fashioned aromatic bitters
- 12 ounces (3 cups) ice cubes
- 1 Ice Ring (page 30)

1. Using vegetable peeler, remove zest from 3 oranges and 1 lime in strips, removing as little white pith as possible. Toss zest with sugar in large bowl. Using potato masher, mash zest and sugar vigorously until mixture is damp, clumpy, and very fragrant, about 2 minutes. Add boiling water and stir until sugar has dissolved, about 2 minutes. Set aside until cool, about 30 minutes. Meanwhile, juice enough oranges to yield 16 ounces juice and limes to yield 8 ounces.

2. Stir orange juice, lime juice, pineapple juice, aged rum, white rum, and bitters into zest mixture until combined. Strain through fine-mesh strainer set over large container; discard zest. Stir ice cubes into punch until fully melted. Cover and refrigerate until well chilled, about 1 hour. (Punch can be refrigerated for up to 3 days.) Stir punch to recombine, then transfer to punch bowl. Add ice ring and garnish with orange slices and lime slices. Serve in chilled punch cups.

Customize Your Cocktail

We like the combination of aged rum and white rum here, but feel free to use aged rum entirely or substitute another unique style of aged rum for the white rum. Additional garnish ideas include sliced tropical fruit, edible flowers, mint sprigs, candied or dried citrus and ginger, and whole cinnamon sticks or star anise pods.

Redcoat's Revenge

Makes 16 cocktails
Sweetness ✦✦✧
Citrusy, Fruity, Herbal

This punch is a great fall refresher. Lemon and ginger form the base, while Pimm's and Old Tom gin lend herbal and fruity flavor. We use apple cider as the weak component, as its apple flavor really shines through and balances out the slight bitterness of the Pimm's.

- 5 lemons, plus lemon slices for garnishing
- 1 (4-inch) piece ginger, sliced thin
- ⅔ cup sugar
- 4 ounces boiling water
- 36 ounces apple cider, chilled
- 22 ounces Pimm's No.1
- 14 ounces Old Tom gin
- 12 ounces (3 cups) ice cubes
- 1 Ice Ring (page 30)
- Apple slices for garnishing

1. Using vegetable peeler, remove zest from lemons in strips, removing as little white pith as possible. Toss zest and ginger with sugar in large bowl. Using potato masher, mash zest, ginger, and sugar vigorously until mixture is damp, clumpy, and very fragrant, about 2 minutes. Add boiling water and stir until sugar has dissolved, about 1 minute. Set aside until cool, about 30 minutes. Meanwhile, juice enough lemons to yield 7 ounces juice.

2. Stir lemon juice, apple cider, Pimm's No.1, and gin into zest mixture until combined. Strain through fine-mesh strainer set over large container; discard solids. Stir ice cubes into punch until fully melted. Cover and refrigerate until well chilled, about 1 hour. (Punch can be covered and refrigerated for up to 3 days.) Stir punch to recombine, then transfer to punch bowl. Add ice ring and garnish with lemon and apple slices. Serve in chilled punch cups.

Customize Your Cocktail

Edible flowers, mint sprigs, candied or dried apples and ginger, and whole cinnamon sticks or star anise pods work well with or in place of the lemon and apple slice garnish.

Clockwise from top: Redcoat's Revenge, Planter's Punch, Regent Punch

Aged *and* Clarified

These two cocktail techniques that seem ultramodern have their roots firmly planted in cocktail history and tradition. Why age or clarify a cocktail? First, each technique offers a unique take on flavor, texture, and overall enjoyment of the cocktail. And second, simply put, like so much else in the cocktail kingdom, it's fun.

First, let's address aging. Think of aging a cocktail as a gift to your future self: Place a batch of your preferred stirred drink in a glass jar and tuck it away for a while. When you taste it again, weeks later, you'll discover a subtle transformation—the harshness of the spirits has softened; the drink feels smoother and more rounded, even creamier, on the tongue; some flavor notes have become less evident while others have grown more prominent. See for yourself by trying the Aged Manhattan (page 271) or Aged Martini (page 273) alongside its nonaged counterpart (page 181 or 155).

While aging spirits is age-old, it's bartender, author, and blogger Jeffrey Morgenthaler who is credited with kick-starting the trend of aging cocktails in wood barrels in the United States in 2009. Morgenthaler in turn cites his inspiration as the "sublime" bottle-aged Manhattans he had experienced a year earlier, created by Tony Conigliaro, a London-based bartender who had been experimenting with bottle-aged cocktails after tasting an exquisite bottle of vermouth almost a century old.

What these individuals found was that when a mixture of spirits, liqueurs, and/or fortified wines are allowed to mingle for an extended time, chemical processes occur that change the aromas, mouthfeel, and flavors of the drink in desirable ways.

Next, let's talk about clarifying, which can refine the texture and smooth out the flavor of a cocktail. There is a centuries-old method that uses milk to clarify alcoholic punches in an effort to stabilize the drink and store it for extended periods. Then there is the modern technique of clarifying cocktails through the use of enzymes or gels. This newer trend is generally tied to food science writer and educator Dave Arnold, who honed his techniques at his New York City cocktail bar Booker and Dax, which was truly ahead of its time with cocktail innovations.

While some cocktail components, like spirits and liqueurs, are already clear, other components are not—think especially about fruit juices, which have suspended particles that scatter light, making them cloudy. Clarification is the process of removing those suspended particles to create a perfectly clear liquid, and thus a perfectly clear cocktail. Elegant and translucent, clarified cocktails like the Tomatini (page 284) feel like alchemy in a glass, tricking the eye as to what the glass actually contains.

What Happens When You Age a Cocktail?

Aging is one of the easiest ways to enjoy a whole new cocktail-drinking experience. Bitter notes and acidity settle down, sweet notes seem more prominent, and the cocktail as a whole feels more rounded on the palate. The process is not difficult and doesn't require much in the way of special equipment, but understanding what's happening and paying attention to the details will help you achieve the best results.

OXIDATION

Even in a sealed environment, there will be some oxygen in the container. The cocktail's exposure to oxygen changes flavors by creating new compounds. For example, ethanol (alcohol) is oxidized to form aldehydes, compounds that at low levels create pleasant fruity, grassy, or nutty aromas and that can subsequently react with other compounds to create more flavors and aromas. (If overoxidized, aldehydes become organic acids, like acetic acid or vinegar.) Oxidation can also dull some elements, particularly volatile ones; for example, gin will lose some of its citrusy aromas. Wine-based ingredients like vermouth are more prone to oxidation than higheralcohol spirits, so drinks with these components may exhibit more oxidation characteristics. When properly controlled, this leads to deliciously nuanced flavors.

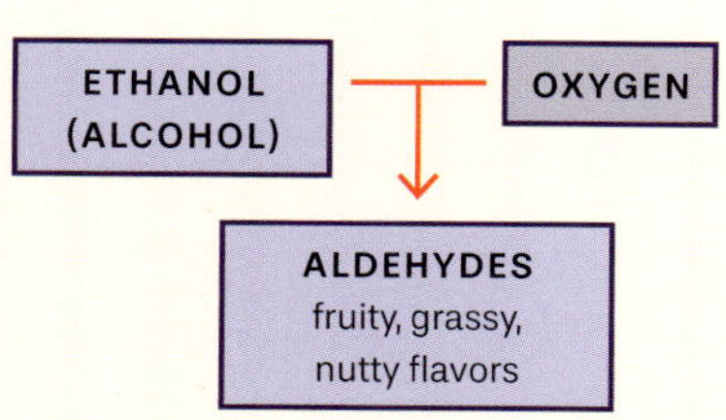

ESTERIFICATION

Besides interacting with oxygen, cocktail ingredients interact with each other to form additional flavor compounds. Esterification is one such reaction and occurs when alcohols interact with acids to form esters, compounds responsible for fruity aromas like banana, pineapple, or apple. Esterification can also affect the mouthfeel of a drink by creating longer-chained esters, which increase a drink's viscosity and perceived "creaminess."

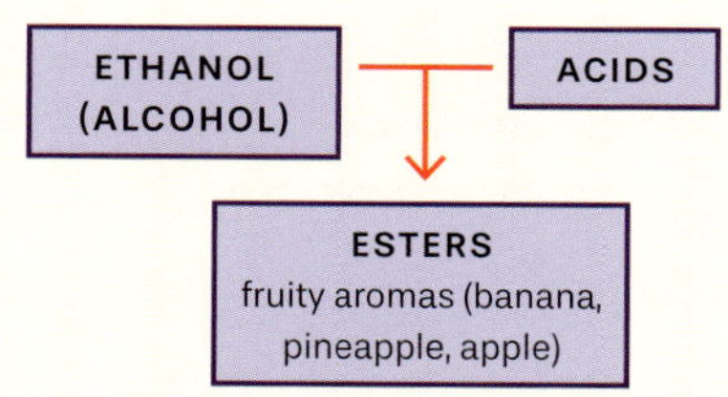

EXTRACTION

If a cocktail is aged using wood, alcohol extracts components from the wood, often resulting in an infusion of toasted, caramel, or vanilla flavors to the drink (depending on the type of wood). Meanwhile, the wood also absorbs components of the cocktail, acting similar to a charcoal filter to remove harsh flavors from the drink.

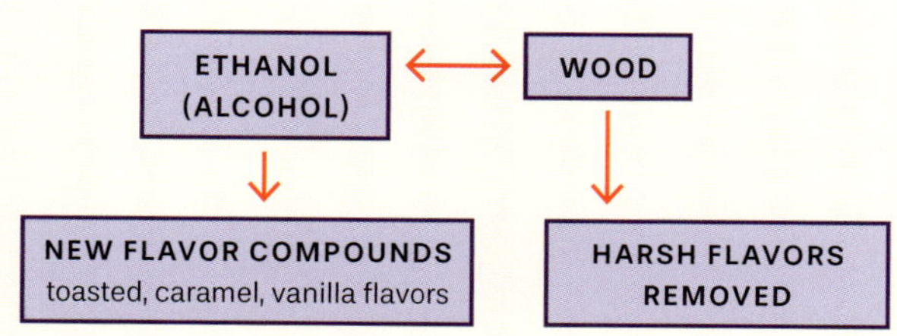

EVAPORATION

If a cocktail is aged in a wood barrel, which is porous, there will be evaporation; this volume loss leads to more concentrated flavors. Evaporation will also occur when a cocktail is aged in a sealed glass vessel, but it will be paired with condensation; so while it accelerates oxidation, it won't result in concentration through volume loss.

Wood Versus Glass

Aging in glass is far more practical than aging in wood for the home bartender. Wood barrels are more costly than glass jars because they require preparation before use—to make sure they are leakproof and to "season" new barrels—and they require continued maintenance once they are in use. Also, every wood barrel is different, and it will change with each use, meaning that aging in barrels can be unpredictable.

Because of the greater ratio of wood surface area to liquid volume in the small, affordable barrels that are used for aging cocktails at home (generally 1 to 2 liters), there is also potential for a cocktail to be overwhelmed by the effects of wood during aging.

If you want to try imparting flavors associated with barrel aging (including vanilla, toast, warm spices, and caramel) while aging in glass, we recommend adding a wood spiral to your glass aging container. This allows for replicable experimentation and more predictable results. Wood spirals are available online or through beer and wine supply stores. There are plenty of options to choose from, in terms of both the type of wood used and how heavily that wood has been charred. While American oak at a level #3 ("medium") char is common for aging spirits in American oak barrels, using a spiral means that you can explore other types of oak—French, for example—or other woods entirely, as well as a range of chars, from light to heavy, to see what flavors you enjoy best.

In the cocktails we tested, we noticed wood-aged flavors emerging after two weeks of adding a level #3 (medium)-char oak spiral to a vessel and found that the balance of a cocktail started to be negatively affected past the four-week mark. However, different cocktails will respond differently, and you should taste frequently after adding a wood spiral. You can continue to age your cocktail after removing the spiral, so experiment at home with different types of spirals and different cocktails.

Getting Started

If you're interested in experimenting with aging cocktails beyond the recipes in this chapter, here are some helpful guidelines.

CHOOSE A SPIRIT-FORWARD COCKTAIL

Most cocktails that are aged are of the stirred variety, with a higher ABV, which means they'll oxidize more slowly, relatively speaking. You generally want to avoid any drinks that contain juice, dairy, or other perishable ingredients if you plan to age your cocktail.

USE A GLASS CONTAINER WITH A TIGHT-FITTING LID

The recipes in this chapter make 20 to 24 ounces each, enough for eight servings, and call for a 1-quart glass container. It doesn't matter whether you choose a wide-mouthed Mason jar or a narrow-mouthed bottle. (If you like, you can repurpose a 750-milliliter liquor bottle.) Just make sure that whatever you choose has a tight-fitting lid or cap.

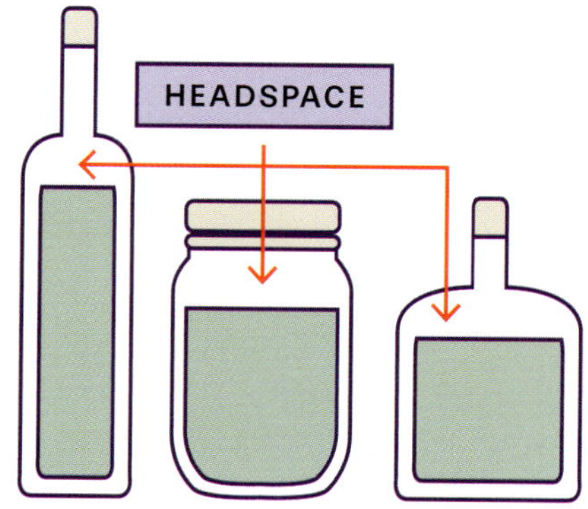

CONTROL THE HEADSPACE

To take advantage of the aging qualities of oxygen, you need a bit of headspace in the glass container. A good guideline is to choose a container that is about three-quarters filled by the cocktail. (As you consume the cocktail, you can transfer it to a smaller container to continue to control the headspace.) If the recipe calls for bitters or measured water, don't add those before aging. Add them when you're ready to serve the cocktail.

LET IT SIT

Place the bottle in a dark, cool location. While some cocktail professionals have experimented with accelerating the aging process through adding heat or light (both of which speed up oxidation and aging), we recommend letting time do the work (in the meantime, relax and enjoy a freshly stirred cocktail).

START TASTING

When developing these recipes, we noticed distinct flavor and aroma differences between a freshly stirred cocktail and an aged cocktail after about one month. You can certainly start tasting your cocktail sooner (after about three weeks, or after two weeks if using oak spirals). Since you can store most aged cocktails for up to a year, keep tasting and note any flavor differences you continue to experience. When it reaches a point that you think is just right, transfer the cocktail to the refrigerator, which will significantly slow down further aging. When ready to serve, proceed just as you would for an unaged version of the cocktail.

Clarified

What Happens When You Clarify a Cocktail?

Removing suspended solid particles from a liquid transforms its appearance and texture and mellows its flavor. There are a number of ways to clarify a cocktail, each of which has its own technique. To clarify at home, we recommend the gel method, though we explain the sedimentation method so you can also try that, if you wish.

APPEARANCE IMPROVES

Clarified cocktails turn crystal clear, presenting themselves as elegant and intriguing. This effect tricks your palate in a delightful way—who expects a Tomatini (page 284) to be transparent?

CARBONATION BECOMES POSSIBLE

Cloudy liquids don't hold carbonation well because each suspended particle is a spot where a bubble can form (known as a nucleation site), then rise to the surface and escape. Using clarified liquids allows you to carbonate drinks you might never expect, leading to new flavor and texture experiences. Try our Pomme de Champagne (page 286), made with fresh Granny Smith apples, or the unexpectedly delicious Sparkling Celery (page 288).

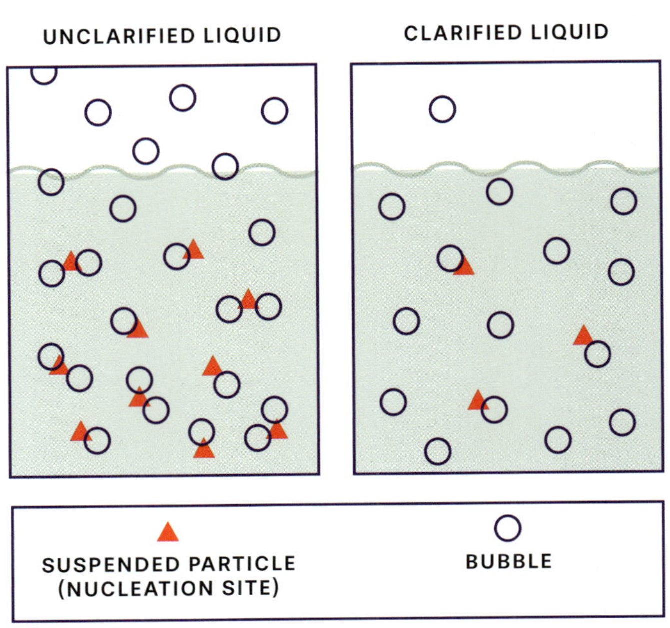

CARBONATE YOUR COCKTAIL

While there are soda makers on the market that carbonate liquids other than water, you need to have a large amount of liquid to use them successfully. A handheld cream whipper, more typically used to make homemade whipped cream and dispense it through the nozzle into swirls and rosettes, makes a perfect device for carbonating a cocktail or two. We like the iSi Gourmet Whip, which is easy to grip and use for both righties and lefties, for novices and experienced users alike.

Clarification Methods

In the process of developing recipes for this book, we explored three primary methods of clarification, each of which has pros and cons. Filtration and sedimentation leave more color, flavor, and aroma in the liquid, but neither creates crystal-clear liquids; plus with at-home sedimentation, the yield of clear liquid can be quite low. Gel clarification creates the clearest liquid, with the caveat being that removing all the particulates from a liquid also removes some flavor, aroma, and color.

FILTRATION

Simply filtering liquids through a fine-mesh strainer, cheesecloth, or coffee filters to remove particles is the easiest and fastest process but will only get you so far, as in most cases it is challenging to get a perfectly clear liquid from filtration alone. Filtration becomes much more effective when used in conjunction with the sedimentation method and compounds that help loosen and separate solid particles from the liquid.

SEDIMENTATION

Also known as racking, this is the most complicated method. Fining agents (compounds that clump particulates based on their electrical charges) or enzymes, such as Pectinex Ultra SP-L, are typically added to a liquid, and the liquid is left to sit. Particles naturally settle out of the liquid by density, and the resulting clear liquid is siphoned off. In high-end bar settings, centrifuges may be used to spin out the sediment sufficiently and quickly; without a centrifuge, one has to rely on time, and the yield is poor, making this an ineffective process for the home bartender.

GEL

The Goldilocks technique for the home bartender is gel clarification, a process in which a liquid is partially solidified into a gel, most commonly with agar-agar (a substance derived from seaweed) or gelatin. The gel is then broken and drained through cheesecloth (coffee filters could also be used); the gel retains the particles and releases a crystal-clear liquid in a process called syneresis, similar to whey leaking from yogurt.

MILK

A fourth way to clarify cocktails is with milk; it's one of the oldest methods of clarification and is key to the clarity of English milk punches, also known as clarified milk punches (see pages 290–293), which rose to popularity during the 18th century. Milk is combined with a cocktail containing citrus juice or another acidic ingredient. The milk curdles, and then the entire mixture is strained to remove the curds, also removing most of the color and cloudiness from the drink. Milk clarification, unlike gel clarification, also removes tannins and other polyphenols that cause astringency in ingredients like black tea or spirits (which were particularly harsh in the past). Also in contrast to gel clarification, where liquid and some flavors are lost during the process, milk clarification adds creamy, luscious flavor and texture to the mixture. For this reason, milk clarification is sometimes referred to as milk washing (see pages 296–297 to learn about fat washing).

Tomatini (page 284) made with unclarified juice (left) versus clarified juice (right)

Getting Started

While all clarification methods have trade-offs, we use the gel clarification method with agar-agar for our clarified cocktails (other than for milk punches) because it results in the clearest liquid, and the process is straightforward and replicable for most juices, making it user-friendly for the home bartender. Following the specific instructions in the recipes, you can clarify most juices with the help of these guidelines.

CLARIFY JUICE, NOT ENTIRE COCKTAILS

Regardless of method, the clarification process removes a portion of the original liquid. In our experience, gel clarification can result in a loss of at least 25 percent; results using filtration or sedimentation will be higher depending on the fruit or vegetable juice used and the thickness of the liquid. For this reason, we recommend clarifying just the juice rather than an entire cocktail.

USE FRESH OR BOTTLED JUICE

While making fresh juice can expand ingredient possibilities, as in our Pomme de Champagne (page 286), we found that in some cases, bottled juice can actually be preferable. For instance, pear puree made from fresh pears is extremely thick and oxidizes quickly, making the clarification process challenging. We found bottled pear juice easier to work with, producing good results. See page 12 for information on making fresh juices.

SIMMER THE AGAR-AGAR IN WATER

Use agar-agar powder, not flakes. In order for agar-agar to work, it needs to be simmered in liquid for a couple of minutes to dissolve it. Instead of heating the juice and potentially losing its fresh flavor and aroma, we heat the agar-agar powder in a small amount of water and then incorporate the juice into that mixture. The most effective ratio of powder to total volume of liquid (water plus juice) is 2 grams powder for every 1,000 grams liquid (approximately 1 teaspoon powder for 32 ounces liquid).

Clarifying with Pectinex Ultra SP-L

Many cocktail professionals use Pectinex Ultra SP-L to clarify juices. This fungi-derived group of enzymes breaks down pectin, the primary compound in fruit and vegetable juices that holds particles in suspension. Adding Pectinex to juice can help separate out particulates more quickly and easily before further filtering (or in the case of high-end cocktail bars, centrifuging) and doesn't affect the flavor or aroma of the liquid. If you'd like to try using Pectinex in our clarified cocktail recipes, you can purchase it online.

We recommend the following method: Microwave 16 ounces of juice in a 1-quart Mason jar until the juice registers 90 degrees, 30 to 60 seconds. Add ⅛ teaspoon of Pectinex, then cover tightly and shake the mixture vigorously for 5 seconds to combine. Allow the mixture to separate for 1 to 1½ hours at room temperature. Line a fine-mesh strainer with cheesecloth or a coffee filter and place it over a large bowl or container. Using a bulb baster, carefully remove the clear liquid without disturbing the sediment and transfer to the prepared strainer.

DRAIN OVERNIGHT FOR BEST RESULTS

After you break up the set gel, the process of the clarified liquid "leaking" out of the gel occurs over several hours. For the greatest yield—in our experience up to 75 percent—allow the gel to drain overnight. Do not squeeze or press on the gel while it drains, as that can cause the agar-agar to drain into the juice.

USE CLARIFIED JUICE WITHIN TWO DAYS

Removing particulates from juice does not mean that you can store it longer; use clarified juice within two days for maximum freshness, or freeze it for up to a month. Agar-clarified juices may develop "agar wisps" during storage—a slight cloudiness at the bottom of the liquid. These are not harmful and can be stirred back into the liquid.

Aged Classics

These cocktails are seemingly disparate, but all follow a similar spirit-forward formula of base spirit + fortified wine and/or liqueur, which makes each one an ideal candidate for aging. While aging in glass alone may not impart additional flavors to a cocktail, it does coax out the best in the flavors that are already present, resulting in a cocktail that feels soft and smooth on the palate. And if you want to add an oak spiral, by all means do so.

The Manhattan is one of the most popular aged cocktails, with many bar menus offering renditions. While it's hard to improve on a freshly and well-made Manhattan, aging this cocktail takes it from classic to legendary. Over time, the peppery astringency of the rye softens and blends with the smoother herbaceousness of the sweet vermouth, creating a new kind of richness. While each component is distinct in a fresh Manhattan, the flavor becomes more integrated and rounded after aging—exponentially more than the sum of its parts.

For our Vieux Nuevo, aging reposado tequila and sherry together unites their savory, almost saline notes, lifted by the herbal, lightly honeyed notes of Bénédictine. Besides the Manhattan, we age another titan: the martini. If you love the pungent juniper qualities and in-your-face alcohol burn of a fresh martini, you might not love this aged version more. But for those seeking a kinder and gentler but still flavorful martini, you've come to the right place.

The Revolver is a new classic, created just after the turn of the 21st century in San Francisco. It was originally made with Bulleit bourbon, hence its name. Bourbon and coffee liqueur age beautifully together, emerging with fused sweet, spicy, nutty, notes. Adding the orange bitters right before serving offers a subtle pop of citrus flavor and aroma without being overwhelming.

Aged Manhattan

Makes 8 cocktails

Sweetness ✦ ✧ ✧

Herbal, Spirit Forward, Toasted

- 16 ounces rye
- 6 ounces sweet vermouth
- 1 teaspoon old-fashioned aromatic bitters, divided
- Cocktail cherries for garnishing

1. Combine rye and vermouth in glass bottle or large Mason jar (do not add bitters). Cover and place in a 50- to 70-degree location away from direct sunlight. Let rye mixture sit until flavors have developed, about 1 month. (Rye mixture can be stored for at least 1 year; flavor will continue to develop over time.)

2. To make 1 cocktail: Gently shake rye mixture to recombine. Add 2¾ ounces rye mixture and ⅛ teaspoon bitters to mixing glass, then fill three-quarters full with ice. Using bar spoon, stir until mixture is fully combined and well chilled, about 1 minute. Strain cocktail into chilled cocktail glass. Garnish with cherries and serve.

Vieux Nuevo

Makes 8 cocktails
Sweetness ✦ ✧ ✧
Herbal, Spirit Forward, Toasted

Though this cocktail blends new-world and old-world spirits an ocean apart, it feels like they were always meant to be together. Fino sherry brings salinity and a savory flavor to the drink. Reposado tequila is aged for a short period in oak barrels, so it's smooth but retains a brightness. Finally, Bénédictine pulls everything together with its herbs and spices. When the mixture is aged, the flavor notes of the sherry come forward and linger on the palate, while the aromatic components of Bénédictine and tequila round out the middle.

- **10 ounces reposado tequila**
- **6 ounces fino sherry**
- **4 ounces Bénédictine**
- **Cocktail cherries for garnishing**

1. Combine tequila, sherry, and Bénédictine in glass bottle or large Mason jar. Cover and place in a 50- to 70-degree location away from direct sunlight. Let tequila mixture sit until flavors have developed, about 1 month. (Tequila mixture can be stored for at least 1 year; flavor will continue to develop over time.)

2. To make 1 cocktail: Gently shake tequila mixture to recombine. Add 2½ ounces tequila mixture to mixing glass, then fill three-quarters full with ice. Using bar spoon, stir until mixture is fully combined and well chilled, about 1 minute. Strain cocktail into chilled cocktail glass. Garnish with cherries and serve.

Customize Your Cocktail

We like making this drink with fino sherry, but you can explore different flavor profiles by using an amontillado, oloroso, or palo cortado sherry. Using blanco tequila instead of reposado will amplify the herbal notes in the cocktail.

Aged Martini

Makes 8 cocktails
Sweetness ✧ ✧ ✧
Herbal, Savory, Spirit Forward

There are those who love martinis for their crisp, intense, spirit-forward brashness—and then there are those who do not. An aged martini might be the preferred drink for the latter set, and a delicious drink in its own right. In the process of aging our favorite 4:1 ratio of London dry gin to dry vermouth (see page 152), we noticed a couple of transformations as the mixture mingled. The prominent citrusy and juniper aromas of gin soften, as does the overall potency of the drink—it's a martini, but more subtle.

16 ounces London dry gin
4 ounces dry vermouth
Brine-cured green olives for garnishing

1. Combine gin and vermouth in glass bottle or large Mason jar. Cover and place in a 50- to 70-degree location away from direct sunlight. Let gin mixture sit until flavors have developed, about 1 month. (Gin mixture can be stored for at least 1 year; flavor will continue to develop over time.)

2. To make 1 cocktail: Gently shake gin mixture to recombine. Add 2½ ounces gin mixture to mixing glass, then fill three-quarters full with ice. Using bar spoon, stir until mixture is fully combined and well chilled, about 1 minute. Strain cocktail into chilled cocktail glass. Garnish with olives and serve.

Customize Your Cocktail

Not a gin drinker? Make an Aged Vodka Martini by substituting vodka for the gin. To make a drier aged martini, reduce the vermouth to 2 ounces; to make a wetter martini, increase it to up to 8 ounces. Or, try an Upside-Down Aged Martini (Julia Child's favorite), with 16 ounces of vermouth and 8 ounces of gin. If you prefer, for the olive garnish you can substitute (or add) a lemon twist.

Aged Revolver

Makes 8 cocktails
Sweetness ✦ ✦ ✧
Nutty, Spirit Forward, Toasted

The revolver is a caffeinated twist on a Manhattan, but it's not just for Manhattan lovers, and it might surprise those who aren't sure they love whiskey cocktails, or even coffee. San Francisco bartender Jon Santer developed this deceptively simple drink in 2004 as an alternative to sweet 'tini drinks and, on the opposite end of the spectrum, overwrought cheffy creations that were popular in the city at the time. Coffee liqueur takes the place of the sweet vermouth that's in a traditional Manhattan, and sweeter bourbon is swapped in for the brasher rye. The coffee taste is subtle, adding depth and a bit of nutty, slightly bitter complexity rather than in-your-face flavor; it pairs well with bourbon's sweet, spicy, and vanilla aromas. When we age the revolver, the components intertwine, and bourbon's caramel notes and perceived sweetness come forward while the coffee flavor recedes a bit. A hit of aromatic orange peel, classically flamed before expressing, brightens up the dark spirits in this smooth and luxurious drink.

- 16 ounces bourbon
- 4 ounces coffee liqueur
- 1 teaspoon orange bitters, divided
- Strips of orange peel for garnishing

1. Combine bourbon and coffee liqueur in glass bottle or large Mason jar (do not add bitters). Cover and place in a 50- to 70-degree location away from direct sunlight. Let bourbon mixture sit until flavors have developed, about 1 month. (Bourbon mixture can be stored for at least 1 year; flavor will continue to develop over time.)

2. To make 1 cocktail: Gently shake bourbon mixture to recombine. Add 2½ ounces bourbon mixture and ⅛ teaspoon bitters to mixing glass, then fill three-quarters full with ice. Using bar spoon, stir until mixture is fully combined and well chilled, about 1 minute. Strain cocktail into chilled cocktail glass.

3. Hold lit match several inches above cocktail. Slowly wave orange peel over flame, zest side facing cocktail, for a few seconds, then quickly squeeze zest to ignite oils; discard peal. Garnish with fresh orange peel, if desired, and serve.

From front to back: Aged Revolver, Vieux Nuevo, Aged Martini

Oak-Aged Negroni

Makes 8 cocktails
Sweetness ✦✦✧
Bitter, Citrusy, Toasted

- 8 ounces London dry gin
- 8 ounces Campari
- 8 ounces sweet vermouth
- 1 (¼-ounce/5-gram) oak spiral (optional)
- Strips of orange peel for garnishing

Customize Your Cocktail

You can make an Oak-Aged Boulevardier by substituting bourbon for the gin.

The Negroni has seduced many cocktail enthusiasts and bartenders worldwide. Whether it's the bold color, intense bittersweet flavor, or the spritz of aromatic orange peel to finish, there's a lot to love. Batching a jar of Negronis gives you more opportunities to partake in this iconic cocktail, and adding an oak infusion spiral allows you to explore a different spin on the classic drink: After a few weeks of aging the drink tastes a bit sweeter and less bitter, with more oak and vanilla coming through and fewer botanical aromas from the gin. Both American and French oak spirals will work here. We developed this recipe using medium char, but feel free to experiment with lighter or heavier chars. The spiral can be rinsed, dried, and stored for future use; the intensity of its flavor will decrease over time. While we really enjoy the flavor that the oak spiral imparts to this cocktail, simply aging a classic Negroni also works really well.

1. Combine gin, Campari, vermouth, and oak spiral, if using, in large Mason jar. Cover and place in a 50- to 70-degree location away from direct sunlight. Let gin mixture sit for about 1 month. Remove oak spiral. (Gin mixture can be stored for at least 1 year; flavor will continue to develop over time.)

2. To make 1 cocktail: Gently shake gin mixture to recombine. Add 3 ounces gin mixture to mixing glass, then fill three-quarters full with ice. Using bar spoon, stir until mixture is fully combined and well chilled, about 1 minute. Strain cocktail into chilled rocks glass half-filled with ice or containing single large ice cube. Pinch orange peel over drink and rub outer edge of glass with peel, then garnish with orange peel and serve.

Oak-Aged Metropolitan

Makes 8 cocktails

Sweetness ✦ ✧ ✧

Fruity, Spirit Forward, Toasted

Also known as a brandy Manhattan, the metropolitan swaps drier rye for brandy, creating a fruitier, smoother, and slightly sweeter drink. Both American and French oak spirals will work here. We developed this recipe using medium char, but feel free to experiment with lighter or heavier chars. The spiral can be rinsed, dried, and stored for future use; the intensity of its flavor will decrease over time. While we really enjoy the flavor that the oak spiral imparts to this cocktail, simply aging a classic metropolitan also works really well.

- 16 ounces brandy
- 8 ounces sweet vermouth
- 1 (¼-ounce/5-gram) oak spiral (optional)
- 1 teaspoon old-fashioned aromatic bitters, divided
- Cocktail cherries for garnishing

1. Combine brandy, vermouth, and oak spiral, if using, in large Mason jar (do not add bitters). Cover and place in a 50- to 70-degree location away from direct sunlight. Let brandy mixture sit for about 1 month. Remove oak spiral. (Brandy mixture can be stored for at least 1 year; flavor will continue to develop over time.)

2. To make 1 cocktail: Gently shake brandy mixture to recombine. Add 3 ounces brandy mixture and ⅛ teaspoon bitters to mixing glass, then fill three-quarters full with ice. Using bar spoon, stir until mixture is fully combined and well chilled, about 1 minute. Strain cocktail into chilled cocktail glass. Garnish with cherries and serve.

PAIR WITH A SNACK

Ham and Cheese Palmiers

Serves 8 to 10
Total Time: 45 minutes, plus 1 hour chilling

These crisp, golden-brown palmiers are an elegant yet ultra-easy salty-savory cocktail snack. To thaw frozen puff pastry, allow it to sit either in the refrigerator for 24 hours or on the counter for 30 minutes to 1 hour.

- 1 (9½ by 9-inch) sheet puff pastry, thawed
- 2 tablespoons Dijon mustard
- Fresh thyme
- 4 ounces thinly sliced deli ham
- 1 cup (2 ounces) grated Parmesan cheese

1. Roll pastry into 12-inch square, then brush with mustard. Mince 2 teaspoons thyme and sprinkle over top. Lay ham evenly over top to edge of pastry and sprinkle with Parmesan. Roll up both sides of dough until they meet in the middle. Wrap log of dough in plastic wrap and refrigerate until firm, about 1 hour.

2. Adjust oven rack to middle position and heat oven to 400 degrees. Line rimmed baking sheet with parchment paper. Trim ends of log, then slice into ⅓-inch-thick pieces with sharp knife. Lay on prepared sheet, about 1 inch apart.

3. Bake until golden brown and crisp, about 25 minutes, rotating sheet halfway through baking. Transfer palmiers to wire rack and let cool completely before serving.

Clarified Cocktails

Starting with some established classic cocktail formulas and concepts, we elevated them by incorporating the pure essence and flavor of clarified fruit juice, using our simplified techniques to create transformed updates.

First we turned to the sidecar, a cocktail in the sour family. This cocktail is traditionally made with brandy (Cognac in the best versions), orange liqueur, and lemon juice. There are some established variations that include pear brandy or pear liqueur with great success. Nowhere is this pear-brandy flavor couple as captivating as in the French practice of capturing an entire pear inside a bottle as it grows (known as prisonnière), later to be filled with a pear-derived brandy. Capturing that essence of pear in a perfectly clear mixed cocktail was our inspiration for this clarified sidecar spin.

Our Hummingbird demonstrates that pineapple juice firmly has a place in an elevated, sophisticated cocktail, in this case alongside an Italian aromatized wine. No longer will you think of it only in terms of tropical cocktails with little umbrellas (although we're certainly not knocking those).

Next we tried our hand at cocktails using fruit that is ordinarily challenging because of density or texture. Our Dew Drop involves making a quick melon puree, which you'll clarify and combine with sake for an ethereally pale green concoction. We went to the savory side with our Tomatini, which will fool your eyes but not your palate with its umami flavor. For maximum visual impact, we call for stirring the Tomatini. While the other cocktails here could also be stirred for the greatest clarity, we enjoy the aerated texture that shaking gives these elegant drinks.

Clair de Pear

Makes 1 cocktail
Sweetness ✦✦✧
Fruity, Nutty, Toasted

This recipe yields enough clarified pear juice to make 6 cocktails. You can also use unclarified juice in this cocktail.

Clarified Pear Juice

- 4 ounces water
- ½ teaspoon agar-agar powder
- 16 ounces unsweetened 100 percent pear juice

Cocktail

- 2 ounces clarified pear juice
- 1½ ounces brandy
- ¼ ounce amaretto
- ¼ ounce lemon juice
- Fresh Bosc or Bartlett pear slice for garnishing

1. For the clarified pear juice: Fill large bowl halfway with ice and water. Whisk water and agar-agar together in small saucepan. Bring to boil over medium-high heat, stirring constantly. Cover, reduce heat to medium-low, and simmer for 2 minutes. Off heat, whisk in pear juice. Transfer juice mixture to medium bowl and set bowl over prepared ice water bath. Place ice bath with juice mixture in refrigerator and let sit, without disturbing, until gel sets, about 30 minutes.

2. Using whisk, gently break up gel into pea-size pieces. Line fine-mesh strainer with triple layer of cheesecloth and place over large bowl or container. Transfer curds to prepared strainer and let drain for at least 30 minutes or overnight. (You will have at least 4 ounces clarified juice after 30 minutes and up to 12 ounces after 12 hours; clarified juice can be refrigerated in airtight container for up to 2 days or frozen for up to 1 month.) Discard solids.

3. For the cocktail: Add pear juice, brandy, amaretto, and lemon juice to cocktail shaker, then fill with ice. Shake mixture until fully combined and well chilled, about 15 seconds. Double-strain cocktail into chilled cocktail glass. Garnish with pear slice and serve.

Customize Your Cocktail

You can make a Clarified Apple Sidecar using clarified apple juice and garnishing with an apple slice.

Hummingbird

Makes 1 cocktail
Sweetness ✦ ✦ ✧
Bitter, Tropical

This elegant drink shows the breadth of pineapple juice, which is for much more than college-party mixers and blending into piña coladas. Pineapple juice performs particularly well in clarified cocktails because it retains a lot of flavor after clarification. Inspired by the Jungle Bird (see page 247), this cocktail proves again how well bitter flavors pair with pineapple's fruitiness and modest acidity. Instead of Campari, as in the Jungle Bird, we pair the pineapple with floral, citrusy, bittersweet Cocchi Americano. Crisp white rum stiffens up the drink, while a modest amount of lemon juice and simple syrup provides sweet-tart balance. This recipe yields enough clarified pineapple juice to make 8 cocktails. You can also use unclarified juice in this cocktail. Lillet Blanc or vermouth bianco (also sometimes labeled blanc or blanco) can be used in place of the Cocchi Americano.

Clarified Pineapple Juice

- 4 ounces water
- ½ teaspoon agar-agar powder
- 16 ounces unsweetened 100 percent pineapple juice

Cocktail

- 1½ ounces clarified pineapple juice
- 1¼ ounces white rum
- ¾ ounce Cocchi Americano Bianco
- 1 teaspoon Simple Syrup (page 458)
- 1 teaspoon lemon juice
- Fresh pineapple slice and/or leaf for garnishing

1. For the clarified pineapple juice: Fill large bowl halfway with ice and water. Whisk water and agar-agar together in small saucepan. Bring to boil over medium-high heat, stirring constantly. Cover, reduce heat to medium-low, and simmer for 2 minutes. Off heat, whisk in pineapple juice. Transfer juice mixture to medium bowl and set bowl over prepared ice water bath. Place ice bath with juice mixture in refrigerator and let sit, without disturbing, until gel sets, about 30 minutes.

2. Using whisk, gently break up gel into pea-size pieces. Line fine-mesh strainer with triple layer of cheesecloth and place over large bowl or container. Transfer curds to prepared strainer and let drain for at least 30 minutes or overnight. (You will have at least 4 ounces clarified juice after 30 minutes and up to 12 ounces after 12 hours; clarified juice can be refrigerated in airtight container for up to 2 days or frozen for up to 1 month.) Discard solids.

3. For the cocktail: Add pineapple juice, rum, Cocchi Americano, simple syrup, and lemon juice to cocktail shaker, then fill with ice. Shake mixture until just combined and chilled, about 5 seconds. Double-strain cocktail into chilled rocks glass half-filled with ice or containing single large ice cube. Garnish with pineapple and serve.

Dew Drop

Makes 1 cocktail
Sweetness ✦✧✧
Fruity, Floral

While some fruit is easily incorporated into cocktails—citrus, pineapple, or cranberry, for example—others, like melon, are more challenging. Fortunately, clarification transforms a sludgy puree into a clear and delicate liquid that captures the essence of the fruit. This crystal-clear, pale celadon cocktail gets sweet flavor from clarified honeydew juice, a perfect complement to mild, floral sake. This recipe yields enough clarified honeydew juice to make 8 cocktails. You can also use unclarified juice in this cocktail; follow straining instructions in step 1, then proceed with making the cocktail.

Clarified Honeydew Juice

- 2½ pounds honeydew, peeled, seeded, and cut into 1½-inch pieces (7 cups)
- 4 ounces water
- ½ teaspoon agar-agar powder

Cocktail

- 1½ ounces junmai ginjō sake
- 1½ ounces clarified honeydew juice, plus honeydew ball for garnishing
- ¼ ounce lemon juice
- ½ teaspoon Simple Syrup (page 458)

1. For the clarified honeydew juice: Working in batches, process honeydew in blender until smooth, about 30 seconds, scraping down sides of blender jar as needed. Strain honeydew puree through fine-mesh strainer set over medium bowl, pressing on solids to extract as much liquid as possible; discard solids.

2. Fill large bowl halfway with ice and water. Whisk water and agar-agar together in small saucepan. Bring to boil over medium-high heat, stirring constantly. Cover, reduce heat to medium-low, and simmer for 2 minutes. Off heat, whisk in honeydew juice. Transfer juice mixture to medium bowl and set bowl over prepared ice water bath. Place ice bath with juice mixture in refrigerator and let sit, without disturbing, until gel sets, about 30 minutes.

3. Using whisk, gently break up gel into pea-size pieces. Line fine-mesh strainer with triple layer of cheesecloth and place over large bowl or container. Transfer curds to prepared strainer and let drain for at least 30 minutes or overnight. (You will have at least 4 ounces clarified juice after 30 minutes and up to 12 ounces after 12 hours; clarified juice can be refrigerated in airtight container for up to 2 days or frozen for up to 1 month.) Discard solids. (You should have 16 ounces juice.)

4. For the cocktail: Add sake, honeydew juice, lemon juice, and simple syrup to cocktail shaker, then fill with ice. Shake mixture until fully combined and well chilled, about 15 seconds. Double-strain cocktail into chilled cocktail glass and garnish with melon ball. Serve.

Tomatini

Makes 1 cocktail
Sweetness ✧ ✧ ✧
Savory

This tomato water martini sharply displays the visual allure of clarified cocktails: Upon first glance, this super-savory stunner has the color and clarity of white wine, but take one sip full of grassy, tomato flavor and you'll hardly believe your eyes. Clarification transforms a thick pink puree of fresh tomatoes into a straw-colored clear liquid brimming with their flavor. Herbal, dry vermouth adds a bit of complexity but keeps this cocktail low in alcohol, nice for sipping with food. This cocktail is a good aperitivo drink, its savoriness opening the appetite like few other cocktails can. This recipe yields enough clarified tomato juice to make 6 cocktails. We do not recommend making this cocktail without clarified juice.

Clarified Tomato Juice

- 2 pounds tomatoes, stemmed and quartered
- ⅛ teaspoon table salt
- 4 ounces water
- ½ teaspoon agar-agar powder

Cocktail

- 2 ounces clarified tomato juice
- ½ ounce dry vermouth
- Fresh Herb Oil with basil (page 455) for garnishing
- Cherry tomato for garnishing

1. For the clarified tomato juice: Process tomatoes and salt in blender until smooth, about 30 seconds, scraping down sides of blender jar as needed. Strain tomato puree through fine-mesh strainer set over medium bowl, pressing on solids to extract as much liquid as possible; discard solids.

2. Fill large bowl halfway with ice and water. Whisk water and agar-agar together in small saucepan. Bring to boil over medium-high heat, stirring constantly. Cover, reduce heat to medium-low, and simmer for 2 minutes. Off heat, whisk in tomato juice. Transfer juice mixture to medium bowl and set bowl over prepared ice water bath. Place ice bath with juice mixture in refrigerator and let sit, without disturbing, until gel sets, about 30 minutes.

3. Using whisk, gently break up gel into pea-size pieces. Line fine-mesh strainer with triple layer of cheesecloth and place over large bowl or container. Transfer curds to prepared strainer and let drain for at least 30 minutes or overnight. (You will have at least 4 ounces clarified juice after 30 minutes and up to 12 ounces after 12 hours; clarified juice can be refrigerated in airtight container for up to 2 days or frozen for up to 1 month.) Discard solids. (You should have 16 ounces juice.)

4. For the cocktail: Add tomato juice and vermouth to mixing glass, then fill three-quarters full with ice. Stir until mixture is just combined and chilled, about 30 seconds. Strain cocktail into chilled cocktail glass. Garnish with basil oil and cherry tomato. Serve.

Clockwise from top: Tomatini, Hummingbird, Dew Drop

Pomme de Champagne

Makes 2 cocktails
Sweetness ✦ ✧ ✧
Fruity, Tart, Toasted

Carbonating a clarified cocktail makes for a one-of-a kind drink, impossible to replicate with store-bought ingredients. Wow guests with this classy cocktail. Tart, fresh Granny Smith apples are our choice for clarified apple juice that has sweet-tart green-apple bite. We add a bit of Scotch for malty background notes that add complexity to the fresh apple flavor, and neutral vodka to prevent the spirits from overwhelming the drink. This drink looks a lot like Champagne and, surprisingly, tastes like it too, but with a hint of fresh apple, and nutty notes on the finish. This recipe yields enough clarified apple juice to make 8 cocktails. For information on making fresh apple juice, see page 12. Do not attempt to make this cocktail without clarified juice. We developed this cocktail using a 16-ounce cream whipper and two CO_2 cartridges. This recipe can be doubled using a 1-quart cream whipper; you may need to adjust the number of CO_2 cartridges to achieve the proper level of carbonation.

Clarified Granny Smith Apple Juice

- 4 ounces water
- ½ teaspoon agar-agar powder
- 16 ounces fresh Granny Smith apple juice

Cocktails

- 3 ounces clarified Granny Smith apple juice
- 3 ounces vodka
- 3 ounces water, chilled

1 ounce Scotch
½ ounce lemon juice
1 teaspoon Simple Syrup (page 458)
Fresh Granny Smith apple slices for garnishing

1. For the clarified apple juice: Fill large bowl halfway with ice and water. Whisk water and agar-agar together in small saucepan. Bring to boil over medium-high heat, stirring constantly. Cover, reduce heat to medium-low, and simmer for 2 minutes. Off heat, whisk in apple juice. Transfer juice mixture to medium bowl and set bowl over prepared ice water bath. Place ice bath with juice mixture in refrigerator and let sit, without disturbing, until gel sets, about 30 minutes.

2. Using whisk, gently break up gel into pea-size pieces. Line fine-mesh strainer with triple layer of cheesecloth and place over large bowl or container. Transfer curds to prepared strainer and let drain for at least 30 minutes or overnight. (You will have at least 4 ounces clarified juice after 30 minutes and up to 12 ounces after 12 hours; clarified juice can be refrigerated in airtight container for up to 2 days or frozen for up to 1 month.) Discard solids.

3. For the cocktails: Combine apple juice, vodka, water, Scotch, lemon juice, and simple syrup in base of cream whipper and chill in freezer until very cold, about 30 minutes, stirring halfway through chilling.

4. Screw cap on cream whipper and charge with 1 CO_2 cartridge. Shake cream whipper for 20 seconds. With nozzle facing up, cover nozzle with paper towel (to catch any small amount of spray) and very slowly vent cream whipper completely. Charge with 1 more CO_2 cartridge and shake cream whipper for 20 seconds. Let cream whipper sit for 5 minutes. With nozzle facing up, cover nozzle with paper towel (to catch any small amount of spray) and very slowly vent cream whipper completely.

5. Unscrew cap and gently pour cocktail into 2 chilled cocktail glasses. Garnish with apple slices and serve.

PAIR WITH A SNACK

Parmesan-Pepper Popcorn

Serves 14 (makes 14 cups)
Total Time: 20 minutes

You'll be planning cocktail parties just to eat this lively, salty, buttery, no-kernel-left-unpopped popcorn next to your drink. The key to perfectly popped stovetop popcorn is to heat three test kernels with vegetable oil in a saucepan until the kernels pop—that means the oil is hot enough. Adding the rest of the kernels off the burner and letting them sit for 30 seconds ensures that all of the kernels heat up evenly. After that, it takes just a few minutes over medium-high heat with the lid slightly ajar for all the corn to pop. The kernels all pop at the same rate—no shaking required.

3 tablespoons vegetable oil
½ cup popcorn kernels
2 tablespoons unsalted butter, melted
1 ounce Parmesan cheese, grated (½ cup)
½ teaspoon pepper
¼ teaspoon table salt

1. Heat oil and 3 popcorn kernels in large saucepan over medium-high heat until kernels pop. Remove pan from heat, add remaining kernels, cover, and let sit for 30 seconds.

2. Return pan to medium-high heat. Continue to cook with lid slightly ajar until popping slows to about 2 seconds between pops. Transfer popcorn to large bowl. Add melted butter and toss to coat. Combine Parmesan, pepper, and salt in bowl. Add to popcorn and toss to combine. Serve.

Sparkling Celery

Makes 2 zero-proof cocktails
Sweetness ✦ ✦ ✧
Spiced, Tart

This sparkling nonalcoholic cocktail is an inspired twist on the beloved Dr. Brown's Cel-Ray soda, which became a mainstay of New York City Jewish delis after being developed in Brooklyn in the late 1800s. While Dr. Brown's version originally used celery seeds for flavor, we use fresh celery stalks, juiced and clarified for a crystal-clear, pale green liquid full of flavor. To sweeten our fizzy beverage, we add an intensely flavored cardamom syrup, a surprisingly compatible pairing that calls you to keep sipping. This recipe yields enough clarified celery juice to make 4 cocktails. For information on making fresh celery juice, see page 12. Do not attempt to make this cocktail without clarified juice. We developed this cocktail using a 16-ounce cream whipper and two CO_2 cartridges. This recipe can be doubled using a 1-quart cream whipper; you may need to adjust the number of CO_2 cartridges to achieve the proper level of carbonation.

Clarified Celery Juice

- 16 ounces fresh celery juice
- 1 tablespoon lemon juice
- 4 ounces water
- ½ teaspoon agar-agar powder

Cocktails

- 6 ounces clarified celery juice
- 4 ounces water, chilled
- 1 ounce Spice Syrup with cardamom (page 459)
- ½ ounce lemon juice
- Celery leaves for garnishing

1. For the clarified celery juice: Fill large bowl halfway with ice and water. Combine celery juice and lemon juice in liquid measuring cup. Whisk water and agar-agar together in small saucepan. Bring to boil over medium-high heat, stirring constantly. Cover, reduce heat to medium-low, and simmer for 2 minutes. Off heat, whisk in celery juice mixture. Transfer juice mixture to medium bowl and set bowl over prepared ice water bath. Place ice bath with juice mixture in refrigerator and let sit, without disturbing, until gel sets, about 30 minutes.

2. Using whisk, gently break up gel into pea-size pieces. Line fine-mesh strainer with triple layer of cheesecloth and place over large bowl or container. Transfer curds to prepared strainer and let drain for at least 45 minutes or overnight. (You will have at least 6 ounces clarified juice after 45 minutes and up to 12 ounces after 12 hours; clarified juice can be refrigerated in airtight container for up to 2 days or frozen for up to 1 month.) Discard solids.

3. For the cocktails: Combine celery juice, water, spice syrup, and lemon juice in base of cream whipper and chill in freezer until very cold, about 30 minutes, stirring halfway through chilling.

4. Screw cap on cream whipper and charge with 1 CO_2 cartridge. Shake cream whipper for 20 seconds. With nozzle facing up, cover nozzle with paper towel (to catch any small amount of spray) and very slowly vent cream whipper completely. Charge with 1 more CO_2 cartridge and shake cream whipper for 20 seconds. Let cream whipper sit for 5 minutes. With nozzle facing up, cover nozzle with paper towel (to catch any small amount of spray) and very slowly vent cream whipper completely.

5. Unscrew cap and gently pour cocktail into 2 chilled highball glasses filled with ice. Garnish with celery leaves and serve.

Customize Your Cocktail

You can experiment with any flavored syrup (pages 458–459) in place of the Spice Syrup with cardamom.

Citrus Milk Punch

Makes 8 cocktails
Sweetness ✦ ✦ ✧
Citrusy, Creamy, Floral

Party like it's 1711 with this historical clarified cocktail. It's based on the oldest known written recipe for milk punch, attributed to a British woman named Mary Rockett. We found it in cocktail historian David Wondrich's book *Punch*. The original features a simple combination of brandy, lemon zest and juice, sugar, and water and is clarified with scalded milk. Our adaptations to Rockett's original recipe are few: We use cold milk in place of hot, add orange peel and orange juice to the lemon for a more complex citrus flavor, and scale it down to make an appropriate 1 quart. (The original makes about twelve 750-milliliter bottles!) The finished drink, served chilled from the freezer, is bright and clean with limoncello-like lemon (and orange) intensity, and the whey that remains after clarification provides velvety body. Take wide, shallow swipes of zest with a vegetable peeler, trying your best to avoid any of the unpleasantly bitter white pith that sits just below. As the brandy-milk mixture drains, don't push or press the liquid through the filter—let it slowly drain through and you'll get the clearest punch possible. You can store the cocktail in a 1-quart Mason jar instead of a bottle.

- 8 ounces brandy
- 6 (3-inch) strips lemon zest plus 2 ounces juice
- 6 (3-inch) strips orange zest plus 2 ounces juice
- 8 ounces whole milk
- 8 ounces warm water
- 3 tablespoons sugar

1. Combine brandy, lemon zest, and orange zest in 4-cup liquid measuring cup. Cover and let sit until flavors meld, at least 12 hours or up to 2 days; discard zest.

2. Place milk in separate 4-cup liquid measuring cup. Stir warm water and sugar into brandy mixture until sugar has dissolved, then stir in lemon juice and orange juice. Pour brandy mixture into milk. Gently stir curds with small spoon and let sit for 30 minutes.

3. Gently pour brandy-milk mixture through fine-mesh strainer set over clean large bowl. Return mixture to now-empty measuring cup; discard solids. Line strainer with paper coffee filter and set over now-empty bowl. Gently pour mixture into prepared strainer and let drain without disturbing, about 1 hour; discard curds. Transfer clarified punch to 1-liter glass bottle. Cover and freeze until well chilled, about 2 hours. Prepare cocktails immediately or transfer to refrigerator and store for up to 1 month; return to freezer and chill for 30 minutes before preparing cocktails.

4. Gently shake punch to recombine, then serve cocktails in chilled punch glasses.

Black Tea–Port Milk Punch

Makes 8 cocktails
Sweetness ✦✦✧
Floral, Toasted, Tropical

- 8 ounces whole milk
- 8 ounces boiling water
- 1 teaspoon black tea leaves
- 3 tablespoons sugar
- 6 ounces ruby port
- 4 ounces Batavia arrack
- 2 ounces lemon juice

This recipe is adapted from ruby punch, a recipe in Jerry Thomas's *How to Mix Drinks, or The Bon Vivant's Companion* from 1862 (but can trace back even further). It features a seriously tasty combination of black tea, ruby port, lemon, and the Indonesian spirit Batavia arrack, which is distilled from both sugarcane and Javanese rice. In its original form (not clarified with milk), the tannins from the black tea and port provide grip and add texture, not to mention deep, inky color. After the drink is clarified with milk, it is full bodied but silky smooth, with a rosé-like color and fruitiness. We prefer the higher quality of loose-leaf tea here; however, a tea bag can be substituted. Remove tea bag from water before adding sugar in step 1. We prefer the nuanced flavor of Batavia arrack in this punch, but aged rum can be substituted. As the tea-milk mixture drains, don't push or press the liquid through the filter—let it slowly drain through and you'll get the clearest punch possible. You can store the cocktail in a 1-quart Mason jar instead of a bottle.

1. Place milk in 4-cup liquid measuring cup. Add boiling water and tea to large bowl and let steep for 4 minutes. Stir in sugar until dissolved, then stir in port, Batavia arrack, and lemon juice. Pour tea mixture into milk. Gently stir curds with small spoon and let sit for 30 minutes.

2. Gently pour tea-milk mixture through fine-mesh strainer set over clean large bowl. Return mixture to now-empty measuring cup; discard solids. Line strainer with paper coffee filter and set over now-empty bowl. Gently pour mixture into prepared strainer and let drain without disturbing, about 1 hour. Transfer clarified punch to 1-liter glass bottle. Cover and freeze until well chilled, about 2 hours. Prepare cocktails immediately or transfer to refrigerator and store for up to 1 month; return to freezer and chill for 30 minutes before preparing cocktails.

3. Gently shake punch to recombine, then serve cocktails in chilled punch glasses.

Infused *and* Fat Washed

Infusing isn't a technique that is particular to cocktails: It's simply the process of extracting flavor from a solid ingredient into a liquid by steeping. When you make tea, you're making an infusion. If you have vanilla extract in your cupboard, you're using an infusion in your cooking. And if you have, say, a bottle of amaretto in your bar cabinet, then you are already working with infused spirits.

The advantage of practicing this technique at home is that it opens up a world of flavor possibilities—including flavors that you may not be able to find in a store or, if you can, that might not taste as good as what you can make yourself. You can also infuse smaller batches of spirits than what you might find on store shelves. Infusing spirits—or finished cocktails—is a fun DIY cocktail project (and homemade infused spirits make extremely popular gifts).

There are a number of ways to make infused cocktails. You can infuse a spirit with a fresh ingredient and use that to make an updated riff on a classic cocktail, as we do in our Makrut Gin and Tonic (page 303), which incorporates makrut lime leaf–infused gin, or the English 75 (page 313), which uses cucumber-infused gin. You can also make an entire cocktail and then let it rest for a while to infuse fresh flavors into it, as with our Strawberry Negroni (page 316). You can even "infuse" a cocktail with smoke using a handheld smoking gun, adding a dramatic smoky flourish in seconds.

One style of infusing that deserves special attention is fat washing. Though bartenders had already been experimenting with it, fat washing started to take off around 2007, when Don Lee, a bartender at the speakeasy-style bar Please Don't Tell (PDT) in Manhattan's East Village, created the Benton's Old-Fashioned, a cocktail that made use of a clever trick of chemistry to saturate whiskey with the flavor of Tennessee country bacon. Bartenders at PDT steeped bacon fat in the whiskey, allowing its flavors to migrate to the alcohol. When the fat was strained off, it left behind a beautifully flavored booze. They called the technique fat washing, and it quickly took off in upscale cocktail bars everywhere as bartenders worked with different combinations of spirits and fats.

Luckily for the home bartender, infusing spirits and cocktails with fresh ingredients and washing them with fats is easy. We explain the techniques and offer plenty of inspiration for getting started—both with these recipes and with your own experimenting.

Infused and Fat Washed

What Is an Infusion?

Infusion describes the process of extracting flavor from a solid ingredient into a liquid ingredient through steeping. The resulting liquid is also known as an infusion. Brewed coffee and flavored vinegars are everyday examples of infusions. In the cocktail world, ingredients such as bitters or lemon vodka are examples of common infusions. But with our techniques, you can infuse spirits with everything from jalapeños to peanut butter.

HOW IS AN INFUSION DIFFERENT FROM A LIQUEUR?

Many liqueurs have a base of ingredients infused into alcohol, sometimes with oils and flavor extracts added as well in order to increase their intensity. Typically a liqueur will also be sweetened so it can be sipped on its own. An infusion, by contrast, is generally unsweetened, just spirit and flavoring, and is typically used as an ingredient in a drink rather than sipped, although any spirit that you enjoy sipping can be infused. If you're partial to sipping bourbon, we think you'll *really* enjoy browned butter–washed bourbon (see page 300), both in our Browned Butter and Maple Old-Fashioned (page 305) and on its own.

Why Infuse?

Flavored spirits have proliferated in recent years, taking up more and more space on store shelves and backbars. Their quality varies wildly. By infusing spirits at home, you can both control the quality of the ingredients and greatly expand your flavor options. Spirits infused with perfectly ripe, seasonal produce such as strawberries or watermelon, or washed with fats such as coconut oil or tahini, will add depth to your home bar, allowing you to be able to make unique, delicious cocktails.

What Can You Infuse?

Fruits, vegetables, herbs, spices, and fats are the ingredients most commonly infused into alcohol. Pretty much any fruit can be used, although we found that some fruits (such as plums, peaches, blueberries, and blackberries) imparted very subtle flavor. At the other end of the flavor intensity spectrum, you can even infuse with Parmesan rinds—which we tried but were not compelled to retry. Infusing alcohol with spices and herbs is done differently, using a process that creates a tincture (see page 464). Here we focus on infusing using fruits, vegetables, and fats.

What Happens When You Fat-Wash?

Fat washing is a type of infusion in which the characteristics of a flavorful fat migrate into a spirit. Our testing results were smashingly successful. The technique differs slightly from other infusions.

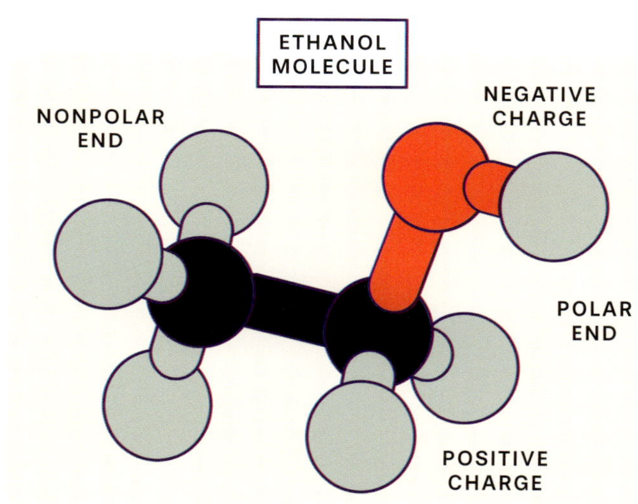

Here's the basic science: A liquid in which other substances can dissolve is called a solvent. Solvents can be grouped into polar solvents (which have molecules with positive and negative charges) and nonpolar solvents (which have uncharged molecules). Water is the classic example of a polar solvent. Oil is a nonpolar solvent.

Polar solvents are able to dissolve polar substances, and nonpolar solvents are able to dissolve nonpolar substances. Many flavor compounds are nonpolar, which means they dissolve nicely in fatty foods but not in water. The smoky, porky compounds in bacon are an example: They're nonpolar, and in a strip of bacon they exist dissolved in the fat.

Ethyl alcohol (the kind we drink) is a special solvent, because an ethanol molecule has a polar part and a nonpolar part. This gives alcohol the ability to dissolve fat-soluble flavor compounds and integrate them into a drink. The alcohol extracts the pure taste of the fat without adding any of the actual fat itself. For example, commercially available coconut-flavored rums often have artificial flavors, whereas infusing rum with unrefined coconut oil adds a clean expression of coconut. We use this rum in our Island Hopper (page 306), which has the flavors of a piña colada but is lighter and fresher.

Imagine this scenario: You take a sip of a drink and a familiar flavor fills your mouth. You've tasted this flavor many times before, but something's different; you've never tasted it in a clear drink. What is it? Then it comes to you: peanut butter! With fat washing, you can add flavors to cocktails that you simply can't find anywhere else and enjoy those strong flavors in a form you likely haven't experienced before. Try peanut butter–washed bourbon in our PBJ (page 306).

Using Fat-Washed Spirits

The act of fat-washing softens some of the harsher edges of spirits and makes them taste smoother. There is a slight change in texture, with fat-washed spirits having a slightly fuller, richer mouthfeel. To highlight these qualities, we had great success using fat-washed spirits in stirred, spirit-forward drinks—like martinis, Manhattans, and old-fashioneds—where we knew the fat-washed spirit would really shine. We found that with many assertive sour-type cocktails (think daiquiri), the interplay of sweetness and acidity could easily overwhelm the subtleties of the fat-washed spirit. To compensate in our Island Hopper sour-type cocktail (page 306), we adjusted the ratios, using only ¼ ounce lime juice and ¼ ounce simple syrup, whereas a conventional sour formula would use ¾ ounce of each.

Infusing and Fat-Washing Cocktails

We also had great success both infusing and fat-washing entire cocktails. The length of time for infusing entire cocktails depends on the ingredient you're using to infuse. For our Strawberry Negroni (page 316), we let quartered strawberries sit in the mixed cocktail for 3 days to infuse with the delicate fruit flavor, whereas the Bloody Marys (pages 318–323), which have much stronger flavoring ingredients, were infused for only 1 day.

Fat-washing entire cocktails is straightforward, and almost any cocktail in our Martini or Manhattan chapters (page 151 or 177) will work well. Try a Vieux Carré (page 196) washed with butter, for example. Simply add the ingredients for your desired cocktail to a Mason jar, scaling them up to achieve 10 ounces of liquid. Then, add your fat of choice in the amount listed in the chart on page 300 and follow the instructions for making a fat-washed spirit. After straining and transferring the cocktail to a storage jar, you can stir individual drinks with ice as you normally would when ready to serve.

Infused and Fat Washed

How to Infuse Spirits

Bartenders take advantage of various methods to infuse, including the use of a sous vide machine and rapid infusions using whipped cream dispensers to create a pressurized environment. These do give a slightly more pronounced flavor, but for the home bartender we felt the amount of extra effort involved wasn't efficient. We found the simplest and most accessible method to be placing a solid in a spirit and letting it steep for a specified amount of time. We also found that infusing for longer than our specified amounts actually reduced the fresh flavor of the final product. Use the charts opposite as a guide to our favorite flavor pairings.

To make about 8 ounces infused spirit:

1. Combine 9 ounces of spirit with solid of your choice in 16-ounce Mason jar.

2. Let sit in cool, dark place for specified amount of infusion time.

3. Strain mixture through fine-mesh strainer set over bowl, then transfer infused spirit to clean 16-ounce Mason jar.

4. Refrigerate infused liquor for up to 3 months. (Liquor will keep indefinitely, but flavor will start to diminish.)

Fruit	Prepped	Amount	Infusion Time	Recommended Spirits (9 oz)
Apple	½-inch pieces	1	3 to 5 days	Vodka, any whiskey
Banana	½-inch-thick slices	1	3 to 5 days	Vodka, white rum
Citrus (lemon, lime, grapefruit, any orange variety)	2-inch strips zest (with as little pith as possible)	½ oz (eight 3-inch strips)	3 to 5 days	Vodka, gin
Makrut lime leaves	½-inch pieces	10 leaves	3 to 5 days	Vodka, gin, white rum
Melon (cantaloupe or honeydew)	½-inch pieces	6 oz (1½ cups)	3 to 5 days	Vodka, white rum, soju
Pear	½-inch pieces	1	3 to 5 days	Vodka, any whiskey
Pineapple	½-inch pieces	5 oz (1 cup)	3 to 5 days	Vodka, white rum, blanco tequila
Strawberry	Hulled and halved	5 oz (1 cup)	3 to 5 days	Vodka, gin
Watermelon	½-inch pieces	6 oz (½ cups)	3 to 5 days	Vodka, white rum

Vegetable	Prepped	Amount	Infusion Time	Recommended Spirits (9 oz)
Bell pepper (any color)	Stemmed, seeded, and chopped	1	3 to 5 days	Vodka, gin
Chile (Fresno or jalapeño)	Stemmed, seeded, and sliced thin	1	1 to 2 days	Vodka, gin, white rum, blanco tequila
English cucumber	Sliced thin	½ (8 oz)	3 to 5 days	Vodka, gin
Fennel	Trimmed and sliced thin	½ (5 oz)	3 to 5 days	Vodka, gin
Lemongrass	Trimmed and sliced thin	1 stalk	3 to 5 days	Vodka, gin, white rum

How to Fat-Wash Spirits

To make about 8 ounces fat-washed spirit:

1. Combine spirit and fat of your choice in 16-ounce Mason jar as follows:

For liquid fats: Combine 10 ounces spirit and fat in jar.

For solid fats: Add 10 ounces spirit to jar. Melt fat in 8-inch skillet over medium-low heat until liquefied, then pour it into jar.

For paste fats: Smear inside of bottom half of jar with paste. Add 10 ounces spirit.

2. Seal jar tightly and swirl gently. Avoid shaking mixture, which could cause it to emulsify and prevent it from properly straining.

3. Lay jar on its side (for liquid and melted solid fats) or stand it upright (for paste fats) and let sit for at least 12 hours or up to 24 hours, gently swirling jar occasionally. (Positioning jar on its side increases surface area of fat's contact with spirit.)

4. Transfer jar to freezer and freeze in same position until fat solidifies, 1 to 3 hours. (If jar is frozen upright for liquid fats, a solid layer will form at top of jar, making it difficult to pour out spirit.)

5. Set paper coffee filter in fine-mesh strainer set over bowl. Strain mixture, then transfer spirit to clean 16-ounce Mason jar.

6. Refrigerate fat-washed liquor for up to 3 months. (Liquor will keep indefinitely, but flavor will start to diminish.)

Fat	State at Room Temp	Amount	Recommended Spirits (10 oz)
Extra-virgin olive oil	Liquid	3 oz	Vodka, gin
Toasted sesame oil	Liquid	½ oz	Vodka, white rum, soju
Unrefined coconut oil	Solid	3 oz	Any rum
Rendered bacon fat	Solid	2 oz	Any whiskey
Unsalted butter	Solid	3 oz	Any whiskey, tequila, brandy, aged rum
Browned butter *	Solid	3 oz	Any whiskey or rum, brandy
Rendered chicken or duck fat	Solid	2 oz	Vodka, gin, brandy
Tahini	Paste	3 oz	Vodka
Peanut butter	Paste	3 oz	Any whiskey

Bonus: Infused Fat

Fat washing also transfers flavor in the other direction: from the spirit to the fat. Leftover butter or peanut butter from fat washing is a delicious way to flavor frostings or use in baking—or anything you use butter or peanut butter for. You can also use leftover oils, such as olive oil or sesame oil, in savory cooking. Try using leftover bacon fat to make cornbread or biscuits.

Smoked Cocktails

Imagine dramatically presenting a guest with a freshly made cocktail that has a little cloud of smoke rolling off it. This is not technically an infusion of smoke, since the drink will have only a surface hit of smokiness rather than being infused all the way through. Think of this as a smoke garnish. Smoke particles will cling to the surface of the cocktail and the interior of the glass, adding a distinct smoky aroma and the impression of an infusion. The process is analogous to expressing the oils from a strip of orange peel over an old-fashioned. When you take a sip, you'll get the distinct aroma of orange, but the drink itself does not contain orange.

We like the Breville/PolyScience Smoking Gun Pro for smoking cocktails at home; it's stable and easy to clean, and allows for precise control of the fan speed. The lighter-weight (and lower-priced) Breville Smoking Gun is also a good option. We developed our recipes using hickory and applewood as smoking materials, but you can experiment with other types of wood chips.

HOW TO ADD SMOKE TO A COCKTAIL

1. Use glass that will have good headspace after adding cocktail, such as rocks glass. Place small saucer or lid over glass after adding cocktail.

2. Following manufacturer's instructions, turn on portable smoke infuser and ignite desired smoking material.

3. Once smoke begins exiting hose, partially lift saucer, place tip of hose in opening, and fill glass with smoke.

4. Quickly remove hose and replace saucer. Turn off smoker and extinguish smoking material. Wait 15 seconds, then remove saucer and serve immediately.

***To Make Browned Butter**
Melt 6 tablespoons unsalted butter in 8-inch skillet over medium-high heat. Cook, swirling skillet and stirring constantly with silicone spatula, until butter is dark golden brown and has a nutty aroma, 1 to 3 minutes. Transfer to bowl and let cool slightly.

Makrut Gin and Tonic

Makrut Gin and Tonic

Makes 1 cocktail
Sweetness ✦ ✧ ✧
Citrusy, Herbal, Tart

Throughout the gin and tonic's long history, bartenders have sought to perfect it, tinkering with ingredient ratios, tonic choices, and styles of gin. One perennial question: Garnish with lemon or lime? We come down firmly on lime's side in our Gin and Tonic (page 95). And in this evolved G&T, we extract flavor from makrut lime leaves, specifically. We infuse gin with the leaves, and their complex flavor provides herbal, intense, and mouth-puckering tang. The garnish? Of course more makrut lime leaves. We think it has the makings of a modern classic. We prefer to make our own tonic water using our homemade Tonic Syrup (page 92); however, you can substitute 6 ounces store-bought tonic water for the tonic syrup and seltzer.

- 2 ounces Makrut Lime–Infused Gin (page 298)
- 1 ounce tonic syrup
- 1 teaspoon lime juice, plus lime wedge for garnishing
- 1 teaspoon Simple Syrup (page 458)
- 5 ounces seltzer, chilled
- Makrut lime leaves for garnishing

Fill chilled highball glass halfway with ice. Add gin, tonic syrup, lime juice, and simple syrup and stir to combine using bar spoon. Add seltzer and, using spoon, gently lift gin mixture from bottom of glass to top to combine. Top with additional ice and garnish with lime wedge and lime leaves. Serve.

Melon Dollar Martini

Makes 1 cocktail
Sweetness ✦ ✧ ✧
Floral, Fruity, Spirit Forward

During our deep dive into infused spirits, we experimented with more than 30 different fruits, vegetables, herbs, spices, and other foods—some with more success than others (let's just say that Parmesan vodka and oyster gin won't be making a comeback). We love all of our infused spirits, but one might stand out above the rest: cantaloupe-infused vodka. Even when using out-of-season, underripe fruit, the result is astonishing: pure, sweet, peak-season melon flavor in liquid form. With such a stellar base, we knew simplicity in the cocktail build was key. To subtly sweeten the cocktail, a touch of orange liqueur is an ideal choice. Its delicate citrus aroma enhances the vodka's melon essence, making each sip taste even fresher.

- 2½ ounces Melon-Infused Vodka with cantaloupe (page 298)
- ¾ teaspoon orange liqueur
- Honeydew or cantaloupe balls for garnishing

Add vodka and orange liqueur to mixing glass, then fill three-quarters full with ice. Using bar spoon, stir until mixture is fully combined and well chilled, about 1 minute. Strain cocktail into chilled cocktail glass. Garnish with melon balls and serve.

Fat-Washed Cocktails

These recipes are drawn from various cocktail families, including old-fashioneds, martinis, and sours. What unites them is their use of fat-washed spirits as the base spirit for each cocktail.

The Browned Butter and Maple Old-Fashioned and the PBJ take bourbon as their base spirit. The first is a classic old-fashioned formula, adding sweetener in the form of maple syrup, plus bitters and ice. The second is our playful but highly elevated take on a beloved flavor combination, combining peanut butter–washed bourbon with a berry liqueur (such as Chambord; or go totally DIY and make our homemade Fruits of the Forest Liqueur on page 466 to use in the drink).

The Island Hopper uses rum washed with coconut oil; the unrefined oil is simply fresh coconut meat pressed to extract its fat, so it has plenty of pure, strong flavor and aroma to add to the rum. This cocktail is based on a sour formula but modifies it a bit by reducing the amount of citrus juice so that the subtlety of the washed spirit still comes through.

Our Olive Oil Martini uses vodka, which we find is an ideal spirit for highlighting the delicate flavors and enhanced richness of texture that emerge when a spirit is washed with olive oil. You could certainly wash gin with olive oil to use instead, if you've got both feet firmly in the gin martini camp. Any extra-virgin olive oil will work, so use your favorite or choose one that has flavors you want to highlight in the infused spirit (grassy or peppery or fruity, for example).

Last but not least, Maizey Days makes the most of butter-washed tequila by pairing it with a Mexican roasted corn liqueur and dark chile liqueur. Washing the tequila with butter enhances its savoriness, the corn liqueur brings a buttery caramel-popcorn flavor, and the chile liqueur adds some brooding spice for a showstoppingly flavorful cocktail.

Browned Butter and Maple Old-Fashioned

Makes 1 cocktail

Sweetness ✦✦✧

Creamy, Spirit Forward, Toasted

- 2 ounces Browned Butter–Washed Bourbon (page 300)
- 1 teaspoon maple syrup
- ⅛ teaspoon old-fashioned aromatic bitters
- Cocktail cherries for garnishing

Add bourbon, maple syrup, and bitters to mixing glass, then fill three-quarters full with ice. Using bar spoon, stir until mixture is just combined and chilled, about 30 seconds. Strain cocktail into chilled rocks glass half-filled with ice or containing 1 large ice cube. Garnish with cocktail cherries and serve.

Customize Your Cocktail

Browned butter–washed rum, brandy, or other whiskeys work here.

PBJ

Makes 1 cocktail
Sweetness ✦ ✦ ✧
Fruity, Nutty, Spirit Forward

A peanut butter and jelly sandwich might not be the first thing that comes to mind when you're crafting an adult beverage, but that's where this cocktail finds its inspiration. It's a must-make destination for our Peanut Butter–Washed Bourbon (page 300), which delivers astonishing depth of flavor—the nuttiness lingers on the palate, as if you'd just taken a big spoonful of peanut butter. For the jelly, we pass on jam and jam syrups, whose flavors struggle to come through. Intense, concentrated berry liqueur, plus a freeze-dried berry rim, brings the cocktail to life. We developed this recipe with Chambord, but other varieties of berry liqueur can be used.

- ¼ cup finely ground freeze-dried berries (optional)
- 2 ounces Peanut Butter–Washed Bourbon (page 300)
- ¼ ounce berry liqueur
- 1 teaspoon Simple Syrup (page 458)

1. Spread ground berries, if using, into even layer on small saucer. Moisten about ½ inch of chilled rocks glass rim by dipping edge of glass in separate small saucer of water. Roll moistened rim in berries to coat. Remove any excess granules that fall into glass. (Leftover ground berries can be stored in airtight container for up to 1 month.)

2. Add bourbon, berry liqueur, and simple syrup to mixing glass, then fill three-quarters full with ice. Using bar spoon, stir until mixture is just combined and chilled, about 30 seconds. Strain cocktail into prepared glass half-filled with ice or containing 1 large ice cube. Serve.

Island Hopper

Makes 1 cocktail
Sweetness ✦ ✧ ✧
Citrusy, Toasted, Tropical

Our coconut oil–washed rum has strikingly pure, precise coconut aroma. It's completely different from artificial-tasting store-bought coconut rum. The Piña Colada (page 428) is the go-to rum-and-coconut cocktail, but we wanted something less rich to really highlight our special coconut-washed rum. Pineapple juice provides the tropical notes, while just a touch of lime juice and simple syrup balances the flavors without overshadowing the delicate coconut. The result? A cocktail with the bright crispness of a daiquiri and the tropical allure of a piña colada. You can also garnish the cocktail with toasted coconut if desired.

- 2 ounces Coconut Oil–Washed Rum (page 300)
- 1 ounce unsweetened 100 percent pineapple juice
- ¼ ounce lime juice, plus lime slice for garnishing
- ¼ ounce Simple Syrup (page 458)

Add rum, pineapple juice, lime juice, and simple syrup to cocktail shaker and shake until combined, about 5 seconds. Pour cocktail into chilled rocks glass half-filled with crushed ice. Top with additional ice and garnish with lime slice. Serve.

Customize Your Cocktail

For some nuttiness, you can substitute orgeat for the simple syrup.

Olive Oil Martini

Makes 1 cocktail
Sweetness ✧ ✧ ✧
Fruity, Savory, Spirit Forward

If you're a martini enthusiast, you might prefer one either zippy and fragrant from the expressed oils of a lemon peel, or deeply savory from a green olive (or three) garnish. This cocktail is for the latter camp. Of course, you can always ratchet up the olive flavor with a dose of funky, salty olive brine in a dirty martini. But olive oil–washing your spirit gives you something even more special. The fresh grassiness of good olive oil lifts the dry, earthy flavors of the vermouth and the vodka's alcoholic strength without a domineering hit of salt. You get an incredibly singular expression of olive, one that is completely clean and precise.

- **2 ounces Olive Oil–Washed Vodka (page 300)**
- **½ ounce dry vermouth**
- **Brine-cured green olives for garnishing**

Add vodka and vermouth to mixing glass, then fill three-quarters full with ice. Using bar spoon, stir until mixture is fully combined and well chilled, about 1 minute. Strain cocktail into chilled cocktail glass. Garnish with olives and serve.

Customize Your Cocktail

Olive oil–washed gin also works here. To make a drier martini, reduce the vermouth to ¼ ounce; to make a wetter martini, increase it to ¾ ounce.

Maizey Days

Makes 1 cocktail
Sweetness ✦ ✧ ✧
Creamy, Spicy, Spirit Forward

A bold and unexpected fusion, the Maizey Days is unabashedly inspired by elote, Mexican street corn. The silky butter-washed tequila base combined with warm ancho chile liqueur, roasty-toasty corn liqueur, and a lime garnish really hits all the right flavor notes. It's a dynamic drinking experience: The first sip is luxuriously rich, and it's followed by slow-building heat and a lingering interplay of corn and lime. Nixta Licor de Elote contributes a unique roasted corn flavor to this cocktail; we also utilize it in the Arroyo (page 173). You can use our homemade Ancho Chile Liqueur (page 468) or store-bought ancho liqueur in this recipe.

- **2 ounces Butter-Washed Tequila (page 300)**
- **¾ ounce Nixta Licor de Elote**
- **¼ ounce ancho chile liqueur**
- **Strip of lime peel for garnishing**

Add tequila, Nixta Licor de Elote, and chile liqueur to mixing glass, then fill three-quarters full with ice. Using bar spoon, stir until mixture is just combined and chilled, about 30 seconds. Strain cocktail into chilled rocks glass half-filled with ice or containing 1 large ice cube. Pinch lime peel over drink and rub outer edge of glass with peel, then garnish with lime peel. Serve.

From left to lower right: Maizey Days, Olive Oil Martini, Island Hopper, PBJ

PAIR WITH A SNACK

Smoked Salmon Crisps

Makes 16 crisps
Total Time: 10 minutes

A dollop of crème fraîche, the briny pop of capers, and a garnish of tender chives elevate this simple smoked salmon nosh into something quite special. You can try dill or tarragon in place of the chives and sour cream instead of crème fraîche. Our preference is for kettle-style potato chips, which tend to be sturdier, to hold the salmon, but you can use your favorite chip.

- 16 large potato chips
- 4 ounces smoked salmon, cut into 16 pieces
- 2 tablespoons crème fraîche
- 16 capers, patted dry
- 1 tablespoon minced fresh chives

Top each chip with piece of salmon, then dollop with crème fraîche and top with caper and light sprinkle of chives. Arrange crisps on serving platter. Serve immediately.

Smoked and Improved Brandy Cocktail

Makes 1 cocktail
Sweetness ✦✦✧
Herbal, Smoky, Toasted

In the late 19th century, cocktails were often very simple—usually just a base spirit, a bit of water, sugar, and perhaps some bitters, the foundation of what we now call the old-fashioned. Then came the improved cocktail, a step forward in complexity; it introduced small quantities of ingredients like absinthe and maraschino liqueur to enhance depth and provide balance. Here, we evolve further—improving an improved cocktail with the transformative power of smoke. This aromatic garnish doesn't just enhance the presentation; it adds an elusive depth of flavor that liquid ingredients alone can't achieve, creating a multisensory experience that lingers long after each sip. Other dry anise-flavored spirits (such as Herbsaint, pastis, or dry anisette) can be substituted for the absinthe. The use of a portable smoker adds another layer of flavor to this cocktail, but you can also enjoy it without smoke, if desired. We developed this recipe using hickory and applewood as our smoking materials, but feel free to experiment with other varieties of wood shavings.

- 2 ounces brandy
- 1 teaspoon maraschino liqueur
- 1 teaspoon Simple Syrup (page 458)
- ⅛ teaspoon absinthe
- ⅛ teaspoon old-fashioned aromatic bitters
- Orange twist for garnishing

1. Add brandy, maraschino liqueur, simple syrup, absinthe, and bitters to mixing glass, then fill three-quarters full with ice. Using bar spoon, stir until mixture is just combined and well chilled, about 1 minute. Strain cocktail into chilled rocks glass.

2. To smoke cocktail, place small saucer or lid over glass. Following manufacturer's instructions, turn on portable smoke infuser and ignite desired smoking material. Once smoke begins exiting hose, partially lift saucer, place tip of hose in opening, and fill glass with smoke. Quickly remove hose and replace saucer. Turn off smoker and extinguish smoking material. Let smoke infuse cocktail for 15 seconds, then remove saucer. Garnish with orange twist and serve.

Customize Your Cocktail

You can use whiskey or rum in place of the brandy.

Smoked New York Sour

Makes 1 cocktail
Sweetness ✦ ✧ ✧
Fruity, Smoky, Tart

As this book's structure has taught, cocktails have families, and little changes—riffs, as you might hear a bartender say—beget entirely new cocktails. The New York sour is a prime example; it's simply a whiskey sour transformed by the addition of a red wine float. This seemingly minor change reshapes the drink—the wine's tannins intertwine with the whiskey and citrus, adding unexpected body to the cocktail and steering the flavor away from the familiar sweet-tart balance of a classic sour. Here, we introduce smoke to complement the spice of the rye, and this additional step leads to yet another new drinking experience. Use a medium-bodied wine, such as a Côtes du Rhône or Pinot Noir, for this cocktail. We developed this recipe using hickory and applewood as our smoking material, but feel free to experiment with other varieties of wood shavings.

- 2 ounces rye
- 1 ounce egg white
- ½ ounce Simple Syrup (page 458)
- ½ ounce lemon juice
- ½ ounce dry red wine

1. Add rye, egg white, simple syrup, and lemon juice to cocktail shaker and vigorously shake until mixture is foamy, about 45 seconds.

2. Fill shaker with ice, then shake mixture until just combined and chilled, about 5 seconds. Strain cocktail into chilled rocks glass half-filled with ice or containing 1 large ice cube. Arrange cocktail spoon concave side down near surface of ice. Gently pour wine onto back of spoon and into cocktail.

3. To smoke cocktail, place small saucer or lid over glass. Following manufacturer's instructions, turn on portable smoke infuser and ignite desired smoking material. Once smoke begins exiting hose, partially lift saucer, place tip of hose in opening, and fill glass with smoke. Quickly remove hose and replace saucer. Turn off smoker and extinguish smoking material. Let smoke infuse cocktail for 15 seconds, then remove saucer. Serve.

English 75

Makes 1 cocktail
Sweetness ✧ ✧ ✧
Herbal, Spirit Forward

You can find cucumber-infused gin on store shelves, and it works well in a gin and tonic. But when you infuse the gin yourself, the result is a world apart, boasting vibrancy and bursting with the crisp, green essence of real cucumber. Here, we take this bright spirit and weave it into a refined spin on the French 75. Instead of overpowering the gin's delicate botanicals and cucumber profile, we use a minimalist sour mix—just ¼ ounce each of lemon juice and simple syrup—to let the aromatics shine. Topping the cocktail with a dry sparkling wine adds savory complexity while lifting the infusion's fragrance into every sip.

- 1 ounce Cucumber-Infused Gin (page 298)
- ¼ ounce lemon juice
- ¼ ounce Simple Syrup (page 458)
- 2½ ounces dry sparkling white wine, chilled
- Cucumber slice for garnishing

Add gin, lemon juice, and simple syrup to cocktail shaker, then fill with ice. Shake mixture until fully combined and well chilled, about 15 seconds. Double-strain gin mixture into chilled flute glass. Slowly add sparkling wine and, using bar spoon, gently lift gin mixture from bottom of glass to top to combine. Garnish with cucumber slice and serve.

Customize Your Cocktail

You can use Cucumber-Infused Vodka instead of gin if you'd like.

Smoked New York Sour

Pimm's Cups

Makes 12 cocktails
Sweetness ✦ ✦ ✧
Bitter, Citrusy, Herbal

No drink is more evocative of English summertime than a Pimm's cup. Go to any society event or even a regular pub and ask for one and they'll know exactly what you're talking about (they'll probably have premixed pitchers waiting). Fruit cups were a Victorian homemade concoction of fruit, liqueurs, and gin, and James Pimm is largely credited with making premixed fruit cups popular by serving them at his fashionable oyster bar in the City of London in the 1840s. By 1865, his aperitif known as Pimm's No.1—a gin-based liqueur with sweet fruit and slightly bitter herbal flavors—was sold prebottled, and now "Pimm's" is synonymous with fruit cups. A Pimm's cup is made by combining Pimm's No.1 with English-style lemonade (which is clear and sparkling, with a sweet-sour balance). It should be infused and lavishly garnished with fruit. The closest substitute for the lemonade we could find in the United States was lemon-lime soda or ginger ale, but both distracted from the spiced, caramelized orange flavor of the Pimm's. Instead we infuse the lemon flavor into the Pimm's by combining the Pimm's with fresh lemon slices and juice, cucumber, and mint in a pitcher and letting it sit and soak up their flavors in the fridge. Simple syrup provides the lemonade with sweetness, and plain seltzer gives it fizz. The result is clean, balanced, and bright. In order to keep the drink sparkling, we gently stir in the seltzer just before serving. The strawberry is a traditional (and properly British) garnish.

- **20 ounces Pimm's No.1**
- **8 ounces Simple Syrup (page 458)**
- **5 lemons (1 sliced thin, 4 juiced to yield 6 ounces), plus extra lemon slices for garnishing**
- **1 English cucumber, sliced thin, divided**
- **½ cup fresh mint leaves, chopped, plus mint sprigs for garnishing**
- **32 ounces seltzer, chilled**
- **Halved strawberries for garnishing**

1. Combine Pimm's, simple syrup, lemon slices and juice, half of cucumber, and mint in serving pitcher or large container. Cover and refrigerate until flavors meld and mixture is well chilled, at least 2 hours or up to 1 day.

2. Gently stir seltzer into Pimm's mixture. Serve in chilled highball glasses filled with ice, garnishing individual portions with extra lemon slices, remaining cucumber slices, mint sprigs, and strawberries.

Strawberry Negroni

Makes 4 cocktails
Sweetness ✦✦✧
Bitter, Fruity, Spirit Forward

- 5 ounces strawberries, hulled and quartered, plus strawberry slices for garnishing
- 4½ ounces London dry gin
- 4½ ounces Campari
- 4½ ounces sweet vermouth

Customize Your Cocktail

Make a slightly tangier Raspberry Negroni by substituting halved raspberries for the strawberries.

Infused cocktails often involve introducing subtle flavor to the entire drink by manipulating a single ingredient in the formula—usually the spirit. A common modern cocktail is a strawberry Negroni, made with strawberry-infused Campari. We love the fruity addition of strawberry to this drink, but it's hard to detect among the already masterfully balanced contrasts in a classic Negroni—bitter and sweet, aromatic and spirit forward, herbal and citrusy. We think the strawberry flavor needs to be bold to compete with these strong flavors. Instead of infusing just one component, the gin or the Campari, we take a different approach: We build the cocktail first and then infuse the whole thing with fresh strawberries. The effect is akin to using the freshest strawberry liqueur imaginable, without upsetting the balance of a drink that's already pretty perfect. You can store the cocktail in a 1-quart Mason jar instead of a bottle if you'd like.

1. Combine strawberries, gin, Campari, and vermouth in 4-cup liquid measuring cup or large container. Cover and place in 50- to 70-degree location away from direct sunlight. Let gin mixture sit until flavors meld, about 3 days. Strain gin mixture into glass bottle or large Mason jar; discard solids. (Gin mixture can be covered and stored in refrigerator for up to 1 month.)

2. To make 1 cocktail: Gently shake bottle to recombine gin mixture. Add 3 ounces gin mixture to mixing glass, then fill three-quarters full with ice. Using spoon, stir until mixture is just combined and chilled, about 30 seconds. Strain cocktail into chilled rocks glass half-filled with ice or containing 1 large ice cube. Garnish with strawberry slices and serve.

The Bloody Mary

Tomato cocktails got their start (in nonalcoholic versions) not long after commercial tomato juice became available in the early 20th century. It's thought that liquor was first added to the mix in the cocktail paradise of 1920s Paris. Just as American bartenders were moving to Europe during this time to circumvent Prohibition, Russians were fleeing to Europe to escape Lenin's regime—and they brought their homeland's vodka with them.

Today, a pitcher of Bloody Marys is a brunchtime favorite. With so many assertive flavors, it can be easy to end up with an unbalanced concoction. We find that a 3:1 ratio of tomato juice to spirit is optimal for both potency and flavor balance. From there, you want to incorporate complementary spicy ingredients: some that add subtle sweetness (such as Worcestershire sauce or gochujang), some that pack a clean punch (such as horseradish or jalapeño brine), and others that bring a burst of spicy heat (like hot sauce or chipotles in adobo). And the brightness of citrus is important for any Bloody Mary.

Branch beyond vodka by stirring up a Bloody Mary with London dry gin. Try our Southwestern rendition, which uses blanco tequila, or our kimchi version, made with soju. No matter which you choose, the key to serving success is patience. Allowing the mixed cocktail to "steep" in the refrigerator for a minimum of two hours infuses the flavors so they can deepen and integrate. If you can let it infuse overnight, so much the better come brunchtime.

And what's any Bloody Mary without an absolute riot of garnishes? Produce such as celery, lemon or lime slices, cucumber spears, cherry tomatoes, sliced chiles, blanched green beans, and fresh herb sprigs work well. And if it's pickled or fermented, it will probably work too. We like cocktail onions; cornichons; olives; pickled chiles, asparagus, or green beans; and kimchi. Finally, there are luxe additions like crisp bacon strips, cubed cheese, poached shrimp, and hard-cooked eggs. Get out your longest skewers and go wild.

Bloody Marys

Makes 12 cocktails
Sweetness ✦ ✧ ✧
Savory, Spicy

- 48 ounces tomato juice
- 16 ounces vodka
- 4 ounces lemon juice, plus lemon slices for garnishing
- 1 ounce Worcestershire sauce
- 4 teaspoons prepared horseradish
- 2 teaspoons pepper
- 1 teaspoon hot sauce
- 12 celery ribs for garnishing

1. Whisk tomato juice, vodka, lemon juice, Worcestershire, horseradish, pepper, and hot sauce together in serving pitcher or large container. Cover and refrigerate until flavors meld and mixture is well chilled, at least 2 hours or up to 1 day.

2. Stir cocktail to recombine, then serve individual portions in chilled highball glasses filled with ice, garnishing with lemon slices and celery ribs.

Berbere-Spiced Bloody Marys

Makes 12 cocktails
Sweetness ✦ ✧ ✧
Savory, Spiced, Spicy

This bold and unconventional take on the Bloody Mary draws its depth from berbere, the richly aromatic spice blend essential to Ethiopian and Eritrean cuisine. With its warm layers of coriander, fenugreek, cardamom, and chile heat, berbere infuses tomato juice with a vibrant, complex kick. Inspired by the frequent use of hot green peppers in Ethiopian cooking, we add pickled jalapeños to introduce grassy, tangy heat for a cocktail that's both spicy and deeply flavorful.

- 48 ounces tomato juice
- 16 ounces vodka
- 4 ounces lemon juice, plus lemon slices for garnishing
- 1 ounce Worcestershire sauce
- 4 teaspoons minced pickled jalapeños plus 2 ounces brine, plus pickled jalapeños for garnishing
- 2 teaspoons berbere
- 1 teaspoon pepper

1. Whisk tomato juice, vodka, lemon juice, Worcestershire, jalapeños and brine, berbere, and pepper together in serving pitcher or large container. Cover and refrigerate until flavors meld and mixture is well chilled, at least 2 hours or up to 1 day.

2. Stir cocktail to recombine, then serve individual portions in chilled highball glasses filled with ice, garnishing with lemon slices and jalapeños.

Customize Your Cocktail

Other aromatic spice blends can work in place of the berbere, like ras el hanout, hawaij, jerk seasoning, or garam masala.

Southwestern Bloody Marys

Makes 12 cocktails
Sweetness ✦ ✧ ✧
Savory, Smoky, Spicy

Hot, smoky chipotles in adobo sauce are central to this Southwestern Bloody Mary. Tequila and lime juice are easy swaps for vodka and lemon juice, creating a drink that tastes familiar yet wholly new. A Tajín rim underscores the punch, spice, and salt in every sip.

- **48 ounces tomato juice**
- **16 ounces blanco tequila**
- **4 ounces lime juice, plus lime wedges for garnishing**
- **1 ounce Worcestershire sauce**
- **2 tablespoons minced canned chipotle chile in adobo sauce**
- **2 teaspoons pepper**
- **¼ cup Tajín Clásico Seasoning (optional)**

1. Whisk tomato juice, tequila, lime juice, Worcestershire, chipotle, and pepper in serving pitcher or large container. Cover and refrigerate until flavors meld and mixture is well chilled, at least 2 hours or up to 1 day.

2. Spread Tajín seasoning, if using, into even layer on small saucer. Moisten about ½ inch of chilled highball glass rims by running lime wedge around outer edge; dry any excess juice with paper towel. Roll moistened rims in Tajín to coat. Remove any excess Tajín that falls into glasses. Stir cocktail to recombine, then serve individual portions in prepared glasses filled with ice, garnishing with lime wedges.

PAIR WITH A SNACK

Deviled Eggs

Makes 12 pieces
Total Time: 20 minutes

Deviled eggs are an ideal pairing for cocktails you might drink prior to primetime. Make them part of a brunch spread or serve them next to an afternoon sipper. Pantry basics make this beloved appetizer a rich counterpoint to spicy or citrusy drinks. This recipe can be doubled. If you don't have a pastry bag, you can use a zipper-lock bag with the corner snipped off to fill the egg halves.

- **6 hard-cooked eggs**
- **2 tablespoons mayonnaise**
- **1 tablespoon sour cream**
- **½ teaspoon distilled white vinegar**
- **½ teaspoon spicy brown mustard**
- **¼ teaspoon sugar**
- **⅛ teaspoon table salt**
- **⅛ teaspoon pepper**

1. Peel eggs and halve lengthwise. Transfer yolks to fine-mesh strainer set over medium bowl. Using spatula, press yolks through strainer into bowl. Stir in mayonnaise, sour cream, vinegar, mustard, sugar, salt, and pepper. (Egg whites and filling can be refrigerated separately for up to 2 days. Wrap egg whites in double layer of plastic wrap. Transfer filling to zipper-lock bag, squeeze out air, and seal.)

2. Arrange egg whites on serving platter. Using spoon or pastry bag fitted with large plain or open-star tip, divide yolk mixture among whites. Serve.

Kimchi Bloody Marys

Makes 12 cocktails
Sweetness ✦ ✧ ✧
Savory, Spicy

In this hypersavory Bloody Mary, we turn to umami-packed Korean ingredients: Fish sauce, gochujang, and kimchi, along with some heat-moderating sesame oil, bring new dimension to this brunch classic. With these additions, the South Korean grain spirit soju makes a logical and delicious spirit choice, but you can substitute vodka for the soju.

- **48** ounces tomato juice
- **16** ounces soju
- **½** cup cabbage kimchi, drained, plus extra kimchi for garnishing
- **4** ounces lemon juice, plus lemon wedge (if using rim garnishes)
- **1** tablespoon fish sauce
- **1** tablespoon gochujang
- **1** teaspoon pepper
- **½** teaspoon toasted sesame oil
- **2** tablespoons gochugaru (optional)
- **2** tablespoons toasted sesame seeds (optional)
- Cucumber slices for garnishing

1. Process tomato juice, soju, kimchi, lemon juice, fish sauce, gochujang, pepper, and sesame oil in blender until smooth, about 1 minute. Transfer mixture to serving pitcher or large container. Cover and refrigerate until flavors meld and mixture is well chilled, at least 2 hours or up to 1 day.

2. Combine gochugaru and sesame seeds, if using, and spread into even layer on small saucer. Moisten about ½ inch of chilled highball glass rims by running lemon wedge around outer edge; dry any excess juice with paper towel. Roll moistened rims in gochugaru mixture to coat. Remove any excess gochugaru mixture that falls into glasses and fill with ice. Stir cocktail to recombine, then serve in prepared glasses, garnishing individual portions with extra kimchi and cucumber slices.

From left: Berbere-Spiced Bloody Marys, Kimchi Bloody Marys, Southwestern Bloody Marys

Citrus & Sage

Makes 8 zero-proof cocktails
Sweetness ✦ ✦ ✧
Citrusy, Floral, Herbal

- 2 red grapefruit, plus grapefruit slices for garnishing
- ⅓ cup sugar
- 6 fresh sage leaves, plus sage sprigs for garnishing
- Pinch table salt
- 8 ounces boiling water plus 20 ounces water, chilled
- 2 cinnamon sticks, divided
- 2 teaspoons Earl Grey tea leaves
- ½ ounce lemon juice
- 2½ ounces (½ cup) blackberries, halved lengthwise

Infusing is an ideal technique for flavoring a complex-tasting zero-proof cocktail without incorporating a lot of cloying fruit juices. Here, we extract every ounce of flavor from fresh grapefruit, while introducing just the right amount of bitterness. To unlock the fragrant grapefruit oils, we muddle its peel with sugar and a hint of salt and then pour in boiling water to dissolve the mixture while infusing it with floral Earl Grey tea, warming cinnamon, and earthy sage. These elements introduce tannins that add structure, body, and satisfying depth to the cocktail. A final touch of lemon juice and the addition of fresh blackberries give each sip juicy brightness. We prefer the higher quality of loose-leaf tea here; however, two tea bags can be substituted.

1. Using vegetable peeler, remove zest from grapefruit, removing as little white pith as possible. Toss zest with sugar, sage leaves, and salt in large bowl. Using potato masher, mash zest mixture vigorously until damp, clumpy, and very fragrant, about 2 minutes. Stir in boiling water, 1 cinnamon stick, and tea until sugar has dissolved, about 1 minute. Set aside until cool, about 30 minutes. While mixture cools, juice grapefruit to yield 6 ounces juice.

2. Stir grapefruit juice and lemon juice into zest mixture until combined. Strain juice mixture through fine-mesh strainer set over 8-cup liquid measuring cup; discard solids. (Juice mixture can be refrigerated for up to 1 day.)

3. Combine juice mixture and chilled water in serving pitcher or large container. Add grapefruit slices, sage sprigs, remaining cinnamon stick, and blackberries. Serve in chilled highball glasses filled with ice, using fruit and sage leaves as garnish.

Aperitivo *and* Digestivo Cocktails

The terms "aperitivo" and "digestivo" refer to both what you drink and when you drink it—and so aperitivi and digestivi are as much states of mind as they are beverages. Though the concepts of before-meal drinks and after-meal drinks are global today, their romantic roots are found throughout Europe. Think of the Italian passeggiata, when residents pour into the street in the predinner hour to savor a stroll and conversation with friends, usually punctuated with a stop for a drink and a snack; or la hora del vermut in Spain, when vermouth and a tapa are enjoyed before lunch. And then, picture lingering at the table at the end of a leisurely meal, after a holiday dinner with family or a celebratory dinner out, wanting a little something to settle your stomach and cap off the evening.

The word "aperitivo" derives from the Latin "aperire," which means "to open." Aperitivi are intended to "open up" one's appetite before a meal with drinks that include herbal elements (to stimulate the appetite) and are not too sweet (which would dull the appetite). Choices—solo or used in cocktails—might include Campari, Aperol, vermouth, or pastis.

Digestivi are intended to help you digest and can range from sweeter liqueurs, including limoncello and Bénédictine, to not-sweet-at-all choices such as grappa or eau de vie. Many digestivi fall into the broad amaro category, which means something bittersweet but with more flavor complexity and often greater alcohol content than a typical aperitivo.

While both aperitivi and digestivi can refer to individual liqueurs or spirits served on their own, they also refer to composed cocktails incorporating these ingredients—and that's where this chapter's recipes come in. Since the individual liqueurs used in these cocktails often share ingredients—including gentian, rhubarb, orange peel, and various herbs, for example—there is sometimes flexibility around when the cocktails may be served. We begin with a duo of classic aperitivo cocktails—the Perfect Kiss (page 330) and the Americano (page 330)—and our Low-jito (page 331) before moving into stronger drinks that are a bridge between the two categories. Then we cap things off with what has become one of the ultimate after-dinner cocktails: the Espresso Martini (page 343).

Aperitivo and Digestivo

Aperitivi

Ranging from vermouths and other aromatized wines such as Lillet to anise-flavored pastis to the so-called red aperitivi, these tend to be lighter in bitterness and lower in alcohol than digestivi and are designed to be enjoyed before a meal. Aperitivi may be made with spirits, wine, or fortified wine, which is combined with flavoring agents; they may be diluted with water and/or sweetened. There are many types of aperitivo; among the most famous are the red ones, which range in alcohol content from about 11 percent to about 25 percent.

RED APERITIVI

Red aperitivi are technically a subcategory within the amaro family, although culturally they are often thought of and consumed in a different way—that is, before a meal rather than after a meal. Here are some of the most popular brands; while they each have a distinct flavor, they are often interchangeable in cocktails.

- **APEROL:** spirit-based, bright orange color, soft bitterness balanced by sweetness, notes of bitter and sweet oranges, rhubarb, and gentian root
- **CAMPARI:** spirit-based, dark carmine-red color, more bitter than sweet, notes of bitter orange, grapefruit, ginseng, and gentian root
- **CAPPELLETTI:** wine-based, bright crimson color, less sweet and drier than others, notes of orange, vanilla, and herbs
- **SELECT:** spirit-based, ruby red color, less sweet and more bitter than Aperol, notes of rhubarb, juniper, and citrus

No-Recipe Aperitivo Cocktails

The Perfect Kiss (page 330) couldn't be simpler: It's equal parts sweet and dry vermouth, served with a twist. Here are some other ultrasimple aperitivo cocktails to try stirred and on the rocks.

- Sweet vermouth, seltzer to taste, orange twist
- Campari, Aperol, or Lillet; seltzer to taste; any citrus twist
- Dry vermouth, tonic water to taste, lemon twist
- Equal parts vermouth bianco and tonic water; sprig of thyme, oregano, or rosemary
- Any style of vermouth, cola to taste

Amari

The cultural home of amari is Italy, though these herbal liqueurs are made all over the world. "Amaro" means "bitter" in Italian, and while the bedrock of these liquids is some bittering flavor agent, their multitude of nuanced flavors—from the barks, roots, herbs, berries, fruits, and flowers used—adds deep complexity to cocktails.

The original purpose of amari was medicinal. Medieval monks in monasteries across the Italian peninsula infused herbs into distilled alcohol as a means of delivering cures for various ailments. Their ingredient options grew as trade expanded. (Venice was a major port for the spice trade during this time period.) As sugar became more available and affordable, that was added to the mix, and suddenly these liqueurs got a whole lot tastier.

To make an amaro, a high-proof neutral spirit (or sometimes wine) is combined with flavoring ingredients, diluted with water, and sweetened to varying degrees. The alcohol content can range from around 15 percent to around 40 percent.

A FEW OF OUR FAVORITE AMARI

There are hundreds of varieties of bottled amari, and whole books have been devoted to this subject. Here's a small sampling of readily available brands worth trying in cocktails such as the Little Baloney (page 191), Fernet Fizz (page 339), and Amaro Vivente (page 344).

- **AVERNA:** spirit-based, bittersweet, notes of orange, licorice, rosemary, and sage
- **CARDAMARO:** wine-based, mildly bitter balanced by sweetness, notes of ginger, almonds, walnuts, and herbs
- **CYNAR:** spirit-based, bittersweet, vegetal, notes of caramel, cinnamon, and orange
- **FERNET-BRANCA:** spirit-based, assertively bitter, notes of peppermint, eucalyptus, resin, and citrus
- **LUCANO:** spirit-based, bittersweet, notes of cardamom, orange peel, pine, and cola
- **MELETTI:** spirit-based, mildly bitter balanced by sweetness, notes of burnt sugar, cinnamon, vanilla, and citrus
- **MONTENEGRO:** spirit-based, bittersweet, notes of orange, cherry, clove, and coriander
- **NONINO:** grappa-based, mildly bitter balanced by sweetness, notes of orange, caramel, and saffron
- **PASUBIO:** wine-based, mildly bitter balanced by sweetness, notes of dark berries, pine, and herbs
- **RAMAZZOTTI:** spirit-based, bittersweet, notes of orange, cinnamon, vanilla, and espresso

Fortified Wines

While vermouth and other aromatized wines like Cocchi Americano and Lillet are considered more appropriate served as aperitivi, fortified wines such as Madeira, port, and sherry can be served, depending on their style, as either aperitivi or digestivi on their own. They are also versatile for cocktail making; we offer our take on a Sherry Cobbler (page 340), using amontillado sherry, as a digestivo.

Nonalcoholic Choices

Several producers offer nonalcoholic products that successfully replicate alcohol-containing aperitivi and amari. To approximate the burn associated with alcohol, producers of nonalcoholic aperitivi and amari may use ingredients such as chiles or ginger. They also use a range of herbs and botanicals like gentian root, bitter orange, Italian chinotto (a type of bitter orange), rhubarb, dandelion root, and more. Some may add glycerin to get closer to the fuller body and viscosity that would typically come from alcohol.

TOP NONALCOHOLIC APERITIVO PICK

- Wilfred's Non-Alcoholic Aperitif: slightly sweet, slightly medicinal, with flavor notes of orange and clove; somewhat reminiscent of Aperol overall

TOP NONALCOHOLIC AMARI PICKS

- Amaro Lucano Zero: made from the same herbs and botanicals as their traditional 130-year-old alcohol-containing version, with notes of citrus, rosemary, and chamomile
- Dr Zero Zero AmarNo: pleasingly bitter, with notes of sage, wormwood, quassia, and orange

Perfect Kiss

Makes 1 cocktail
Sweetness ✦ ✦ ✧
Bitter, Herbal

We think the distinct characteristics of and interplay among the many botanical elements of vermouth make the fortified wine deserving of more prominence. Even in a Negroni (page 332), where sweet vermouth is combined in equal parts with gin and Campari, the intense flavor of the Campari tends to steal the show. The answer is the Perfect Kiss, which combines sweet vermouth with an equal measure of dry vermouth for a cocktail that showcases their lightly bitter, herbal, floral, and fruity flavor nuances. The only addition is a bright lemon twist.

- 1½ ounces sweet vermouth
- 1½ ounces dry vermouth
- Lemon twist for garnishing

Add sweet vermouth and dry vermouth to mixing glass, then fill three-quarters full with ice. Stir until mixture is just combined and chilled, about 30 seconds. Strain cocktail into chilled rocks glass half-filled with ice or containing 1 large ice cube. Garnish with lemon twist and serve.

Americano

Makes 1 cocktail
Sweetness ✦ ✧ ✧
Bitter, Citrusy, Herbal

This low-alcohol cocktail is a perfect introduction to the bittersweet charms of Campari and the elegant complexity of sweet vermouth. It's a close relative of the aperitivo known as the Milano-Torino, which combines equal parts Campari (from Milan) and vermouth (from Turin). At some point along the way, soda water was added to the Mi-To, as it's known in Italy. Cocktail historians claim this bittersweet, bubbly refresher became known as the Americano when it grew popular among American tourists and expats in Italy during Prohibition. This drink's main players coexist in perfect balance, with the more bitter, astringent qualities of the Campari softened by the gently spiced, sweetly herbal notes of the vermouth.

- 1½ ounces Campari
- 1½ ounces sweet vermouth
- 5 ounces seltzer, chilled
- Orange slice for garnishing

Fill chilled highball glass halfway with ice. Add Campari and sweet vermouth and stir to combine using bar spoon. Add seltzer and, using spoon, gently lift Campari mixture from bottom of glass to top to combine. Top with additional ice and garnish with orange slice. Serve.

Customize Your Cocktail

Try other another aperitivo, such as Aperol or Select, or an amaro such as Cynar, in place of the Campari.

Low-jito

Makes 1 cocktail
Sweetness ✦✧✧
Bitter, Citrusy, Herbal

Inspired by the Mojito (page 77) but adjusted to be lower in alcohol, the Low-jito substitutes aromatized wine for the rum, specifically Cocchi Americano, which has a gentle herbaceousness and lots of grapefruit aromatics. Another drink, the Spanish rebujito, helped us get there. That one, depending on what bartender is making it, looks like a shandy or a mojito made with sherry. Cocchi Americano is an equally appealing starring player in this drink, which you might enjoy more than one of. Lillet Blanc or vermouth bianco (also sometimes labeled blanc or blanco) can be used in place of the Cocchi Americano Bianco.

- ⅓ **cup fresh mint leaves, plus mint sprig for garnishing**
- ½ **ounce Simple Syrup (page 458)**
- 2 **ounces Cocchi Americano Bianco**
- ¾ **ounce lime juice**
- 4 **ounces seltzer, chilled**

1. Add mint leaves and simple syrup to base of cocktail shaker and muddle until fragrant, about 30 seconds. Add Cocchi Americano and lime juice, then fill with ice. Shake mixture until just combined and chilled, about 5 seconds.

2. Double-strain into chilled highball glass half-filled with ice. Add seltzer and, using bar spoon, gently lift Cocchi Americano mixture from bottom of glass to top to combine. Top with additional ice and garnish with mint sprig. Serve.

The Negroni

Complex in flavor, gorgeous in color, and perfectly balanced between sweet and bitter, the Negroni is a timeless beauty. Accepted lore has it that circa 1919, in a bar in Florence, Italy, a particular Count Camillo Negroni ordered his Americano aperitivo cocktail (page 330) with gin in place of carbonated water. Thus the Negroni cocktail was born, although it took a couple of decades before it appeared in print.

Today it's wildly popular, with countless variations and even an entire Negroni Week event held in cocktail bars worldwide every spring, which has over the years raised millions of dollars for charitable causes. As in the Americano, the alcoholic ingredients for the Negroni are mixed in equal parts. (We tested versions made with different ratios of gin, Campari, and sweet vermouth, but we found that given the aromatic intensity of each element, increasing any one in proportion to the others created an imbalance.)

The Negroni is considered a classic aperitivo, even though the addition of gin makes it stronger than many other cocktails in this category. It has a distinct and enjoyably crisp bitterness that pairs perfectly with such savory and piquant appetizers as olives and cheese—and this is how it's often enjoyed, predinner, throughout Italy.

For our coffee version, we add coffee liqueur to the existing trinity of ingredients, which contributes deep, round flavor; reducing the Campari ensures the drink isn't too bitter. For a lighter, spritzier version, swap the gin for prosecco or another sparkling wine and you'll have the sbagliato (Italian for "wrong" or "mistaken"), which emerged in Milan in the 1960s. And sub in rye (or bourbon) for the gin and you have the richer, spicier boulevardier, thought to have been invented by an American expat in Paris during the 1920s and regularly enjoyed by him at Harry's New York Bar, operated by legendary bartender Harry MacElhone.

Classic Negroni

Makes 1 cocktail
Sweetness ✦✦✧
Bitter, Citrusy, Spirit Forward

- 1 ounce London dry gin
- 1 ounce Campari
- 1 ounce sweet vermouth
- Strip of orange peel for garnishing

Add gin, Campari, and vermouth to mixing glass, then fill three-quarters full with ice. Using bar spoon, stir until mixture is just combined and chilled, about 30 seconds. Strain cocktail into chilled rocks glass half-filled with ice or containing 1 large ice cube. Pinch orange peel over drink and rub outer edge of glass with peel, then garnish with orange peel. Serve.

Customize Your Cocktail

Try another aperitivo or amaro, such as Aperol, Cynar, Amaro Averna Siciliano, or Amaro Montenegro in place of the Campari. Or try another spirit, such as brandy, rum, or vodka.

Coffee Negroni

Makes 1 cocktail
Sweetness ✦✦✦
Bitter, Spirit Forward

This recipe is the classic, with a little pick-me-up: coffee liqueur. In a classic Negroni, the ratio of gin, vermouth, and Campari is 1:1:1; here the coffee liqueur is the star of the show, and the recipe gets a slight rejiggering to achieve balance. The profile pairs perfectly with the classic orange peel, as well as some espresso beans to hint at what's in the glass.

- 1 ounce coffee liqueur
- ¾ ounce London dry gin
- ¾ ounce sweet vermouth
- ½ ounce Campari
- Strip of orange peel for garnishing
- Espresso beans for garnishing

Add coffee liqueur, gin, vermouth, and Campari to mixing glass, then fill three-quarters full with ice. Using bar spoon, stir until mixture is just combined and chilled, about 30 seconds. Strain cocktail into chilled rocks glass half-filled with ice or containing 1 large ice cube. Pinch orange peel over drink and rub outer edge of glass with peel, then garnish with orange peel and espresso beans. Serve.

Negroni Sbagliato

Makes 1 cocktail
Sweetness ✦✦✧
Bitter, Citrusy

While this cocktail's name translates to "wrong Negroni," there is a lot that is right about this lighter, bubblier variation. The story goes that the drink was created by accident at Bar Basso in Milan in the late 1960s when a bartender, Mirko Stocchetto, grabbed a bottle of sparkling wine instead of gin and guessed that it might make for a refreshing and fizzy addition to the mixture of bittersweet Campari and herbal sweet vermouth. Given the cocktail's continued popularity today, clearly he wasn't wrong. While prosecco is traditional, any style of dry sparkling white wine will work well here.

- 1 ounce Campari
- 1 ounce sweet vermouth
- 2 ounces dry sparkling white wine, chilled
- Orange twist for garnishing

Add Campari and vermouth to mixing glass, then fill three-quarters full with ice. Using bar spoon, stir until mixture is fully combined and well chilled, about 1 minute. Strain into chilled flute glass. Slowly add sparkling wine and, using spoon, gently lift Campari mixture from bottom of glass to top to combine. Garnish with orange twist and serve.

Boulevardier

Makes 1 cocktail

Sweetness ✦ ✦ ✧

Bitter, Citrusy, Toasted

Erskine Gwynne was an American expat of epic reputation across Paris during the 1920s, a bon vivant and man-about-town who founded a literary and cultural magazine called, aptly, *The Boulevardier* (the name means someone who frequents Parisian boulevards). While the boulevardier is basically a Negroni made with whiskey, you could instead think of the reverse, a Negroni as a boulevardier variation, since the recipe for the boulevardier appeared in print long before the Negroni. Gwynne is also credited with inventing this deceptively simple cocktail. Originally this cocktail called for equal parts bourbon or rye, Campari, and sweet vermouth. However, we prefer when this cocktail leans closer to a Manhattan, with a smaller ratio of Campari (and vermouth) to the whiskey. This allows the drink to walk the fine line between bitter and sweet while maintaining a rich, lush texture.

- 1½ ounces rye
- ¾ ounce Campari
- ¾ ounce sweet vermouth
- Strip of orange peel for garnishing

Add rye, Campari, and vermouth to mixing glass, then fill three-quarters full with ice. Using bar spoon, stir until mixture is just combined and chilled, about 30 seconds. Strain cocktail into chilled rocks glass half-filled with ice or containing 1 large ice cube. Pinch orange peel over drink and rub outer edge of glass with peel, then garnish with orange peel. Serve.

Fridge Door Negronis

Makes 8 cocktails

Sweetness ✦ ✦ ✧

Bitter, Citrusy, Spirit Forward

It's aperitivo hour any hour when there are Negronis in the fridge. Just make sure you have a salty snack at the ready as well. You can store the cocktail in a 1-quart Mason jar instead of a bottle if you'd like.

- 8 ounces London dry gin
- 8 ounces Campari
- 8 ounces sweet vermouth
- 8 ounces water
- Strips of orange peel for garnishing

1. Combine gin, Campari, vermouth, and water in 1-liter glass bottle. Cover and freeze until well chilled, about 2 hours. Prepare cocktails immediately or transfer to refrigerator and store for up to 1 month; return to freezer and chill for 30 minutes before preparing cocktails.

2. Gently shake bottle to recombine, then serve cocktails in chilled rocks glasses half filled with ice or containing 1 large ice cube. Pinch orange peels over drinks and rub outer edges of glasses with peels, then garnish with orange peels. Serve.

From left: Fridge Door Negronis, Negroni Sbagliato, Coffee Negroni, Boulevardier

PAIR WITH A SNACK

Easy Cheese Straws

Makes 14 straws
Total Time: 30 minutes, plus 30 minutes cooling

To thaw frozen puff pastry, let it sit either in the refrigerator for 24 hours or on the counter for 30 minutes to 1 hour.

- **2 ounces Parmesan cheese, grated (1 cup)**
- **¼ teaspoon table salt**
- **¼ teaspoon pepper**
- **1 (9½ by 9-inch) sheet puff pastry, thawed**

1. Adjust oven racks to upper-middle and lower-middle positions and heat oven to 425 degrees. Combine Parmesan, salt, and pepper in bowl. Roll pastry into 10½-inch square on lightly floured counter. Sprinkle pastry with half of Parmesan mixture and press to adhere. Flip pastry and repeat with remaining Parmesan mixture.

2. Using sharp knife or pizza cutter, cut dough into fourteen ¾-inch-wide strips. Gently twist ends of strips in opposite directions and transfer to 2 parchment paper–lined baking sheets. Bake until fully puffed and golden brown, about 10 minutes, switching and rotating sheets halfway through baking. Let cool completely before serving. (Straws can be stored in airtight container for up to 3 days.)

VARIATION

Sweet and Spicy Straws

Combine 1 tablespoon sugar, 2 teaspoons chili powder, and ⅛ teaspoon ground cinnamon in bowl. Substitute sugar mixture for Parmesan mixture.

Fernet Fizz

Absinthe Frappé

Makes 1 cocktail
Sweetness ✦ ✦ ✧
Herbal

This classic New Orleans cocktail is believed to have first been served in the 1870s at a coffeehouse at the site of what is now the Old Absinthe House in New Orleans. And as you might surmise by the establishment's name, they're still serving it. Sweet anise and mint provide a double dose of digestive power for the perfect drink after a large meal. The first taste is pretty strong, but it smooths out with each sip. Other dry anise-flavored spirits (such as Herbsaint, pastis, or dry anisette) can be substituted for the absinthe.

- 2 ounces absinthe
- ½ ounce Simple Syrup (page 458)
- ⅓ cup fresh mint leaves, plus mint sprig for garnishing
- 3 ounces seltzer, chilled

Add absinthe, simple syrup, and mint to cocktail shaker, then fill with ice. Shake mixture until fully combined and well chilled, about 15 seconds. Double-strain absinthe mixture into chilled rocks glass half-filled with ice. Add seltzer and, using bar spoon, gently lift absinthe mixture from bottom of glass to top to combine. Top with additional ice and garnish with mint sprig. Serve.

Fernet Fizz

Makes 1 cocktail
Sweetness ✦✦✧
Bitter, Creamy, Herbal

Sharply medicinal and aggressively aromatic, fernet might be the most notorious member of the amaro family, and a divisive beverage. Fernet-Branca is 78 proof, barely sweetened, oak-aged, and a cultish favorite of the hospitality world, where industry insiders celebrate the end of a difficult shift with a round. Looking around the world for inspiration for a fernet cocktail that most everyone would love, we discovered that fernet and cola is the de facto national drink of Argentina. But we felt that the soda exacerbated the most astringent elements of the fernet rather than tamed them. We did like the bubbles, so we switched to seltzer. Bourbon is an excellent spirit pairing, as its sweet charred-oak elements meld with the fernet. Finally, an egg white gives a softer mouthfeel to the drink and a beautiful pearlescent head. These elements together make fernet far more universally palatable.

1 ounce bourbon
¾ ounce Simple Syrup (page 458)
½ ounce egg white
½ ounce Fernet-Branca
¼ ounce lemon juice, plus lemon twist for garnishing
1½ ounces seltzer, chilled

1. Add bourbon, simple syrup, egg white, Fernet-Branca, and lemon juice to cocktail shaker and vigorously shake until mixture is foamy, about 45 seconds.

2. Fill shaker with ice, then shake mixture until fully combined and well chilled, about 15 seconds. Double-strain cocktail into chilled flute glass. Slowly pour seltzer over top of cocktail. Garnish with lemon twist and serve.

Sherry Cobbler

Makes 1 cocktail
Sweetness ✦ ✦ ✧
Citrusy, Fruity, Savory

Despite this cocktail's fruity profile, the sherry cobbler—one of the oldest cocktails, from the early 1800s—isn't named for a dessert. Some say the name comes from the old ice industry, where "cobbled" meant small pieces (what we now call "crushed" ice). The sherry cobbler is also thought to be the first drink served conveniently with a straw. The cocktail has come in and out of fashion throughout history, and as a fully flavored, fortified wine-based cocktail (read: low-alcohol) it is having a fresh resurgence with the no/low trend. The fruit hits the palate first, then there is a very dry finish from the sherry, which lingers, resulting in a balanced, refreshing, easy-to-drink cocktail.

- 1 (¼-inch) slice orange, quartered, plus orange slice for garnishing
- 4 raspberries, plus extra raspberries for garnishing
- 4 fresh mint leaves, plus mint sprig for garnishing
- ½ ounce Simple Syrup (page 458)
- 2 ounces amontillado sherry

1. Add orange pieces, raspberries, mint, and simple syrup to mixing glass and muddle until mint is fragrant, orange pieces and raspberries have broken down, and all juice has been expressed, about 30 seconds. Add sherry and stir, using bar spoon, until mixture is combined.

2. Double-strain cocktail into chilled rocks glass half-filled with crushed ice. Top with additional ice and, using spoon, gently lift cocktail from bottom of glass to top to evenly distribute. Top with more crushed ice to form mound above rim of glass. Garnish with orange slice, extra raspberries, and mint sprig and serve.

Customize Your Cocktail

We like making this drink with dry amontillado sherry, but you can explore other flavor profiles by using a fino, oloroso, or palo cortado sherry. Blackberries are a nice choice in place of the raspberries.

Widow's Kiss

Makes 1 cocktail
Sweetness ✦✦✦
Herbal, Spirit Forward

This classic cocktail first appeared in George Kappeler's 1895 *Modern American Drinks* and was further popularized after it appeared in the 1900 edition of Harry Johnson's famous *Bartenders' Manual*. This after-dinner drink is quite sweet from the Chartreuse and further from the very herbal Bénédictine. These two liqueurs shine beyond the base spirit, brandy, which melds beautifully into the drink. You can substitute Strega for the yellow Chartreuse in this cocktail.

- 1½ ounces brandy
- ¾ ounce yellow Chartreuse
- ¾ ounce Bénédictine
- ⅛ teaspoon old-fashioned aromatic bitters

Add brandy, Chartreuse, Bénédictine, and bitters to mixing glass, then fill three-quarters full with ice. Using bar spoon, stir until mixture is fully combined and well chilled, about 1 minute. Strain cocktail into chilled cocktail glass and serve.

Sherry Cobbler

The Espresso Martini

While traditionally considered a digestivo, the espresso martini has been adopted by many Gen Zers as their anytime, anywhere cocktail of choice—and with good reason, considering its eye-opening deliciousness. Drinks based on combinations of coffee and spirits abound throughout the world, but none has as big a fan club as the espresso martini. Typically consisting of vodka, coffee liqueur, and espresso, this cocktail is shaken to create a thin layer of crema—just as one would find on an espresso.

Served in a martini glass with a garnish of three espresso beans floating atop the foam (signifying health, wealth, and happiness), this drink was developed by London-based bartender Dick Bradsell in the early 1980s. His original drink used Kahlúa and Tia Maria in addition to vodka and espresso.

The espresso martini is not really a "martini" in the classical sense. It was one of the many, many creations of the late 20th-century all-things-tini era, when you-name-it was combined in an oversized cocktail glass and called a martini. Many of those kitchen-sink drinks are best left in the previous millennium, but the espresso martini has come back thanks to its tried-and-true formula: a base spirit combined with balanced sweet and bitter elements.

To add variety to this modern classic, we swap in mezcal or Amaro Averna for the vodka, or brandy and a touch of orange liqueur for a French-inspired take. Whichever version you choose, the cocktail will taste best with freshly made and chilled espresso; you can substitute an equal amount of cold-brewed coffee, if needed. We recommend our homemade Coffee Liqueur (page 467) for extra pizzazz, though store-bought coffee liqueur works.

All of these cocktails are equally appealing as an after-dinner sip and as a cocktail hour pick-me-up at the start of the evening; we'll let you decide the best time to shake them up.

Espresso Martini

Makes 1 cocktail
Sweetness ✦ ✧ ✧
Bitter, Creamy, Nutty

Depending on the sweetness of your coffee liqueur, you may want to add the simple syrup.

- **1½ ounces vodka**
- **¾ ounce brewed espresso, chilled**
- **¾ ounce coffee liqueur**
- **1 teaspoon Simple Syrup (page 458) (optional)**
- **Espresso beans for garnishing**

Add vodka, espresso, coffee liqueur, and simple syrup, if using, to cocktail shaker, then fill with ice. Shake mixture until fully combined and well chilled, about 15 seconds. Double-strain cocktail into chilled cocktail glass. Garnish with espresso beans and serve.

Customize Your Cocktail

Make a Lattetini by adding ½ ounce heavy cream to the shaker with the vodka. Consider modifying the flavor of your cocktail by utilizing other flavors of simple syrup.

Amaro Vivente

Makes 1 cocktail
Sweetness ✦ ✦ ✧
Bitter, Creamy, Herbal

As it combines two common after-dinner offerings, Amaro Averna and a cup of coffee, this espresso martini variation is the ultimate digestivo. As with many amari, it's packed with the flavors of its region of origin, Sicily. Like Sicilian wines, it has a bold, rich character, redolent of Mediterranean spices and fruit dried in the sun. And, as an echo of some of Sicily's most famous desserts, alongside which it is often consumed, the amaro has a pronounced candied orange note, with hints of bitter chocolate. These qualities make it the perfect pairing for the espresso, with its also-bold, fruity notes.

- **1½ ounces Amaro Averna Siciliano**
- **1 ounce brewed espresso, chilled**
- **½ ounce coffee liqueur**
- **Orange twist for garnishing**

Add amaro, espresso, and coffee liqueur to cocktail shaker, then fill with ice. Shake mixture until fully combined and well chilled, about 15 seconds. Double-strain cocktail into chilled cocktail glass. Garnish with orange twist and serve.

Customize Your Cocktail

Try another amaro such as Amaro Lucano, Amaro Montenegro, or Amaro Nonino Quintessentia in place of the Amaro Averna.

Bone in Her Teeth

Makes 1 cocktail
Sweetness ✦ ✧ ✧
Bitter, Creamy, Smoky

Espresso martinis and mezcal have soared to wild popularity on very similar timelines. Combine them, which happens to be a very good idea, and you might make the hottest cocktail on the scene. Some people like their espresso martini creamy, often achieved by adding heavy cream or Irish cream liqueur. Instead, here we use cream of coconut to add great texture and a hint of pleasing coconut flavor to offset the smoky and bitter flavors of the spirit and coffee, while avoiding the artificial taste that cream liqueurs can sometimes carry. To pull out the coconut flavor, we garnish the foamy-topped (as the name suggests) cocktail with toasted coconut.

- **1¼ ounces mezcal**
- **¾ ounce brewed espresso, chilled**
- **½ ounce coffee liqueur**
- **1 tablespoon cream of coconut**
- **Toasted coconut for garnishing**

Add mezcal, espresso, coffee liqueur, and cream of coconut to cocktail shaker, then fill with ice. Shake mixture until fully combined and well chilled, about 15 seconds. Double-strain cocktail into chilled cocktail glass. Garnish with toasted coconut and serve.

I Woke Up Like This

Makes 1 cocktail

Sweetness ✦ ✧ ✧

Bitter, Citrusy, Spirit Forward

Like the amaro in the Amaro Vivente, brandy is a classic after-dinner choice, often served after espresso. But why not combine the two? With its subtle sweetness and typical flavor notes of dried fruits, spice, and caramel or vanilla, brandy makes a beautiful pairing with espresso. Orange liqueur complements both brandy and espresso and further seals the deal.

- 1¼ ounces brandy
- ¾ ounce brewed espresso, chilled
- ½ ounce coffee liqueur
- ½ ounce orange liqueur
- Freshly grated cinnamon for garnishing

Add brandy, espresso, coffee liqueur, and orange liqueur to cocktail shaker, then fill with ice. Shake mixture until fully combined and well chilled, about 15 seconds. Double-strain cocktail into chilled cocktail glass. Garnish with grated cinnamon and serve.

Fridge Door Espresso Martinis

Makes 8 cocktails

Sweetness ✦ ✧ ✧

Bitter, Creamy, Nutty

For the espresso martini superfan: These can be made ahead and frozen for a couple of hours or stored in the refrigerator for quite some time. You can store the cocktail in a 1-quart Mason jar instead of a bottle if you'd like.

- 12 ounces vodka
- 8 ounces water
- 6 ounces brewed espresso, chilled
- 6 ounces coffee liqueur
- 1½ ounces Simple Syrup (page 458) (optional)
- Espresso beans for garnishing

1. Combine vodka, water, espresso, coffee liqueur, and simple syrup, if using, in 1-liter glass bottle. Cover and freeze until well chilled, about 2 hours. Prepare cocktails immediately or transfer to refrigerator and store for up to 1 month; return to freezer and chill for 30 minutes before preparing cocktails.

2. Shake bottle vigorously to recombine and aerate, then serve cocktails in chilled cocktail glasses. Garnish with espresso beans and serve.

Customize Your Cocktail

Make Fridge Door Lattetinis by adding 4 ounces heavy cream with the vodka.

From left: I Woke Up Like This, Amaro Vivente, Bone in Her Teeth, Fridge Door Espresso Martinis

PAIR WITH A SNACK

Chocolate Chip–Orange Cannoli Dip

Serves 6 to 8 (makes 1¾ cups)
Total Time: 10 minutes, plus 30 minutes chilling

Inspired by Italian cannoli, we created a shareable version in the form of a luxurious dip. We stir together a filling of ricotta and mascarpone sweetened with confectioners' sugar and a hint of vanilla, and serve it with the "shell" on the side. As a nod to flavors popular in Italian bakeries, we stir in mini chocolate chips and orange zest. Serve with broken cannoli shells, pizzelle, speculoos cookies, butter wafers, broken sugar cones, graham crackers, Florentine cookies, or vanilla wafers.

- 6 ounces (¾ cup) whole-milk ricotta cheese
- 6 ounces (¾ cup) mascarpone cheese
- ½ cup (2 ounces) confectioners' sugar
- ¼ cup (1½ ounces) mini chocolate chips, plus extra for serving
- ¾ teaspoon vanilla extract
- ¼ teaspoon grated orange zest
- ⅛ teaspoon table salt

Using wooden spoon or silicone spatula, stir all ingredients in large bowl until evenly combined, breaking up any large pieces of mascarpone by pressing them against side of bowl. Cover and refrigerate until chilled, at least 30 minutes. (Cannoli dip can be refrigerated for up to 3 days; stir to recombine before serving.) Sprinkle with extra mini chocolate chips before serving.

Wine *and* Beer Cocktails

If you treat the term "cocktail" a little loosely, then wine and beer mixed drinks could be considered the original cocktails. Millennia before distilling was successfully achieved, Bronze Age humans were improving the flavor of their wine and beer by mixing them with various ingredients (whatever they had on hand, and sometimes even mixing the two together). Ancient Greeks and Romans combined their wine with spices, fruit, honey, and various liquids. Sometimes the concoction was heated. Recipes for flavored wine even appeared in the ancient Roman cookbook *De Re Coquinaria*, believed to be authored by nobleman (and gourmand) Marcus Gavius Apicius.

Wine in its various forms appears in a lot more cocktails than you might initially think. Champagne, vermouth, sherry, port, and Madeira feature in countless mixed drinks. The wine cocktails in this chapter focus primarily on drinks made with still, unfortified wine. The most famous still-wine cocktail is probably sangria, and we offer five different styles for every occasion or mood, using different wines (including sparkling), liqueurs, and fresh fruits. Because the Iberian Peninsula has such a strong culture of mixed drinks made with wine, we share our takes on tinto de verano and kalimotxo.

A duo of sake-based cocktails serves as a bridge between the wine and beer recipes. Sometimes called rice wine, sake is made from grain rather than fruit. The brewing and production process for sake (which involves fermenting rice with koji mold and yeast) is closer to that of beer than to the wine-making process.

Though they're not as common now, mixed drinks made with beer have been enjoyed in the United States since its founding. During Revolutionary times, beer was often mixed with rum and various spices or citrus juice. And flip was a drink that involved beer, sugar, and sometimes eggs, served hot.

What takes the title of most famous beer cocktail is up for debate. At its simplest a beer cocktail can be a black and tan, which is equal parts pale ale and stout; a snakebite, which is equal parts lager and hard cider; or a black velvet, which is equal parts stout (traditionally Guinness) and Champagne. And of course there's the boilermaker, which is a beer with a shot of liquor—sometimes served alongside and sometimes dropped into the pint glass. No recipes are needed for such simple ratios, but we do give you several shandy recipes, along with the Michelada (page 366), the spicy Mexican beer cocktail, and a couple of creative new beer and cider spritzes.

Wine and Beer

Wines for Cocktails

Choose cheap: Save the expensive wines for drinking on their own. Because wine cocktails include other strongly flavored ingredients, such as fruit, liqueurs, or sweeteners, less-expensive wines are just fine. We stick with medium- to full-bodied red wines that are fruit forward and have tannins on the smoother side, such as Merlot, Grenache, Pinot Noir, or Malbec. Choose a medium-acidity, lightly fruity white wine, such as Pinot Grigio or unoaked Chardonnay.

Consider boxed: Boxed wines have come a long way in terms of quality and no longer deserve to be maligned. They hold a strong advantage for cocktail making, since the airtight bag in the box preserves the wine's flavor, aroma, and color for 6 to 8 weeks, maybe even longer if you store it in the refrigerator. An open bottle of wine, on the other hand, will stay good for a week at most, even if refrigerated.

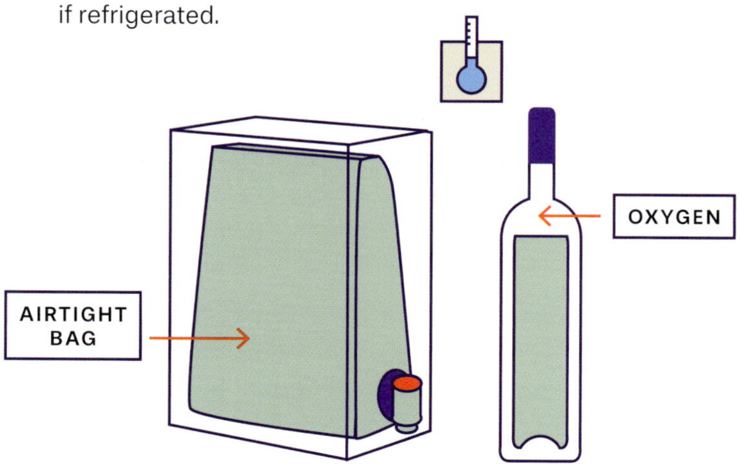

Beers for Cocktails

While certain styles are better for certain cocktails, a good baseline beer for most cocktails (and most of the recipes in this chapter) is a light lager or pilsner. We also like the slightly sweeter, fruitier profile of wheat beer in our Peach Cruiser (page 364) and the creamy texture of stout in our Gingered Beer (page 365).

Nonalcoholic Wine and Beer

With numerous high-quality commercial options available, nonalcoholic wine and beer make great cocktails. They can be produced in different ways.

DEALCOHOLIZED WINE AND BEER

Dealcoholized wine and beer are made using a similar process for removing the alcohol: vacuum distillation. The boiling point for alcohol is 173 degrees Fahrenheit under normal conditions, but in a vacuum it evaporates at much lower temperatures (around 60 degrees). So, the alcohol can be "cooked off" without heating the wine or beer, thus avoiding any unpleasant off-flavors. This process leaves the liquid with less than 0.5 percent alcohol by volume. To reestablish flavor balance in wine, producers add ingredients such as sugar, fruit juice, and/or grape must (freshly crushed or pressed grape juice), plus sometimes carbon dioxide for carbonation or glycerin for texture. For beer, volatile flavor compounds are captured at the start and then added back into the beer after the dealcoholizing process.

WINE ALTERNATIVES AND WINE PROXIES

A second method of producing nonalcoholic wine is to begin with a slightly fermented base, such as kombucha or kvass (an Eastern European drink), or something nonfermented like verjuice (tart juice from unripe grapes) or tea. Fruit juice concentrates and extracts are added to replicate some flavor aspects of wine, along with a myriad of savory ingredients to add balance and complexity, including salt, black peppercorns, chicory root, pine needles, or wine tannin.

LIMITING ALCOHOL PRODUCTION IN BEER

Another way to produce nonalcoholic beer is to limit the creation of alcohol in the first place. Brewer's yeast, part of the *Saccharomyces* genus, invariably converts sugar into alcohol, but it's possible to control the process so that less alcohol is produced. Brewers start with a mash containing a smaller amount of fermentable sugar so that the yeast has less to work with. Fermenting this mash at a temperature just a couple of degrees above freezing alters the yeast's metabolism so that it produces a full complement of desirable flavor compounds while producing very little alcohol. The behavior of yeast can also be controlled by limiting the amount of oxygen in the mash and stopping the fermentation early. There are also methods that involve using different species of yeast that are unable to convert some types of sugar to alcohol.

TOP NONALCOHOLIC WINE PICKS

- **SPARKLING:** Thomson & Scott Noughty Non-Alcoholic Sparkling Chardonnay. We also like Sovi's The Wild Child Sparkling Orange Non-Alcoholic Wine (made with white grapes using a skin-contact fermentation).
- **WHITE:** Leitz Eins Zwei Zero Alcohol-Free Chardonnay
- **RED:** Sovi Reserve Red Non-Alcoholic Wine

TOP NONALCOHOLIC BEER PICKS

- **LAGER:** Heineken 0.0 and O'Doul's
- **WHEAT:** Drink'in the Sun from Mikkeller and Heavenly Body Golden Wheat from Wellbeing Brewing
- **ALE:** Upside Dawn Golden Ale from Athletic Brewing Co. and Omission Good to Go Golden
- **INDIA PALE ALE (IPA):** Untitled Art West Coast Style IPA (boldly bitter) and Samuel Adams Just the Haze IPA (East Coast style, fruitier and hazier)
- **STOUT:** Guinness 0 and All Out from Athletic Brewing Co.

Chill Out–But Quickly

The fastest way to cool down a bottle of wine is to wrap the bottle in a wet dish towel and place it in the freezer. Since cooling occurs when heat is transferred away from an item, the water in the towel—a much more efficient conductor of heat than air—will quickly freeze, dropping the temperature of the wine to 50 degrees in only 30 minutes. (Once the wine is fully chilled, the towel will be frozen solid. To release it from the bottle, place it very briefly under warm running water.)

Add Bitters to Your Beer

The practice of adding bitters to beer has been around for a long time. In the United States, it's an open secret in the bartender community because it makes a light beer a lot tastier. Use potable bitters like aperitivi (see Stock Car Spritz on page 368) or amari or nonpotable bitters (those you don't drink on their own, like old-fashioned aromatic bitters). Start with a few drops and adjust to your palate. Here are some combinations to try.

- **LAGERS AND PILSNERS:** Peychaud's bitters or old-fashioned aromatic bitters
- **WHEAT BEERS:** orange or lemon bitters
- **PALE AND GOLDEN ALES:** grapefruit bitters
- **IPAS:** Bittermens Scarborough Savory Herbal Bitters
- **AMBER AND RED ALES:** Amaro Montenegro
- **PORTERS AND STOUTS:** amari such as rabarbaro (made using rhubarb), sfumato (a smoky version of rabarbaro), or fernet (made with a varied blend of herbs and spices)
- **SOURS:** Cynar or The Pathfinder Hemp and Root (a nonalcoholic amaro)

Sangria

From its ancient roots in Spain and Portugal, sangria has grown to become a party drink mainstay around the world. Many people think of sangria as an unruly collection of fruit chunks in overly sweetened wine, but that needn't be the case. To create robust sangria with fresh flavor, simpler is generally better.

People living on the Iberian Peninsula were adding flavor enhancements to their wine as far back as about 1000 BC. Evolution of these basic wine "punches" continued through the centuries, right up until the region was conquered by the Moors in the early 700s. Although the Moors didn't forbid alcohol outright, consumption waned under their rule. Wine drinking didn't return in force until the late 15th century.

Sangria as we know it today hit its stride in the 18th and 19th centuries, making its way to the Caribbean, where it was adapted according to local ingredients and known as sangaree. It was during this time that it started to become popular in Mexico—and to this day it's ubiquitous on Mexican restaurant menus. Its popularity in the United States dates back to the 1964 World's Fair in New York City, when Spain's pavilion featured the drink, to the delight of fairgoers.

Depending on the wine, different liqueurs and fruits will complement it best to create a balanced sangria. We also find that using whole citrus fruit (not trimming away the peel and pith) makes an important contribution to flavor.

Our classic red wine version uses oranges and lemons, with orange liqueur complementing and deepening the citrus fruitiness. With white wine, we love the crisp taste of apples and oranges highlighted with brandy. Rosé is a natural pairing with berries and floral liqueur. Our festive sparkling sangria starts to get a little unruly (but not too much!) with oranges, lemons, limes, and strawberries.

Pro tip: Unless you're using sparkling wine, don't serve your sangria immediately after making it. Letting it rest in the refrigerator for a couple of hours, if possible, smooths the edges and mellows and marries the flavors.

Classic Sangria

Makes 12 cocktails
Sweetness ✦✦✧
Citrusy, Fruity

- 2 (750-ml) bottles dry red wine
- 4 ounces orange liqueur
- 4 ounces Simple Syrup (page 458)
- 3 oranges (2 sliced thin, 1 juiced to yield 4 ounces)
- 2 lemons, sliced thin

1. Combine all ingredients in serving pitcher or large container. Cover and refrigerate until flavors meld and mixture is well chilled, at least 2 hours or up to 8 hours.

2. Stir sangria to recombine, then serve in chilled wineglasses half-filled with ice, garnishing individual portions with macerated orange and lemon slices.

Customize Your Cocktail

Use fruit that's in season or on hand. Limes (sliced), apples (sliced, chopped), or berries would be nice. Experiment with different varieties of red wine or try white wine.

White Wine Sangria

Makes 12 cocktails
Sweetness ✦ ✦ ✧
Citrusy, Fruity

While red wine sangria may be the archetypal version, other wines work very well. White wine makes a lighter, more refreshing drink that works well with crisp apples (and some apple juice). Brandy, rather than orange liqueur, rounds out the flavors.

- 2 (750-ml) bottles dry white wine
- 4 ounces brandy
- 4 ounces unsweetened 100 percent apple juice
- 4 ounces Simple Syrup (page 458)
- 2 oranges, sliced thin
- 2 Granny Smith apples, cored and sliced thin

1. Combine all ingredients in serving pitcher or large container. Cover and refrigerate until flavors meld and mixture is well chilled, at least 2 hours or up to 8 hours.

2. Stir sangria to recombine, then serve in chilled wineglasses half-filled with ice, garnishing individual portions with macerated orange and apple slices.

Rosé Sangria

Makes 12 cocktails
Sweetness ✦ ✦ ✧
Floral, Fruity

For a particularly summery sangria, rosé and mixed berries are a perfect seasonal combo. For the liqueur, this pairing calls for something more floral and delicate, so we use elderflower liqueur. We reinforce the fruitiness in this sangria with pomegranate juice.

- 2 (750-ml) bottles dry rosé wine
- 4 ounces elderflower liqueur
- 4 ounces unsweetened 100 percent pomegranate juice
- 2 ounces Simple Syrup (page 458)
- 10 ounces strawberries, hulled and halved (2 cups)
- 5 ounces (1 cup) blackberries, blueberries, or raspberries

1. Combine all ingredients in serving pitcher or large container. Cover and refrigerate until flavors meld and mixture is well chilled, at least 2 hours or up to 8 hours.

2. Stir sangria to recombine, then serve in chilled wineglasses half-filled with ice, garnishing individual portions with macerated berries.

Sparkling Sangria

Makes 12 cocktails
Sweetness ✦✦✧
Citrusy, Fruity

The sangria at the Columbia Restaurant in Ybor City, Florida, a Spanish-Cuban hot spot with more than 120 years of history, is the inspiration for this recipe. In place of red or white wine, the restaurant adds some bubbles to their sangria with the sparkling Spanish wine cava. Following their lead, we use a combination of cava (or another dry sparkling wine—white or red), brandy, and orange liqueur, with citrus fruits to yield a delightfully lively punch. Of course because this sangria is meant to sparkle, it is served immediately after mixing and, with lots of juiced citrus, it's plenty flavorful.

- 2 (750-ml) bottles dry sparkling white wine, such as cava or prosecco, chilled
- 6 ounces brandy
- 6 ounces orange liqueur
- 6 ounces Simple Syrup (page 458)
- 2 oranges (1 sliced thin, 1 juiced to yield 4 ounces)
- 3 lemons (1 sliced thin, 2 juiced to yield 2 ounces)
- 3 limes (1 sliced thin, 2 juiced to yield 1½ ounces)
- 5 ounces strawberries, hulled and halved (1 cup)

Combine all ingredients in serving pitcher or large container. Serve immediately in chilled wineglasses half-filled with ice, garnishing individual portions with macerated fruit.

Spiced Pear Sangria

Makes 12 cocktails
Sweetness ✦✦✧
Fruity, Spiced

Who says sangria is only for summer? For this fall-flavored sip that's just as fruity and refreshing as the traditional version, we swap in pear (juice and slices) for the standard citrus (liqueur and slices). Amaretto and brandy, both of which pair nicely with pear, add the appropriate warm, round profile.

- 2 (750-ml) bottles dry white or red wine
- 4 ounces amaretto
- 4 ounces brandy
- 4 ounces Spice Syrup with cardamom (page 459)
- 4 ounces unsweetened 100 percent pear juice
- 3 ounces lemon juice
- 2 Bartlett or Bosc pears, sliced thin
- 3 (3-inch) strips of lemon peel

1. Combine all ingredients in serving pitcher or large container. Cover and refrigerate until flavors meld and mixture is well chilled, at least 2 hours or up to 8 hours.

2. Stir sangria to recombine, then serve in chilled wineglasses half-filled with ice, garnishing individual portions with macerated pear slices.

Clockwise from top: Spiced Pear Sangria, Sparkling Sangria, Rosé Sangria, White Wine Sangria

PAIR WITH A SNACK

Marinated Manchego

Serves 6 to 8
Total Time: 25 minutes, plus 25 hours sitting and chilling

Wine loves cheese. Marinating Manchego is a way to add more depth to the cheese so it pairs with a very flavorful wine cocktail. You can serve the marinating oil with bread for dipping.

- ¾ cup extra-virgin olive oil, plus extra as needed
- 8 garlic cloves, smashed and peeled
- 6 (3-inch) strips orange zest
- 8 sprigs fresh thyme
- 3 bay leaves
- ½ teaspoon table salt
- ¼ teaspoon red pepper flakes
- 8 ounces Manchego cheese, cut into rough ¾-inch cubes

1. Combine oil, garlic, orange zest, thyme sprigs, bay leaves, salt, and pepper flakes in small saucepan and cook over medium-low heat until garlic begins to turn golden, about 10 minutes. Set aside and let cool completely.

2. Place Manchego in 16-ounce Mason jar. Using tongs or fork, transfer garlic, orange zest, thyme sprigs, and bay leaves to jar with Manchego. Pour oil mixture over Manchego, pressing down cheese as needed to submerge it. If needed, add extra oil to cover cheese. Cover jar with lid and refrigerate for at least 24 hours. Let come to room temperature before serving.

Tinto de Verano

Makes 1 cocktail

Sweetness ✦ ✧ ✧

Citrusy, Fruity

Think of tinto de verano as a fruity, light sparkling instant sangria for one. As the name suggests (it translates to "summer red wine"), it's perfect for those hot summer months when a refreshing drink is welcome. In Spain, this drink is typically built with equal parts dry, fruity red wine and either a lightly sweetened seltzer or a more citrusy soda, and it's served over lots of ice. Some variations add sweet vermouth, which we like for the herbal complexity it brings to a relatively straightforward cocktail. Instead of store-bought sodas, which can make the drink too sweet, we like the customizability of using simple syrup, lemon juice, and seltzer to build our bubbly component instead.

- 4 ounces dry red wine, chilled
- ¾ ounce sweet vermouth
- ½ ounce Simple Syrup (page 458)
- ½ ounce lemon juice, plus lemon slice for garnishing
- 4 ounces seltzer, chilled

Fill chilled highball glass halfway with ice. Add wine, vermouth, simple syrup, and lemon juice and stir to combine using bar spoon. Add seltzer and, using spoon, gently lift wine mixture from bottom of glass to top to combine. Top with additional ice. Garnish with lemon slice and serve.

Kalimotxo

Makes 1 cocktail

Sweetness ✦ ✧ ✧

Bitter, Citrusy, Fruity

Kalimotxo, a Basque specialty that consists of equal parts red wine and cola, has long been enjoyed throughout the Iberian Peninsula, often to upgrade the taste of lower quality wine. But, as legend has it, the drink was truly popularized at a Basque Country festival in 1972. Festival organizers received several cases of wine that had gone off, so to make the wine palatable, they cut it with cola. Now the easy-to-drink cocktail is a beloved bar staple across Spain. To add just a bit of complexity to this straightforward drink, we incorporate a dash of both orange and aromatic bitters, and garnish with the traditional orange slice.

- 4 ounces dry red wine, chilled
- ⅛ teaspoon orange bitters
- ⅛ teaspoon old-fashioned aromatic bitters
- 4 ounces cola, chilled
- Orange slice for garnishing

Fill chilled rocks glass halfway with crushed ice. Add wine, orange bitters, and aromatic bitters and stir to combine using bar spoon. Slowly add cola and, using spoon, gently lift wine mixture from bottom of glass to top to combine. Top with crushed ice and garnish with orange slice. Serve.

Customize Your Cocktail

Make a Zero-Proof Kalimotxo by using nonalcoholic red wine and nonalcoholic bitters.

Kalimotxo

Gathered Clouds

Gathered Clouds

Makes 1 cocktail
Sweetness ✧ ✧ ✧
Fruity, Spirit Forward

This beautiful, aptly named sake cocktail is made with junmai nigori, which is cloudy rice sake. The sake is unfiltered, so some of the kasu—the particulate matter composed of the processed rice and yeast—is retained, leading to a creamy, mouth-filling texture that builds up the body of a drink and helps the sake stand up to other flavorful ingredients. Here those flavors are floral (gin and elderflower liqueur) and citrus (orange bitters and lemon). You'll find this cocktail satisfying and balanced any day, cloudy or not. We appreciate the creamy texture the nigori sake adds to this cocktail; however, a junmai ginjō sake also works well here (the cocktail will not have the cloudy appearance if you use a different sake).

- 2½ **ounces junmai nigori sake**
- ½ **ounce London dry gin**
- 1 **teaspoon elderflower liqueur**
- ⅛ **teaspoon orange bitters**
- **Lemon coin**

Add sake, gin, elderflower liqueur, and bitters to mixing glass, then fill three-quarters full with ice. Using bar spoon, stir until mixture is fully combined and well chilled, about 1 minute. Strain cocktail into chilled cocktail glass. Pinch lemon coin over drink, then discard. Serve.

Kappa Cocktail

Makes 1 cocktail
Sweetness ✦ ✧ ✧
Citrusy

Named for the water-dwelling, cucumber-loving creatures in Japanese folklore, this sake cocktail is inspired by spa water, or cucumber water. The simple, pleasant flavors of lemon juice and cucumber elevate the aromatics of the sake without overpowering it, as undiluted genshu sake is a variety that likes to stand out. We prefer the bolder flavor of a junmai genshu sake in this cocktail; however, a junmai ginjō sake also works well here.

- 2 **ounces junmai genshu sake**
- ½ **ounce Simple Syrup (page 458)**
- ½ **ounce lemon juice**
- 1 **(1-inch) piece English cucumber, sliced thin, plus cucumber slice for garnishing**

Add sake, simple syrup, lemon juice, and cucumber slices to cocktail shaker, then fill with ice. Shake mixture until fully combined and well chilled, about 1 minute. Double-strain cocktail into chilled cocktail glass. Garnish with cucumber slice and serve.

The Shandy

In England in the 1850s, beer was mixed with ginger beer and called a shandygaff—and it quickly became a warm-weather pub favorite. By the late 1800s, it had become well-known enough in America that a recipe appeared in Harry Johnson's *Bartenders' Manual.*

By the end of the century, though, ginger beer was on the outs in favor of a sparkling lemony soft drink, and "gaff" was dropped from the name. This lemony shandy is still a pub favorite in England today, generally made with a light style of beer (think lager or pilsner) and still with a sparkling lemon mixer.

When this lemony shandy first came to America, something got lost in translation. In England, "lemonade" refers to a bubbly beverage, whereas in America, lemonade refers to a still, cloudy drink. The former is preferred for shandy making. Our bright and bubbly version is closer to the British version of the shandy because we start by making a fresh lemonade concentrate from lemon juice and simple syrup. Then we dilute it with seltzer instead of still water, adding beer at the same time.

Although the radler has a separate origin story from the shandy, the two are certainly close siblings. The radler emerged in Munich in the 1920s, supposedly from an inventive beer garden owner who was running low on beer and mixed what he had with some citrus juice in an effort to serve all his customers (who happened that day to be cyclists, the German for which is "radler"). Whereas a shandy typically uses a lemon drink as the nonalcoholic component, a radler can use any fruit juice. Our refreshing take uses grapefruit juice and skips the seltzer. Like shandies, radlers are made with light-style beers such as lagers or pilsners.

Expanding this family, our Peach Cruiser uses wheat beer and peach nectar—a flavor combination popular in France. And we offer an homage to the original shandygaff with the Gingered Beer, which calls for stout and ginger syrup.

Shandy

Makes 1 cocktail
Sweetness ✦ ✧ ✧
Bitter, Citrusy

- ¾ ounce lemon juice, plus lemon slice for garnish
- ¾ ounce Simple Syrup (page 458)
- 6 ounces pilsner or light lager, chilled
- 6 ounces seltzer, chilled

Add lemon juice and simple syrup to chilled highball glass and stir to combine using bar spoon. Slowly add beer and seltzer and, using spoon, gently lift lemon mixture from bottom of glass to top to combine. Garnish with lemon slice and serve.

Customize Your Cocktail

If you'd like to simplify your shandy, you can use 6 ounces of Italian-style lemon soda in place of the lemon juice, simple syrup, and seltzer. Create a Zero-Proof Shandy by using a nonalcoholic pilsner or light lager.

Radler

Makes 1 cocktail
Sweetness ✦ ✧ ✧
Bitter, Citrusy

A session beverage is one that's low enough in alcohol that it can be enjoyed in multiples over the day. All shandies are session beverages, but the radler, which means "cyclist" in German, was created to hydrate cyclists throughout the day while having the effect of allowing them to continue on their route responsibly. The radler is different from a shandy in that it can be made with citrus fruits other than lemon. Here, equal parts grapefruit juice and beer, sweetened with simple syrup, can refresh through strenuous activity—or a lazy day on a lawn chair.

- 6 ounces grapefruit juice, plus grapefruit slice for garnishing
- 1¼ ounces Simple Syrup (page 458)
- 6 ounces pilsner or light lager, chilled

Add grapefruit juice and simple syrup to chilled highball glass and stir to combine using bar spoon. Slowly add beer and, using spoon, gently lift grapefruit mixture from bottom of glass to top to combine. Garnish with grapefruit slice and serve.

Customize Your Cocktail

Create a Zero-Proof Radler by using a nonalcoholic pilsner or light lager.

Peach Cruiser

Makes 1 cocktail
Sweetness ✦ ✧ ✧
Fruity, Toasted

Wheat and peaches go together: Desserts are an obvious marriage of the two, but we're also thinking about the South American drink mote con huesillo, which combines reconstituted dried peaches and wheat berries. This light and refreshing wheat beer shandy is inspired by that combination. We developed this recipe using a German-style hefeweizen, but other wheat beers will also work.

- 2 ounces peach nectar
- 6 ounces wheat beer, chilled
- 4 ounces seltzer, chilled
- Peach slice for garnishing

Add peach nectar to chilled highball glass. Slowly add beer and seltzer and, using bar spoon, gently lift peach nectar from bottom of glass to top to combine. Garnish with peach slice and serve.

Customize Your Cocktail

Create a Zero-Proof Peach Cruiser by using a nonalcoholic wheat beer, pilsner, or light lager.

Gingered Beer

Makes 1 cocktail
Sweetness ✦ ✦ ✧
Spiced, Spicy, Toasted

Stout's dark color tricks some into thinking it's heavy when really it's quite light in body, similar to a pale ale, and perfect for a shandy. The characteristic color comes from dark-roasting the barley in the malting process, which creates roasty, toasty, chocolaty flavors. The stout's molasses notes pair well with ginger and soda in this zippy shandy that reminds us of a moist ginger cake, especially with the nutmeg garnish. We prefer to use our homemade Ginger Syrup (page 93), but store-bought versions will also work.

- 2 ounces ginger syrup
- 6 ounces stout, chilled
- 4 ounces seltzer, chilled
- Freshly grated nutmeg for garnishing

Add ginger syrup to chilled highball glass. Slowly add beer and seltzer and, using bar spoon, gently lift ginger syrup from bottom of glass to top to combine. Garnish with grated nutmeg and serve.

Customize Your Cocktail

Create a Zero-Proof Gingered Beer by using a nonalcoholic stout beer or malta.

Michelada

Makes 1 cocktail
Sweetness ✧ ✧ ✧
Citrusy, Savory, Spicy

- ¼ cup Sriracha Rim Salt (page 453) (optional)
- 2 ounces lime juice, plus lime wedge for garnishing
- ½ ounce hot sauce
- ¼ ounce Worcestershire sauce
- 12 ounces light lager, chilled

Customize Your Cocktail

While we prefer the heat of our Sriracha Rim Salt here, you can substitute the Citrus Rim Salt or Herb Rim Salt from page 453, Tajín Clásico Seasoning, or plain kosher salt. Create a Zero-Proof Michelada by using a nonalcoholic light lager.

A michelada is incredibly satisfying on a blisteringly hot day—or great as a hangover cure. Believed to have first been made in Mexico, the michelada has lots of regional variations. This drink only recently found broad popularity in other places (with beer brands offering pre-made versions), though many people tend to conflate it with the chelada and add tomato juice. One constant is fresh lime, and a generous 2 ounces of lime juice adds the refreshing tartness we desire. To balance that tartness, we add doses of Worcestershire sauce and hot sauce; a thicker hot sauce contributes a bit of body. Our sriracha rim salt gives every sip a bit more heat. To ensure that everything is well blended, we combine the flavorful seasoning ingredients in the glass before pouring in the beer. Mexican lager is traditional here, but other light lagers will also work. We recommend Cholula and Tapatío hot sauces for their flavor and thicker consistency. If using a thinner, more vinegary hot sauce such as Tabasco, start with half the amount called for and consider dropping the volume of lime juice; adjust to your taste after mixing.

1. Spread rim salt, if using, into even layer on small saucer. Moisten about ½ inch of chilled pint glass rim by running lime wedge around outer edge; dry any excess juice with paper towel. Roll moistened rim in salt to coat. Remove any excess salt that falls into glass; set aside.

2. Fill prepared glass halfway with ice. Add lime juice, hot sauce, and Worcestershire and stir to combine using bar spoon. Add beer and, using spoon, gently lift lime mixture from bottom of glass to top to combine. Top with additional ice and garnish with lime wedge. Serve.

Stock Car Spritz

Makes 1 cocktail
Sweetness ✦ ✦ ✧
Bitter, Citrusy

Many countries throughout Europe, particularly in places with a colder climate, have traditions of both brewing lagers and making bitter liqueurs. Long before lots of flavors were added to beers, in many of these places there had been a custom of pouring a bitter liqueur into a lager. The combination of light-bodied, bottom-fermented beer and intensely flavored liqueur is a beautiful marriage, as in this cocktail. Sure, an Aperol spritz refreshes, but this drink feels right for more casual occasions, when the wineglass and prosecco aren't right—in a backyard instead of a piazza. In fact, in a pinch you can even build the drink in the bottle or can (the density of the Aperol will do the mixing for you).

- 2 ounces Aperol
- 10 ounces light lager, chilled
- Orange slice for garnishing

Add Aperol to chilled highball glass. Slowly add beer and, using bar spoon, gently lift Aperol from bottom of glass to top to combine. Garnish with orange slice and serve.

Customize Your Cocktail

You can substitute Campari or Select Aperitivo for the Aperol. Make a Zero-Proof Stock Car Spritz by using a nonalcoholic light lager and a nonalcoholic aperitif, such as Wilfred's.

PAIR WITH A SNACK

Garlic-Parsley Crispy Chickpeas

Serves 4
Total Time: 35 minutes

Fried chickpeas are as poppable as any other crunchy snack, from popcorn to chips to nuts, with a satisfying savor that pairs nicely with these cocktails. Do not rinse the chickpeas after draining them, and be sure to dry them as thoroughly as possible before frying.

- 2 (15-ounce) cans chickpeas, drained
- 2 cups vegetable oil
- 1 tablespoon minced fresh parsley
- 3 garlic cloves, minced
- ½ teaspoon table salt

1. Spread chickpeas into even layer over clean dish towel. Cover chickpeas with second clean dish towel, then press and gently roll chickpeas between towels to remove as much moisture as possible. Transfer chickpeas to large saucepan (no need to discard any loosened or separated skins). Add oil and cook over medium-high heat, stirring occasionally, until chickpeas are deep golden brown and crispy, 27 to 32 minutes, adjusting heat as needed to maintain oil temperature between 325 and 350 degrees.

2. Using spider skimmer or slotted spoon and allowing excess oil to drain back into saucepan, transfer chickpeas to large bowl. Add parsley, garlic, and salt and toss until evenly combined. Transfer to serving bowl. Serve. (Chickpeas can be stored in airtight container for up to 2 days.)

Cider 66

Makes 1 cocktail

Sweetness ✦✦✧

Citrusy, Floral, Fruity

The French 75 (page 42) is a classic cocktail that combines gin or brandy with lemon, sugar, and sparkling wine. Here we lean into the apple notes of brandy and substitute dry sparkling cider for the sparkling wine. This makes a very drinkable, fruity cocktail with accessible style. We developed this recipe using dry hard cider (sometimes labeled cidre and usually stocked with beers); do not confuse this with sparkling cider from the grocery store, which is much sweeter.

- 1 ounce brandy
- ½ ounce lemon juice, plus lemon twist for garnishing
- ½ ounce Simple Syrup (page 458)
- 3 ounces dry sparkling cider, chilled

Add brandy, lemon juice, and simple syrup to cocktail shaker, then fill with ice. Shake mixture until fully combined and well chilled, about 15 seconds. Double-strain brandy mixture into chilled flute glass. Slowly add sparkling cider and, using bar spoon, gently lift brandy mixture from bottom of glass to top to combine. Garnish with lemon twist and serve.

Customize Your Cocktail

Bourbon works well in place of the brandy.

Flips *and* Nogs

I flip, you flip, we all flip for flips and nogs. While a general definition of eggnog—milk, eggs, sugar, spices, and traditionally a spirit—is well known, flips don't enjoy the same recognition, having largely fallen out of fashion in the 20th century. But like nogs, flips are decadent, flavorful, and a delicious path to holiday (or anytime) cheer.

Flips are made up of a liquor, liqueur, and/or fortified wine (such as sherry) shaken with a whole egg or an egg yolk and sweetened with sugar. They are historically distinguished from eggnog by their lack of dairy—although as is common in our modern cocktail times, this line has become blurred.

Early versions of flips started to appear in the 1600s and were drinks of ale and rum to which sugar (sometimes molasses) and spices (particularly nutmeg but also cinnamon, cloves, and others) were added. Soon eggs began to be added, and eventually the ale began to be omitted. These flips were served hot—a feat often achieved by sticking a hot fire poker into the mug. Contemporary flips are mostly served cold, shaken with ice.

Although from a technique perspective, a nog is essentially a flip with dairy added, the history of eggnog actually goes back farther. Eggnog likely originated from Britain's early medieval "posset" of warm milk mixed with ale or wine, flavored with whatever spices were available. By the 13th century, monks (who tended to have better food access than the general population) were including eggs in their possets.

The drink started to become associated with the winter holiday season (and adopted its modern name) with the rise of the American colonies in the 1700s. There was no shortage of chickens and cows to provide the necessary ingredients, and spirits were plentiful. Rum made from molasses imported from the Caribbean was cheaper than spirits from Europe and was frequently used. Those in Pennsylvania and the Southern colonies were more likely to use whiskey. George Washington's extant recipe calls for brandy, whiskey, rum, and sherry!

Physicians in the 19th century often prescribed eggnog for recovering patients because of the vitamins and minerals found in the dairy and eggs and the believed medicinal properties of the spices (even though these "prescriptions" often included brandy).

In addition to a variety of flips and nogs made with different spirits, you'll also find eggnog-adjacent creamy drinks here. Our Southern Milk Punch (page 390) could be thought of as an eggless eggnog. And the Brandy Alexander (page 392) enhances heavy cream with crème de cacao for a truly indulgent dessert cocktail.

Flips and Nogs

Fundamental Formula

- flip = spirit + egg (whole or yolk) + sugar
- nog = spirit + egg + cream or milk + sugar

BUILD ON THE FUNDAMENTALS

To build on the classic Brandy Flip (page 375), incorporate a fortified wine or liqueur in addition to the base spirit, as in our Ruby Flip (page 376); or swap the spirit for a liqueur, as in our Fernet Flip (page 377). Our nonalcoholic Peanut Butter Flip (page 381) incorporates a small amount of nut butter to achieve its well-rounded texture. To build on Classic Eggnog (page 382), add flavors by using low-liquid ingredients such as espresso powder, lemon zest, or pumpkin puree. To skip the eggs, try Southern Milk Punch (page 390) or Tahini-Rose Russian (page 390), which adds richness using tahini.

Why Use Eggs in Cocktails?

Eggs have been used in cocktails for centuries to enrich flavor, body, and texture.

WHOLE EGGS add rich eggy flavor and creamy texture. Nogs and flips typically use whole eggs, with many eggnog recipes including additional egg yolks to achieve the desired richness.

EGG YOLKS add a stronger, slightly sweeter flavor than whole eggs do. Certain flip recipes may use egg yolks only, but these are less common. We like the more rounded flavor and texture that whole eggs bring to flips.

EGG WHITES create a foamy texture by trapping air bubbles when shaken and offer a round, silky mouthfeel without affecting flavor. They also soften the sharp qualities of acidic ingredients, making for more balanced flavors. Egg whites can be used in sours (see page 203) and sometimes fizzes.

Fresh or Pasteurized?

Our eggnog recipes call for making an egg custard base. Tempering the eggs with hot milk and then cooking the mixture to 160 degrees kills any potential bacteria. Our flip recipes call for adding a raw egg to the cocktail.

If you use fresh eggs in cocktails, follow commonsense guidelines. The fresher the egg, the safer it's likely to be to consume raw. Check the dates on the container, including the Julian date, which is a three-digit number below the sell-by or expiration date. The Julian date tells you the day of the year the eggs were packed (for example, 050 is February 19). Make sure none of the eggs are cracked or damaged, store them in the coldest part of your refrigerator (40 degrees or colder; that's not the door, which is subject to temperature fluctuations). Wash the eggs before cracking them and examine them after you crack them open. If any part looks cloudy or discolored, do not use it. And wash your hands thoroughly—both before and after cracking them open.

You can use pasteurized eggs in cocktails. Larger supermarkets carry in-shell pasteurized eggs. You can also purchase pasteurized whole eggs, egg yolks, and egg whites in cartons; check ingredient labels to ensure you are buying eggs with no additives, which may affect the texture or flavor of your cocktail. One whole egg equals about 1¾ ounces of pasteurized egg product. To pasteurize eggs at home, see page 397.

Frozen Egg White Assets

Leftover egg whites—whether those egg whites are from making eggnogs or from baked goods—freeze well, so you should save them for use in cocktails that call for egg whites only, such as our Aperol Sour (page 224), Amaretto Sour (page 211), or Bitter with the Sweet (page 221). We freeze the whites in 1-ounce portions in standard-size ice cube trays. Once they're frozen, you can pop out the cubes and store them in a zipper-lock freezer bag in the freezer. Simply add a frozen cube to a cocktail shaker for the dry-shake step, adjusting the shaking time to 1 minute 15 seconds.

Dairy Fat Differences

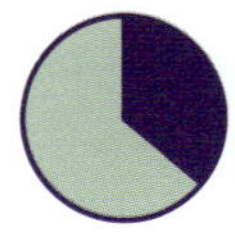

HEAVY CREAM (also labeled as heavy whipping cream) contains 36 percent or more milk fat. This is the cream we call for in our flips and nogs.

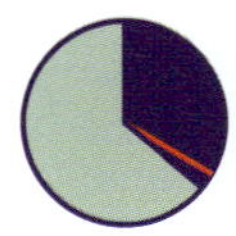

CREAM (sometimes called whipping cream) contains 30 to 36 percent milk fat. You can substitute this for heavy cream in our recipes, but you may end up with a less rich cocktail.

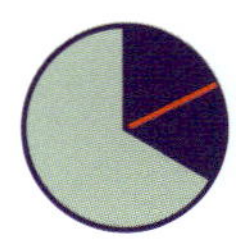

LIGHT CREAM is 18 to 30 percent milk fat. We use it in our Southern Milk Punch (page 390) to bring a fuller body than whole milk would do. (Don't substitute half-and-half, which is lower in milk fat.)

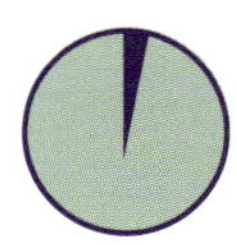

WHOLE MILK contains about 3.25 percent milk fat. For the best flavor and texture, we suggest you use whole milk in these recipes rather than a lower-fat version.

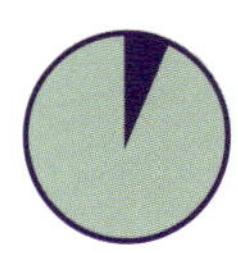

EVAPORATED MILK, which contains about 6.6 percent milk fat, is made by slowly heating milk to remove about half its water, a process that caramelizes its lactose, resulting in a light golden color and mildly sweet flavor. We use it in our Coquito (page 394).

COCONUT MILK is made by combining grated coconut flesh with hot water and then straining out the liquid. For the Cocochai (page 393) and the Coquito (page 394), buy canned full-fat coconut milk rather than canned light coconut milk or the refrigerated variety in a carton. Shake the can before opening it; otherwise, you may find that it has separated into coconut cream and watery liquid.

CREAM OF COCONUT is sweetened and thickened with emulsifiers. It's what you want for our Coquito (page 394).

The Flip

The flip began as a sailor's drink. In the 1600s, the flip was known in England as a mixture of rum, ale, and sometimes molasses, poured back and forth between two pitchers to achieve an airy, smoothly mixed texture. As with many drink traditions, it made its way across the pond to the American colonies, where it became a mainstay in taverns, heated with a red-hot fire poker plunged into the liquid to caramelize the sugars and make it froth (or "flip," as the process was referred to at the time). It was also in the colonies that adding eggs became more common, resulting in a richer, creamier drink.

Over time, the ale largely disappeared from the mix, and eventually cold flips arrived on the scene. The first written reference to a flip made without heating the egg was in E. A. Simmons's 1874 book *The American Bar-Tender, or The Art and Mystery of Mixing Drinks*, which includes cold flips made with brandy, whiskey, gin, and sherry.

Flips seemed to have had their pop culture moment in the mid-1800s, being enthusiastically referred to in *Moby-Dick* by Herman Melville as well as in novels by Harriet Beecher Stowe and Charles Dickens. The popularity of flips has flagged over the past hundred or so years, at least in part due to concern about the safety of consuming raw eggs and the lack of a commercially available alternative (an advantage that eggnog holds over flips).

We think it's time for home bartenders to start shaking more flips, and with the availability of pasteurized eggs, it becomes worry-free. We suggest using a Boston shaker when dry-shaking eggs for cocktails, as it typically has more room than a cobbler shaker for the expansion of the egg foam.

The brandy flip is one of the classics, and it's easy to customize by using a flavored simple syrup, or incorporating a fortified wine like port, or even swapping out the brandy for an assertive amaro. One sip and you'll flip.

Brandy Flip

Makes 1 cocktail
Sweetness ✦✦✧
Creamy, Spirit Forward, Toasted

- 2 ounces brandy
- 1 large egg
- ½ ounce Simple Syrup (page 458)
- Freshly grated nutmeg for garnishing

1. Add brandy, egg, and simple syrup to cocktail shaker and vigorously shake until mixture is foamy, about 45 seconds.

2. Fill shaker with ice, then shake mixture until fully combined and well chilled, about 15 seconds. Double-strain cocktail into chilled cocktail glass. Garnish with grated nutmeg and serve.

Customize Your Cocktail

You can garnish the cocktail with other freshly grated spices such as cinnamon, star anise, or allspice. Make a Sherry Flip by substituting a dry amontillado, oloroso, or palo cortado sherry for the brandy.

Spiced Brandy Flip

Makes 1 cocktail
Sweetness ✦✦✧
Creamy, Spiced, Toasted

Brandy always pairs well with spice and citrus. Here especially, the flavors complement the richness of the flip and recall holiday mulling blends that match baking spice with orange peel. Shaking an orange coin with the rest of the ingredients introduces the aromatic orange oil more evenly through the drink than expressing it as a garnish can. The orange aroma elevates this flip while reminding us of high-quality brandy-based orange liqueurs, and the grated star anise provides a lovely licorice-y finish.

- 2 ounces brandy
- 1 large egg
- ½ ounce Spice Syrup (page 459)
- 1 orange coin (see page 450)
- Freshly grated star anise for garnishing

1. Add brandy, egg, spiced syrup, and orange coin to cocktail shaker and vigorously shake until mixture is foamy, about 45 seconds.

2. Fill shaker with ice, then shake mixture until fully combined and well chilled, about 15 seconds. Double-strain cocktail into chilled cocktail glass. Garnish with grated star anise and serve.

Ruby Flip

Makes 1 cocktail
Sweetness ✦✦✧
Creamy, Fruity, Toasted

Ruby port is one of the most loved after-dinner drinks. Here it adds fruitiness that stands out in each creamy sip of this pretty cocktail.

- 1 large egg
- 1 ounce brandy
- 1 ounce ruby port
- ½ ounce Simple Syrup (page 458)
- Freshly grated nutmeg for garnishing

1. Add egg, brandy, port, and simple syrup to cocktail shaker and vigorously shake until mixture is foamy, about 45 seconds.

2. Fill shaker with ice, then shake mixture until fully combined and well chilled, about 15 seconds. Double-strain cocktail into chilled cocktail glass. Garnish with grated nutmeg and serve.

Fernet Flip

Makes 1 cocktail
Sweetness ✦✦✧
Bitter, Creamy, Herbal

Why choose between a digestif or a dessert after dinner when you can have both in a single glass? Bitter, herbaceous fernet takes the flip in a totally different direction, the liqueur offsetting the sweet creaminess of the egg.

- **2 ounces Fernet-Branca**
- **1 large egg**
- **¾ ounce Simple Syrup (page 458)**
- **Freshly grated star anise for garnishing**

1. Add Fernet-Branca, egg, and simple syrup to cocktail shaker and vigorously shake until mixture is foamy, about 45 seconds.

2. Fill shaker with ice, then shake mixture until fully combined and well chilled, about 15 seconds. Double-strain cocktail into chilled cocktail glass. Garnish with grated star anise and serve.

Customize Your Cocktail

You can substitute your favorite amaro for the fernet.

Makes 1 cocktail
Sweetness ✦ ✦ ✧
Creamy, Spiced, Spirit Forward

James Flip

We know shaking an egg into a cocktail smooths sharp edges. In our James Flip (which we named for the inventor of Pimm's No.1, James Pimm), we really test the limits by employing two bar weapons: funky, complex Jamaican rum and herbal Pimm's. And the flip formula passes with flying colors: When emulsified with the egg, the rum and the Pimm's create a surprising cocktail with cohesive flavor and unexpected depth. A dusting of cinnamon enhances the rum's warm spice notes, making for a well-rounded and inviting flip.

- 1 large egg
- 1 ounce aged Jamaican rum
- 1 ounce Pimm's No.1
- ½ ounce Simple Syrup (page 458)
- Freshly grated cinnamon for garnishing

1. Add egg, rum, Pimm's, and simple syrup to cocktail shaker and vigorously shake until mixture is foamy, about 45 seconds.

2. Fill shaker with ice, then shake mixture until fully combined and well chilled, about 15 seconds. Double-strain cocktail into chilled cocktail glass. Garnish with grated cinnamon and serve.

Customize Your Cocktail

We enjoy the complex flavor of Jamaican rum in this cocktail, but feel free to experiment with other styles of aged rum.

Peanut Butter Flip

Makes 1 zero-proof cocktail
Sweetness ✦✦✦
Creamy, Nutty

This drink's a dream for all peanut butter lovers (and as it's a zero-proof cocktail, we really mean all). This might be one of the most decadent drinks you've ever tasted, perfect for dessert—ideally after a lighter dinner. If you'd like, a peanut butter cup garnish is a playful touch.

- 1 large egg
- 1 ounce heavy cream
- ¾ ounce Simple Syrup (page 458)
- 1 tablespoon creamy peanut butter
- Freshly grated nutmeg for garnishing

1. Add egg, heavy cream, simple syrup, and peanut butter to cocktail shaker and vigorously shake until mixture is foamy, about 45 seconds.

2. Fill shaker with ice, then shake mixture until fully combined and well chilled, about 15 seconds. Double-strain cocktail into chilled cocktail glass. Garnish with grated nutmeg and serve.

Customize Your Cocktail

Try replacing the peanut butter with other nut and seed butters, such as almond butter or tahini. Make a Spiked Peanut Butter Flip by adding 1 ounce of Scotch or bourbon to the cocktail shaker with the egg.

PAIR WITH A SNACK

Salty Snack Bark

Makes 16 pieces
Total Time: 15 minutes, plus 30 minutes cooling

Something sweet—but also a little bitter, salty, and texturally compelling—is the perfect accompaniment to these creamy drinks. While making candy doesn't sound like a quick treat, this bark is; we temper the chocolate easily in the microwave. We developed this recipe using Ghirardelli 60% Cacao Bittersweet Chocolate.

- 1 pound bittersweet chocolate, chopped fine, divided
- ⅔ cup crushed kettle-cooked potato chips
- ⅔ cup crushed thin pretzels

1. Line rimmed baking sheet with parchment paper.

2. Microwave 12 ounces chocolate in medium bowl at 50 percent power, stirring often with silicone spatula, until about two-thirds melted, 1½ to 2½ minutes (chocolate should be fluid but still lumpy). Remove bowl from microwave and add remaining 4 ounces chocolate. Stir and mash until chocolate is just melted and smooth, about 3 minutes. (If lumps remain, return chocolate to microwave at 50 percent power for no more than 5 seconds at a time, stirring after each interval, until fully melted.)

3. Working quickly, use offset spatula to spread chocolate evenly over prepared sheet. Sprinkle with chips and pretzels and gently press into chocolate. Let sit until chocolate is set, about 30 minutes (if your kitchen is warm, you can let bark set up briefly in refrigerator).

4. Transfer bark to cutting board; discard parchment. Cut or break into pieces. Serve. (Bark can be stored at room temperature for up to 2 weeks.)

Eggnog

Add milk and/or cream to a flip, and you've got an eggnog. Over the past century, eggnogs have become relegated to the winter holidays, but that wasn't always the case. "Nog" was once a term for strong beer, and it also may have referred to a wooden cup used for drinking.

In simpler forms, eggnog has been around since the 1200s. Its modern form comes into clearer view in the 18th century, when eggnog caught on in the American colonies. The combination of dairy and eggs with alcohol was serendipitous, since the alcohol acted as a natural preservative, allowing the drink to be stored for a while. Additionally, the richness of the dairy and egg worked well to mask the astringency of the alcohol of that era. Colonial eggnogs could be quite heady—George Washington was said to favor an eggnog so strong that only his most courageous guests would partake during his parties at Mount Vernon.

As for eggnog's Christmastime association—in those olden days, though eggnog was made nearly year-round, dairy and eggs became harder to come by in winter, so eggnog became reserved for special occasions during those months. It was once a tradition to have a glass for breakfast on Christmas Day (or, if you were lucky, on each of the twelve days of Christmas).

And what's more satisfying on a wintry day than a cocktail that's practically a meal? If you've only had commercial versions, you're in for a treat. We like our homemade nog full of cozy spices, such as nutmeg, cinnamon, and ginger, and sometimes enhanced with other flavors, including espresso, lemon, or pumpkin spice.

We first temper the eggs with hot milk to help prevent curdling. It's also important to stir the custard constantly; if it does begin to curdle, remove it from the heat immediately and pour it into a bowl set over a larger bowl of ice water to stop the cooking, then strain as directed. We spike the nog with spirit and spices, and finally whisk in heavy cream whipped to soft peaks for a superluxurious mouthfeel.

Classic Eggnog

Makes 8 cocktails
Sweetness ✦✦✦
Creamy, Spiced, Toasted

Freshly grated nutmeg is best here; if using preground nutmeg, reduce the amount to ¼ teaspoon.

- **6 large eggs plus 2 large yolks**
- **½ cup plus 2 tablespoons sugar**
- **¼ teaspoon table salt**
- **32 ounces whole milk**
- **8 ounces brandy**
- **1 tablespoon vanilla extract**
- **½ teaspoon freshly grated nutmeg, plus extra for garnishing**
- **4 ounces heavy cream, chilled**

1. Whisk eggs and yolks, sugar, and salt in medium bowl until thoroughly combined, about 30 seconds. Bring milk to simmer in large saucepan over medium-high heat, stirring occasionally.

2. When milk comes to simmer, remove from heat and, whisking constantly, slowly pour into egg mixture to temper. Return milk-egg mixture to saucepan. Place over medium-low heat and cook, stirring constantly and scraping edges of saucepan with spatula, until mixture reaches 160 degrees, 2 to 5 minutes.

3. Immediately pour custard through fine-mesh strainer into large bowl. Whisk in brandy, vanilla, and nutmeg. Cover and refrigerate until base registers 40 degrees, at least 3 hours or up to 3 days. (Alternatively, base can be chilled to 40 degrees in about 1½ hours by placing bowl in ice bath filled with 6 cups ice, ½ cup water, and ⅓ cup table salt.)

4. Vigorously whisk cream in separate chilled bowl until soft peaks just begin to form, about 60 seconds. Whisk whipped cream into chilled eggnog until fully incorporated. Serve in chilled punch cups, garnishing individual portions with extra nutmeg.

Customize Your Cocktail

Bourbon or aged rum are also good options for eggnog.

Caffè Eggnog

Makes 8 cocktails
Sweetness ✦✦✦
Creamy, Spiced, Toasted

If a latte is your forever coffee order, this eggnog variation might become your new standard. The roasty bitterness of the espresso powder with the smooth caramel notes of aged rum make every sip deeply satisfying. Ground cinnamon (instead of nutmeg) and an optional espresso bean garnish complete the coffeehouse flavor profile—and offer the aroma of one too.

- **6 large eggs plus 2 large yolks**
- **½ cup plus 2 tablespoons sugar**
- **¼ teaspoon table salt**
- **32 ounces whole milk**
- **8 ounces aged rum**
- **2 tablespoons instant espresso powder**
- **1 teaspoon vanilla extract**
- **½ teaspoon ground cinnamon**
- **4 ounces heavy cream, chilled**
- **Espresso beans for garnishing (optional)**

1. Whisk eggs and yolks, sugar, and salt in medium bowl until thoroughly combined, about 30 seconds. Bring milk to simmer in large saucepan over medium-high heat, stirring occasionally.

2. When milk comes to simmer, remove from heat and, whisking constantly, slowly pour into egg mixture to temper. Return milk-egg mixture to saucepan. Place over medium-low heat and cook, stirring constantly with spatula, until mixture reaches 160 degrees, 2 to 5 minutes.

3. Immediately pour custard through fine-mesh strainer into large bowl. Whisk in rum, espresso powder, vanilla, and cinnamon. Cover and refrigerate until base registers 40 degrees, at least 3 hours or up to 3 days. (Alternatively, base can be chilled to 40 degrees in about 1½ hours by placing bowl in ice bath filled with 6 cups ice, ½ cup water, and ⅓ cup table salt.)

4. Vigorously whisk cream in separate chilled bowl until soft peaks just begin to form, about 60 seconds. Whisk whipped cream into chilled eggnog until fully incorporated. Serve in chilled punch cups, garnishing individual portions with espresso beans, if using.

Customize Your Cocktail

We like the complexity that aged rum adds to this eggnog spin, but you can use brandy or bourbon. Reposado tequila would also be a great complement to the espresso.

Lemon-Almond Eggnog

Makes 8 cocktails
Sweetness ✦✦✦
Citrusy, Creamy, Toasted

This brandy and amaretto eggnog is like no other we've encountered: It tastes like a beautiful lemon-almond cake but with the same silky, fluffy texture of our original eggnog. To achieve marked lemon flavor amid all the dairy, we add some lemon zest to the milk as it simmers so the citrus oils migrate to the drink. Adding some lemon juice right before serving ensures there's fresh lemon flavor at the finish.

- 6 large eggs plus 2 large yolks
- ½ cup sugar
- ¼ teaspoon table salt
- 32 ounces whole milk
- 1 tablespoon grated lemon zest plus 2 tablespoons juice, divided, plus extra lemon zest for garnishing
- 6 ounces brandy
- 2 ounces amaretto
- 1 teaspoon vanilla extract
- 4 ounces heavy cream, chilled

1. Whisk eggs and yolks, sugar, and salt in medium bowl until thoroughly combined, about 30 seconds. Bring milk and lemon zest to simmer in large saucepan over medium-high heat, stirring occasionally.

2. When milk mixture comes to simmer, remove from heat and, whisking constantly, slowly pour into egg mixture to temper. Return milk-egg mixture to saucepan. Place over medium-low heat and cook, stirring constantly with spatula, until mixture reaches 160 degrees, 2 to 5 minutes.

3. Immediately pour custard through fine-mesh strainer into large bowl. Whisk in brandy, amaretto, and vanilla. Cover and refrigerate until base registers 40 degrees, at least 3 hours or up to 3 days. (Alternatively, base can be chilled to 40 degrees in about 1½ hours by placing bowl in ice bath filled with 6 cups ice, ½ cup water, and ⅓ cup table salt.)

4. Vigorously whisk cream in separate chilled bowl until soft peaks just begin to form, about 60 seconds. Whisk whipped cream and lemon juice into chilled eggnog until fully incorporated. Serve in chilled punch cups, garnishing individual portions with extra lemon zest.

Pumpkin Spice Eggnog

Makes 8 cocktails
Sweetness ✦✦✦
Creamy, Spiced, Toasted

Eggnog takes on spice very well, as it's classically finished with freshly grated nutmeg. Here we dial the spice up with our own homemade pumpkin spice blend, plus some actual pumpkin. (We believe in putting the pumpkin into pumpkin spice.) The canned squash adds a touch more body, and its savoriness keeps the spice and sweetness in check.

- 6 large eggs plus 2 large yolks
- ½ cup plus 2 tablespoons sugar
- ¼ teaspoon table salt
- 32 ounces whole milk
- 8 ounces bourbon
- ¾ cup canned unsweetened pumpkin puree
- 1 teaspoon vanilla extract
- ¾ teaspoon ground cinnamon, plus extra for garnishing
- ¼ teaspoon ground allspice
- ¼ teaspoon ground ginger
- ¼ teaspoon freshly grated nutmeg, plus extra for garnishing
- 4 ounces heavy cream, chilled

1. Whisk eggs and yolks, sugar, and salt in medium bowl until thoroughly combined, about 30 seconds. Bring milk to simmer in large saucepan over medium-high heat, stirring occasionally.

2. When milk comes to simmer, remove from heat and, whisking constantly, slowly pour into egg mixture to temper. Return milk-egg mixture to saucepan. Place over medium-low heat and cook, stirring constantly with spatula, until mixture reaches 160 degrees, 2 to 5 minutes.

3. Immediately pour custard through fine-mesh strainer into large bowl. Whisk in bourbon, pumpkin, vanilla, cinnamon, allspice, ginger, and nutmeg. Cover and refrigerate until base registers 40 degrees, at least 3 hours or up to 3 days. (Alternatively, base can be chilled to 40 degrees in about 1½ hours by placing bowl in ice bath filled with 6 cups ice, ½ cup water, and ⅓ cup table salt.)

4. Vigorously whisk cream in separate chilled bowl until soft peaks just begin to form, about 60 seconds. Whisk whipped cream into chilled eggnog until fully incorporated. Serve in chilled punch cups, garnishing individual portions with extra cinnamon and nutmeg.

Customize Your Cocktail

You can also use aged rum or brandy here.

Egg Notnog

Makes 8 zero-proof cocktails
Sweetness ✦✦✦
Creamy, Spiced

Most store-bought eggnog is already nonalcoholic, but it tends to be a bit thin and flat-tasting, and it often includes flavorings and additives. We think it's really worth making your own for better texture and taste. Homemade nonalcoholic eggnog is often just nutmeg-scented egg custard, which is nice, but we wanted to mimic the traditional brandy twang. Root beer does the trick to capture the spirit's complex vanilla and savory notes. Cutting back on some of the sugar keeps the sweetness in check.

- 6 large eggs plus 2 large yolks
- ⅓ cup sugar
- ¼ teaspoon table salt
- 32 ounces whole milk
- 4 ounces root beer
- 1 teaspoon vanilla extract
- ½ teaspoon freshly grated nutmeg, plus extra for garnishing
- 4 ounces heavy cream, chilled

1. Whisk eggs and yolks, sugar, and salt in medium bowl until thoroughly combined, about 30 seconds. Bring milk to simmer in large saucepan over medium-high heat, stirring occasionally.

2. When milk comes to simmer, remove from heat and, whisking constantly, slowly pour into egg mixture to temper. Return milk-egg mixture to saucepan. Place over medium-low heat and cook, stirring constantly with spatula, until mixture reaches 160 degrees, 2 to 5 minutes.

3. Immediately pour custard through fine-mesh strainer into large bowl. Whisk in root beer, vanilla, and nutmeg. Cover and refrigerate until base registers 40 degrees, at least 3 hours or up to 3 days. (Alternatively, base can be chilled to 40 degrees in about 1½ hours by placing bowl in ice bath filled with 6 cups ice, ½ cup water, and ⅓ cup table salt.)

4. Vigorously whisk cream in separate chilled bowl until soft peaks just begin to form, about 60 seconds. Whisk whipped cream into chilled eggnog until fully incorporated. Serve in chilled punch cups, garnishing individual portions with extra nutmeg.

Nutrition
Facts

Clockwise from top left: Lemon-Almond Eggnog, Caffè Eggnog, Pumpkin Spice Eggnog, Egg Notnog

PAIR WITH A SNACK

Crunchy Chocolate Haystacks

Makes about 20 haystacks
Total Time: 25 minutes

Complete a festive holiday spread with eggnog and these simple, irresistibly crunchy no-bake cookies.

- 1 cup (6 ounces) bittersweet chocolate chips
- 2 teaspoons vegetable oil
- 3 ounces (1½ cups) chow mein noodles
- ½ cup dry-roasted salted peanuts

Line rimmed baking sheet with parchment paper. Microwave chocolate chips in bowl at 50 percent power, stirring occasionally, until melted and smooth, 2 to 4 minutes. Stir in oil until combined. Using silicone spatula, gently fold in noodles and peanuts until evenly coated. Drop heaping 1-tablespoon portions of noodle mixture onto prepared sheet in high mounds and refrigerate until set, about 15 minutes, before serving.

Tahini-Rose Russian

Makes 1 cocktail

Sweetness ✦ ✦ ✧

Creamy, Floral, Nutty

A white Russian isn't just indulgent; it deserves recognition for its remarkable interplay of bitterness, sweetness, creaminess, and alcoholic strength. To elevate it in the modern cocktail conversation, we apply a couple of elegant and nuanced touches. Rather than simply stirring in heavy cream, we lightly whip it, and we flavor it with tahini and rose water. The cream floats to the top so every sip pairs bitter coffee with the nutty, floral sweet cream.

- 2 ounces heavy cream
- 1 teaspoon tahini
- 1 teaspoon Simple Syrup (page 458)
- ⅛ teaspoon rose water
- 2 ounces vodka
- 1 ounce coffee liqueur
- Toasted sesame seeds for garnishing

1. Vigorously whisk cream, tahini, simple syrup, and rose water in chilled bowl until slightly thickened and frothy, about 30 seconds; set aside.

2. Add vodka and coffee liqueur to mixing glass, then fill three-quarters full with ice. Using bar spoon, stir until mixture is just combined and chilled, about 30 seconds. Strain cocktail into chilled rocks glass half-filled with ice. Dollop reserved tahini whipped cream over top and garnish with sesame seeds. Serve.

Southern Milk Punch

Makes 1 cocktail

Sweetness ✦ ✦ ✧

Creamy, Toasted

Two very different types of cocktails share the name "milk punch." The version that is more commonly associated with the South is creamy and rich (find the other version on pages 291 and 292). Often called brandy milk punch, bourbon milk punch, or New Orleans milk punch, it's made with milk, nutmeg, and brandy, bourbon, and/or rum—it's almost like an eggless eggnog. It's often a day drink, equally as fitting on a holiday morning, for a birthday lunch, or at a tailgate. Using light cream in this brandy cocktail gives the drink a full body without masking the flavor of the booze. If you can't find light cream, you can substitute 1 ounce milk plus 1 ounce heavy cream.

- 2 ounces light cream
- 1¼ ounces brandy
- ½ ounce Simple Syrup (page 458)
- ½ teaspoon vanilla extract
- Freshly grated nutmeg for garnishing

1. Add light cream, brandy, simple syrup, and vanilla to cocktail shaker and vigorously shake until mixture is foamy, about 45 seconds.

2. Fill shaker with ice, then shake mixture until just combined and chilled, about 5 seconds. Double-strain cocktail into chilled rocks glass. Garnish with nutmeg and serve.

Tahini-Rose Russian

Cocochai

Brandy Alexander

Makes 1 cocktail
Sweetness ✦✦✦
Creamy, Toasted

Who is the Alexander in brandy Alexander? No one really knows! But we can assume he was a fan of the decadent and delicious. The enriched drink may have been popular during Prohibition, though there are conflicting reports of what spirit was at its core. At least by 1937, William J. Tarling was confident enough that brandy was the base spirit of the drink that he titled it simply Alexander in the *Café Royal Cocktail Book*. It's like an (ice-cold) hot cocoa for adults. White (clear) and dark crème de cacao both work.

- 1 ounce brandy
- 1 ounce crème de cacao
- 1 ounce heavy cream
- Freshly grated nutmeg for garnishing

1. Add brandy, crème de cacao, and heavy cream to cocktail shaker and vigorously shake until mixture is foamy, about 45 seconds.

2. Fill shaker with ice, then shake mixture until fully combined and well chilled, about 15 seconds. Double-strain cocktail into chilled cocktail glass. Garnish with grated nutmeg and serve.

Customize Your Cocktail

Aged rum works in place of the brandy. You can make a Gin Alexander with gin or a Tequila Alexander with blanco or reposado tequila.

Cocochai

Makes 1 zero-proof cocktail
Sweetness ✦ ✦ ✧
Creamy, Nutty, Spiced

You don't need alcohol to make a cocktail great, and you don't need eggs to make it foamy. This tea cocktail is frothed with lush coconut milk. We were inspired by the layering of another caffeinated drink, Vietnamese coffee, in which lower-density coffee naturally floats above higher-density condensed milk. Liberal amounts of sweetened condensed milk can be too cloying for a cocktail, however, so in our "upside-down" tea version, we layer coconut milk on top of spiced black tea. We shake the milk, which creates gorgeous open bubbles and a frothy texture that's rich but light. The buoyant bright-white milk floats strikingly atop the dark tea. For the best flavor, we brew our own chai, simmering black tea leaves with cardamom, cinnamon, peppercorns, and cloves, all toasted for depth, and slices of fresh ginger. A boldly flavored tea such as Assam is ideal for this recipe; alternatively, use Irish or English breakfast tea. We prefer the higher quality of loose-leaf tea here; however, three tea bags can be substituted.

Chai Concentrate

- ½ cinnamon stick
- 1 star anise pod
- 5 green cardamom pods
- 5 peppercorns
- 3 whole cloves
- 18 ounces water
- 1 (1-inch) piece ginger, sliced thin
- 1 tablespoon black tea leaves

Cocktail

- 3 ounces chai concentrate
- 1 ounce Simple Syrup (page 458)
- 4 ounces coconut milk
- ¼ teaspoon vanilla extract
- Freshly grated cinnamon for garnishing

1. For the chai concentrate: Place cinnamon stick and star anise on cutting board. Using back of heavy skillet, press down firmly until spices are coarsely crushed; transfer to medium saucepan. Crush cardamom pods, pepper-corns, and cloves and add to saucepan. Toast spices over medium heat, stirring frequently, until fragrant, 1 to 2 minutes.

2. Add water and ginger and bring to boil. Cover saucepan, reduce heat, and simmer mixture for 10 minutes. Stir in tea, cover, and simmer for 10 minutes. Off heat, let tea and spices steep for 10 minutes. Strain mixture through fine-mesh strainer into bowl; discard solids. Let concentrate cool completely, then transfer to storage container and refrigerate until chilled, about 30 minutes. (You should have about 12 ounces tea concentrate, enough for 4 cocktails. Concentrate can be refrigerated for up to 1 week.)

3. For the cocktail: Fill chilled highball glass halfway with ice. Add chai concentrate and simple syrup and stir to combine using bar spoon. Top with additional ice, leaving room for coconut milk.

4. Add coconut milk and vanilla to cocktail shaker, then fill with ice. Shake mixture until frothy, about 15 seconds. Arrange spoon concave side down near surface of ice. Gently strain coconut mixture onto back of spoon and into cocktail. Garnish with cinnamon and serve.

Coquito

Makes 8 cocktails
Sweetness ✦✦✦
Creamy, Nutty, Spiced

- 1 (15-ounce) can cream of coconut
- 1 (14-ounce) can coconut milk
- 1 (12-ounce) can evaporated milk
- 10 ounces aged rum
- 1 teaspoon vanilla extract
- ½ teaspoon ground cinnamon
- ½ teaspoon freshly grated nutmeg, plus extra for garnishing

Coquito (meaning "little coconut" in Spanish) is a celebrated holiday drink among Puerto Rican families. It can have eggs but more often doesn't; a blend of coconut and dairy products provides its creamy but not superthick texture. Like many holiday sippers, there are nuances to each family's coquito recipe that make it their own. This version is served over ice—but some folks prefer drinking it chilled, without ice. With both a can of coconut milk and a can of cream of coconut, it has plenty of creamy coconut richness. Vanilla, cinnamon, and nutmeg provide warm spiciness. Blending the drink right before serving time ensures that everything is fully combined; plus it gives the cocktail a delightful bit of frothiness. Different families suggest using different kinds of rum. Whichever you decide, we suggest looking for a Puerto Rican brand such as Don Q or Palo Viejo. Freshly grated nutmeg is best here; if using preground nutmeg, reduce the amount to ¼ teaspoon.

1. Whisk all ingredients together in large bowl or container. Cover and refrigerate until well chilled, at least 1 hour or up to 3 days.

2. Just before serving, working in 2 or 3 batches, transfer mixture to blender and process until slightly frothy, about 1 minute per batch; transfer to chilled pitcher. Serve individual portions in chilled rocks glasses filled with ice, garnishing individual portions with extra nutmeg.

Eggs in Cocktails

Using eggs in cocktails adds an extra step to the process, but it yields undeniable rewards. Incorporating an egg white—as we do in the Ramos Gin Fizz (page 72), Amaretto Sour (page 211), and Foggy Day (page 221)—adds silky texture without discernible flavor. That's because egg whites are largely just protein and water.

The texture comes via shaking. Vigorously shaking a cocktail aerates it, forcing thousands of minuscule bubbles into the liquid. Typically the bubbles rise to the surface and dissipate quickly. Egg white proteins, however, link together and trap those bubbles on the surface of the cocktail, forming a lush, long-lasting froth.

Using a whole egg adds a touch of flavor in addition to texture. A cocktail made with a whole egg won't be as frothy as one made with egg white, because an egg yolk's makeup is one-third fat. The fat from the yolk interacts with the foaming proteins from the white, preventing them from trapping as much air. But in cocktails such as the flips and nogs in this chapter, that extra fat offers lush texture with rich, mellow flavor.

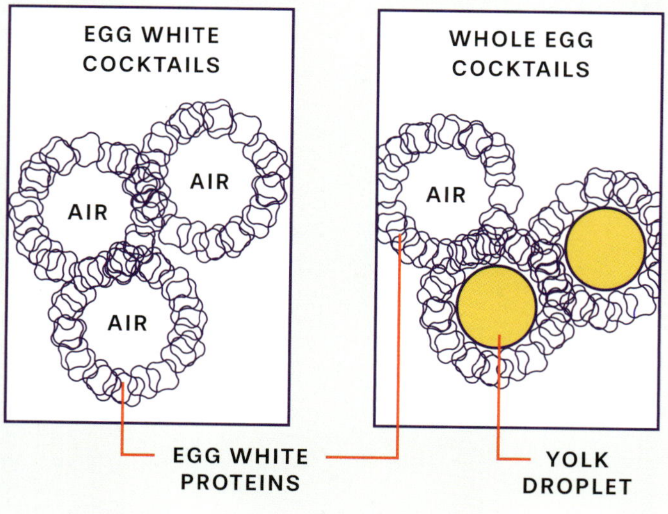

Cocktails made with egg whites or whole eggs benefit from dry shaking—that is, shaking the ingredients together first before adding ice, then adding ice and shaking a second time. This two-step shake distributes the egg throughout the cocktail and also begins to denature the proteins in the egg so that they'll readily link up into a foam. Ice is omitted from the dry shake so as not to overdilute the cocktail; egg whites also emulsify faster at warmer temperatures.

Those egg proteins also bond to astringent flavor compounds in the spirit, such as the oaky tannins of a whiskey, softening those compounds and leaving the drink tasting rounder and smoother.

As we do with other shaken cocktails, we double-strain shaken cocktails made with eggs. Double straining (see page 27) not only removes ice shards, but also traps any tiny stray bits of egg that may be lingering.

SOUS VIDE PASTEURIZED EGGS

Does the alcohol in a cocktail instantly kill off any germs in a raw egg? No: It's important to still be aware that there's a raw ingredient in the drink. If that is a major concern for you, you'll want to use pasteurized eggs.

While you can buy pasteurized whole eggs (in cartons and in the shell) and pasteurized egg whites in cartons, you can use a sous vide circulator at home to pasteurize eggs in the shell, after which they can be refrigerated and used normally. Pasteurized eggs are slightly more viscous than unpasteurized eggs but can still be used for the same purposes.

To pasteurize eggs: Heat a sous vide water bath to 135 degrees. Use tongs or a ladle to gently place up to a dozen eggs in the bath. Let sit for 90 minutes. Remove the eggs from the bath, chill under cold running water, and refrigerate for up to five weeks.

Cooked-Egg Cocktails

In the case of our eggnog recipes (pages 382–389), the goal is a rich, plush-textured drink infused with warm spices—but without a head of foam. We achieve this by making a basic custard: whole eggs and extra egg yolks cooked with milk. In order to prevent the egg proteins from heating too fast and curdling into scrambled eggs, we temper the eggs.

First, mixing the eggs with plenty of sugar means that the proteins are separated from each other and can't combine easily to form curds. Next, slowly adding hot milk to the mixture allows the eggs to heat up gradually without overcooking. Finally, gentle cooking causes the egg proteins, which are by now nicely spread out through the milk, to denature and then tangle together into a delicate matrix, thickening the liquid into a lush custard.

GENTLE HEAT Careful cooking keeps the network of egg proteins loose and smooth.

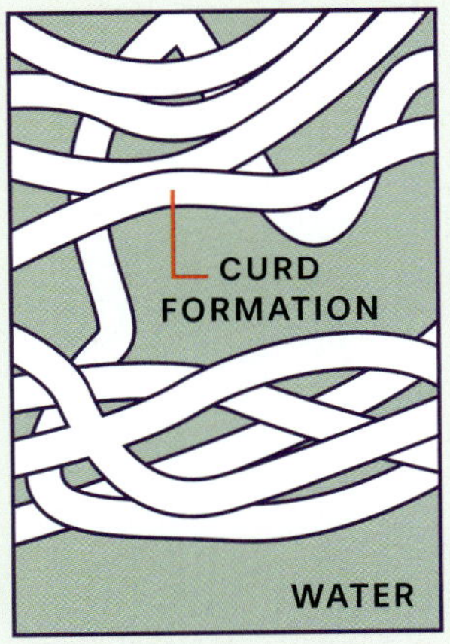

HIGH HEAT Fast cooking can cause egg proteins to clump together, pull apart, and separate from the liquid surrounding them.

Warmed *and* Mulled

When cold weather creeps in, nothing warms the bones (and the belly) like a warm drink. From spiked hot chocolate to mulled wine, heated cocktails are an enjoyable way to keep your spirits up through a long winter. Warmed and mulled cocktails are more than just a respite from the chill, though. As a category, they have a long and storied association with festivity, ritual, hospitality, and comfort.

In Bronze Age China, warm wine was poured from ritual vessels during ancestor worship. In ancient Rome, soldiers on the march drank mulled wine flavored with spices and honey. Since at least as early as the 12th century, people in Britain sipped hot ale (or wine or cider) called wassail during their harvest celebrations. In pre-colonial Mesoamerica, Mayan royalty and warriors drank chocolate as a ceremonial drink, spiked not with alcohol but with chiles. The list goes on; with a basic formula of alcohol (or other liquid) + flavorings + heat, it's a category that showcases human innovation.

In Europe during the age of humoral medicine, warmed and mulled drinks shifted from luxurious to medicinal, prescribed for all kinds of illnesses. Versions of the Hot Toddy (page 402) were suggested as common-cold cures for all ages well past that era. Gradually hot cocktails shifted back toward luxury, becoming an inextricable part of winter holiday festivities. This was especially true in England; at the end of Charles Dickens's *A Christmas Carol*, a newly reformed Scrooge decides to give his poor clerk a raise "over a Christmas bowl of smoking bishop." (See our take on the Smoking Bishop on page 418.) Today, throughout Europe as well as in the United States, mulled and spiked hot drinks are a classic holiday tradition.

Temperature isn't the only marker for these drinks. Heat changes the way our taste buds perceive flavor. Sweetness, bitterness, and umami are all experienced as more intense in a hot drink than in a cold one. Additionally, aromas of ingredients like liquors and spices are heightened in a hot drink, which plays into our perception of their potency. For these reasons, ingredient ratios in heated cocktails may be approached differently than they are in chilled cocktails; however, dilution and balance are still essential.

This is a great category for nonalcoholic drinks, too. Enjoy the fruit of the harvest with Mulled Cider (page 420) or enhance your afternoon cuppa with our Southern Spiced Tea (page 413). Curl up by the fire and sip away.

Warmed and Mulled

Our Favorite Mulling Spices

There are many spices to mull over when flavoring warm beverages, but here are the ones we reach for the most often. Try mixing and matching these core spices with additional flavorings such as citrus zest, citrus juice, and vanilla bean to discover a wide world of mulled drinks.

- **Allspice berries:** light warm flavor; peppery bite
- **Black peppercorns:** assertive flavor; mild heat
- **Cardamom pods:** slightly sweet; peppery and floral
- **Cinnamon sticks:** strong warm flavor; sweet spiciness
- **Cloves (whole):** strong warm flavor; sweet spiciness
- **Coriander seeds:** floral and citrusy
- **Star anise pods:** sweet and spicy; hints of licorice

GET THE MOST FROM YOUR MULLING SPICES

When making mulled drinks, we call for cracked spices. Cracking whole spices rather than grinding them into powder (or buying them preground) makes their flavor more pronounced and also makes them easier to filter from the finished cocktail. There's no shrapnel from stray seeds and no lingering fine spice dust to settle at the bottom of your vessel and potentially burn.

Some of our recipes also begin by toasting cracked or whole spices in a dry saucepan. Toasting spices helps release their essential oils, bringing out their fullest flavor and aroma to give your cocktail a major boost. (This applies to any recipe calling for whole spices, not just cocktails.)

When you then add liquid to the spices (in the same saucepan) and allow it all to simmer, the spices' oils quickly infuse the drink with their flavor. None of this would be possible without heat—simply adding whole spices to a glass of cold wine or cider would change very little about the flavor.

How to Crack and Toast Spices

1. Crack whole spices such as peppercorns, allspice berries, coriander seeds, and cardamom pods between underside of large saucepan and cutting board. (A mortar and pestle will also make quick work of them.) Cinnamon sticks can be broken by hand into several pieces. Cloves can be left whole.

2. Toast spices in saucepan over medium heat, shaking saucepan occasionally, until fragrant, 1 to 3 minutes. Proceed with recipe. (Strain spices out when finished making cocktail.)

What Is Mead?

Too often relegated to the pop-culture province of Vikings and Renaissance faires, mead is making a comeback. Sometimes called "honey wine," mead is made from fermented honey and is in a category all its own. This ancient beverage fell out of favor in Europe once beer and wine became more widely and cheaply available. Its popularity has continued elsewhere, notably in Ethiopia and Eritrea, where tej—a traditional honey wine often flavored with gesho leaves—has been a favorite for centuries, and in the Yucatán, where xtabentún, made from a local wildflower, has been enjoyed since the Mayan era. In recent years, there's been a growing interest in mead that mirrors the rise of the craft beer movement. We use a semisweet mead in our recipe for Mulled Mead with Star Anise and Ginger (page 417) for its unique, not-too-sweet honeyed floral notes reminiscent of a medium-dry white wine.

Hot Chocolate for Grown-Ups

Our Spiked Hot Chocolate (page 410) uses bittersweet chocolate and unsweetened cocoa powder. For the ultimate adult hot chocolate, choose high-quality chocolate products.

Cocktailing (or cooking) with bittersweet chocolate doesn't automatically mean you should reach for your favorite snacking bar. You want a bar that has a rich chocolate flavor balanced by a bit of fruitiness. Since you're incorporating it into a hot drink, it's important to use a bar that has a creamy, smooth texture and melts well. We like the Ghirardelli 60% Cacao Bittersweet Chocolate Premium Baking Bar and the Chocolove Organic Dark 73% Chocolate Bar.

For unsweetened cocoa powder, whatever you like for making from-scratch hot cocoa is a good choice for cocktails. Dutch-processed or natural doesn't matter; products with a higher fat content and lower starch content will make the silkiest cocktails. We especially like Valrhona Cocoa Powder.

Keep Warm Drinks Warm with a Slow Cooker

Several recipes in this chapter, including Classic Mulled Wine (page 414), Mulled Cider (page 420), and Southern Spiced Tea (page 413), make big batches. You can keep these drinks warm over very low heat on the stovetop, but if you're hosting a gathering and don't want to have to monitor the stovetop all night, consider the slow cooker. Make the drinks ahead on the stovetop, then transfer everything to a slow cooker and keep warm on a low setting. Most of these recipes will fit in a 2-quart slow cooker; you will need a 4-quart one for the Ponche Navideño (page 422).

You can even take this a step further and create a hot drink station of sorts. Set out a ladle and festive mugs and serve additional garnishes on the side. Depending on the flavor profile of your drink, consider cinnamon sticks, citrus slices, or citrus zest strips so that guests can customize their cocktail.

Reheat Warmed Cocktails Properly

When making big batches of warmed or mulled cocktails you might have leftovers. Don't throw them away; they'll generally keep for a few days in the refrigerator. It's important to reheat them gently in order to preserve all of their flavor notes, so don't just stick a mug in the microwave. Instead, gently warm the liquid in a saucepan over low heat until it's steaming. Don't allow the drink to come to a boil; that will change the flavor and drive off the more delicate nuances of the wine and spirits used.

Hot Toddy

Makes 1 cocktail
Sweetness ✦ ✧ ✧
Citrusy, Spirit Forward, Toasted

- 5 ounces boiling water
- 1½ ounces brandy
- ½ ounce lemon juice, plus lemon slice for garnishing
- 1 tablespoon honey
- Cinnamon stick for garnishing

Hot toddies have been hailed as a cure-for-what-ails-you for hundreds of years. The hot beverage essentially comprises a spirit, hot water, sometimes citrus or spices, and a sweetener. Today this is usually honey or maple syrup; palm sap or jaggery appeared in what some think was the original hot toddy, created during British colonial rule in India. While some versions of this delicious cup of comfort contain herbal tea, we prefer to keep our toddy pure and simple with just boiling water. We like brandy, and we use a modest hand when it comes to the ratio of brandy to water. As for the lemon juice and honey, we opt for a balanced approach and use an equal amount of each. Just stir everything together, wrap your hands around the steaming cup, and enjoy all winter long.

Stir all ingredients together in warmed mug until combined and honey has dissolved. Garnish with lemon slice and cinnamon stick. Serve.

Customize Your Cocktail

Make a Scotch Hot Toddy by substituting brewed hot black tea for the boiling water and Scotch for the brandy. You can also make an Amaro Hot Toddy by substituting amaro for the brandy and orange juice for the lemon juice.

The Irish Coffee

We don't know who was the first to mix up the concoction now known as the Irish coffee, but there's a pretty good Irish tale surrounding how and where it achieved liftoff: Foynes Airport in Limerick, Ireland. The story goes that one night in 1943, a flight leaving Limerick was forced to turn around several hours in and wait for better weather. To ease the shivering discomfort of the passengers, the chef at the terminal's restaurant, Joe Sheridan, provided them with his own personal hangover cure: hot coffee spiked with Irish whiskey. The drink was a hit and soon became part of the restaurant's official menu.

Foynes was a hub for seaplanes and flying boats, a short-lived mode of passenger air transport that could be as luxurious as an ocean liner. Many wealthy and important people came through the airport—so in an effort to impress, Sheridan gussied up what he called his Gaelic coffee with a cream float on top. Before long, the drink was known internationally and became especially popular in American bars. It has lingered on pub menus ever since, long after Foynes closed and Sheridan himself quit the bottle for good. In a 1995 Saint Patrick's Day edition of *The Bakersfield Californian*, Sheridan is quoted in an interview saying, "It's odd to think it all came out of my hangover."

Maybe it's the convivial Irish spirit, or maybe it's because ultimately this is an alcoholic coffee drink decadently topped with whipped cream, but Irish coffee has a tendency to veer toward excess—either too heady or too sweet. We like a coffee-to-whiskey ratio of 4:1 in our version, plus simple syrup and hand-whipped cream that's light enough to float on top but not so whipped that it doesn't smoothly incorporate into the rich coffee. It's a perfect cocktail for experimentation; we love flavoring the simple syrup and/or swapping out the whiskey for rum, brandy, or even mezcal and incorporating liqueurs such as an amaro or crème de cacao.

Irish Coffee

Makes 1 cocktail
Sweetness ✦✦✧
Bitter, Creamy

- 2 ounces heavy cream
- ¾ ounce Simple Syrup (page 458), divided
- 4 ounces brewed hot coffee
- 1 ounce Irish whiskey

1. Whisk cream and ¼ ounce simple syrup in chilled bowl until soft peaks just begin to form, about 30 seconds; set aside.

2. Add coffee, whiskey, and remaining ½ ounce simple syrup to warmed mug and stir to combine. Dollop whipped cream over top. Serve.

Customize Your Cocktail

Irish whiskey is traditional here, but rye and Tennessee whiskey also work well.

Zesty Irish Coffee

Makes 1 cocktail
Sweetness ✦ ✦ ✧
Bitter, Citrusy, Creamy

Whiskey and orange are a common pairing, and we love how orange also brightens the deep flavors of the hot coffee. In addition to the orange liqueur in this recipe, we sweeten things with orange-flavored simple syrup so the flavor really comes through.

- **2 ounces heavy cream**
- **½ ounce Citrus Syrup with orange (page 458), divided**
- **4 ounces brewed hot coffee**
- **¾ ounce Irish whiskey**
- **¼ ounce orange liqueur**
- **Orange twist for garnishing**

1. Whisk cream and ¼ ounce citrus syrup in chilled bowl until soft peaks just begin to form, about 30 seconds; set aside.

2. Add coffee, whiskey, orange liqueur, and remaining ¼ ounce simple syrup to warmed mug and stir to combine. Dollop whipped cream over top. Garnish with orange twist and serve.

Caribbean Coffee

Makes 1 cocktail
Sweetness ✦ ✦ ✧
Bitter, Creamy, Nutty

Orgeat and rum give this coffee drink a decidedly tropical twist. These ingredients' almond and caramel notes, respectively, blend beautifully with coffee to make it extra sweet and nutty.

- **2 ounces heavy cream**
- **¾ ounce orgeat syrup, divided**
- **4 ounces brewed hot coffee**
- **1 ounce aged rum**

1. Whisk cream and ¼ ounce orgeat syrup in chilled bowl until soft peaks just begin to form, about 30 seconds; set aside.

2. Add coffee, rum, and remaining ½ ounce orgeat syrup to warmed mug and stir to combine. Dollop whipped cream over top. Serve.

Keoke Coffee

Makes 1 cocktail
Sweetness ✦ ✦ ✧
Bitter, Creamy, Toasted

This luxurious after-dinner drink likely emerged from the sunny shores of California in the 1960s. As the story goes, bartender George Bullington in Del Mar created this indulgent coffee cocktail, which was subsequently named "Keoke" (Hawaiian for "George") at the suggestion of a Hawaiian patron. Whereas Irish coffee relies on the bold character of whiskey, the Keoke substitutes fruitier, softer brandy for its foundation. The addition of crème de cacao introduces sweet chocolate notes that move the drink in a delicious mocha direction. While some recipes include coffee liqueur, we found its inclusion to be redundant when paired with the coffee, rendering the drink overly sweet.

- 2 ounces heavy cream
- ½ ounce Simple Syrup (page 458), divided
- 4 ounces brewed hot coffee
- ½ ounce brandy
- ½ ounce crème de cacao
- Cacao nibs or grated bittersweet chocolate for garnishing

1. Whisk cream and ¼ ounce simple syrup in chilled bowl until soft peaks just begin to form, about 30 seconds; set aside.

2. Add coffee, brandy, crème de cacao, and remaining ¼ ounce simple syrup to warmed mug and stir to combine. Dollop whipped cream over top. Sprinkle with cacao nibs and serve.

MonMez Coffee

Makes 1 cocktail
Sweetness ✦ ✦ ✧
Bitter, Floral, Smoky

This modern coffee cocktail draws inspiration from the M&M or "Monte y Mezcal" shot that became an industry favorite in the early 2010s. It is an equal-parts blend of Amaro Montenegro and mezcal, designed to be either shot or sipped. In this cocktail, the amaro enhances the coffee's floral and fruity notes, while the mezcal introduces a subtle smokiness for a remarkably balanced and interesting drink.

- 2 ounces heavy cream
- ¾ ounce Simple Syrup (page 458), divided
- 4 ounces brewed hot coffee
- ½ ounce Amaro Montenegro
- ½ ounce mezcal
- Grapefruit coin for garnishing

1. Whisk cream and ¼ ounce simple syrup in chilled bowl until soft peaks just begin to form, about 30 seconds; set aside.

2. Add coffee, Amaro Montenegro, mezcal, and remaining ½ ounce simple syrup to warmed mug and stir to combine. Dollop whipped cream over top. Pinch grapefruit coin over drink, then garnish with grapefruit coin. Serve.

Customize Your Cocktail

Try another amaro such as Amaro Ramazzotti.

From left: Keoke Coffee, MonMez Coffee, Caribbean Coffee, Zesty Irish Coffee

PAIR WITH A SNACK

Pistachio-Orange Stuffed Dates

Makes 9 dates
Total Time: 15 minutes

Aromatic, nutty, crunchy pistachios and floral orange zest augment and add complexity to chewy, caramelly dates for a beautiful bite to accompany an after-dinner drink.

- 9 pitted Medjool dates
- 3 tablespoons pistachios, chopped
- ½ teaspoon grated orange zest
- ¼ teaspoon flake sea salt

Using paring knife, cut slit down length of each date, without cutting through entirely. Combine pistachios, orange zest, and salt in bowl. Working with 1 date at a time, gently open date at slit and stuff with 1 teaspoon pistachio mixture. Serve. (Dates can be refrigerated for up to 1 month.)

Spiked Hot Chocolate

Makes 1 cocktail
Sweetness ✦✦✦
Creamy, Toasted

- 2 ounces heavy cream
- ¾ ounce Simple Syrup (page 458), divided
- 1 tablespoon nonfat dry milk powder
- 1 tablespoon unsweetened cocoa powder, plus extra for garnishing
- 6 ounces whole milk
- 1½ ounces bittersweet chocolate, chopped fine
- 1 ounce bourbon
- ¼ teaspoon vanilla extract

Customize Your Cocktail

We like bourbon in this drink, but aged rum or brandy will also work well.

Hot chocolate is a treat; spiking it makes it even more special and gives the chocolate further dimension. We've made a simple version for whenever the craving hits—no special occasion needed. For the base, whole milk is just rich enough without being too heavy—we also add milk powder for depth. Unsweetened cocoa powder brings the backbone of chocolaty complexity, while the melted bittersweet chocolate ensures big flavor and richness. Bourbon's caramelly flavor works well in chocolate desserts, including in this sweet whipped cream–topped sipper.

1. Whisk cream and ¼ ounce simple syrup together in chilled bowl until soft peaks begin to form, about 30 seconds; set aside.

2. Whisk milk powder and cocoa together in medium saucepan. Slowly whisk in milk until incorporated and no lumps remain. Bring to simmer over medium-high heat, stirring occasionally. Off heat, immediately whisk in chocolate until melted and smooth. Stir in bourbon, vanilla, and remaining ½ ounce simple syrup. Transfer cocktail to warmed mug. Top with whipped cream and dust with extra cocoa. Serve.

Emoliente

Makes 4 zero-proof cocktails
Sweetness ✦ ✦ ✧
Citrusy, Herbal, Toasted

Often sold on the streets of Lima, Peru, emoliente is a warm barley-based beverage made with herb infusions, syrups, and extracts. It's a fabulous alternative to tea, with a sweet-tart profile, a uniquely nutty flavor, and a thick, soothing texture. It also happens to be very good for you, packed with nutrients, minerals, and fiber. We found several common denominators to emoliente: toasted barley, flaxseeds, horsetail, and cat's claw. Horsetail is a grassy-tasting fern, while cat's claw is a bitter, woody vine found in the tropical jungles of South and Central America. The toasted barley gives a nutty flavor to the brew, and flaxseeds provide texture. To meld these flavors, we introduce lemon juice and honey. Keeping the drink at a simmer for half an hour allows for proper extraction of the thickening qualities of flaxseeds and for adequate reduction and concentration of flavor. Roasted unhulled barley kernels (sometimes known as toasted barley) give this beverage its distinctive caramel hue and nutty flavor; do not substitute pearl barley. Dried horsetail and cat's claw bark can be purchased at specialty tea shops, health stores, or online.

- 1 cup roasted barley
- ½ cup flaxseeds
- ¼ cup dried horsetail, crumbled into 1-inch pieces
- 1 stick (2½ inches long by 1 inch wide) cat's claw bark
- 64 ounces water
- 3 tablespoons lemon juice, plus extra for seasoning
- 2 tablespoons honey, plus extra for seasoning

1. Bring barley, flaxseeds, horsetail, cat's claw, and water to simmer in large saucepan and cook until liquid is reduced by half, 30 to 35 minutes.

2. Strain mixture through fine-mesh strainer into heat-safe bowl; discard solids. Return barley mixture to now-empty saucepan and stir in lemon juice and honey. (Emoliente can be refrigerated for up to 1 week; mixture will thicken once chilled but loosen again after bringing to brief simmer before serving.) Serve in warmed mugs.

Customize Your Cocktail

Make Spiked Emoliente by adding 4 ounces of pisco, cachaça, white rum, or vodka with the lemon juice. You can also spike individual portions by adding 1 ounce of the spirit to individual mugs.

Southern Spiced Tea

Makes 8 zero-proof cocktails
Sweetness ✦✦✦
Citrusy, Herbal, Spiced

Southern spiced tea was popular in the late 1800s among Southeastern United States elites who adapted it from Russian tea culture. Eventually, recipes called for Tang and instant tea, but ours is wholly homemade. If you use store-bought orange juice, use the lesser amount of sugar. We prefer the higher quality of loose-leaf tea here; however, 12 tea bags can be substituted.

- 48 ounces water
- ¾–1 cup sugar
- 2 cinnamon sticks, plus extra for garnishing
- 1 teaspoon whole cloves
- 3 (3-inch) strips orange zest plus 16 ounces juice, plus orange slices for garnishing
- ¼ cup black tea leaves
- 3 ounces lemon juice, plus lemon slices for garnishing

1. Bring water, sugar, cinnamon sticks, cloves, and orange zest to boil in large saucepan over high heat, whisking often. Off heat, stir in tea, cover, and let steep for 5 minutes.

2. Strain mixture through fine-mesh strainer into heat-safe bowl; discard solids. Return tea mixture to now-empty saucepan and stir in orange juice and lemon juice. (Tea can be refrigerated for up to 1 week; bring to brief simmer before serving.) Serve in warmed mugs, garnishing individual portions with orange slices, lemon slices, and extra cinnamon sticks.

Southern Spiced Tea

Mulled Wine

Adding spices to wine is a practice that goes way back—recipes exist from ancient Greece and Rome. The flavor profile of these spiced wines was often a complex mix of savory and sweet: Saffron, black pepper, bay leaves, honey, dates, and mastic (a piney resin from the mastic tree) could all be found in the same mixture.

By the late Middle Ages, a type of mulled wine called hippocras or hypocras became popular in Europe. It was so named because it was drained through a conical cloth bag called a Hippocratic sleeve, which in turn took its name from the Greek physician Hippocrates, who would use the same sort of sieve to filter impurities from water. Hippocras bears a closer resemblance to the flavor of modern mulled wines, as it was often made with cinnamon, ginger, and nutmeg.

Though it may not be the go-to cold-weather drink in the United States, mulled wine is an essential wintertime beverage in Europe's colder climes. Germany has glühwein; Sweden has glögg; France has vin chaud. And every year, Christmas market vendors across the continent and the British Isles serve cup after cup of steaming mulled wine to warm the fingers and stomachs of holiday shoppers.

Badly made versions of mulled wine can be reminiscent of cough syrup—excessively sweet and overspiced, with a harsh taste of alcohol from too much of an added spirit like brandy or rum. We offer here a set of warming wines with a mild alcohol kick, deep but not overwhelming spice notes, and some welcome fruitiness. (See page 350 for information on how to choose wines for cocktails.) The combination of red wine with cinnamon, cloves, allspice, and black pepper—all simmered low and slow for full flavor and then fortified with a hit of brandy at the end—will warm even the chilliest hearts. There are also versions featuring white wine with cardamom and coriander; mead with star anise and ginger; and equal parts red wine and port with roasted oranges and cloves—a vintage Victorian recipe known as the smoking bishop.

Classic Mulled Wine

Makes 8 cocktails

Sweetness ✦ ✦ ✧

Bitter, Fruity, Spirit Forward

- 3 cinnamon sticks, broken into pieces, plus extra for garnishing
- 10 whole cloves
- 1 teaspoon allspice berries, cracked
- ½ teaspoon black peppercorns, cracked
- 2 (750-ml) bottles dry red wine
- ½ cup sugar, plus extra for seasoning
- 4 (3-inch) strips orange zest, plus orange slices for garnishing
- 2 ounces brandy

1. Toast cinnamon stick pieces, cloves, allspice berries, and peppercorns in large saucepan over medium heat, shaking saucepan occasionally, until fragrant, 1 to 3 minutes. Add wine and sugar and bring to simmer. Reduce heat to low, cover, and simmer gently for 15 minutes. Off heat, add orange zest and let sit until flavors meld, about 15 minutes.

2. Strain wine mixture through fine-mesh strainer into heat-safe bowl; discard solids. (Wine mixture can be refrigerated for up to 1 week.) Return wine mixture to now-empty saucepan, stir in brandy, and season with extra sugar to taste. Heat over medium-low heat until mixture begins to steam but not simmer. Serve in warmed mugs, garnishing individual portions with orange slices and extra cinnamon sticks.

Customize Your Cocktail

Make Zero-Proof Mulled Wine by omitting the brandy and using nonalcoholic red wine.

Mulled White Wine with Vanilla and Cardamom

Makes 8 cocktails
Sweetness ✦ ✦ ✧
Floral, Fruity, Spiced

Mulled wine is traditionally made with red, but it doesn't have to be: This bright version made with white wine and scented with cardamom and vanilla proves it. We toast cardamom, bay leaves, coriander, allspice, and black pepper, which give herbal, citrus, and spice notes; a few strips of lemon zest dropped in at the end reinforce the citrusy elements. For added complexity, we stir in some Cocchi Americano, which adds tropical fruit and floral notes—and just a touch of bitterness—to the brew. We recommend saving the vanilla bean after straining the wine mixture and using it to make Vanilla Rim Sugar (page 454). Lillet Blanc or vermouth bianco (also sometimes labeled blanc or blanco) can be used in place of the Cocchi Americano Bianco.

- 6 green cardamom pods, cracked, plus extra for garnishing
- 5 bay leaves
- 2 teaspoons whole coriander seeds, cracked
- ½ teaspoon whole allspice berries, cracked
- ¼ teaspoon black peppercorns, cracked
- 2 (750-ml) bottles dry white wine
- ½ cup sugar, plus extra for seasoning
- 1 vanilla bean
- 2 (3-inch) strips lemon zest, plus extra strips for garnishing
- 2 ounces Cocchi Americano Bianco

1. Toast cardamom pods, bay leaves, coriander seeds, allspice berries, and peppercorns in large saucepan over medium heat, shaking saucepan occasionally, until fragrant, 1 to 3 minutes. Add wine, sugar, and vanilla bean and bring to simmer. Reduce heat to low, cover, and simmer gently for 15 minutes. Off heat, add lemon zest and let sit until flavors meld, about 15 minutes.

2. Strain wine mixture through fine-mesh strainer into heat-safe bowl; discard solids. (Wine mixture can be refrigerated for up to 1 week.) Return wine mixture to now-empty saucepan, stir in Cocchi Americano, and season with extra sugar to taste. Heat over medium-low heat until mixture begins to steam but not simmer. Serve in warmed mugs, garnishing individual portions with extra cardamom pods and extra strips of lemon zest.

Customize Your Cocktail

Make Zero-Proof Mulled White Wine with Vanilla and Cardamom by omitting the Cocchi Americano Bianco and using nonalcoholic white wine.

Mulled Mead with Star Anise and Ginger

Makes 8 cocktails
Sweetness ✦✦✦
Fruity, Spiced, Spicy

Drunk by the ancient Romans and said to be the nectar of the gods in Greek mythology, mead is an old beverage that's the starting place for this new mulled drink. Punchy fresh ginger, licorice-y star anise, and warming allspice complement the honey flavor of the mead. We add lemon and orange zest off heat, where they gently release their aroma into the drink. A handful of sweet golden raisins is a fitting finishing touch for this golden elixir. We developed this recipe using a semisweet mead without added flavors. If mead is unavailable, you can substitute a dry, fruity white wine such as Sauvignon Blanc, Riesling, or Pinot Grigio.

- **2 whole star anise pods, plus extra for garnishing**
- **½ teaspoon whole allspice berries, cracked**
- **2 (750-ml) bottles semisweet mead**
- **1 (2-inch) piece ginger, sliced ¼ inch thick, plus extra ginger slices for garnishing**
- **2 (3-inch) strips lemon zest**
- **2 (3-inch) strips orange zest**
- **½ cup golden raisins**
- **Honey for seasoning**

1. Toast star anise pods and allspice berries in large saucepan over medium heat, shaking saucepan occasionally, until fragrant, 1 to 3 minutes. Add mead and ginger and bring to simmer. Reduce heat to low, cover, and simmer gently for 15 minutes. Off heat, add lemon zest and orange zest and let sit until flavors meld, about 15 minutes.

2. Strain mead mixture through fine-mesh strainer into heat-safe bowl; discard solids. (Mead mixture can be refrigerated for up to 1 week.) Return mead mixture to now-empty saucepan, stir in raisins, and season with honey to taste. Heat over medium-low heat until mixture begins to steam but not simmer. Serve in warmed mugs, garnishing individual portions with macerated raisins, extra star anise pods, and extra ginger slices.

Smoking Bishop

Makes 8 cocktails
Sweetness ✦✦✧
Citrusy, Fruity, Spiced

Part of a family of mulled drinks called "ecclesiastics" that were popular in Victorian England, the smoking bishop and similar drinks like the smoking cardinal and smoking pope were ways to poke fun at the Catholic Church in the largely Protestant country. Often served in a mitre-shaped punch bowl, the smoking bishop's purple color mimics that of the typical bishop's robe. As for the "smoking" moniker, it could represent the characteristic roasting of the oranges (traditionally the bitter Seville variety) that infuse the wine mixture with flavor, or the "smoky" vapors that rise from the surface of the drink while it heats. Regardless of how this citrus- and clove-scented mulled drink got its name, it's much too good to be relegated to the history books.

- **4 oranges, plus orange slices for garnishing**
- **26 whole cloves, divided, plus extra for garnishing**
- **1 (750-ml) bottle dry red wine**
- **½ cup sugar, plus extra for seasoning**
- **1 (750-ml) bottle ruby port**
- **1 ounce lemon juice**
- **2 cinnamon sticks**

1. Adjust oven rack to middle position and heat oven to 350 degrees. Thoroughly scrub and dry oranges. Using skewer, poke 5 holes in each orange, then insert 1 clove in each hole. Place oranges on aluminum foil–lined rimmed baking sheet and roast, rotating oranges every 20 minutes, until browned on several sides, about 1 hour.

2. Whisk wine and sugar in large bowl until sugar has dissolved. Add roasted oranges (oranges should be partially or entirely submerged), cover, and let sit at room temperature for at least 8 hours or up to 24 hours.

3. Set fine-mesh strainer over large saucepan. Transfer oranges to cutting board and cut in half. Squeeze orange halves into prepared strainer (you should have about 8 ounces juice); discard solids and spent orange halves. Add red wine mixture, port, lemon juice, cinnamon sticks, and remaining 6 cloves to saucepan. Heat over medium-low heat until mixture begins to steam but not simmer. Off heat, remove cinnamon sticks and cloves and season with extra sugar to taste. (Mulled wine can be refrigerated for up to 1 week; gently warm before serving.) Serve in warmed mugs, garnishing individual portions with orange slices studded with extra cloves.

Clockwise from top left: Smoking Bishop, Mulled Mead with Star Anise and Ginger, Mulled White Wine with Vanilla and Cardamom

Mulled Cider

Makes 12 zero-proof cocktails
Sweetness ✦✦✦
Fruity, Spiced

Mulled cider is a zero-proof treat, but it has an intoxicating aroma when it's bubbling away on the stovetop. Our concentrated version tastes even better than it smells, with a prominent rounded, sweet-and-tart apple flavor complemented by brown sugar, orange zest, and spices. As for spices, we found that less was more: We use cinnamon, black pepper, coriander seeds, and cloves, and each comes through clearly in the final cider, providing sweetness, savoriness, and piquant notes. The amount of brown sugar will vary depending on the sweetness of the apple cider; start with the lesser amount and add more as needed.

- 1 cinnamon stick, broken into pieces, plus extra sticks for garnishing
- ½ teaspoon black peppercorns, cracked
- ½ teaspoon coriander seeds, cracked
- 7 whole cloves
- 2 quarts apple cider
- 1–3 tablespoons packed brown sugar
- 4 (3-inch) strips orange zest, plus orange slices for garnishing
- Apple slices for garnishing

1. Toast cinnamon stick pieces, peppercorns, coriander seeds, and cloves in large saucepan over medium heat, shaking saucepan occasionally, until fragrant, 1 to 3 minutes. Add cider and sugar and bring to simmer, using wide, shallow spoon to skim off any foam that rises to surface. Reduce heat to low, cover, and simmer gently for 15 minutes. Off heat, add orange zest and let sit until flavors meld, about 15 minutes.

2. Strain cider mixture through fine-mesh strainer into heat-safe bowl; discard solids. (Mulled cider can be refrigerated for up to 1 week; gently warm before serving.) Return cider mixture to now-empty saucepan and heat over medium-low heat until mixture begins to steam but not simmer. Serve in warmed mugs, garnishing individual portions with apple slices, orange slices, and extra cinnamon sticks.

Customize Your Cocktail

Make Brandied Mulled Cider by stirring 16 ounces of brandy into the strained cider mixture. Bourbon or aged rum also work well. You can make Pumpkin Spice Mulled Cider by increasing the cinnamon sticks to 2 and substituting ½ teaspoon of whole allspice berries and ⅛ teaspoon of ground nutmeg for the peppercorns and coriander seeds. Then, cut 1 vanilla bean in half lengthwise. Using the tip of a paring knife, scrape out the seeds and substitute the bean and seeds for the orange zest.

PAIR WITH A SNACK

Baked Brie with Honeyed Apricots

Serves 8 to 10
Total Time: 30 minutes

This sweet-savory Brie preparation is a real crowd-pleaser. Served in a cast-iron skillet, it remains warm and gooey through leisurely cocktail party snacking. Cutting the Brie into pieces and combining it with the seasoned apricots (rather than topping a whole wheel) means that every bite gets all of the complex flavors. Be sure to use a firm, fairly unripe Brie for this recipe. Serve with baguette slices, crackers, or Melba toast.

- ¼ cup chopped dried apricots
- ¼ cup honey, divided
- 1 teaspoon minced fresh rosemary
- ¼ teaspoon table salt
- ¼ teaspoon pepper
- 2 (8-ounce) wheels firm Brie cheese, rind removed, cheese cut into 1-inch pieces
- 1 tablespoon minced fresh chives

1. Adjust oven rack to middle position and heat oven to 400 degrees. Microwave apricots, 2 tablespoons honey, rosemary, salt, and pepper in medium bowl until apricots are softened and mixture is fragrant, about 1 minute, stirring halfway through microwaving. Add Brie and toss to combine.

2. Transfer mixture to 10-inch cast-iron skillet and bake until cheese is melted, 10 to 15 minutes. Drizzle with remaining 2 tablespoons honey and sprinkle with chives. Serve.

Ponche Navideño

Makes 12 zero-proof cocktails

Sweetness ✦✦✧

Floral, Fruity, Spiced

- 96 ounces water
- ½ ounce whole, dried hibiscus flowers (about ½ cup)
- 2 (6-inch) stalks sugarcane
- 12 ounces tejocotes, ends trimmed
- 8 ounces piloncillo
- 2 (6-inch) tamarind pods, shelled and deveined
- 1 cup prunes
- 2 (4-inch) Ceylon cinnamon sticks
- 1 pound guava, cut into ½-inch-thick wedges
- 1 large Gala or Fuji apple, peeled, cored, and cut into ¾-inch pieces

Mexican ponche Navideño ("Christmas punch") is a winter drink infused with fruit and warm spices. While recipes vary from person to person, the preparation typically involves simmering such ingredients as tejocotes (a sweet-sour fruit that resembles crab apples), tamarind pods, piloncillo (raw cane sugar), guava, and cinnamon sticks in water until the spices release their flavors and the fruits become tender. Until 2015, tejocotes were banned from being imported to the United States, so during the holiday season they became the most smuggled item over the USA-Mexico border. Happily, tejocotes now appear in the United States, especially in the fall and winter in Latin markets. It is common for their skin to be covered in black dots or patches. If you can't find them, crab apples are a suitable alternative. Use whole, dried hibiscus flowers, not ones that have been cut and sifted. If you can find only cut and sifted flowers, use the weight listed, not the volume. This recipe calls for piloncillo, also known as panela or panocha. Granulated cane sugar can be substituted. The delicate flavor of Ceylon cinnamon is preferred here; if substituting cassia cinnamon, reduce the amount to two 3-inch sticks.

1. Bring water to boil in Dutch oven over high heat. Reduce heat to low, add hibiscus, and let steep for 10 minutes. Using slotted spoon, discard hibiscus.

2. Using sharp knife, remove outer peel from sugarcane stalks. Halve each stalk lengthwise, then cut each half lengthwise into 3 strips. Add sugarcane, tejocotes, piloncillo, tamarind pods, prunes, and cinnamon to pot and bring to boil. Reduce heat to medium-low, cover, and simmer, stirring occasionally, until flavors meld and piloncillo has fully dissolved, about 20 minutes.

3. Stir in guava and apple and simmer, covered, until softened, about 10 minutes. (Ponche can be refrigerated for up to 3 days; gently warm before serving.) Serve in warmed mugs, garnishing individual portions with tejocotes, sugarcane, guava, and apple.

Customize Your Cocktail

Make Spiked Ponche Navideño by adding 12 ounces of blanco tequila, white rum, or vodka to the ponche after simmering the guava. You can also spike individual portions by adding 1 ounce of the spirit to individual mugs.

Frozen *and* Blended

Cocktails requiring a blender are usually frozen drinks—but not always. All the cocktails in this chapter are blended, but not all are frozen. Either way, the blender is an invaluable tool for crafting smoothly textured cocktails with plenty of body.

Frozen blended drinks are one of the new kids on the cocktail block, getting their start in the late 1950s. We have one Omar Knedlik of Kansas City to credit for them. The Dairy Queen franchise operator supposedly stored some soda in his freezer when the soda machine in his restaurant broke. When the soda went slushy, presumably his eyes went wide. He began selling the semi-frozen soda as "the coldest drink in town," and customers flocked to it. Not long after, Knedlik repurposed some parts (some say from a car air conditioner, some say from an old ice cream machine) to build the first frozen beverage machine. He patented it, calling it the ICEE.

In the mid-1960s, 7-Eleven bought some ICEE machines, eventually christening their product the Slurpee. Based on sales volume alone, the Slurpee is the world's most popular frozen beverage. To no one's surprise, frozen drinks eventually came to include alcohol. Indeed, Dallas restaurateur Mariano Martinez credited the Slurpee machine as the inspiration for his invention of the frozen margarita machine in 1971. Our frozen cocktails bring bartending techniques to the forefront by using fresh ingredients rather than artificial ones or premade mixes.

The nonfrozen blended drinks in this chapter also happen to be nonalcoholic. Agua fresca ("fresh water") is a beverage that's popular throughout Latin America. These drinks are made with fruits, vegetables, seeds, or grains; water, and a sweetener; they can also include herbs, flowers, or nuts. An agua fresca is like a complex juice that has been lengthened with water and served over ice (often with a straw) to make it more thirst-quenching and refreshing. Ingredients can be muddled, mashed, or juiced, but the blender makes preparation very efficient.

Aguas frescas have a long history. It's believed that they originated in Tenochtitlán, which is now Mexico City, where the Aztecs muddled together local fruits, adding ice from nearby dormant volcanoes. Their attraction did not wane over the centuries, expanding throughout Latin America and becoming especially popular in areas where sugarcane was grown. Aguas frescas arrived in the United States around the 1940s, spreading their refreshment outward from the Southwest.

Frozen and Blended

Best Blending Techniques

The blender has a unique ability to handle liquid, making it better than a food processor when it comes to producing uniformly smooth blended cocktails. In the narrow confines of a blender jar (as opposed to the wide bowl of a food processor), the ingredients form a vortex that keeps them in near-constant contact with the blades. As the blades spin, the contents are drawn down into the blades and back up again before being drawn back down into the blades at high speed.

Blenders

If you plan on making blended cocktails, you'll need a good blender. Here are a few we recommend.

- **VITAMIX 5200:** This top-notch, high-end blender, which comes with a tamper accessory, produces fine texture without incorporating excess air. Its narrow jar, which helps it blend so efficiently, does make scraping out the contents a minor challenge.
- **BREVILLE FRESH & FURIOUS:** This blender is compact yet still powerful enough to process any cocktail efficiently. It automatically stops every 60 seconds, and its timer makes tracking recipe stages very easy. It's easy to operate and is a great piece of equipment in the midprice range.
- **BRAUN TRIFORCE POWER BLENDER:** Also midpriced, this quiet blender is easy to operate, with a clear, well-labeled interface and speed dial. The touchscreen buttons are very sensitive, however, making it easy to accidentally activate a setting you don't want.

ORDER IS IMPORTANT

To create an effective vortex, add the ingredients in the order specified. This allows the ingredients to process quickly without the need for stopping, stirring, and starting up again. Solids and ice give the blades something to grip, while liquid thins the ingredients so the blades can turn. We add liquids first, then solids, then ice.

TECHNIQUE AND TIME MATTER FOR TEXTURE

For the most effective blending, starting on low speed and ramping up to high is best. Increase the speed gradually, one power level at a time (whatever that looks like on your blender). This helps maintain the vortex without sloshing ingredients up the side of the blender, ensuring everything properly breaks down. Don't overblend, as this can warm up your frozen cocktail. Aim for a smooth, homogeneous texture, keeping in mind that the thickness of blended cocktails may vary depending upon the ingredients.

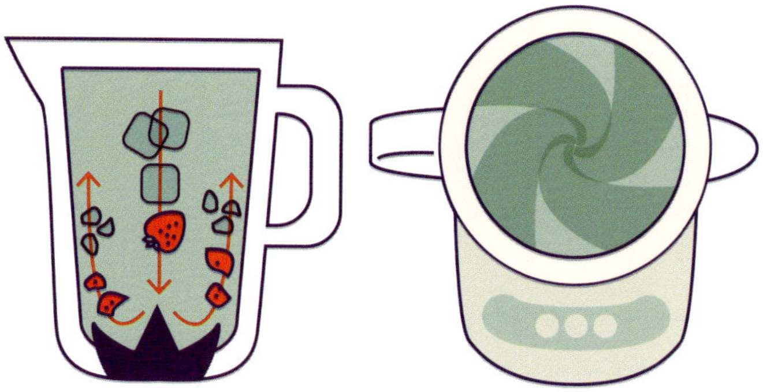

Cuckoo for Canned Coconut

Coconut products bring delicious flavor and luxurious texture to cocktails, but they can be confusing. Canned coconut milk and coconut cream are not interchangeable with the coconut milk or creamer available in cartons with the dairy milk alternatives. The latter products are more diluted and meant to replace dairy milk and cream. And cream of coconut—what you want for luscious Piña Coladas (page 428)—is entirely different.

Cream of coconut: Cream of coconut is a product based on coconut milk that contains sweeteners, thickeners, and emulsifiers. Coco López is the best-known brand, but there are other good brands available. Cream of coconut and coconut cream are not interchangeable.

Coconut cream: To make this unsweetened product, shredded coconut meat is steeped in hot water, the meat is pressed or mashed to release as much liquid as possible, and the mixture is strained. Coconut cream uses a 4:1 ratio of coconut meat to liquid.

Coconut milk: Made using the same process as coconut cream, coconut milk uses a 1:1 ratio of coconut meat and water. Coconut milk is also unsweetened.

Coconut water: If you crack open a coconut, the thin liquid that pours out is mellow, lightly sweet coconut water. Sold in cans and cartons, it's popular for sports drinks, smoothies—and cocktails. It makes a good nonalcoholic substitution for rum in some drinks in this chapter, including the Frozen Hurricanes (page 438).

Measuring Frozen Fruits (and Ice)

Frozen fruits, which are picked and frozen at their peak ripeness, are perfect for using in frozen and blended cocktails, contributing flavor without bringing down the temperature or diluting the texture of the finished drink. We offer both weight and cup measures for the frozen fruits and measured ice in this chapter. If you choose to measure either by the cup, here's how. Although we usually reserve liquid measuring cups for liquid ingredients, we find it easier to measure chunky frozen fruit or ice in a glass liquid measuring cup rather than a dry measuring cup. Place the fruit or ice in the glass measuring cup and then gently press down so it spreads somewhat to the edges of the glass. Continue as needed until you reach the amount called for in the recipe.

Frozen Juice Concentrates

So far this book has been all about fresh juices. When it comes to frozen and blended cocktails, we pivot to frozen. If you were to use fresh juices in frozen cocktails, you would need to add sweetener and more ice, which in turn would overdilute your cocktail. The frozen juice concentrates we use—orange, lemonade, and limeade—provide intense fruit flavors while adding their sweetening and chilling qualities. Following this principle, we also freeze some of the wine for our Peach-Strawberry Frosé (page 440) in ice cube trays so that we can use these iced-wine cubes when blending the drink.

Piña Coladas

Makes 4 cocktails
Sweetness ✦✦✦
Creamy, Tropical

Puerto Rico's official drink is a magical combination of pineapple, coconut, and rum. Here we've made the frozen version, blending frozen pineapple for a luscious final texture. Equal parts cream of coconut and heavy cream give the drink great, not-too-sweet coconut flavor with the right consistency. The choice of rum is yours: White rum holds its own, while aged rum adds spiced caramel notes.

- 6 ounces white or aged rum
- 4 ounces cream of coconut
- 4 ounces heavy cream
- 12 ounces (3 cups) frozen pineapple chunks
- 8 ounces (2 cups) ice cubes
- Fresh pineapple slices for garnishing

Add rum, cream of coconut, heavy cream, pineapple, and ice to blender (in that order) and process until smooth, about 1 minute, scraping down sides of blender as needed. Adjust consistency with water as needed. Pour into chilled rocks glasses and garnish with pineapple slices. Serve.

Customize Your Cocktail

Add a rum float by arranging a bar spoon concave side down over the cocktail. Gently pour ½ ounce of aged rum onto the spoon. Make Zero-Proof Piña Coladas by susbtituting 6 ounces coconut water for rum.

Mudslides

Makes 4 cocktails
Sweetness ✦✦✦
Creamy, Nutty

The Wreck Bar & Grill at Rum Point on Grand Cayman claims to have created the mudslide in the 1970s when a customer asked for a white Russian but the bar didn't stock cream. A quick-thinking bartender substituted Irish cream liqueur, and the mudslide was born. We've made the frozen version, taking this island treat to the next level by incorporating coffee ice cream for a thick drink with reinforced flavor. Garnishing with a dollop of whipped cream, chocolate shavings, and a cocktail cherry is, literally, the cherry on top of the most indulgent frozen mudslides we've ever had. We like the flavor of coffee ice cream, but vanilla ice cream also works well.

- 4 ounces vodka
- 4 ounces coffee liqueur
- 4 ounces Irish cream liqueur
- ½ pint premium coffee ice cream
- 1 pound (4 cups) ice cubes
- Whipped cream for garnishing
- Chocolate shavings for garnishing
- Cocktail cherries for garnishing

Add vodka, coffee liqueur, Irish cream, ice cream, and ice to blender (in that order) and process until smooth, about 1 minute, scraping down sides of blender jar as needed. Adjust consistency with water as needed. Pour into chilled rocks glasses and garnish with whipped cream, chocolate shavings, and cocktail cherries. Serve.

The Spirited Slush

Ice cream truck slushes equal happy summertime childhood memories for many. Retailers such as 7-Eleven and Sonic let us carry that simple pleasure into adulthood. And the spirited slushes here are truly grown-up, adding alcohol to the equation, using fresh ingredients, and moderating sugar levels. So what makes a slush a slush? It's like a drinkable flavored ice of sorts, made using fruit, juice, ice, and of course spirits. The combination of both fruit pieces and fruit juice is what distinguishes it from other dairy-free frozen cocktails like Frozen Margaritas (page 437) or Peach-Strawberry Frosé (page 440).

In developing these recipes, we had a lot of fun with spirit-fruit pairings. Our Bourbon-Cherry Slush came about because the lush, red-fruit flavor of cherries goes beautifully with the oaky, caramel-vanilla notes of bourbon. Think about the old-fashioned or a bourbon Manhattan (or even a cherry cola) as a more typical cocktail example of this combination; as with those cocktails, old-fashioned aromatic bitters enhance the flavors. Three other versions swap out the bourbon for vodka, tequila, or rum and swap in different fruits for the cherries to take the flavor profiles in entirely different directions.

Using frozen fruit and frozen juice concentrates in these slushes ensures intense fruity flavor while also meaning these slushes aren't seasonally dependent. The fruit adds sweetness and a dominant flavor. Enhancing the main fruit with complementary juice concentrates (orange with cherry, lime with mango) boosts the overall fruity, fun taste that we expect from traditional nonalcoholic slushes.

With every frosty sip, these slushes will conjure up that familiar ice cream truck jingle and remind you that even as a grown-up, it's nice to relax and enjoy a frosty treat—whether it's summertime or not.

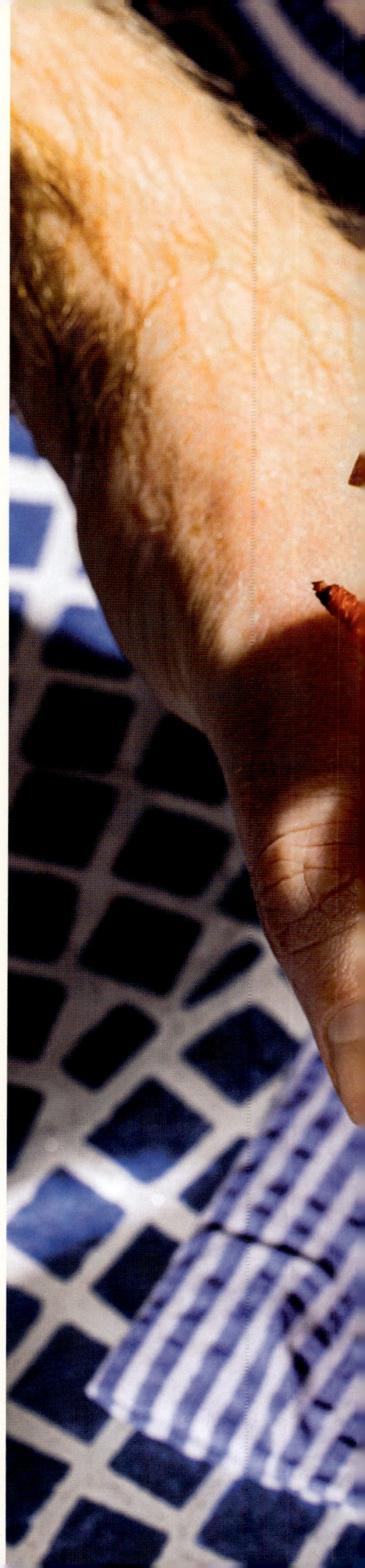

Bourbon-Cherry Slush

Makes 4 cocktails
Sweetness ✦✦✧
Citrusy, Fruity, Toasted

- 8 ounces bourbon
- 8 ounces water, plus extra as needed
- 1 teaspoon old-fashioned aromatic bitters
- ¾ cup frozen orange juice concentrate
- 12 ounces (3 cups) frozen sweet cherries
- 8 ounces (2 cups) ice cubes
- Orange slices for garnishing

Add bourbon, water, bitters, orange juice concentrate, cherries, and ice to blender (in that order) and process until smooth, about 1 minute. Adjust consistency with extra water as needed. Pour into chilled rocks glasses. Garnish with orange slices and serve.

Customize Your Cocktail

You can substitute Tennessee whiskey, lightly smoky blended Scotch, or aged rum for the bourbon. Make Zero-Proof Cherry Slush by omitting the bourbon and increasing the water to 16 ounces.

Strawberry-Lemonade Slush

Makes 4 cocktails

Sweetness ✦✦✦

Citrusy, Fruity, Tart

This sweet-tart slush is as refreshing as a nostalgic Popsicle but with way more fruit flavor. We use lemonade concentrate and frozen strawberries as the base, as they both pack a tasty punch and help the drink stay ice cold during blending. We use vodka for the spirit because its neutral flavor doesn't interfere with the citrus and berry.

- 8 ounces vodka
- 8 ounces water, plus extra as needed
- ¾ cup frozen lemonade concentrate
- 12 ounces (3 cups) frozen strawberries
- 8 ounces (2 cups) ice cubes
- Lemon slices for garnishing
- Halved fresh strawberries for garnishing

Add vodka, water, lemonade concentrate, frozen strawberries, and ice to blender (in that order) and process until smooth, about 1 minute. Adjust consistency with extra water as needed. Pour into chilled rocks glasses. Garnish with lemon slices and strawberry halves. Serve.

Customize Your Cocktail

Make Zero-Proof Strawberry-Lemonade Slush by omitting the vodka and increasing the water to 16 ounces. You can use tequila in place of the vodka.

Skinny Dipper

Makes 4 cocktails

Sweetness ✦✦✦

Tart, Tropical

It's not a frozen beverage lineup without a blue drink, bu we didn't love the taste of the blue curaçao in the classic blue-hued cooler, the blue Hawaii. We went a totally dif- ferent route, making a very beachy banana cocktail with complementary rum and bright lime. Blending a little food coloring into the mixture gives us the right color with the flavor we love. You can make your own frozen banana chunks by cutting 12 ounces of bananas into 1-inch pieces and freezing them until firm.

- 8 ounces white rum
- 8 ounces water, plus extra as needed
- ½ teaspoon blue food coloring (optional)
- ¾ cup frozen limeade concentrate
- 12 ounces (3 cups) frozen banana chunks
- 8 ounces (2 cups) ice cubes
- Cocktail cherries for garnishing

Add rum; water; food coloring, if using; limeade concentrate; bananas; and ice to blender (in that order) and process until smooth, about 1 minute. Adjust consistency with extra water as needed. Pour into chilled rocks glasses. Garnish with cocktail cherries and serve.

Customize Your Cocktail

Make Zero-Proof Skinny Dipper by substituting 8 ounces of coconut water for the rum.

Takes Two to Mango

Makes 4 cocktails
Sweetness ✦✦✧
Spicy, Tart, Tropical

Mangonada, a Mexican frozen layered drink of blended mango, lime juice, savory chamoy sauce, and chile-lime seasoning, provides inspiration for this simpler mango-chile slush. Here, the fruit flavor comes from frozen mango and limeade concentrate, which get palate-awakening savor from Tajín seasoning both blended into the drink and used to rim the glasses. Dried chili-lime mango slices also make an excellent garnish here.

- ¼ **cup plus 2 teaspoons Tajín Clásico Seasoning, divided**
- **Lime wedges for garnishing**
- 8 **ounces blanco or reposado tequila**
- 8 **ounces water, plus extra as needed**
- ¾ **cup frozen limeade concentrate**
- 12 **ounces (3 cups) frozen mango chunks**
- 8 **ounces (2 cups) ice cubes**

1. Spread ¼ cup Tajín into even layer on small saucer. Moisten about ½ inch of 4 chilled rocks glass rims by running lime wedge around outer edge; dry any excess juice with paper towel. Roll moistened rims in Tajín to coat. Remove any excess Tajín that falls into glasses; set aside.

2. Add tequila, water, limeade concentrate, mango, ice, and remaining 2 teaspoons Tajín to blender (in that order) and process until smooth, about 1 minute. Adjust consistency with extra water as needed. Pour into prepared rocks glasses. Garnish with lime wedges and serve.

Customize Your Cocktail

Make Zero-Proof Takes Two to Mango by substituting 8 ounces of coconut water for the tequila.

From left to right: Strawberry-Lemonade Slush, Takes Two to Mango, Skinny Dipper

Frozen Margaritas

Makes 4 cocktails
Sweetness ✦✦✧
Citrusy, Tart

It's believed that the world's first frozen margarita machine made its debut in Dallas in 1971. Now it's a mainstay companion for nachos, tacos, and more at Tex-Mex restaurants. If you only know the sickly sweet, too-icy machine slush, get ready for a revelation. Our from-scratch frozen version has tangy, true citrus flavor and a perfect consistency. Rather than squeezing, sweetening, and freezing juice from fresh limes, we opt for frozen limeade concentrate (made with real limes), which offers a balance of lime flavor and sweetness, and also helps create the ideal semifrozen texture when it's combined with ice.

- 2 tablespoons Citrus Rim Salt (page 453) (optional)
- Lime wedges for garnishing
- 6 ounces blanco or reposado tequila
- 4 ounces orange liqueur
- ¾ cup frozen limeade concentrate
- 1¼ pounds (5 cups) ice cubes

1. Spread rim salt, if using, into even layer on small saucer. Moisten about ½ inch of 4 chilled rocks glass rims by running lime wedge around outer edge; dry any excess juice with paper towel. Roll moistened rims in salt to coat. Remove any excess salt that falls into glasses; set aside.

2. Add tequila, orange liqueur, limeade concentrate, and ice to blender (in that order) and process until smooth, about 1 minute, scraping down sides of blender jar as needed. Adjust consistency with water as needed. Pour into prepared glasses. Garnish with lime wedges and serve.

Customize Your Cocktail

While we prefer using our Citrus Rim Salt here, you can substitute another flavored rim salt from page 453 or plain kosher salt.

Frozen Hurricanes

Makes 4 cocktails
Sweetness ✦ ✦ ✧
Citrusy, Tart, Tropical

The hurricane, served in its namesake curved glass, is one of the best-known tropical drinks created in America in the 1940s. The creation of this fruity relative of the daiquiri (see page 204) is credited to New Orleans tavern owner Pat O'Brien, and it's one of many iconic cocktails famously associated with the Big Easy. However, the frozen versions you typically find floating down Bourbon Street these days are pumped from giant machines, mix-based, garishly red from dye, and laden with artificial ingredients and often harsh, cheap booze. We wanted to put the quality back into this drink.

Three fruits—passion fruit, orange, and lime—flavor our version. For the prominent passion fruit element, we use frozen passion fruit puree and for the orange element, a freezer staple, orange juice concentrate. We need only an ounce of lime juice, so fresh works fine here. Aged rum is our choice for this cocktail; it provides deep, rich flavor while still allowing the fruit juices to shine. A bit of sweetness from richly colored grenadine balances the sour notes of the passion fruit in this delightful frozen rum punch.

8 ounces aged rum
8 ounces water, plus extra as needed
2 ounces grenadine
1 ounce Simple Syrup (page 458)
1 ounce lime juice, plus lime wedges for garnishing
¾ cup frozen orange juice concentrate
½ cup frozen passion fruit puree
1 pound (4 cups) ice cubes
Cocktail cherries for garnishing

Add rum, water, grenadine, simple syrup, lime juice, orange juice concentrate, passion fruit puree, and ice to blender (in that order) and process until smooth, about 1 minute, scraping down sides of blender jar as needed. Adjust consistency with extra water as needed. Pour into chilled hurricane glasses. Garnish with lime wedges and cocktail cherries and serve.

Customize Your Cocktail

Create Zero-Proof Frozen Hurricanes by substituting 8 ounces of coconut water for the rum.

Florentine Freezes

Makes 4 cocktails
Sweetness ✦✦✧
Bitter, Citrusy

While we love Negronis (see page 333) almost any time of year, we offer a frozen riff on the classic for the most scorching summer days. To lighten up the strong flavors, we opt to use fruit juice in place of the typical vermouth. Orange juice concentrate tempers both the herbal spiciness of the Campari and the botanical notes of the gin. Proving that not all frozen drinks need to have a sweet and tart flavor profile, our Florentine freeze achieves a complex herbal-bittersweet flavor profile that's molto delizioso.

- 4 ounces Campari
- 4 ounces London dry gin
- 4 ounces water, plus extra as needed
- ¾ cup frozen orange juice concentrate
- 1 pound (4 cups) ice cubes
- Orange slices for garnishing

Add Campari, gin, water, orange juice concentrate, and ice to blender (in that order) and process until smooth, about 1 minute, scraping down sides of blender jar as needed. Adjust consistency with extra water as needed. Pour into chilled hurricane glasses. Garnish with orange slices and serve.

Peach-Strawberry Frosé

Makes 4 cocktails

Sweetness ✦ ✧ ✧

Fruity, Tart

- 1 (750-ml) bottle rosé wine
- 3 ounces Simple Syrup (page 458)
- 4 ounces (1 cup) frozen strawberries
- 4 ounces (1 cup) frozen peaches
- Fresh strawberry slices for garnishing

You may find frosé—frozen rosé wine blended with other ingredients—churning away in countertop machines at restaurants. But the pretty-in-pink fruit-forward wine cocktail is simple to make at home. While some recipes call for pouring wine right from bottle to blender, we discovered that freezing some of the wine first in ice cube trays promotes a fine-textured slush. Many recipes call for strawberries and lemon juice, but we found this combination overwhelms the wine. Instead, combining equal parts strawberries and peaches results in a light, fresh fruitiness that enhances the wine. Along with the wine ice cubes, using frozen fruit eliminates the need for regular ice cubes. Use a fruitier rather than a drier rosé for this cocktail.

1. Measure out and reserve 10 ounces wine and refrigerate until ready to use. Divide remaining wine between 2 ice cube trays and freeze until firm, about 2 hours. (Frozen wine cubes can be transferred to zipper-lock bag and kept frozen for up to 2 months.)

2. Add reserved wine, simple syrup, frozen strawberries, peaches, and frozen wine cubes to blender (in that order) and process until smooth, about 1 minute, scraping down sides of blender jar as needed. Adjust consistency with water as needed. Pour into chilled wineglasses. Garnish with strawberry slices and serve.

Customize Your Cocktail

Add complexity to this cocktail by substituting citrus or herb syrups (see pages 458 and 459) for the simple syrup. Create Zero-Proof Peach-Strawberry Frosé by using nonalcoholic rosé or white wine. You can also make Peach Frieslings by substituting off-dry (slightly sweet) Riesling for the rosé, omitting the strawberries, and increasing the peaches to 2 cups.

Frozen Watermelon Coolers

Makes 4 zero-proof cocktails
Sweetness ✦✦✧
Fruity, Citrusy

On a hot summer's day, watermelon in any form is a quintessential thirst quencher. So, transforming this succulent fruit into a vibrant, crowd-pleasing nonalcoholic cocktail seems like a no-brainer. Watermelon is watery enough before ice is added, so we simply freeze half of our watermelon before blending the drink. We accent our fruit base with fresh lime juice for a tangy profile. Just a little bit of simple syrup, balanced with some salt, brings out the sweet and tart flavors even further. Depending on the sweetness of your watermelon, you may need to add the greater amount of simple syrup.

- 3 pounds peeled seedless watermelon, cut into 1-inch pieces (10 cups), divided
- 2 tablespoons Citrus Rim Salt (page 453) (optional)
- 2 ounces lime juice, plus lime wedges for garnishing
- ½–1 ounce Simple Syrup (page 458)
- ¼ teaspoon table salt

1. Spread 2 cups watermelon into single layer on large plate and freeze until firm, about 2 hours.

2. Spread rim salt, if using, into even layer on small saucer. Moisten about ½ inch of 4 chilled highball glass rims by running lime wedge around outer edge; dry any excess juice with paper towel. Roll moistened rims in salt to coat. Remove any excess salt that falls into glass; set aside.

3. Add remaining 8 cups fresh watermelon, lime juice, simple syrup, and salt to blender and process until smooth, about 30 seconds, scraping down sides of blender jar as needed. Add frozen watermelon and process until smooth, 30 to 60 seconds. Adjust consistency with water as needed. Pour into prepared glasses. Garnish with lime wedges and serve.

Customize Your Cocktail

While we prefer to use our Citrus Rim Salt here, you can substitute another flavored rim salt from page 453 or plain kosher salt. You can make Spiked Frozen Watermelon Coolers by adding 8 ounces vodka, white rum, or blanco tequila to the blender with the fresh watermelon.

PAIR WITH A SNACK

Cóctel de Camarón

Serves 4 to 6
Total Time: 45 minutes

This Mexican dish consists of cooked shrimp tossed with chopped vegetables in a bright tomato sauce. We prefer untreated shrimp; if your shrimp are treated with salt or additives such as sodium tripolyphosphate, do not add the salt in step 1. The balanced flavor of Valentina, Cholula, or Tapatío hot sauce works best here.

- **1¼ pounds large shrimp (26 to 30 per pound), peeled, deveined, and tails removed**
- **¼ teaspoon table salt, plus salt for cooking shrimp**
- **1 cup V8 juice, chilled**
- **½ cup ketchup**
- **3 tablespoons lime juice, plus lime wedges for serving**
- **2 teaspoons hot sauce, plus extra for serving**
- **½ English cucumber, cut into ½-inch pieces**
- **1 cup finely chopped red onion**
- **1 avocado, halved, pitted, and cut into ½-inch pieces**
- **¼ cup chopped fresh cilantro**
- **Saltines**

1. Bring 3 cups water to boil in large saucepan over high heat. Stir in shrimp and 1 tablespoon salt. Cover and let stand off heat until shrimp are opaque, about 5 minutes, shaking saucepan halfway through. Fill large bowl halfway with ice and water. Transfer shrimp to ice bath and let cool for 3 to 5 minutes. Cut each shrimp into 3 pieces.

2. Combine V8 juice, ketchup, lime juice, hot sauce, and salt in large bowl. Add cucumber, onion, and shrimp and stir until evenly coated. Stir in avocado and cilantro. Portion cocktail into individual glasses and serve, passing saltines, lime wedges, and extra hot sauce separately.

Honeydew-Lemon Aguas Frescas

Makes 8 zero-proof cocktails
Sweetness ✦ ✦ ✧
Citrusy, Floral, Fruity

Agua fresca means "fresh water" and is the catchall term for a variety of Mexican beverages made by combining fruits, vegetables, grains, seeds, or flowers with sugar and water. This melon version is hydrating and fresh, perfect for brunch guests or an afternoon refresher. We derive sweetness from the melon itself and a bit of agave nectar. Honeydew melon has a juicy but mild flavor, so we enliven it with just enough lemon juice to punch up the drink without turning it sour. This beverage keeps for days, so if you make it ahead, you have a better-than-bottled beverage to grab from the fridge all week. Because honeydew melons vary in sweetness, we started by tasting our honeydew to determine how much agave nectar to incorporate into the agua fresca. Depending on the sweetness of your honeydew, you may need to add the greater amount of agave syrup.

- **2½ pounds honeydew, peeled, seeded, and cut into 1½-inch pieces (8 cups)**
- **16 ounces water**
- **3 ounces lemon juice, plus lemon slices for garnishing**
- **½–1 ounce agave syrup**
- **¼ teaspoon table salt**

Working in 2 batches, process honeydew and water in blender until smooth, about 30 seconds. Strain mixture through fine-mesh strainer into pitcher or large container, pressing on solids to extract as much liquid as possible; discard solids. Stir in lemon juice, agave, and salt. (Agua fresca can be refrigerated for up to 5 days; stir to recombine before serving.) Serve in chilled highball glasses filled with ice, garnishing individual portions with lemon slices.

Customize Your Cocktail

You can make Spiked Honeydew-Lemon Aguas Frescas by adding 8 ounces of vodka, white rum, or blanco tequila with the lemon juice. You can also make Watermelon-Lime Aguas Frescas by substituting watermelon for the honeydew and lime juice for the lemon juice.

Horchata

Makes 4 zero-proof cocktails
Sweetness ✦✦✦
Creamy, Nutty, Spiced

Horchata has countless variations across Latin America, the Carribean, and parts of Spain. Our rice and almond version, flavored with cinnamon, is a style typical to Mexico. This sweet, cold, creamy agua fresca, made with relatively few ingredients, is the perfect foil for spicy food. Toasting the almonds and cinnamon adds depth to this drink. We strain the blended horchata through a nut milk bag to simplify the usual process of straining through cheesecloth; this ensures perfectly smooth horchata with no chalkiness or grit. A bit of fresh lime zest adds brightness against the backdrop of rich rice and almond milk and warm cinnamon. Finally, we stir in some milk for body. Ceylon cinnamon is relatively subtle and floral and is traditional here, but you can use any variety of cinnamon sticks. You will need a 12 by 12-inch reusable nut milk bag for this recipe.

- 1 cup slivered almonds
- 2 (4-inch) Ceylon cinnamon sticks, coarsely crumbled, plus freshly grated cinnamon for garnishing
- 24 ounces water
- 1 cup raw long-grain white rice
- ½ cup sugar
- 2 teaspoons vanilla extract
- 1 (2-inch) strip lime zest
- ¼ teaspoon table salt
- 14 ounces whole milk

1. Toast almonds and cinnamon sticks in 12-inch skillet over medium heat until fragrant and almonds are just beginning to turn golden, 5 to 8 minutes.

2. Transfer almond mixture to blender. Add water, rice, sugar, vanilla, lime zest, and salt and process until smooth, about 1 minute, scraping down sides of blender jar as needed. Open nut milk bag and place in medium bowl. Pour mixture into nut milk bag, leaving bag in bowl. Close bag and drape enclosure over edge of bowl. Cover bowl with plastic wrap and refrigerate for at least 2 hours or up to 24 hours.

3. Lift nut milk bag above bowl to strain remaining liquid through bag. When liquid no longer runs freely, firmly squeeze bag to extract as much liquid as possible; discard solids. (You should have 18 ounces horchata base.) Whisk milk into horchata base. (Horchata can be refrigerated for up to 3 days; stir to recombine before serving.)

4. Pour horchata into chilled highball glasses filled with ice. Garnish with ground cinnamon and serve.

Customize Your Cocktail

You can substitute any nondairy milk for the milk. You can make Horchata Borracha (Drunken Horchata) by substituting 6 ounces of white rum or vodka for the milk.

The
Backbar

Cocktail Garnishes

Just as you eat with your eyes first, you drink with them too, and a cocktail is often better with a bauble. This could be as simple as a wedge of citrus or as intricate as an elegantly tied twist of peel; as quick as a string of jarred Manzanilla olives or as thoughtful as homemade stuffed olives filled with blue cheese and bacon. Never skip your garnishes, as their aroma can add necessary nuance to every sip of a well-balanced cocktail.

FRESH CITRUS GARNISHES

Citrus is the most ubiquitous garnish. This could mean a simple lime wedge or a coin of zest topping an egg foam. Citrus zest is a tool for expressing citrus oil into a cocktail, adding the finishing touch of flavor, aroma, and texture. When we want the lightest touch—as in our Aviation (page 229), which boasts delicate floral flavor—we simply twist the zest over the glass before placing it on the rim. For a strong burst of brightness, we use a wide strip of peel and pinch it over the top of the drink to express the oils before rubbing the outer edge of the glass. And for the most dramatic option, we flame the citrus, which expresses and also lightly caramelizes the oils.

How to Make a Citrus Coin

For garnishing: Using sharp slicing knife, slice 1-inch disk of zest, avoiding as much white pith as possible.

For muddling: Slice citrus a little deeper so that it includes a small amount of pulp.

How to Make Citrus Wedges

1. Trim ends of citrus, if desired, then halve pole to pole. Arrange each half, cut side down, on cutting board and cut lengthwise into ½- to ¾-inch wedges.

2. Remove seeds from each wedge and trim away any white membrane from narrow end of wedge.

How to Make a Citrus Twist

1. Using channel knife, remove 3- to 4-inch strand of peel, working around circumference of citrus in spiral pattern to ensure continuous piece.

2. Curl strand tightly over cocktail to establish uniform twist, then place in cocktail or on edge of glass.

ELEVATE YOUR CITRUS TWIST

Citrus twists can vary in appearance. To create a thicker twist, use a Y-shaped vegetable peeler to remove a 1-inch-wide strip of zest, then slice the zest lengthwise into slender strips. You can also modify the shape of twists by tying them into knots or artfully securing them to the rim of the glass (see page 452). There's lots of inspiration in the photographs throughout this book.

How to Make a Citrus Strip

1. Using Y-shaped vegetable peeler, remove 2- to 3-inch strip, working from pole to pole of citrus and avoiding as much white pith as possible.

2. With index finger and thumb of both hands, hold strip, pith side facing you, horizontal to surface of cocktail. Pinch zest to express oils onto cocktail. Rub outer edge of glass with peel, then place in cocktail.

ELEVATE YOUR CITRUS STRIP

Citrus strips serve a serious purpose, but you don't have to be so serious with their presentation. You can easily create a variety of geometric shapes by trimming the edges of the strips with a paring knife before expressing the oils onto the cocktail. You can also weave them onto cocktail skewers, after expressing them, by themselves or with other garnishes.

How to Perch a Citrus Peel on the Rim

1. Cut 2-inch strip of citrus peel into elongated diamond shape.

2. Cut 1-inch slit down center of peel.

3. Curl strip into bowed shape and use slit to secure to rim of glass.

How to Flame a Citrus Peel

1. Hold lit match few inches above cocktail. Hold citrus coin or strip, zest side toward flame, just above flame.

2. Slowly wave zest over flame for a few seconds to warm oils, then quickly squeeze zest to express oils over flame and ignite. Discard zest.

TIPS FOR FLAMING SUCCESS

- ◊ The fresher the citrus, the more oils there will be in the peel and, thus, the more impressive the flame will be (and the more flavor you'll extract).
- ◊ This technique works best for oranges and very fresh lemons; limes generally don't have enough oils to create the desired effect.
- ◊ Create the flame away from yourself and others.
- ◊ Note: The flame lasts for just a quarter of a second or less.

RIM SALTS AND SUGARS

Certain cocktails spring to life when garnished with a bit of salt. Others win some sweetness and an elevated touch from a glimmer of sugar. We've created easy flavored rim salts and sugars that can be used to add a whiff of aroma or a hint of spice—in addition to saltiness or sweetness—to complement certain cocktails. These recipes are easy to make and keep on hand and can be doubled. They can be stored in an airtight container for up to 1 month; break up clumps as needed before using.

Citrus Rim Salt

Makes about ½ cup

- ½ cup kosher salt
- 1 tablespoon grated lime zest (2 limes), orange zest, lemon zest, or grapefruit zest

Combine salt and zest in bowl, then spread onto large plate. Microwave, stirring occasionally, until mixture is dry and no longer clumps, about 2 minutes. Let cool completely, about 15 minutes. Transfer mixture to food processor and pulse until zest is finely ground, 5 to 10 pulses.

Sriracha Rim Salt

Makes about ½ cup

- ½ cup kosher salt
- ⅓ cup sriracha

Combine salt and sriracha in bowl, then spread onto large plate. Microwave, stirring occasionally, until mixture is only slightly damp, 6 to 8 minutes. Let cool completely, about 15 minutes. Transfer mixture to food processor and pulse until finely ground, 5 to 10 pulses.

Berry Rim Salt

Makes about ½ cup

You can find freeze-dried berries in the baking or natural foods aisle of most well-stocked supermarkets.

- 1 cup freeze-dried strawberries, blueberries, or raspberries
- ½ cup kosher salt

Working in batches, process berries in spice grinder until finely ground, about 30 seconds. Transfer to bowl and whisk in salt until combined.

Herb Rim Salt

Makes about ½ cup

- ½ cup kosher salt
- ½ cup minced fresh basil, dill, or tarragon

Using your hands, rub salt and basil in large bowl until well combined. Spread mixture into even layer on parchment paper–lined rimmed baking sheet. Let sit at room temperature, away from direct sunlight, until completely dry, 36 to 48 hours, stirring every 12 hours to break up any clumps.

Vanilla Rim Sugar

Makes about ½ cup

1 vanilla bean
½ cup sugar, divided

Cut vanilla bean in half lengthwise. Using tip of paring knife or spoon, scrape out seeds. Using fingers, rub vanilla seeds and 2 tablespoons sugar together in medium bowl until combined. Whisk in remaining 6 tablespoons sugar. Transfer sugar mixture and spent vanilla bean halves to airtight container and let sit until flavors meld, about 2 days.

Pumpkin Spice Rim Sugar

Makes about ½ cup

½ cup sugar
2 teaspoons ground cinnamon
1 teaspoon ground ginger
½ teaspoon ground nutmeg
½ teaspoon ground allspice

Whisk all ingredients in bowl until combined.

Smoky Chile Rim Sugar

Makes about ½ cup

½ cup sugar
1 teaspoon chipotle chile powder
½ teaspoon smoked paprika

Whisk all ingredients in bowl until combined.

How to Create a Salt or Sugar Rim

1. Moisten about ½ inch of glass rim by running citrus wedge around outer edge, or by dipping edge of glass in small saucer of water; dry any excess liquid with paper towel.

2. Spread ¼ cup rim salt or sugar (for up to 4 glasses) into even layer on small saucer, then roll moistened rim in salt or sugar to coat. Remove any excess granules that fall into glass.

ELEVATE YOUR GLASS RIM

Any finely ground mixture will work on the rim of your glass. Consider using spice or seed blends, such as za'atar or shichimi togarashi. You can also change up the presentation by extending the seasoning beyond the rim. Moisten the side of the glass with the citrus wedge (or lightly brush it with water), then roll the moistened surface in the garnishing mixture of your choice. Or, moisten and coat only one portion of the glass rim so that you can enjoy the cocktail both with and without the garnish.

COCKTAIL GARNISHES

ELEVATED ADORNMENTS

While you could buy these garnishes in jars, the homemade versions look and taste extra luxe. They finish a drink with flavor, texture, substance—and style.

Dehydrated Citrus Slices

Makes 2 cups

Get creative when a recipe calls for a citrus wedge or slice garnish. Dehydrating citrus—from lemons to limes to pomelos to grapefruit—concentrates its flavor and gives it an elegant stained-glass appearance. This recipe will work with any variety of citrus fruits. Be sure to thoroughly wash and dry citrus before slicing. To double, arrange citrus slices on 2 baking sheets and adjust oven racks to upper-middle and lower-middle positions.

- 8 ounces citrus, ends trimmed, sliced crosswise ⅛ inch thick

Adjust oven rack to middle position and heat oven to 200 degrees. Set wire rack in rimmed baking sheet and spray rack with vegetable oil spray. Arrange citrus slices in single layer on prepared rack. Bake until dry to the touch, 2½ to 3½ hours. Remove sheet from oven and let slices cool completely. (Citrus slices can be stored in zipper-lock bag for up to 1 month.)

Fresh Herb Oil

Makes about ½ cup

Herb oil adds a pop of vibrancy when drizzled on a cocktail. The key to its bright hue is blanching and shocking the herbs: Blanching collapses the plants' cells, intensifying their green color, and partially deactivates the enzyme that causes oxidation; shocking stops the cooking to keep the herbs tasting fresh. If you don't use all of the oil within 4 days of making it, you can freeze the remainder for up to 1 month.

- 1½ ounces fresh basil, cilantro, dill, mint, parsley, and/or tarragon leaves
- ⅔ cup vegetable oil

1. Fill large bowl halfway with ice and water. Bring 6 cups water to boil in large saucepan. Add basil and cook until tender but still bright green, about 30 seconds. Immediately drain basil in fine-mesh strainer, then submerge strainer and basil in prepared ice bath. Let sit until well chilled, about 2 minutes. Remove strainer from ice bath and let drain.

2. Transfer basil to salad spinner and spin to remove excess water. Spread over clean, dry dish towel. (If you don't have a salad spinner, pat basil dry with clean dish towel and squeeze thoroughly to remove excess water.) Line clean, dry fine-mesh strainer with quadruple layer of cheesecloth and set over liquid measuring cup or bowl.

3. Transfer basil to blender. Add oil and process until basil is very finely pureed and oil is bright green, about 1 minute. Transfer mixture to prepared strainer and let drain until oil has fully passed through cheesecloth, about 1 hour.

4. Fold edges of cheesecloth over remaining basil puree and gently squeeze to extract any remaining oil; discard solids and cheesecloth. Transfer oil to glass jar or glass dropper bottle. (Basil oil can be refrigerated for up to 4 days; gently shake to recombine before using.)

Cocktail Cherries

Makes 2 cups

The garishly bright-red cherries that garnish everything from ice cream sundaes and fruitcakes to baked hams and cocktails are a far cry from the original maraschino cherry. Maraschinos originated in Croatia in the 19th century, when Marasca cherries were preserved in liqueur. This tradition has been preserved in several high-quality commercial versions, including Luxardo's Original Maraschino Cherries. Since store-bought options can be expensive, we created a homemade option. We hit the sweet (and delicately sour) spot when we soaked jarred sour Morello cherries (similar to but more accessible than Marascas) in a syrup made from unsweetened 100 percent cherry juice and sugar. The key to the syrup was to reduce the juice before adding sugar. You can substitute other jarred or canned sour cherries for the Morellos; their weight after draining should be 12 ounces.

- 8 ounces unsweetened 100 percent cherry juice
- 1 cup sugar
- 1 (24-ounce) jar pitted dark Morello cherries in light syrup, drained

1. Bring cherry juice to simmer in medium saucepan over medium-high heat and cook until juice has reduced to 4 ounces, about 5 minutes. Off heat, whisk in sugar until dissolved.

2. Meanwhile, place 1-pint Mason jar in bowl and set under hot running water until heated through, 1 to 2 minutes; shake dry.

3. Using slotted spoon, gently pack cherries into hot jar. Using funnel and ladle, pour hot syrup over cherries to cover; you may have some leftover syrup. Let jar cool completely, about 30 minutes. Cover and refrigerate for 12 hours before serving. (Cherries can be refrigerated for up to 2 months.)

Cocktail Onions

Makes about 2 cups

When brined in a flavorful spiced liquid, mild, naturally sweet pearl onions become the signature garnish for the Gibson (page 156), the pickled onion–lover's riff on the gin martini. Or set out a bowl of them for garnishing when you serve Bloody Marys (page 319). We prefer to use fresh pearl onions for their bright flavor and firm texture and do not recommend using frozen pearl onions in this recipe. Look for onions that are no larger than 1 inch in diameter. Blanching them in boiling water for 1 minute makes it easy to remove their skins. The additives commonly found in table salt (iodine and anticaking agents) can produce off-flavors and hazy brines when making pickles, but canning salt, which is often called pickling or preserving salt and is specifically designed for pickle making, doesn't contain additives. This salt also has a very fine grain and dissolves quickly in water. However, you can swap kosher salt for the canning salt: If substituting Morton's Kosher Salt, increase the amount called for here to 2¼ teaspoons; if using Diamond Crystal Kosher Salt, increase the amount to 3 teaspoons.

- 12 ounces small pearl onions
- 4 ounces distilled white vinegar
- 2 ounces dry vermouth
- 1 tablespoon sugar
- 1½ teaspoons canning salt
- 1 teaspoon juniper berries, lightly crushed
- 1 teaspoon coriander seeds
- ½ teaspoon black peppercorns
- 2 (2-inch) strips lemon zest

1. Bring 2 quarts water to boil in large saucepan. Fill large bowl halfway with ice and water. Add onions to boiling water and cook for 1 minute. Drain onions, then transfer to prepared ice bath; drain again. Using paring knife, shave off root ends and tips of onions, then peel off skins.

2. Bring vinegar, 4 ounces water, vermouth, sugar, salt, juniper berries, coriander seeds, and peppercorns to boil in now-empty saucepan over medium-high heat, stirring occasionally to dissolve sugar and salt. Add onions, return to simmer, and cook for 2 minutes.

3. Meanwhile, place 1-pint Mason jar in separate bowl and set under hot running water until heated through, 1 to 2 minutes; shake dry.

4. Place zest strips in hot jar. Using slotted spoon, pack onions into jar. Using funnel and ladle, pour hot vinegar mixture over onions to cover; you may have some leftover brine. Let jar cool completely, about 30 minutes. Cover and refrigerate for 12 hours before serving. (Onions can be refrigerated for up to 2 months.)

Cocktail Onions

Stuffed Olives with Hazelnuts, Parmesan, and Anchovies

Makes 12 stuffed olives

While you can easily top savory cocktails with pimento-stuffed Manzanilla olives (in the number of your choice) straight from the jar, and Castelvetrano olives are a popular choice, sometimes a nice dry cocktail is divine with the extra salinity, savor, and heft of some impressively stuffed olives. We like to prepare for cocktail parties with these recipes. Food-handling gloves make it easy to stuff the olives with your fingers, but a small spoon will also work. This recipe can easily be doubled or tripled.

- 1½ teaspoons finely chopped Parmesan cheese
- 1½ teaspoons finely chopped toasted hazelnuts
- 2 anchovies, finely chopped
- 12 pitted large green olives

Combine Parmesan, hazelnuts, and anchovies in small bowl. Using gloved hands, evenly stuff olives with Parmesan mixture. (Olives can be refrigerated for up to 24 hours.)

Stuffed Olives with Bacon and Blue Cheese

Substitute 1 tablespoon crumbled blue cheese and 1 teaspoon finely chopped crisp bacon for Parmesan, hazelnuts, and anchovies.

Stuffed Olives with Preserved Lemon and Calabrian Chile

Substitute 1 tablespoon finely chopped preserved lemon, ½ teaspoon jarred crushed Calabrian chiles, and ¼ teaspoon za'atar for Parmesan, hazelnuts, and anchovies.

Syrups, Shrubs, and Purees

Sugar in some form is a fundamental building block of cocktails; sometimes it's used to provide an unequivocal sweetness; other times, it is a ncte in a chord of flavors, used to balance acidic, bitter, savory, or other flavors. These are some ways we incorporate sweetness in our cocktails.

Simple Syrup

Makes about 8 ounces

Syrups dissolve more easily than other forms of sugar in cocktails. Simple syrup is one of the most ubiquitous cocktail additions, and it should be a constant of your home bar. Our method is quick: We (simply) stir warm water and sugar together. We also developed several flavored syrups; these require brief cooking but result in fruit or spice infusions that can add dimension to your drinks. Simple syrup can be refrigerated for up to 1 month; shake well before using.

- ¾ cup sugar
- 5 ounces warm tap water

Whisk sugar and warm water in bowl until sugar has dissolved. Let cool completely, about 10 minutes, before transferring to airtight container.

Citrus Syrup

- ¾ cup sugar
- 5 ounces water
- 1 tablespoon grated lemon, lime, orange, or grapefruit zest

Heat sugar and water in small saucepan over medium heat, whisking often, until sugar has dissolved, about 5 minutes; do not boil. Stir in zest and let syrup cool completely, about 30 minutes. Strain syrup through fine-mesh strainer into airtight container, pressing on solids to extract as much syrup as possible; discard solids.

Berry Syrup

This recipe works best with frozen berries. Feel free to use a single type of berry or a combination of berries.

- ¾ cup sugar
- 5 ounces water
- 6 ounces (about 1 cup) frozen blackberries, blueberries, raspberries, and/or chopped strawberries

Heat sugar and water in small saucepan over medium heat, whisking often, until sugar has dissolved, about 5 minutes; do not boil. Stir in berries and let syrup cool completely, about 30 minutes. Strain syrup through fine-mesh strainer into airtight container (do not press on solids); discard solids.

Herb Syrup

Avoid delicate herbs like basil, dill, and tarragon.

- ¾ cup sugar
- 5 ounces water
- 1 fresh rosemary sprig, 12 fresh thyme sprigs, or ½ cup fresh sage leaves

Heat sugar and water in small saucepan over medium heat, whisking often, until sugar has dissolved, about 5 minutes; do not boil. Stir in rosemary and let syrup cool completely, about 30 minutes. Strain syrup through fine-mesh strainer into airtight container; discard solids.

Spice Syrup

If a recipe calls for Spice Syrup, feel free to use a single spice or combination of spices. If you don't have a mortar and pestle, you can rock the bottom edge of a skillet over the spices on a cutting board until they crack.

- 1 ounce allspice berries, cardamom pods, whole cloves, cinnamon sticks, and/or star anise pods
- 7 ounces water
- ¾ cup sugar

Working in batches, lightly crush spices with mortar and pestle. Combine spices, water, and sugar in small saucepan and bring to boil over medium-high heat. Reduce heat to low, cover, and simmer for 5 minutes. Let cool completely, about 30 minutes. Strain syrup through fine-mesh strainer into airtight container; discard solids.

Tea Syrup

Use loose-leaf tea in this recipe.

- ¾ cup sugar
- 5 ounces water
- 2 ounces (¾ cup) black or green tea leaves

Heat sugar and water in small saucepan over medium heat, whisking often, until sugar has dissolved, about 5 minutes; do not boil. Stir in tea and let steep for 15 minutes. Strain syrup through fine-mesh strainer into airtight container, pressing on solids to extract as much syrup as possible; discard solids. Let syrup cool completely, about 15 minutes.

Orgeat Syrup

Makes about 8 ounces

Orgeat syrup is an indispensable ingredient in tropical cocktails, with its rich texture, nutty flavor, and light perfume. A homemade version is a special way to elevate your tropical drinks. A little orange blossom water (a traditional addition) stirred in at the end lends an enchanting hint of floral aroma.

- 5 ounces blanched whole, sliced, or slivered almonds, toasted and cooled
- 1 cup sugar
- 8 ounces water
- ¼ teaspoon orange blossom water

1. Pulse almonds in food processor until finely chopped, about 30 pulses.

2. Heat sugar and water in small saucepan over medium heat, whisking often, until sugar has dissolved, about 5 minutes; do not boil. Off heat, stir in almonds, cover, and let sit at least 12 hours or up to 24 hours.

3. Set fine-mesh strainer over medium bowl and line with triple layer of cheesecloth that overhangs edges. Transfer almond mixture to prepared strainer and let drain until liquid no longer runs freely, about 10 minutes. Pull edges of cheesecloth together to form pouch, then firmly squeeze pouch to extract as much syrup from pulp as possible; discard pulp. Stir in orange blossom water. (Orgeat Syrup can be refrigerated in airtight container for up to 1 month. Shake gently before using.)

Grenadine

Grenadine

Makes about 8 ounces

This garnet-colored syrup gives cocktails a bright punch of flavor and an unmistakable hue. It's traditionally made from pomegranate juice. But now one of the most ubiquitous commercial brands lists only high-fructose corn syrup, preservatives, natural and artificial flavors, and artificial colors on its label. For our very real version, we substitute pomegranate juice for the water in our Simple Syrup (page 458) formula and include a touch of allspice as a warm counterpoint. We suggest the small amount of tangy pomegranate molasses for even deeper flavor.

- ¾ cup sugar
- 5 ounces unsweetened 100 percent pomegranate juice
- 8 allspice berries, lightly crushed
- ½ teaspoon pomegranate molasses (optional)

Heat sugar, pomegranate juice, allspice berries, and pomegranate molasses, if using, in small saucepan over medium heat, whisking often, until sugar has dissolved, about 5 minutes; do not boil. Let cool completely, about 30 minutes, then strain through fine-mesh strainer into airtight container. (Grenadine can be refrigerated for up to 1 month; shake well before using.)

Cranberry Shrub Syrup

Makes about 8 ounces

Sweetened vinegar-and-fruit syrups (also sometimes called drinking vinegars), shrubs have been around for a long time. Evidence of acidulated fruit beverages around the world goes back centuries; the version popping up in modern American glasses is believed to have evolved from the fruit-and-vinegar preserves of 17th-century England, continued here by colonists as a way to preserve seasonal fruit. Modern bar menus abound with cocktails (which also, confusingly, can be called shrubs) made from these versatile concoctions, but you can also simply add 1 to 2 ounces of shrub syrup (to your taste) to 6 ounces of seltzer for an amazing thirst quencher.

- 8 ounces (2 cups) fresh or frozen cranberries
- 1 cup sugar
- 6 ounces water
- 1 ounce white wine vinegar

1. Bring cranberries, sugar, and water to boil in large saucepan over high heat. Reduce heat to medium-low, cover, and simmer until cranberries are beginning to break down, about 5 minutes.

2. Remove saucepan from heat and use potato masher to crush cranberries. Set fine-mesh strainer over medium bowl and line with triple layer of cheesecloth that overhangs edges. Transfer cranberry mixture to prepared strainer and let drain until liquid no longer runs freely and mixture is cool enough to touch, about 30 minutes. Pull edges of cheesecloth together to form pouch, then gently squeeze pouch to extract as much syrup as possible; discard solids. Whisk in vinegar. (Shrub syrup can be refrigerated for up to 1 month; shake well before using.)

Berry Shrub Syrup

This recipe works best with frozen berries.

- 5 ounces (1 cup) frozen blueberries, blackberries, and/or raspberries, chopped
- 5 ounces (1 cup) frozen strawberries, chopped
- 1 cup sugar
- 2 ounces white wine vinegar

1. Toss blueberries and strawberries with sugar in bowl. Cover and refrigerate for 24 hours, stirring occasionally.

2. Strain berry mixture through fine-mesh strainer into medium bowl, pressing on solids to extract as much liquid as possible; discard solids. Whisk in vinegar.

Peach Shrub Syrup

We like the convenience of frozen peaches, but you can use an equal weight of peeled and chopped fresh peaches.

- 10 ounces (2 cups) frozen peaches, thawed and chopped
- 1 cup sugar
- 6 ounces water
- 2 ounces cider vinegar

1. Bring peaches, sugar, and water to boil in large saucepan over high heat. Reduce heat to medium-low, cover, and simmer, stirring occasionally, until peaches are soft and beginning to break down, about 10 minutes.

2. Remove saucepan from heat and use potato masher to crush peaches until uniform in texture. Strain mixture through fine-mesh strainer into medium bowl, pressing on solids to extract as much liquid as possible; discard solids. Whisk in vinegar.

Berry Puree

Makes about ½ cup

There are times when a little extra body is welcome in cocktails. Our berry purees easily add sweetness with fresh seasonal flavor to cocktails, like our Strawberry Gin and Tonic (page 96) (which you can certainly make any berry–flavored). Or, add them to sparkling wine for a variation on the Bellini (page 40). The type of berries used as well as their ripeness will affect the sweetness of the puree. Start with 2 tablespoons of sugar, then add more to taste in step 2. Additional sugar should be stirred into the warm puree immediately after straining so that the sugar will readily dissolve.

- 5 ounces (1 cup) frozen blackberries, raspberries, and/or chopped strawberries
- 1 ounce water
- 2 tablespoons sugar
- Pinch table salt

1. Heat berries, water, sugar, and salt in small saucepan over medium heat, stirring occasionally, until berries have softened and sugar has dissolved, about 2 minutes.

2. Process mixture in blender until smooth, about 20 seconds, scraping down sides of blender jar as needed. Strain mixture through fine-mesh strainer into bowl, pressing on solids to extract as much puree as possible; discard solids. Let cool completely. (Puree can be refrigerated for up to 4 days; stir to recombine before using.)

Tinctures and Bitters

Tinctures—of which bitters is a subcategory—are infusions (usually alcohol infusions; sometimes glycerin infusions) that add concentrated flavor hits to cocktails in tiny amounts (eye-dropper amounts) that don't alter the consistency of the drink. Our recipes are lovely to have in your home bar to add distinctiveness to cocktails, and they also make great gifts. You can store either in a jar and measure out the desired amount or in glass dropper bottles, though we prefer the dropper bottles for the tinctures, which are extremely potent in small amounts.

Old-Fashioned Aromatic Bitters

Makes about 16 ounces

These homemade bitters are familiar enough to use wherever their commercial counterparts are called for, yet original enough for you to make personalized and unique cocktails. Our blend of flavoring agents is woodsy and earthy, with notes of dried fruit plus just a hint of warm spice that would be a perfect fit for classic cocktails like the Old-Fashioned (page 123) or the Manhattan (page 181). We cover our flavoring agents with 100-proof vodka and let the mixture steep for two weeks before straining and sweetening. If you can't find 100-proof vodka, substitute 80-proof vodka and add 1 week to the infusion time. We recommend storing your bitters in a cool, dark place to prevent oxidation. Gentian root chips and dried mugwort are bittering agents; you can purchase them, along with dried orange peel, online or in specialty spice shops; look for ¼-inch chips.

- 16 ounces 100-proof vodka
- ¼ cup raisins, chopped
- 2 tablespoons (½ ounce) dried orange peel
- 2 tablespoons (½ ounce) gentian root chips
- 2 tablespoons dried mugwort
- 8 green cardamom pods
- 10 allspice berries, lightly crushed
- 4 whole cloves
- 1 ounce Simple Syrup (page 458)

1. Add vodka, raisins, orange peel, gentian root chips, mugwort, cardamom pods, allspice berries, and cloves to 1-quart Mason jar. Cover and shake to combine. Place jar in a 50- to 70-degree location away from direct sunlight and let mixture sit until flavors have developed, about 2 weeks, shaking mixture once every other day.

2. Set fine-mesh strainer over 4-cup liquid measuring cup or medium bowl and line with triple layer of cheesecloth. Strain infused vodka mixture through prepared strainer, pressing on solids to extract as much liquid as possible; discard solids. Stir in simple syrup. Transfer bitters to clean jar or divide among glass dropper bottles. (Bitters can be stored for up to 1 year; gently shake before using.)

Orange Bitters

Makes about 16 ounces

To create our orange bitters—delicious in the Fireside (page 130), Chancellor (page 195), and Aperol Sour (page 224), among other drinks—we use a combination of fresh sour orange zest (with its exquisitely floral aromas) and lemon. Quassia bark provides a backbone of clean, piney bitterness, and lightly floral coriander seeds round out the citrus flavors. Sour oranges (also known as Seville, bigarade, bitter, or marmalade oranges) can be found in Latin American and Caribbean grocery stores. If you can't find them, substitute the zest of a sweet orange variety (such as navel). If you can't find 100-proof vodka, substitute 80-proof vodka and add 1 week to the infusion time. You can purchase quassia bark chips online or in specialty spice shops.

- 16 ounces 100-proof vodka
- 24 (3-inch) strips sour orange zest (3 oranges)
- 8 (3-inch) strips lemon zest
- 2 tablespoons (½ ounce) quassia bark chips
- 1½ teaspoons coriander seeds
- 2 ounces Simple Syrup (page 458)

1. Add vodka, orange zest, lemon zest, quassia bark chips, and coriander seeds to 1-quart Mason jar. Cover and shake to combine. Place jar in a 50- to 70-degree location away from direct sunlight and let mixture sit until flavors have developed, about 2 weeks, shaking mixture once every other day.

2. Set fine-mesh strainer over 4-cup liquid measuring cup or medium bowl and line with triple layer of cheese-cloth. Strain infused vodka mixture through prepared strainer, pressing on solids to extract as much liquid as possible; discard solids. Stir in simple syrup. Transfer bitters to clean jar or divide among glass dropper bottles. (Bitters can be stored for up to 1 year; gently shake before using.)

Cherry-Fennel Bitters

Makes about 16 ounces

Dried cherries, toasted almonds, and vanilla create a base blend for botanicals: sarsaparilla root for its herbal bitterness, fennel seeds and star anise for their pungent aromas, dried hibiscus flowers for tartness and gorgeous color, and quassia for pineyness. We love these bitters in the Sazerac (page 128) and Amaretto Sour (page 211). If you can't find 100-proof vodka, substitute 80-proof vodka and add 1 week to the infusion time. Any dried cherries except for unsweetened sour cherries will work. Look for the botanicals online or in specialty spice shops.

- 16 ounces 100-proof vodka
- ½ vanilla bean, halved lengthwise
- ¾ cup chopped dried cherries
- ¼ cup slivered almonds, toasted
- 2 tablespoons (½ ounce) sarsaparilla root chips
- 2 tablespoons (½ ounce) quassia bark chips
- 2 teaspoons dried hibiscus flowers
- ½ teaspoon fennel seeds
- ½ star anise pod
- 1½ ounces Simple Syrup (page 458)

1. Add vodka, vanilla bean, cherries, almonds, sarsaparilla root chips, quassia bark chips, hibiscus flowers, fennel seeds, and star anise pod to 1-quart Mason jar. Cover and shake to combine. Place jar in a 50- to 70-degree location away from direct sunlight and let mixture sit until flavors have developed, about 2 weeks, shaking mixture once every other day.

2. Set fine-mesh strainer over 4-cup liquid measuring cup or medium bowl and line with triple layer of cheese-cloth. Strain infused vodka mixture through prepared strainer, pressing on solids to extract as much liquid as possible; discard solids. Stir in simple syrup. Transfer bitters to clean jar or divide among glass dropper bottles. (Bitters can be stored for up to 1 year; gently shake before using.)

Herb Tincture

Makes about 2 ounces

Herb tinctures are made by infusing a high-proof neutral alcohol with fresh herbs, and they can be added by the drop to enliven water, lemonade, cocktails, and other beverages. They keep for months, so you can continue to enjoy the flavor of your herbs long after fresh herbs would have wilted. Typically, tinctures are made by steeping whole herbs in alcohol for several hours, but Senior Science Research Editor Paul Adams found that blending the herb leaves (omitting stems to avoid their bitterness) with the alcohol in a blender cut the infusion time to 30 minutes. After that, we strain the liquid through a coffee filter paired with a double layer of cheesecloth. This recipe works well with any herb you like, from rosemary to basil to makrut lime leaves. Rather than mix herbs, we recommend making several individual tinctures to flavor your cocktails. Because this tincture is incredibly concentrated, we like to store it in a glass dropper bottle; only 1 or 2 drops are needed to flavor most cocktails.

- 4 ounces 190-proof grain alcohol
- 1 ounce fresh herb leaves

1. Process grain alcohol and herbs in blender until herbs are finely chopped and dispersed in alcohol, about 30 seconds. Transfer alcohol mixture to small bowl and let steep for 30 minutes.

2. Set fine-mesh strainer over liquid measuring cup or small bowl and line with paper coffee filter followed by double layer of cheesecloth. Strain vodka mixture through prepared strainer until all liquid has filtered through, about 15 minutes; discard solids. Transfer tincture to glass dropper bottles or clean jar. (Tincture can be stored for up to 1 year; gently shake before using.)

Spice Tincture

Makes about 2 ounces

We like to use our spice tincture to add concentrated flavor where the texture or appearance of the spice in a cocktail might be distracting. And it can flavor more than just cocktails: Think drinks like sparkling water, hot chocolate, or even baked goods. This recipe works well with a variety of dried whole spices, including allspice berries, cardamom pods, cinnamon sticks, cloves, coriander seeds, and dried chiles. Rather than mix spices into a blend, we recommend making tinctures of individual spices to flavor your cocktails. Because this tincture is incredibly concentrated, we like to store it in a glass dropper bottle; only 1 or 2 drops are needed to flavor most cocktails.

- 4 ounces 190-proof grain alcohol
- 2 ounces whole spices

1. Process grain alcohol and spices in blender until spices are finely chopped and dispersed in alcohol, about 30 seconds. Transfer alcohol mixture to small bowl and let sit for 30 minutes.

2. Set fine-mesh strainer over liquid measuring cup or small bowl and line with paper coffee filter followed by double layer of cheesecloth. Strain vodka mixture until all liquid has filtered through, about 15 minutes; discard solids. Transfer tincture to glass dropper bottles or clean jar. (Tincture can be stored for up to 1 year; gently shake before using.)

Liqueurs and Vermouths

Making homemade liqueurs is the ultimate cocktail DIY. These all-purpose recipes are the building blocks of many cocktails and also delicious enough to drink on their own or give as a gift.

Orange Liqueur

Makes about 16 ounces

Orange liqueur is known by many labels commercially. Triple sec and curaçao are generic category examples; Cointreau and Grand Marnier are high-end brand names. For our version, a blend of fresh and dried orange peels gives us the best balance of floral and pungent orange flavors. We use brandy for its well-rounded flavors. Mature (read: pricier) brandies yield a smoother product, with Cognac leading the pack. We suggest a moderately priced brandy that has been aged for at least two and preferably more than four years. You can purchase dried orange peel online or in specialty spice shops; look for pieces that are approximately ¼ inch in size.

- 12 ounces brandy
- 5 (3-inch) strips orange zest
- 1½ teaspoons dried orange peel
- 4 ounces Simple Syrup (page 458)

1. Add brandy, orange zest, and orange peel to 1-pint Mason jar. Cover and shake to combine. Place jar in a 50- to 70-degree location away from direct sunlight and let mixture sit until flavors have developed, about 1 week, shaking mixture once every other day.

2. Set fine-mesh strainer over 4-cup liquid measuring cup or medium bowl and line with triple layer of cheesecloth. Strain infused brandy mixture through prepared strainer, pressing on solids to extract as much liquid as possible; discard solids. Stir in simple syrup. Transfer liqueur to glass bottle or clean jar. (Liqueur can be stored for up to 1 year; gently shake before using.)

Limoncello

Makes about 32 ounces

Italians often end grand meals with a small chilled glass of this palate-cleansing liqueur. Making limoncello is a simple process in which strips of lemon zest are steeped in a neutral spirit to extract flavors and aromas from the zest. Traditionally this takes a month or longer, but for speedier gratification, we turn to the blender. Processing the zest with vodka extracts the flavor compounds mechanically and creates more surface area on which the alcohol acts to extract flavors more quickly. After a week, our processed zest yields as much flavor as strips that are steeped for a month. Over time, a fine sediment (of innocuous pith residue) may form on the surface of the liqueur; if you like, repeat straining through cheesecloth (or simply shake it).

10	ounces vodka
40	(3-inch) strips lemon zest (4 large lemons)
1½	cups sugar
18	ounces water

1. Process vodka and lemon zest in blender until finely ground, about 30 seconds. Transfer vodka mixture to 1-quart Mason jar. Cover, place jar in a 50- to 70-degree location away from direct sunlight, and let sit until flavors have developed, about 1 week, shaking mixture once every other day.

2. Set fine-mesh strainer over 4-cup liquid measuring cup or medium bowl and line with triple layer of cheesecloth. Strain infused vodka mixture through prepared strainer, pressing on solids to extract as much liquid as possible; discard solids.

3. Heat sugar and water in small saucepan over medium heat, whisking often, until sugar has dissolved, about 5 minutes; do not boil. Let cool completely, about 30 minutes. Stir syrup into vodka mixture. Transfer limoncello to glass bottle or clean jar and refrigerate until well chilled, about 2 hours, before serving. (Limoncello can be refrigerated for up to 1 year; gently shake before using.)

Arancello

Substitute 40 (3-inch) strips of sour orange zest (4 oranges) for the lemon zest.

If you can't find sour oranges, substitute 20 (3-inch) strips of sweet orange zest (such as navel), 10 (3-inch) strips of lemon zest, and 8 (2-inch) strips of lime zest for the sour orange zest.

Crema di Limoncello

Substitute 16 ounces of half-and-half for the water.

Fruits of the Forest Liqueur

Makes about 16 ounces

Inspired by such iconic berry liqueurs as Chambord (made from black raspberries) and crème de cassis (made from black currants), we created this intense yet balanced berry-flavored liqueur that can be used whenever these luxurious liqueurs are called for. Liqueur made from freeze-dried berries is bright and bold—and can be made any time of year. Using combinations of at least two types of berries results in liqueur bursting with complex, exquisite flavors that are far more interesting than liqueurs made using just any one type of berry. Try this liqueur in the Royal Berry (page 46) and the Frutti de Bosco Punch (page 54).

12	ounces vodka
1	ounce freeze-dried blackberries, blueberries, and/or raspberries
½	ounce freeze-dried strawberries
4	ounces Simple Syrup (page 458)

Limoncello

1. Add vodka, blackberries, and strawberries to 1-pint Mason jar. Cover and shake to combine. Place jar in a 50- to 70-degree location away from direct sunlight and let mixture sit until flavors have developed, about 1 week, shaking mixture once every other day.

2. Set fine-mesh strainer over 4-cup liquid measuring cup or medium bowl and line with triple layer of cheesecloth. Strain infused vodka mixture through prepared strainer, pressing on solids to extract as much liquid as possible; discard solids. Stir in simple syrup. Transfer liqueur to glass bottle or clean jar. (Liqueur can be stored for up to 1 year; gently shake before using.)

Floral Liqueur

Makes about 16 ounces

Dried flowers are easy to work with, they are readily available online and in specialty shops, and they infuse quickly into a spirit—so there's no stopping you from making homemade floral liqueur. Since elderflower liqueur is ubiquitous, we decided to focus on more-unsung blossoms. A single strip of lemon zest balances the floral fragrances with just a hint of fresh citrus aroma. Try lavender liqueur as an alternative to the crème de violette typically called for in the Aviation (page 229). Chamomile liqueur, when combined with Scotch and a thyme-infused syrup in the Seelie Sipper (page 233), will bring you to the Scottish heathland. Jasmine liqueur adds its heady aroma to our Kiwi Blossom (page 78). Be sure to use food-grade dried flowers (available online or in specialty spice shops) to make these liqueurs; other types likely have been sprayed with pesticides or treated with chemicals.

- 14 ounces vodka
- ¼ ounce dried chamomile flowers, jasmine flowers, lavender flowers, or rose petals
- 1 (3-inch) strip lemon zest
- 2 ounces Simple Syrup (page 458)

1. Add vodka, flowers, and lemon zest to 1-pint Mason jar. Cover and shake to combine. Place jar in a 50- to 70-degree location away from direct sunlight and let mixture sit until flavors have developed, about 2 days, shaking mixture occasionally.

2. Set fine-mesh strainer over 4-cup liquid measuring cup or medium bowl and line with triple layer of cheesecloth. Strain infused vodka mixture through prepared strainer, pressing on solids to extract as much liquid as possible; discard solids. Stir in simple syrup. Transfer liqueur to glass bottle or clean jar. (Liqueur can be stored for up to 1 year; gently shake before using.)

Coffee Liqueur

Makes about 16 ounces

Rich and earthy, with hints of chocolate, whispers of vanilla, and a trace of toasted nuttiness, this liqueur—whether shaken into an Espresso Martini (page 343), tipped into a cup of coffee, served over ice, stirred into cake batter, or drizzled over ice cream—gives the perfect buzz. Infusing coffee beans in alcohol for one week achieves the best flavor; any longer and the flavors verge on bitter. We add a small amount of cacao nibs and a piece of vanilla bean to the coffee and liquor to create delicate flavor harmonies. Adding a small amount of brandy to the vodka base contributes caramel and oaky notes. For a more intensely flavored liqueur, use dark-roast coffee beans; we do not recommend using light-roast beans. You can substitute 1½ teaspoons cocoa powder for the cacao nibs, but the resulting liqueur will be slightly cloudy.

- 8 ounces vodka
- 4 ounces brandy
- ½ cup medium-roast coffee beans
- 1½ teaspoons cacao nibs
- ¼ vanilla bean, halved lengthwise
- 4 ounces Simple Syrup (page 458)

Coffee Liqueur

1. Add vodka, brandy, coffee beans, cacao nibs, and vanilla bean to 1-pint Mason jar. Cover and shake to combine. Place jar in a 50- to 70-degree location away from direct sunlight and let mixture sit until flavors have developed, about 1 week, shaking mixture once every other day.

2. Set fine-mesh strainer over 4-cup liquid measuring cup or medium bowl and line with triple layer of cheesecloth. Strain infused vodka mixture through prepared strainer; discard solids. Stir in simple syrup. Transfer liqueur to glass bottle or clean jar. (Liqueur can be stored for up to 1 year; gently shake before using.)

Tea Liqueur

Makes about 16 ounces

As with flowers, the flavor compounds of delicate tea leaves extract easily into alcohol. We settled on black and green teas for making our tea liqueurs for their flavors and availability. Black teas (such as Assam, Ceylon, and Darjeeling, which are sometimes enhanced with additional flavors to make such familiar blends as English breakfast, Irish breakfast, Earl Grey, and masala chai) are made from oxidized tea leaves and are bold, tannic teas. One of our favorite black teas, Lapsang souchong, is smoke-dried, with a unique woodsy-smoky flavor. Green teas are made from unoxidized tea leaves and have bittersweet, grassy notes. They are sometimes enhanced with additional flavor elements (such as roasted popped brown rice to make genmaicha tea). Any of these styles can be used. This liqueur can be made overnight; so, if on Thursday you start making your tea liqueur, by Friday you could be sipping on a Hole in One (page 76).

- 14 ounces vodka
- 1 tablespoon dried black or green tea
- 2 ounces Simple Syrup (page 458)

1. Add vodka and tea to 1-pint Mason jar. Cover and shake to combine. Place jar in a 50- to 70-degree location away from direct sunlight and let mixture sit until flavors have developed, about 24 hours, shaking mixture occasionally.

2. Set fine-mesh strainer over 4-cup liquid measuring cup or medium bowl and line with triple layer of cheesecloth. Strain infused vodka mixture through prepared strainer, pressing on solids to extract as much liquid as possible; discard solids. Stir in simple syrup. Transfer liqueur to glass bottle or clean jar. (Liqueur can be stored for up to 1 year; gently shake before using.)

Ancho Chile Liqueur

Makes about 16 ounces

Fruity, smoky, and mildly spicy, ancho chiles (which are actually dried ripe poblanos) are a natural fit for infusing into tequila. This liqueur works great in our Old Poblano (page 134), and it also makes a delicious substitute for tequila in our Fresh Margarita (page 214) or other tequila-based cocktails. Adding a hint of cinnamon deepens the spicy complexity of the liqueur. Simple syrup tempers and balances the heat of the chiles. We use blanco tequila because of its clean, comparatively neutral flavor and its price point. You can substitute more expensive reposado tequila or añejo if you plan to sip your liqueur on its own (over ice is nice), where its flavors can be fully enjoyed. Although our favorite base spirit for this liqueur is tequila, vodka or bourbon will also work well. For a spicier liqueur, include the chile seeds when steeping. Experiment with flavors by substituting an equal weight of dried guajillo, pasilla, or New Mexico chiles for the ancho.

- 12 ounces blanco tequila
- ½ dried ancho chile (¼ ounce), stemmed, seeded, and torn into 1-inch pieces
- ¼ cinnamon stick
- 4 ounces Simple Syrup (page 458)

1. Add tequila, chile, and cinnamon stick to 1-pint Mason jar. Cover and shake to combine. Place jar in a 50- to 70-degree location away from direct sunlight and let mixture sit until flavors have developed, about 1 week, shaking mixture once every other day.

2. Set fine-mesh strainer over 4-cup liquid measuring cup or medium bowl and line with triple layer of cheesecloth. Strain infused tequila mixture through prepared strainer, pressing on solids to extract as much liquid as possible; discard solids. Stir in simple syrup. Transfer liqueur to glass bottle or clean jar. (Liqueur can be stored for up to 1 year; gently shake before using.)

Mole Chile Liqueur

Add ½ teaspoon cacao nibs and 1 teaspoon coffee beans to the jar with the ancho chile.

Dry Vermouth

Makes about 32 ounces

This homemade vermouth might just make your next Gin Martini (page 155) the best you've ever had. Herbal and grassy, its winey acidity is balanced by a touch of simple syrup to take the edge off the bittering agents. Commercial vermouth makers extract botanical flavors using a combination of distillation and maceration. Here, we add botanicals to a jar with a small amount of the fortifying spirit; after 24 hours, the vodka extracts a complex and vibrant array of aromas. To that base, we add enough wine to achieve the proper level of alcohol by volume. We prefer to use Pinot Grigio, but you can substitute your favorite unoaked dry white wine. You can purchase dried wormwood, chamomile flowers, and quassia bark chips online or in specialty spice shops; look for chips that are approximately ¼ inch in size.

- 6 ounces vodka
- 1 (3-inch) strip orange zest
- 1 bay leaf
- 1 teaspoon dried wormwood
- 1 teaspoon dried chamomile flowers
- 1 teaspoon dried sage
- 6 juniper berries, lightly crushed
- ½ teaspoon coriander seeds
- ½ teaspoon dried thyme
- ¼ teaspoon black peppercorns
- ¼ teaspoon quassia bark chips
- 2 whole cloves
- 1 green cardamom pod
- ½ star anise pod
- 20 ounces Pinot Grigio
- 1½ ounces Simple Syrup (page 458)

1. Add vodka, orange zest, bay leaf, wormwood, chamomile flowers, sage, juniper berries, coriander seeds, thyme, peppercorns, quassia bark chips, cloves, cardamom pod, and star anise pod to 1-quart Mason jar. Cover and shake to combine. Place jar in a 50- to 70-degree location away from direct sunlight and let mixture sit until flavors have developed, about 24 hours, shaking mixture occasionally.

2. Set fine-mesh strainer over 8-cup liquid measuring cup or large bowl and line with triple layer of cheesecloth. Strain infused vodka mixture through prepared strainer, pressing on solids to extract as much liquid as possible; discard solids. Stir in wine and simple syrup. Transfer vermouth to glass bottle or clean jar. (Vermouth can be refrigerated for up to 3 months; gently shake before using.)

Sweet Vermouth

Makes about 32 ounces

Indispensable to the Manhattan (page 181), Classic Negroni (page 333), and Americano (page 330), sweet vermouth plays a special role in defining how good—or how mediocre—these classics can be. For our home-made version, we use the same basic method as for our Dry Vermouth (page 469), but we add golden raisins for their concentrated fruity sweetness, and we emphasize the warmer spices and floral flavors while keeping the herbal notes in balance. For enriched sweetening and to contribute to the color, we make an easy stovetop caramel syrup, adding it to our mixture of aromatized wine and vodka. The hibiscus flowers bring it closer to the garnet shade of commercial vermouths. We prefer to use Pinot Grigio, but you can substitute your favorite unoaked dry white wine. You can purchase dried wormwood, chamomile flowers, hibiscus flowers, and quassia bark chips online or in specialty spice shops; look for chips that are approximately ¼ inch in size. Both whole and cut hibiscus flowers will work here. For an accurate measurement of boiling water, bring a full kettle of water to a boil and then measure out the desired amount.

- 6 ounces vodka
- ½ cup golden raisins, chopped
- 2 (3-inch) strips orange zest
- 1 bay leaf
- 1 teaspoon dried wormwood
- 1 teaspoon dried chamomile flowers
- 6 juniper berries, lightly crushed
- ½ teaspoon quassia bark chips
- ½ teaspoon coriander seeds
- ½ teaspoon dried sage
- ½ teaspoon dried thyme
- ¼ teaspoon black peppercorns
- 4 whole cloves
- 2 green cardamom pods
- ½ star anise pod
- 2 teaspoons dried hibiscus flowers
- 4 ounces boiling water, plus 2 ounces water
- ¾ cup sugar
- 20 ounces Pinot Grigio

1. Add vodka, raisins, orange zest, bay leaf, wormwood, chamomile flowers, juniper berries, quassia bark chips, coriander seeds, sage, thyme, peppercorns, cloves, cardamom pods, and star anise pod to 1-quart Mason jar. Cover and shake to combine. Place jar in a 50- to 70-degree location away from direct sunlight and let mixture sit until flavors have developed, about 24 hours, shaking mixture occasionally.

2. Set fine-mesh strainer over 8-cup liquid measuring cup or large bowl and line with triple layer of cheese-cloth. Strain infused vodka mixture through prepared strainer, pressing on solids to extract as much liquid as possible; discard solids. Set aside.

3. Combine hibiscus flowers and boiling water in bowl and let steep for 5 minutes. Strain through fine-mesh strainer into separate bowl, pressing on solids to extract as much liquid as possible; discard solids.

4. Combine sugar and remaining 2 ounces water in medium saucepan. Bring to boil over medium-high heat and cook, without stirring, until mixture is amber-colored around edges of saucepan. Reduce heat to low and continue to cook, swirling saucepan occasionally, until caramel is evenly dark amber, 3 to 5 minutes. Off heat, carefully whisk in hibiscus tea (mixture will bubble and steam) until syrup is smooth. Immediately transfer caramel to separate bowl and let cool completely, about 30 minutes.

5. Stir wine and caramel into infused vodka mixture. Transfer vermouth to glass bottle or clean jar. (Vermouth can be refrigerated for up to 3 months; gently shake before using.)

Cocktails by Flavor

Bitter

Citrusy

Creamy

Floral

Fruity

Herbal

Nutty

Savory

Smoky

Spiced

Spicy

Moscow Mule (page 107)
Mexican Mule (page 108)
Orchard Mule (page 108)
Once in a Blue Mule (page 109)
Bourbon Mint Tea Mule (page 109)
Hibiscus-Lime Buck (page 113)
Bitter and Bubbly (page 116)
Old Poblano (page 134)
Spicy Margarita (page 216)
Tumbleweed (page 222)
Smoke and Mirrors (page 223)
Tongue Thai'd (page 254)
Maizey Days (page 307)
Bloody Marys (page 319)
Berbere-Spiced Bloody Marys (page 320)
Southwestern Bloody Marys (page 321)
Kimchi Bloody Marys (page 322)
Gingered Beer (page 365)
Michelada (page 366)
Mulled Mead with Star Anise and Ginger (page 417)
Takes Two to Mango (page 433)

Spirit Forward

New-Fashioned Gin and Tonic (page 99)
Old-Fashioned (page 123)
Cinnamon Old-Fashioned (page 124)
Berry Old-Fashioned (page 124)
Fridge Door Old-Fashioned (page 125)
Fond du Lac Old-Fashioned (page 126)
Sazerac (page 128)
Tequila Old-Fashioned (page 129)
Fireside (page 130)
Ti' Punch (page 131)
Caramelized Banana Old-Fashioned (page 132)
Old Poblano (page 134)
Fly by Night (page 134)
Irish Godfather (page 135)
Promise Us Paradise (page 136)
From Beirut with Love (page 142)
Mint Julep (page 145)
Gin Martini (page 155)
Dirtiest Martini (page 156)
Gibson (page 156)
Sherry Martini (page 157)
Fridge Door Martinis (page 157)
Vesper (page 160)
Herb Martini (page 161)
El Capitán (page 163)
Jabberwocky (page 163)
Martinez (page 165)
Martinez, but Make It Citrusy (page 166)
Tuxedo (page 166)
Fridge Door Martinez (page 167)
Hanky Panky (page 168)
Las Palmas (page 170)
Arroyo (page 173)
Bijou (page 173)
Manhattan (page 181)
Black Manhattan (page 182)
Palmetto (page 183)
Fridge Door Manhattans (page 183)
Monte Carlo (page 186)
Little Baloney (page 191)
Helia Bravo (page 191)
Rosita (page 192)
Rumsicle (page 195)
Chancellor (page 195)
Vieux Carré (page 196)
Smoky Peat (page 196)
Sidecar (page 225)
Yellowlegs (page 230)
Aged Manhattan (page 271)
Vieux Nuevo (page 272)
Aged Martini (page 273)
Aged Revolver (page 274)
Oak-Aged Metropolitan (page 279)
Melon Dollar Martini (page 303)
Browned Butter and Maple Old-Fashioned (page 305)
PBJ (page 306)
Olive Oil Martini (page 307)
Maizey Days (page 307)
English 75 (page 313)
Strawberry Negroni (page 316)
Classic Negroni (page 333)
Coffee Negroni (page 334)
Fridge Door Negronis (page 335)
Widow's Kiss (page 341)
I Woke Up Like This (page 345)
Gathered Clouds (page 361)
Brandy Flip (page 375)
James Flip (page 378)
Hot Toddy (page 402)
Classic Mulled Wine (page 414)

Tart

Champagne Cocktail (page 36)
Mimosa (page 39)
Bellini (page 40)
Poinsettia (page 40)
French 75 (page 42)
ATK 25 (page 43)
Lovage or Leave It (page 45)
Bubbles and Blooms (page 45)
Royal Berry (page 46)
Frutti di Bosco Punch (page 54)
Summer Stone-Fruit Punch (page 54)
Tom Collins (page 71)
New Englander (page 75)
Raspberry Lime Rickey (page 81)
Doctor's Orders (page 103)
Tamarind and Tonic (page 103)
Hibiscus-Lime Buck (page 113)
Caipirinha (page 146)
Daiquiri (page 205)
Basil Daiquiri (page 206)
Strawberry Daiquiri (page 206)
Fridge Door Daiquiris (page 207)
Celery Gimlet (page 208)
Whiskey Sour (page 208)
Amaretto Sour (page 211)
Fresh Margarita (page 214)
Spicy Margarita (page 216)
Watermelon Margarita (page 217)

Toasted

Tropical

Index

Note: Page references in *italics* indicate photographs.

G

H

N

O

Q

R

S

T

V

W

Y

Z